C000090590

THE **MADNESS** OF **KNOWLEDGE**

STEVEN CONNOR

THE
MADNESS
OF
KNOWLEDGE

ON WISDOM,
IGNORANCE
AND
FANTASIES
OF
KNOWING

REAKTION BOOKS

Published by
REAKTION BOOKS LTD
Unit 32, Waterside
44–48 Wharf Road
London N1 7UX, UK
www.reaktionbooks.co.uk

First published 2019
Copyright © Steven Connor 2019

All rights reserved

No part of this publication may be reproduced,
stored in a retrieval system, or transmitted,
in any form or by any means, electronic, mechanical,
photocopying, recording or otherwise,
without the prior permission of the publishers

Printed and bound in Great Britain
by TJ International, Padstow, Cornwall

A catalogue record for this book is available
from the British Library

ISBN 978 1 78194 072 9

CONTENTS

'But I don't want to go among mad people', Alice remarked.

'Oh, you can't help that', said the Cat: 'we're all mad here. I'm mad. You're mad.'

'How do you know I'm mad?' said Alice.

'You must be', said the Cat, 'or you wouldn't have come here.'

Alice didn't think that proved it at all.

Lewis Carroll, *Alice's Adventures in Wonderland*

INTRODUCTION

> ... never stop a Psychopath
> From following his vocation!
> *Punch*, 17 January 1885

Like the word 'scientist', put into play at the British Association for the Advancement of Science in the early 1830s, 'epistemology' is a thoroughly modern word. It was proposed in the *English Review* in 1847 as a translation of Johann Gottlieb Fichte's *Wissenschaftslehre*, 'after the analogy of *technology*', according to its author's explanation.[1] It is a curious reflection that, although one would surely have to say that the entire conception and contour of Greek philosophy was epistemological, in the sense that it was concerned with how secure and reliable knowledge was to be separated from mere *doxa*, the attempt to turn knowing on to the conditions and possibility of knowing itself seems to have had to wait until the nineteenth century to be named, if not exactly to be known.

There were a few near misses and half-chances. In a treatise completed around 1688, though not published until 1731, Ralph Cudworth gives us the term *epistemonical*, meaning something like 'capable of being known'. Having affirmed that 'the Entity of all Theoretical Truth is nothing else but Clear Intelligibility, and whatever is Clearly Conceived, is an Entity and a Truth', implying that falsehoods have no positive existence at all, he assures his reader that 'no Man ever was or can be deceived in taking that for an Epistemonical Truth which he clearly and distinctly apprehends, but only in Assenting to Things not clearly apprehended by him'.[2] Epistemony, signifying the condition of knowability, the nonexistent term from which the nonce-word epistemonical would derive, might perhaps have caught on, but in the event never found any more takers – until now, I suppose.

The *epistem-* prefix also appears in the form of allegorical names, most famously and definingly that of Epistemon in Rabelais' *Gargantua and Pantagruel* (1532–64), who embodies the powers of learning (and who suggestively loses his head in a battle, but has it sewn back on). James IV of Scotland casts his *Daemonologie* (1597) in the form of a debate between Philomath (the lover or seeker of learning) and Epistemon (the knower), and Thomas Heywood invents an Epistemus in 1609. Guy Miège's *Dictionary of Barbarous French*, an adaptation of Randle Cotgrave's 1611 *Dictionary of the French and English Tongues*, defines an *epistemon* as a teacher.[3]

Just as there seemed to be no word for what a lot of people had been up to for a long time before the arrival of the word 'epistemology', so there seems to me to be no word for what has also been a strongly pervasive phenomenon, namely the production and development of complex states of feeling and imaginative projection in relation to knowledge. *Epistemopathy*, the uncomely term I mean to employ for this, would need to be broader and fuzzier in its application than epistemology, precisely because it would not aim at exact knowledge as such, but rather at the spectrum of feeling exacted by the idea, the ambition and even, we must often feel constrained to say, the fantasy of knowledge, whether exact or not. So it must encompass not just questions of what can be known for sure, and how, but the investments in all the accessory and executive functions of knowing, for example wondering, enquiring, discovering, arguing, reasoning, teaching and learning. Epistemopathy's concern, in short, will be with the concern with knowledge. 'All men naturally desire knowledge', Aristotle writes in the opening words of the *Metaphysics*.[4] Epistemopathy has a care for that desire, along with passions incident to it and its absence – because ignorance, too, is no mere omission, or remission, of knowledge, but itself a kind of mission, or even, as Jacques Lacan observes, a passion.[5]

The word 'knowledge' is not a very precise or satisfactorily inclusive term for the areas I mean to consider, which might at different times be more accurately designated as memory, intelligence, reason, understanding, belief, expertise, wisdom, cognition or just plain thinking. But in that it is a word that has increasingly soaked up these kinds of associations, its very lowest-common-denominator sogginess is actually itself rather usefully expressive of the way in which we think – by which we often mean feel – about knowledge. One of the singular things about our thinking about all the different forms of knowing and knowledge is precisely this tendency to scrunch them into singularity.

The epistemological itch may be thought of as intrinsic to modern philosophy, in the sense that the 'know thyself' of Delphi coils, like Alice's flamingo-mallet, into the commandment 'Know thy knowing' that impels the inquiries of Descartes and Kant. There might be thought to be something essentially or tendentially modern about the exercise of epistemology, in that it must always constitute a fold or fissure within accepted understandings, as knowledge turns away from the putatively knowable world to investigate its own conditions of possibility. But we must also say that there is an epistemopathic payload within every epistemology, an excited yearning, for instance, to strive for a kind of self-realization and self-government in knowledge. Peter Sloterdijk has made the arresting claim that there has never really been any religion, understood in its own terms, since all forms of religious doctrine and devotion are better understood as ascetological or anthropotechnic projects of self-formation and -transformation.[6] We might similarly surmise that the function of the more metaphysical kind of theological thinking that has kept the universities busy for centuries has been to allow for the impassioned and sustained elaboration, at once untrammelled by experiment or experience and yet, perhaps for that reason, arming itself with ferociously austere internal logical constraints, of a kind of artificial intelligence or epistemotechnic, a miracle-making kind of thinking in thin air. This kind of theology, the elaboration of knowledge systems concerning inexistent objects and relations of fantastic complexity (literally fantastic, in the sense that they permit the development of a fantasy of complexity itself), is an epistemology that, in the absence of anything but imaginary objects, and in its joyously earnest capacity to multiply those objects and their relations without limit, is unalloyed epistemopathy, the rapturous attempt of knowledge to feel, fuel and feed its own powers of self-generation. This is really not as bad as it perhaps sounds, though it is quite as weird. As a young academic, I had plenty of theology practice in the passion for the abstract encouraged by the metaphysical peelings and parings of the literary theory that held sway during the 1980s.

It should already be becoming clear that I am using the word 'epistemopathy' in two different ways: to refer both to the forms of feeling at work in knowledge and to the formal investigation of them – epistemopathology, as it might be, but on second thought had perhaps better not, given the negative charge carried by the word 'pathological'. The kind of feeling suggested by derivations from the Greek *pathos* is often morbid (neuropath, osteopath, homeopath), though I am interested by the fork that occurs in the path of the word 'psychopath'. Up to 1884, a psychopath was equivalent to a psychopathist and designated one who studied or treated disorders of the mind. And then, in 1885, the *Pall Mall Gazette* used the word 'psychopath' to mean not the student of mental disorder but the subject of that study, quoting a Russian psychiatrist, Ivan Balinsky, on 'the psychopath . . . a type which has only recently come under the notice of medical science'.[7] Balinsky was defending a murderess named Semenova who had confessed to the murder of a child named Sarah Becker. In fact the public debut of the word used in this new way had been the week before, in a poem about the case entitled 'A Merry Medico' that appeared in *Punch* on 17 January:

The Doctor framed a new defence,
There never was a lamer;
For why? – She was a 'Psychopath,'
And therefore you can't blame her! . . .

To gain their end they'll put to death
Their nearest blood relation;
So never stop a Psychopath
From following his vocation![8]

I hope it will be clear when I am using epistemopathy to refer to a phenomenon under investigation and when I intend to refer to the investigation of that phenomenon, though I acknowledge there will be times when it is not easy to shear them cleanly one from the other. Perhaps this is a hint that there is an inquisitive twitch within every feeling we have of knowledge, an impulse to get to know the feeling we have of knowing.

I cannot take all the credit for having invented the term epistemopathy, which means at least that I need not take the complete rap for it either. It was deployed in this sense by the psychologist Sigmund Koch in 1981 in describing himself as 'the modest founder of a discipline given to the study of misfirings of the scholarly and creative impulse: the field soon to be widely known as the science of "cognitive pathology", the metatheory of which is "epistemopathologistics"'.[9] Though cheerfully admitting, even ten years later, that the field 'as yet has but one practitioner', Koch persisted with the claim to be 'the founder of the new science of "cognitive pathologistics"', the purpose of which is 'the diagnosis of the many epistemopathies that pervade modern scholarship'.[10] But my use of the term extends beyond psychopathology. Where epistemology inquires into the truth, or *logos*, of knowing, epistemopathy takes, or rather, perhaps, aspires to form as its object the *pathos* of knowledge, that is, the inner or subjective life of knowing – the rapture and rue we may feel about it and its accessory and executive actions of learning, thinking, arguing, doubting, wondering and forgetting.

THE MATTERING OF KNOWLEDGE

Chapter One, 'Will to Knowledge', will suggest that what governs modern thought and feeling regarding knowledge is not the concern with truth and the effort to purify it of error and prejudice, slowly escorting *pathos* towards *logos*, but something like the opposite, in the growing suspicion that knowledge is not easily to be purged of a seemingly inborn will to knowledge. The idea that investigative thinking may be a kind of psychopathology moves through the work of Schopenhauer, Nietzsche and Freud but is articulated most emphatically in Nietzsche's conception of the will to knowledge as a will to power.

And yet (though perhaps we do not yet know if it is an 'and yet'), the modern period is characterized by a vast formalization and autonomization of knowledge, in the forms of expertise and information. The coming of electronic forms of information technology is only the most recent stage of this. We may say that modern epistemopathy is characteristically concerned with the negotiation of the growing gap between personal knowledge, that is, the knowledge embodied in subjects who know their knowing (or think they do) as consciousness, and the various forms of artificial intelligence, or knowledge that need not know, or need to know, itself. It is the gap between knowledge as lived out and what will be described in Chapter Eight as *exopistemology*. In one sense, it is the tension between the -*pathic* and the -*logical*, between the feeling of knowing and knowing without feeling, even if, at the same time, this tension is the adjutant ague of epistemopathy itself.

So epistemopathy does not mean a kind of feelingful knowledge, a knowledge impelled and palpitant with affect (maybe all knowledge is of this kind); rather it is knowledge-feeling, the feelings we build and sustain about knowledge. Of course, feeling is not the opposite of knowing. It is not just that feeling is a necessary accessory to understanding and judgement. It is that feeling is knowing's manner and method, the how or *quomodo* of knowing. Feeling is not just a form of knowing, it is the formality of all knowing, in the necessity for all knowing to take some form and fulfil some aim. Having no uninflected form or zero degree, knowing must always have some tone, temper or purport through which it is lived and acted out. This is particularly the case whenever people try to persuade themselves that they or others are in possession of what they might call 'objective' knowledge, knowledge uncontaminated by any sort of subjective feeling, because the putation of objects is one of the strongest exercises of subjective desire, force and excitement, in that concupiscence of the austere known to all aspiring thinkers, that can be imagined. The epistemopathy I wish to encourage will make it its business to account for the large and various class of these knowledge-feelings. There is no particular zone of the spectrum of feelings which characterizes knowing-feelings. Knowing-feelings will include irritation, rage, envy, lust, misery, boredom and melancholy just as much as satisfaction, assurance, excitement and triumph.

Epistemopathy is therefore the mattering of knowledge, beyond the mere matter of its facts. An epistemopathic project of this kind is obviously vulnerable to self-referential scorpions. How is one to conduct what might be regarded as an epistemopathic investigation without being drawn back into epistemological questions of what can be precisely or securely known (though now not about the world, but about the world of knowing)? There is always, I think, a tendency for epistemopathy to displace and disguise itself as epistemology: how can I know for sure that this is what I or others feel about knowledge? The fact of this mattering can obviously be turned into an object of philosophical inquiry, for example in the utilitarian tradition that runs from Hume's declaration that 'Reason is, and ought only to be the slave of the passions, and can never pretend to any other office than to serve and obey them',[11] through to the claims for the utility of reason in the work of William James and, with any luck, beyond. James writes that 'For a thing to be valid . . . is the same as to make itself valid. When the whole universe seems only to be making itself valid and to be still incomplete (else why its ceaseless changing?) why, of all things, should knowing be exempt? Why should it not be making itself valid like everything else?', a formulation which certainly sounds close to my idea of the mattering of knowledge.[12] All I can say is that questions about the certainty of the knowledge we might have about our feelings about knowledge are indeed questions that might be put; but they are not the only ones, and for the most part they are not the kind of questions I will be sponsoring in this book.

It has been put to me that I might as well refer to this prospect and perspective as a phenomenology of knowledge and have done with it. It is indeed striking how little work there has been even within the phenomenological tradition of philosophy on questions of knowledge. Again, it appears to be very hard to keep an inquiry into the phenomenology of knowledge from becoming an inquiry into phenomenological kinds of knowledge, in which knowledge gets a pinfall on phenomenology rather than the reverse. Where most philosophers worry and wonder about what kinds of claim phenomenology might have to be knowledge, or what phenomenology can contribute towards knowledge, the idea behind epistemopathic inquiry would be to bracket both of those questions.[13]

The principal reason that I am inhibited from calling the inquiry undertaken here a phenomenology of knowledge is to avoid confusion with the very different thing that is signalled by Ernst Cassirer's use of the phrase as the title of the third volume of *The Philosophy of Symbolic Forms*, which was subtitled *The Phenomenology of Knowledge* (1929). Cassirer makes it clear in his preface that his phenomenology is not that of Husserl but that of Hegel, such that

> in speaking of a phenomenology of knowledge I am using the word 'phenomenology' not in its modern sense but with its fundamental signification as established and systematically grounded by Hegel. For Hegel, phenomenology became the basis of all philosophical knowledge, since he insisted that philosophical knowledge must encompass the totality of

cultural forms and since in his view this totality can be made visible only in the transitions from one form to another. The truth is the whole – yet this whole cannot be presented all at once but must be unfolded progressively by thought in its own autonomous movement and rhythm. It is this unfolding which constitutes the being and the essence of science. The element of thought, in which science is and lives, is consequently fulfilled and made intelligible only through the movement of its becoming.[14]

So, for Cassirer, the phenomenology of knowledge does not refer to reflection on the consciousness and experience of knowledge – the feeling of knowing – but the process whereby knowledge moves historically through various different contingent modes and manifestations to a condition of completeness. Such an ambition might in fact provide an occasion for a phenomenology of knowledge in the sense in which I conceive it – the 'modern' sense of the word from which Cassirer distinguishes his own – for the story of the self-unfolding historical adventure of thought is one of the strongest of the fantasy-formations driving both philosophy and history.

Epistemological uncertainty of the kind proposed by Nietzsche, James, Wittgenstein and Dewey implies that epistemology must not only take account of epistemopathy but also move closer to it. But epistemopathy need not be promoted into or cashed out as a kind of epistemology, since it ought to be seen as itself in the reckoning with all forms of thinking and knowing, whether philosophical or not. There can be no fully epistemopathic knowledge, since the pathos of knowing is always at work in knowledge and will always ask in its turn to be accounted for. Epistemopathy is not a knowing, though it is inseparable from knowing, and precisely because of this inseparability is resistant to being something simply known. Epistemopathy is, if you must, applied epistemology, epistemology brought to bear on the world, and, more particularly for my present purposes, the world bearing down on epistemology.

TRUE FANTASY

Knowing is taken up with truth. You can only know something if it is true. It makes no sense to say that I know that Paris is situated at the

North Pole. It turns out, a little oddly and also perhaps alarmingly, that this relation is reversible. That is, not only can you only know things that are true, all true things must be, if not necessarily known, then certainly knowable – *epistemonical* in Cudworth's still-stillborn locution, for which, look, we seem suddenly to have found a use. Many have wanted to believe in ineffable truths, truths too subtle or splendid to be available to human knowledge, but this must be mere word-magic, something therefore to be banished from epistemology, though a hugely important part of epistemopathy. This necessary knowability of all knowledge is concerning because it seems to make truths dependent on and even accessory to the ability for them to be known, that is, apprehended in the ways we recognize as knowing, where we would probably prefer things to be the other way round, that is, for knowability to be dependent on truth.

I will be greatly preoccupied through this book with fantasies of knowledge – not just things we think we know, but, more powerfully, and so less tractably, things we wish we knew about knowledge. This includes fantasies in the ordinary sense of false beliefs about what one knows (I imagine I know how to speak Italian or know my way round calculus but when it comes to the pinch, I don't really). It also includes desirous deliberation about what it may be possible to know in principle, either for an individual or for a collective, along with fantasies about what one merely wishes it were possible to know. In such cases the word 'fantasy' implies mistaken understanding, whether impelled by egotism, vanity, immoderate desire or just plain error. As Francis Bacon put it, 'The human understanding is not composed of dry light, but is subject to influence from the will and the emotions, a fact that creates fanciful knowledge; man prefers to believe what he wants to be true.'[15]

But I will use the word 'fantasy' largely in a sense distinct from that of false or deluded belief, or Bacon's 'fanciful knowledge' (his Latin is 'quod vult scientias', 'what-you-like science'). My use of the word will principally imply the force of emotional investment. Here it is much less easy to distinguish true from false. Here the fantasy may be a matter instead of the value ascribed to knowledge and its significance for the knower. It may still be possible to point to exaggeration, eccentricity and imprudence in these kinds of investment, but these will have no necessary relation to the correctness or incorrectness of the knowledge sought or obtained. The reasonableness of reason is one of the ways we invest fantasy in it. Investment need not imply any particular kind of personal interest. A group or institution may have an investment in a particular valuing of knowledge in that it gives them a rationale for existence. But investment always implies some interest, in the strong sense that one's being is held in some way to be compact or bound in with the object of the investment.

Fantasy in this sense may often be defined as the charge imparted or imputed to knowledge. Very often this will involve desiring representation, or wishful thinking, the latter a phrase that sounds impeccably seventeenth-century but only seems to arise in the 1930s, perhaps influenced by psychoanalysis. Various kinds of desire may be indirectly satisfied in fantasy, through what is familiarly known as wish-fulfilment: the desire to be home, the desire to be young, to be old, to be powerful, immortal, helpless, safe, fed, free. But the primary desire in knowledge-fantasy relates reflexively to fantasy and desire themselves: my wish for certain things may be satisfied through fantasy, but the desire of fantasy itself is the desire for the fantasy (noun-substantive) produced by my fantasy (verb gerund) to be real, or at least to seem sufficiently actual. Perhaps we must go further still and say that the desire for there to be such a thing as the real, beyond any contingent matters of what may happen to be the case, is the ultimate force of fantasy. Fantasy is at work not just because we may wish certain unreal things to be real – elves, angels, irrational numbers – but because we wish, indeed require, there to be a Real, and for us, as we so revealingly say, to be able to *realize* it. Nothing is more suffused with desire than the burning-ice idea of that which is beyond all delusion and desire. We can never be indifferent to this kind of indifference to us.

Fantasy is therefore the thought that thinking might make it so. We cannot think of anything without fantasy. Fantasy always interposes itself between thought and its object. This is because there must always be a fantasy of thinking which comes between our thinking and itself and seems to make it knowable. There are mental operations going on all the time, but you can only consciously think via a fantasy of thinking, one which seems to say, 'now there is thinking, and this is it'. Central to the inquiries conducted in this book will be the fact that we can never quite know, or capture for thought, what that 'I am thinking' actually is, and so may require the cooperation (the co-agitation, or moving together, of which *cogitare* is the compressed form) of fantasy.

This is an important secondary component of the drive to know, which may not just be the desire to exercise power through knowing, a power that creates objects of knowledge: it may also be the expression of the fantasy attaching to thinking itself, the fantasy not simply of appropriating and penetrating that which is to be known, but of substituting for it, as though the being depended (epistemonically, again) on the knowing and not vice versa. In this sense the fantasy of knowing is an expression of Freud's formula for magical thinking, the 'omnipotence of thoughts', the fantasy of knowledge's creativity or capacity to bring the world into being, or sustain it in being.[16] Far from objectifying the world, by making it the docile theme of my knowledge, as so many have charged, fantasy may also perform its magical office through the animation of the world. This need not take the grotesque form of a Friar Bacon or Frankenstein flinging together a bundle of body parts to pantomime the mechanical functions of a living being. It is a much more powerful exercise of the mind to conceive a cosmos that is infinitely beyond the powers of that mind. There is a secret majesty in the humility of the mind that abases itself before the certainty that the cosmos is infinitely beyond the powers of knowing: for it hides from itself the knowledge that, if this were absolutely true, there would be no occasion for it to occur to that mind that it might be so. In one sense, such a thought of immensity makes the conceiving mind an inconceivably paltry thing; in another, it magnifies the mind by seeming to exempt it from the conditions of its own thought, as in Francis Quarles's ethereally nested epigram of 1718:

> My soul, what's lighter than a feather? Wind.
> Than wind? The fire. And what than fire? The mind.
> What's lighter than the mind? A thought. Than thought?
> This bubble world. What than this bubble? Nought.[17]

The mind is both lighter than the lightest thing (fire) and yet denser and more substantial than the epiphenomenal ebullition of the world, which is lighter even than thought's own thought of it. So the more attenuated the world gets, the more exquisitely the mind may seem to exert and exalt its power. This is a distinctive form of the lust that impels theological and metaphysical inquiries, the lust after the power to create that which goes beyond one's powers of creation and govern that which exceeds all possibilities of government (except those of knowing and the pseudo-knowing of naming); the unknowable, the inconceivable, the ineffable, along with the whole extended clan of *un*-s and *in*-s and *non*-s. When the mystic quails before the ravishing splendour or immensity of the world, she is really pumping up the dream of being the onlie begetter of transcendence, recognition the sister of cognition. Self-transcendence always harbours the dream of the transcendent self, exercised not in any kind of physical power but in the imaginary executive of knowing. In one sense, the mind must strain its capacities to and beyond its limit; in another sense, no work is required at all beyond the simple addition of the prefix un- or in- to words like certainty and conceivability.

The pleasure in this power can secrete itself in unexpected places. Heisenberg's uncertainty principle, as popularly explicated, maintains that all phenomena at a sub-atomic scale are subject to an observer effect, meaning that the very action of observing the behaviour of an object changes that behaviour, by forcing it to stop its dithering about the kind of thing it is, particle or wave. This may be seen as a troublesome disruption, to be sure, putting a limit on absolute knowledge; but it can also be seen as an assertion of the impossibility for an object to be indifferent to the knowing actions which force it, as it were, to make up its absent mind. Little could be more gratifying than the idea that nothing in the universe is immune to the action of human inquiry. Paradoxically, this idea is epistemopathically indistinguishable from the apparently opposite apprehension that everything in the universe is numbly immune to mind.

This necessary fantasy of the conformity of mind and world – conformity not only in the sense that the world is subordinated to thought, but also in the conviction that they must con-form, that is, share a form – becomes apparent in the principle of coherence bias. This is the powerful prejudice to accord belief to things that seem more rather than less organized, where *organized* will often, though not invariably, mean exhibiting agents and chains of intelligible consequence in something like a narrative form. This is a kind of reflexivity in that, in recognizing as knowable things that are susceptible to orderly sequences and arrangements, the mind is saluting and accrediting something like its own constitution, and certainly its own powerful prejudice, in favour of more rather than less organized structures. We may see the work of fantasy in the pleasurable reward the mind gives itself when it apprehends something which mirrors its own structures and expectations. Why should such a prospect of compliant accordance give pleasure? Because such structures are parsimonious, to borrow the Occamite formula, and, though parsimony is valued in its own terms by many scientists, we may also surmise that the drive to coherence exercises its force over the idea of parsimony because incoherence is cognitively and affectively expensive. To fantasize is to economize, precisely in order to make something thinkable. If Jerome S. Bruner, Jacqueline J. Goodnow and George A. Austin are right in the claim made in their *A Study of Thinking* of 1956 that thinking is the way in which an organism *'reduces the complexity of its environment'* – a claim followed and expanded in the systems theory of Niklas Luhmann, for whom a system is an understandable zone of reduced complexity – then it is often fantasy that executes the work and registers the reward of this economization.[18] Despite what one might think, fantasy often exists to cut short some kind of intolerably long story of ifs and buts. We do not ourselves merely make the saving, since we are constituted in our ways of thinking to *be* it.

In short, the madness of knowledge will often therefore consist essentially in the demand that knowledge must make sense (in short). That is, for something to be known or knowable, it must move the knower and the world in the direction of order and simplicity. This will not always involve obvious simplification, and may sometimes give the impression of increasing complexity rather than reducing it. But calling something complex can often be a way of letting yourself off having to think about it any more. Complexity cannot be thought in itself, and the knowledge of complexity will always involve a scansion, narrativizing or orchestration of the complex within a containing frame that will make it knowable as a system of divergences. One needs only to think of the relentless homogenizing – that is, the move defiantly upstream from diversity – that has occurred to the contemporary idea of 'diversity', which has come to mean 'strictly regulated proportions', rather than unpredictable variety. Even if it were possible to know a state of pure chaos – that is, pure, uncompressible unpredictability, pure divergence with no norm or regularity from which the divergence would take place – simply recognizing it as this limit state would itself be a kind of containment or compression of it. Because it is a matter of moving from complexity to information, from disorder to disorder, this process is expressible mathematically – and probably expressible in no other way – as a cancelling out in the interests of reduction of the many to the one. The principle of parsimony will always make it more plausible to speak of Capitalism, or Neoliberalism, or Globalization, or Terrorism or the Clash of Civilizations than to take account of the swirling, turbid, unregistrable mixture of causation and contingency that might otherwise have to be figured into the equations. This is the madness of knowledge: that we can only know the knowable and can never know if it is possible to know anything else. We can never know whether knowledge is more than the adjustment of the world to our focal length. Even knowing that fact must bend the knee, epistemonically as it may be, to knowledge's own law of conformity.

There are other senses in which one may speak of the madness of knowledge. There is, most dramatically and familiarly, the idea that knowledge can go mad and that the lust for knowledge therefore anticipates or leads to this madness. It would have to be acknowledged that, where it used to be poetry that was to madness near allied, it is now science, or its idiot half-brother 'science' – the first the name for a range of practices of experimental investigation, the second the fantasy, at once envious and self-given, in which, as T. S. Eliot writes, 'the giving famishes the craving', of an omnipotent, godlike power.[19] Madness is sometimes thought of as a wild disordering of thought, the scattering of reason and the dissolution of all regularity, but we have had to become used to the fact that madness is in fact much more likely to take the form of an excessive reduction to rule. The delusions of schizophrenics could not be more uniform if they were assigned by a Central Bureau of Paranoid Systems. (But then, Perhaps They Are . . .) It is hard to be sure whether delusions about magical systems of thought-control (fairies, spirits, angels, devils, rays, energies) have always themselves been systematic, or whether we have only lately become systematically interested in them. Human societies structured around belief tended to make the distinction between reason and madness irrelevant, since reason had always itself frankly taken the form of systematic, wish-fulfilling delusion. But ever since the seventeenth century, when knowledge began to separate from belief, madness has operated more and more in apposition rather than opposition to systematic reason. During this period it has become possible for the exercise of reason to become not only unreasonable but irrational. The easy access to forms of self-broadcasting provided by the Internet has revealed to us all how easy it is for humans to surrender to the kind of systematic delusions of systematicity that are characteristic of an intense moral, emotional and religious investment in knowledge and the pressure to make known that it encourages. The figures of the mad scientist, master criminal or evil genius are familiar embodiments of this kind of knowledge gone mad. In a world of systems in which there is a sense of being threatened – not by evil, but by secret knowledge and, increasingly, by knowledge *that nobody knows* (with the diabolical cast that the innocent word 'algorithm', which simply means a logical procedure, has recently taken on, for example) – the only reasonable response is more and countervailing knowledge. Necessarily this is a knowledge that can be known and that we can make our own, underpinning the existence of a knowing subject: epistemophilia can thereby mutate into epistemopathology.[20] For some time the word 'irrationality' has usefully named the phenomenon not of nonrationality but of mad reason, of a rationality pushed to the point of obsession or absurdity. The problem with reason is precisely that it can become so unreasonable. The oscillation between the words 'reasonable' and 'rational' is telling: reasonableness is the moderator of rationality. It may seem rational to cull a large proportion of existing humans in the interest of reducing carbon emissions and depredation of the environment, but to most it would seem unreasonable.

But there is another, milder yet much more pervasive form of knowledge-madness, which would correspond to the state signalled by being 'mad for' or 'crazy about' something or someone. Here what is meant is often an immoderate, if often also admirable, attachment or devotion. This is the kind of excited infatuation, which may not always amount to fatuity, with which this book will largely be concerned. Such devotion may often cloud judgement, though the question of how to ensure correct judgements will not be found to be much to the fore in this book (though not because such questions are unimportant).

Another minor form of the full-blown madness of knowledge is the operation of noetic fantasy in the form of magical thinking, whether defined specifically in terms of Freud's omnipotence of thoughts or more broadly as thought's 'I thought as much' self-congratulation. Thinking about magical thinking can sometimes be caught up in contemporary forms of critique which see magic as part of a lifeworld that has been the victim of denigration and domination by rationalist modernity. The point of inquiring into magical thinking then comes to be either to expunge it or to protect and exalt it. Randall Styers goes further than most in the second direction, maintaining that

> scholarly discourses on magic have regularly conformed to the interests of the dominant classes of Europe and America seeking to regulate and control both their colonial possessions and their domestic populations, especially the troublesome groups on the margins of society.[21]

But there are other ways of thinking than proposing this kind of life-or-death contest. It will scarcely be possible to emerge on one side or the other, the magical or the rational, with regard to magical thinking, simply because it will be impossible to locate oneself fully within or beyond its orbit. Nor will it be possible for thinking to be aligned otherwise with some kind of domination, if only because the power of letting be will always still be a power. That is why epistemopathy is not the name for a disease of knowing, or for its cure. Rather, it is an inquiry into what, and with what, we feel about knowing.

It might sound as though being strongly and decidedly for or against magical thinking would be just the kind of evidence of feeling that ought to be considered by an epistemopathic study. To be sure – but identifying this kind of yes/no feeling is very far from exhausting the possibilities. The drive to know may well be accompanied by decisive feelings, or the desire for decision, but it may, and perhaps always must, also be accompanied by more mixed and shifting complexions of feeling. Whether we take note of it or not, feeling is always at work in the work of knowing, even and especially in the itinerant or suspensive conditions we call surmising, supposing, doubting or wondering. 'You may imagine his thoughts as he sat there in the dark not knowing what to think', Samuel Beckett writes in *Company*.[22] The gentle redemption of this joke is that one can indeed imagine such 'thoughts', or rather the peculiar yet familiar feeling of not quite knowing what you think about something, while perhaps carefully wanting not quite to be sure.

Let us return to the relations between fantasy and truth. As I remarked earlier, philosophers since Plato have agreed that you cannot really know something that is not true; you must know it, as we oddly say, 'in truth'. Truth is what can be shown to be true, and *so must be so shown*. There can be no unnecessary or merely given truth. Truth may not just happen to be, for truth is what exerts its traction between the statement *x* and the statement 'it is true that *x*'. Truth must be forced into being, for it is itself the very force of being true, which is a *must* of being known and shown. This is phenomenology and not ontology, of course. It is only for us, those of us worked on, up and over by the idea of the force of truth, that truth exercises a force; only to creatures like us who have the relation to knowing that we do does it seem that things must be forced into the condition of truth. If there is a way things really are, then there just is, and there would be no *having to be* about it. Why is truth necessarily to be known? This is an epistemic variation on the question: if there really were an omnipotent God, why would He have any need of being praised or believed in?

Fantasy is the engine of this imperative force and the force of this imperative engine. I do apologize for all these nasty inversions, and wish I could promise that this is the end of them. Not only is truth 'a property of sentences', as Richard Rorty proposes, but those sentences always operate in an imperative mood.[23] In fact, truth is not just itself imperative, it is imperiousness itself. Fantasy is both outcome and author of this demand that the truth actively and imperatively *be*, rather than passively existing. Truth, as *troth*, that in which we can have trust, cannot in fact be trusted to happen to be. This is not just the will to power but the will to cede to truth the power to empower the will. The will to power is at work in the will to be powerless in front of the truth. I see no way out of this paradox except through the fantasy that tightens its slipknot. If I mitigate the fantasy of knowing the truth then I intensify the fantasy, which can only in fact pass through me, of letting the truth be in my despite.

It is hard to think of fantasy in this way, because fantasy has the reputation of being the untrue, and therefore of being an idle, childish or slipshod evasion of the demands of truth. Fantasy is thought to compensate for the harshness and austerity of how things are; it makes it possible to live, even if at the cost of living a lie. Fantasy is associated with the excessive – to say something is fantastic is to say that it goes far beyond the necessary minimum that characterizes truth, where the latter is always held by contrast to be simple, immutable and absolute. 'That is simply not the case', we insist; but there can be nothing that is *simply* not the case, because being not-something must always be marginally more complicated (take away the number you first thought of) than the simple being of it.

So the inquiries conducted in this book will depend on the principle that fantasy is by no means the opposite of truth, it is rather its executive force. Truth is in fact the outcome of the twinned relation of fantasy and force – for fantasy is always force and force always phantasmal (never, of course, merely or entirely phantasmal, precisely because it always exercises a real force, and thereby the force of the Real itself). Fantasy exists as the way in which we transitively *exist* things as existing, the way we insist that they be, even and perhaps especially when we insist that that being is independent of us – and thus never more so than in our fantasies of the kinds of force that qualify as absolutely immune or indifferent to our coercion: hurricanes, mathematics, time, death, taxes and so on. This is why we force on to such things the status of unforced force, though the force that such things exercise over us is one that we have given to them, through a complex but impassioned disavowal that enables us to be taken up in its operations. Truth is the ungovernable and implacable force that we force on things. It follows that the operations of those whose business is truth, or who make truth their business – lawyers, priests, pundits, journalists, medics, media-folk and academics – must be riddled and red-handed with fantasy. What kind of imagination is this, so reason-ridden? What kind of reason is this, so dream-driven?

It would be wearisome and self-regarding for me to go on too long about this, but of course there is a considerable epistemic yield from the very way in which I am here evoking the work of fantasy, in which every investment in knowledge can be described as a kind of fantasy. If I am claiming knowledge of all this, then may it not be my own act of fantasy – the cackling, self-hugging fantasy of being the only one, or among the only ones, to be in the know about the workings of fantasy – and to be able to descry its operations everywhere except in myself? It would be hard to deny that the temptation of this aquiline, alpine perspective is at least sometimes a powerful component in the professional fantasy-life of academics in the humanities and those who feel the ripples of its gravitational waves. I can feel it, as I know you can, verily swelling in me now. There is nothing more powerful than fantasy; and no fantasy more powerful than the fantasy of having power over fantasy through knowledge. And then the power of exposing that fantasy, and so on, we must suppose, in glumness or glee. My aim in this book is not to snap my fingers, awaken us from this trance of epistemological command and bring us bump back into the room, but rather to try to articulate something of what it is like to be in the thick of these inside-out arrogations and abrogations.

These sentiments are readable as having relation to something like what is called the politics of truth, or what determines the possibility at any one time of being, in terms Michel Foucault borrowed from Georges Canguilhem, 'in the true'.[24] I would fall in with this formulation on condition that we acknowledge that the idea of politics is one of the areas in which the phantasmal force of the will to truth operates most potently. There is assuredly a politics of fantasy, but all politics is also itself fantasy – not only fantasy, of course, because the implication of force in fantasy means that nothing is only fantasy. The politics of fantasy – a denunciation, say, of the ideology of equality, or consumer happiness – is the way in which the idea of fantasy is used to make stick a certain fantasy of truth, in the sense of a certain wish-for-truth-to-be. Slavoj Žižek has claimed that ideology is never more in evidence than when we claim that we have moved beyond ideology. But the work done by the word 'ideology' for Žižek is exemplary: rather than promising the truth beneath the raree-show or fairylights of appearance, the truth of ideology is that there is always and only more ideology:

> This is probably the fundamental dimension of 'ideology': ideology is not simply a 'false consciousness', an illusory representation of reality, it is rather this reality itself which is already to be conceived as 'ideological' – *'ideological' is a social reality whose very existence implies the non-knowledge of its participants as to its essence* – that is, the social effectivity, the very reproduction of which implies that the individuals 'do not know what they are doing'. *'Ideological' is not the 'false consciousness' of a (social) being but this being itself in so far as it is supported by false consciousness'.*[25]

Let us not shrink from reading the gratification that comes from reading and writing such sentences. For academics, truth-fantasy is inseparable from epistemophilia, from the longing to know; and the fantasy of the power that we want to believe comes from knowing the truth of things, from knowing what truth wants us to know and make known.

AS WE KNOW

Michel Serres has repeatedly said that all the evil of the world comes from the *libido d'appartenance*, the libido of belonging: not nothing but evil, one should be careful to note, but still, all the evil there is going.[26] I would prefer to say that all the evil of the world comes from the libido of truth, since libido is just the will to truth, and the libido of belonging is the fantasy of the truth of belonging. I cannot indulge that sense of belonging without building for myself the belief that there is some community to which I not only might but do belong. Most of the ceremonies that cement belonging depend upon investing some belief or tradition with the power of willed truth. If it is not true in itself, we invest it with our own power performatively to give it this status.

Of course we do not always know what we are saying or what we are doing. What is more, we do not always know what we do not know about what we say and do. Indeed, since we so rarely inquire into what it actually means to know something (where 'means' means 'feels like'), because it seems we do not need to inquire, we really know very little about what and how we know. What is more, we often seem not to want to know about such things – otherwise we might have shown more interest in them than we have over the centuries we have been haggling over epistemology. That is because while we seem to know what it means to know the different things we know – your computer password, how to baste a chicken and drive a car, the rules of English word order – we do not have much of what could count as *experience* of them. To have experience, to be 'experienced' or 'expert', does not rule out my having an experience of knowing what knowing something is like, but it renders it unnecessary. I simply appear to myself to know the things I know, because my knowing seems simply to pop up just at the point at which it is needed. I don't have to press the intercom to an internal librarian who trills 'just a moment, sir' and shortly afterwards slips the required folder on to my desk. Or, more disconcertingly, the knowledge on which I have taught myself to count deserts me, making me wonder if it was ever even there: how could I not have known that I did not really know this? This means that I may often in fact assume I know all kinds of things that I in fact do not.

This is concerning because what we are is dependent not on what we feel or do, what we look like or where we live, but on what we know. Our knowledge – of facts, memories, capacities, likelihoods – is at once the most important and the most fragile, evanescent part of us. And yet, set your face as flint and *sapere audere* as much as you like, but a lucky right cross, a ripped cerebral artery or a few neuro-fibrillary tangles are all it takes to nix large parts of what you thought you infallibly knew and ergo were.

A thought 'occurs to' me. I am 'lost in thought'. It seems to be intrinsic to thinking that I cannot precisely coincide with it. When anyone has ever said 'a penny for your thoughts', it has always left me at a loss and penniless. In part it is because I don't really seem to have things I could call 'thoughts' unless I am marshalling my mental activity into the form of propositions, like this. And yet, at the same time, thoughts seem like things, they seem to be productions of some kind, and not just processes. My thoughts seem, like my words, to be separate from me, once they have been, as I say, as I find myself saying, had.

When I remarked to a philosopher friend that I found it interesting that I didn't have anything that could count as a feeling of how I knew things, he said, like the White Rabbit in the trial in *Alice's Adventures in Wonderland*, '*Un*interesting, I think you mean'. Which left me dispiritedly, and of course silently, beginning to find it interesting that such a thing might seem to anyone, even a philosopher, to be of no interest. For much of epistemology seems to be taken up with the question of how we can be sure of what we know, and what we can know, where 'being sure' presumably means not having to check every time. Epistemopathy, the feeling of having knowledge and the feeling we may have for knowledge more generally, operates in this space in which knowledge is always to be had, as it were, on account. Like so much else, my knowledge is actually a matter of conjecture or probability: to say I know something is to say only that I take there to be a high chance of my being able to invoke or deploy it as required. So, I am not only surrounded by people who I assume have knowledge, and am myself assumed by other people to have certain kinds of knowledge; I represent for and to myself what Jacques Lacan calls the *sujet-supposé-savoir*, the subject-supposed-to-know.[27] I seem not to be inward with the knowledge I suppose to be somewhere inside me. The knowing of the knowing subject must be supposed, which is pretty much the same word as substituted, put under, or even understood, in the sense in which an absent part of speech may be said to be 'understood'. All this supposition and presumption makes knowing subject to the work of fantasy and perhaps inextricable from it. The thing I will be calling fantasy is what helps me suppose that I am the person that I am supposed to be, and that I know who that is.

If it is hard to be quite sure what it means, or is like, for an individual subject to know something, it is even harder to understand what kind of experience there could be of collective knowing. In this respect, collective knowing is like collective memory or collective feeling (about which I have had my extended say elsewhere) in that there is no conceivable way for knowledge to be known collectively in the absence of something like a collective subject to do the feeling or remembering.[28] We must say that collective knowledge requires not just a subject supposed to know, but a supposed collective subject of knowing.

And yet it feels as though there is something essentially collective about all knowing. Human beings find it almost intolerably difficult to keep any kind of knowledge to themselves. Like a joke, knowledge needs to be transmitted or made intelligible. Of course, there is such a thing as secret knowledge, but, as I will be proposing in Chapter Three, 'Secrecy', even secret knowledge is social, in that it is usually held in common by a cabal or select group rather than by an individual.

No society or social system is directly or immediately knowable or experienceable. A society can only ever be known or experienced through objectifications, which are themselves approximations to a kind of fantasy. It is not right to think of rituals, performances, ceremonies or institutions as the expression or manifestation of something that exists in latent form. Latent existence is not existence at all, which is why there is so much pressure to *exist* ideas of what is latent of underlying. A society is the fantasy that individual members or observers of that society have of it. And yet that fantasy is not merely perspectival, for fantasy is never a merely atomic or individual phenomenon. There is always a fantasy of the social, but it is prevented from being 'merely' a fantasy through the existence of a sociality of fantasy. Systems and collectives are phantasmal, but these fantasies are systematic and collective.

The collectivity of knowledge is suggested by the very elusiveness of the experience of knowing. I know what it is like to recognize something that I know, and I know what it is like to think I know something (I think), but the things I know seem somehow to be withdrawn from the possibility of being experienced; to know something means to know it without having to know you know it, which is why we rely so much on various acts of telling or spelling out to provide the proof that we do indeed know what we know – and that we know that we know it. And this doubling, in knowing that we know that, means that our knowing must be able to go beyond us. The fact that this telling or spelling out is necessarily in a language that is not our own – otherwise it would not itself be intelligible or even perhaps known to be a language – may suggest to us that knowledge can neither originate in or remain with us, but must precisely be part of what 'we know'. If we are *Homo sapiens*, the very existence of such a phrase makes it clear that, if we have knowledge, it is a knowledge held in common and capable of being preserved and passed on.

It is commonly assumed that, if divinity has been dispelled by knowledge, then knowledge may supply the place of that absconded or ostracized divinity. There is at least one sense in which knowledge retains its divine features. Paul writes to the Colossians that in God 'are hid all the treasures of wisdom and knowledge' (Colossians 2:3). The idea that God is a kind of infinite archive of knowledge beyond human knowing – and that religious faith involves what the King James rendering of Paul's Greek calls the 'acknowledgment of the mystery of God' (Colossians 2:2) – suggests in advance the possibility of a kind of deification of knowledge, which, in modernity, may survive the dissolution of the idea of God as its carrier or container while retaining its occult and unencompassable character. Perhaps all this survives in a vestigial way in the exaltation implied in the phrase 'look up', in the sense of consult or search for, recorded from 1632.

More than ever before we have the sense of a collective archive of knowledge, maintained for the use of, and accessible by, the 'we' I have just invoked, which at once transcends any individual and is yet, in some abstract sense, available to them. In the place of religious faith, yet isomorphic with it, there is the faith in knowledge, the assumption amounting itself almost to certainty of the prodigious extent of the things that 'we know'. Though this knowledge is known only by this abstract 'we', the knowing we, or first-person-plural supposed-to-know, is itself only the hypostasis, the imaginary bearer or, literally, 'understander' of the knowledge itself.

Chapter Five, 'Imposture', is concerned with the history of the values and feelings attached to pretended knowledge. But it might be said that epistemopathy allows us to recognize that there must be an element of imposture in all knowing. Epistemopathy can help make sense of the ways in which we play at knowing, or, put somewhat less dismissively, act out the various games of knowledge. The theatrics of knowing require scenery and properties, both rhetorical – as in the formalized exchanges involved in interrogation and answer, for example, discussed in Chapter Four, 'Quisition' – and physical – as in the scenes, spaces and occasions of knowledge examined in Chapter Seven, 'Epistemotopia'. There must always be a *mise en scène* of knowing, which makes it difficult to know what, if anything, is behind the scenes.

PLEASURE OF KNOWING

It may appear that my focus on fantasy has emphasized negative emotions, and especially those of aggression and anxiety. A great deal of epistemopathic import might be said about the abundant harvest of pleasure that is reaped in academic and para-academic writing both from the creation and maintaining of various kinds of anxiety and, more importantly, the vengeful and triumphant attribution of states of anxiety to culpable actors in the past. Men, white people, the rich and powerful of all kinds are to be shown gnawed at by anxiety at their wickedness or unearned privilege, though only dimly and uneasily (hence anxiety rather than out-and-out wretchedness), lest they seem by that token less mired in ignorance and in need of the corrective explications of future know-alls. But it is important to recognize that knowledge-feelings are not always saturnine or sable-hued. The affective work of knowing seems essential both to pleasure and to survival.

Knowledge requires, for example, a blend of constancy and change. Indeed, it may be understood as supplying a bridge between these two principles, for knowing allows both for the securing of a world that will continue in existence without my perception or experience of it and the possibility of adaptation in and to that world. This is much more than an abstract principle, because constancy and change are themselves both strongly invested with feeling. This leads Lawrence Friedman to the proposal that affective investment plays a central role in knowledge; feelings are not just marks of emphasis, a kind of italicizing of items of special interest in the world, but rather constitute the fundamental relations between self and world that are necessary both for knowledge and for psychological flourishing. It is feeling that allows for the blend of conservation and adventure because the trust in the constancy of the world that knowledge gives, and the consequent trust we transfer to knowledge itself, are what is required to allow us to test, speculate and explore: Friedman suggests plausibly that 'an affective bond to the environment enables an infant to limit and thus withstand and be able to assimilate novel stimuli.'[29] Knowing is caught up in the play of accommodation and assimilation, as evoked in Friedman's summary of Jean Piaget's studies of the action of play:

> the patterns that will develop into logical thought are ways of righting a balance which impinging stimuli have upset. This tendency to equilibrium is what it means to be an organism. It is an expression of the fact that if an organism is to adapt, it must allow the environment to affect it, but it must limit the ensuing change so as to be able to retain something of its own organization and identity.[30]

Friedman sees the figure of the mother as essential to this emotional interplay of adaptation to the world and assimilation of the world to the self:

> the mother's style of cognition provides for her child not just a way of being receptive to the influx of stimuli, but a way that bears with it a guarantee of the child's own integrity. The mother's style is a safe model because it is the style of someone who is also the satisfier and therefore respecter of his needs. Epistemologically formulated: the child's needs and drives are familiar to him, and his mother who is so involved in meeting these shares this familiarity. Her familiarity enables the child to 'recognize', or make sense out of, or assimilate, or tolerate, the unfamiliar diversity of experience if seen through her eyes.[31]

We might even be justified in seeing consciousness itself as the product of a hedonic system of reward and pain. All creatures behave in ways that tend towards the maximization of pleasure and the avoidance of pain, and it is getting to be quite easy to build machines that obey this principle. One way of thinking of consciousness is as the intensification through internalization of this instinctual system, an intensification which allows decision-making to complement simple action and reaction. Crucially, it both prescribes and permits temporal deepening – the capacity to remember and to anticipate, comparing past with future circumstances.

An important component of subjectivity is the capacity for selective attention, the willed direction of one's being towards particular objects of perception. Indeed, Bruno van Swinderen identifies subjectivity with the capacity for selective attention, which he seems to have demonstrated in fruit flies.[32] Selective attention need not involve consciousness, and indeed Jakob von Uexküll's work seems convincingly to suggest that a species may simply amount (or reduce) to a kind of selective attention to an environment.[33] But selective attention can also act to tune or enhance the instinctual predispositions that constitute a species. Selective attention can optimize instinct. And it can also begin to optimize itself, directing and correcting its own forms of attention.

Perception and attention are both directed by relations of care; we notice the things that matter to us, which is to say, the things that may give us reward or cause displeasure. This selective attention, consciousness as instinct-optimization, allows for an interesting reversal. Consciousness maximizes reward, but the very capacity to pay attention may create its own reward system. Because we notice what we care about, we come to care about our noticing. First, selective attention enhances pleasure; then pleasure is further enhanced by a selective attention to the capacity for selective attention. The pleasure of knowing x can become the pleasure of knowing that I can know x.

For relatively highly developed organisms like human beings this pleasure can in time become primary. Organisms subject to this form of what may be called hedonic recursion can begin to care more and more for the quality of their consciousness as well as their consciousness of the qualities of their world. They may even come to live for the sake of developing the pleasures and rewards of that consciousness and in some cases be given a salary for it, and even legalized protection against any interference with its desire to fulfil itself as and where it lists. For creatures capable of this kind of self-relation the unexamined life may come to seem not worth living. The pleasure of conscious reflection on consciousness may even allow for feelings and behaviour that seem to override questions of what may seem objectively to conduce to the organism's well-being or survival. If consciousness comes into being at the behest of a utilitarian pleasure principle, then it can also deploy that principle for its own ends, to further the ever more autonomous drive to thinking and knowing, along with its promised yield of pleasure-knowledge. Thinking begins as the dumb instrument of life, but then begins to find ways of bending life into its own service. Even the most powerful and vital reward system, that of sexual pleasure, can be overtaken by the epistemophilic principle, sexual desire becoming ever more entangled with curiosity, such that the act of sexual congress becomes known as 'knowing', especially in religious language, an act which frequently leads to 'conceiving': the Vulgate 'Adam vero cognovit [Hebrew יָדַע, *yada*] Havam uxorem suam' being rendered in the late fourteenth-century Wycliffite Bible as 'Adam forsothe knew Eue his wijf' (Genesis 4:1).[34] The Freudian view of curiosity attempts to maintain the dominion of instinct, seeing knowing as an indirect form of sexual gratification; the view maintained in this book is that knowing can become primary, subduing and enveloping sexual pleasure for its own ends.

Something of this may be involved in the curious phenomenon of sexual identity. It is of course not unknown for human beings to band together on the basis of their likes and dislikes – we, the sausage-eaters, will never capitulate to the life-denying nutarians; we, pure-of-heart abhorrers of pigs as we are, will never sink to the vile quadruped depravities of the pork-pie perverts. Like having red hair or pale skin, thinking you know what you like to eat furnishes you with a way of knowing what distinguishes you – a weak but serviceable substitute for knowing who you are, otherwise an extremely tricky procedure among beings who are in almost every respect so irritatingly indistinguishable from each other. But to believe that who you are can be conveniently summarized by reference to the nature of your sexual preferences is a truly strange capitulation to the force of synecdoche. We may surmise, I think, that the pleasure of what is nowadays presented as the almost religious function of acknowledging your sexuality – which must, it seems, be confessed in the proclaiming way you confess a faith, as a secret that with obedient defiance you steadfastly refuse to keep – is a pleasure impelled to a large degree by the fantasy of self-knowing. Affirmation of this kind is noesis in the imperative mode. Knowing what you like underpins liking what you know. The apparently spontaneous act of recognizing the things that give you pleasure – especially pleasures that we assume are cardinal like eating and sex – becomes a substitute for knowing yourself. I like knowing that I am the sort of person who likes object *x*. The pleasure is intensified if I can persuade myself to believe that liking object *x* (sausages, frottage) phobically precludes liking object *y* (marmalade, bestiality). The pleasure must in part be that of not allowing oneself to recognize the tangled nest of substitutions and approximations that make up one's assurance about such things.

COGNITUS INTERRUPTUS

These reflections on the pleasures of thought may throw some light on the fear of death. While such a fear seems like a goodish thing for an organism to evolve, as a kind of extension and intensification of the desire to avoid pain, Freud thought that 'the organism's puzzling determination (so hard to fit into any context) to maintain its own existence in the face of every obstacle' was a phenomenon in need of explanation.[35] This apparent anomaly may in fact be nothing more than a tautology, since none of the organisms that indeed exhibit what Freud saw as the rational desire to reduce tension and complexity by immediately saying 'no thanks' to life are going to survive to have the Freudian question put to them. What looks like an 'instinct' for survival is bound to be highly developed in the kinds of entities that tend to survive. They don't mean to survive; their meaning is just that they are the ones who have.

Knowing is intimately allied with death. If human beings are, as some of them sometimes claim, the only creatures on earth who truly know that they are going to die, then what they know and the fact that they know what they know and know that they know it, is tuned and tempered by the imminence of death. In one sense death is an insuperable limit to knowledge, for I know that I, living, will never know what death is – or at least won't know my own, and, to be frank, that is the only one that I am really interested in. And yet death is also an enabling condition of knowledge in that what I know may be the only thing of my own that will survive my death. If my being is a being-toward-death, then it is also for that reason a being-in-knowing toward that death. For we cannot say that there is first of all death and then, adventitiously associated with it, the knowledge of death, as though the two might perfectly well be disjoined, at least not for us. For human beings, because they know the fact of death – because they know that there will be something that we will absolutely never know, knowing that death will be the absolute end of all knowledge – the knowing of death is in fact the whole of death. Death, unknowable, is nevertheless taken up entirely in knowledge. It is, despite the existence of at least one other candidate, all we know on earth and all we need to know. So not only is death nothing but the ways in which we know of it, whether statistically or physiologically, but there is no knowledge of anything that is not tinged by the fact that we know it only for the time being, the time-being that keeps us hanging around for the end of being-in-time. Knowledge, then, is the whole of death, and mortality the whole of knowledge.

We can, of course, attempt to evade that knowledge, through various kinds of happy-ever-after post-operative scenarios, but none of them can succeed in expunging the knowledge that some explanation is needed, that there is something to be accounted for in that apparent extinction of feeling and knowing that occurs at the end of physiological life. The absolute limit to knowledge that is immanent to knowing is cognate with the more minor and accessory forms of limit that are intrinsic to all forms of knowing. Knowledge is not only shadowed by the non-knowledge of death, it is also characterized, I will be arguing in Chapter Six, 'Unknowing', by an active relation to forms of unknowing. To know something is always to be aware of how much we know and what we do not yet know.

Yet it remains puzzling to some that the prospect of the absence of consciousness should be a source of anxiety or pain. Philosophers since Lucretius have struggled to understand, or have pretended not to understand, how nothingness can be a source of fear. There is a striking tension between the pleasure to be had from contemplating the end of pain and the pain of contemplating the end of contemplation. It is nicely captured in Philip Larkin's mockery, in his poem 'Aubade' (1977), of the Stoic mockery of the fear of death, in which he points out that it is no good at all saying we should not fear what we cannot feel, since not being able to feel is exactly the thing we dread.[36] Larkin is scarcely the first to enter this objection: Aureng-Zebe says it too in John Dryden's play of the same name: 'Death, in it self, is nothing; but we fear / To be we know not what, we know not where'.[37] 'Aubade' moves towards the awareness that the awareness of death cannot be had, or at least held, so will have itself to be done away with. In this, Larkin's poem attempts a substitution about which it is not quite forthright. It tells us that the fact of death cannot be known, so that the knowledge that we in fact always have of its necessity cannot for long be tolerated. But there is a kind of pleasure in knowing that abstract fact about our knowing, a pleasure that may provide a sort of counter-weight to our dread. This pulls against the fact that the poem does not seem to have much confidence in anything except knowledge-evasion – the numbing routines of work, socializing or drink. Indeed, 'Aubade' actually offers itself as an instance of this numbing, thereby seeming to face up to the impossibility of facing up to death. This is a little cognitive ruse, or bit of epistemohedonic apparatus, that enables the poem to imagine that it is in fact confronting what it is evading, by styling its own evasion as a sort of facing-up.

I will confess that I have both suffered and profited all my life from the terror of unemployment, which, given the kind of employ-ment that has improbably turned out to have been gainful for me, means not being able to think, or having nothing to think about. I once heard Anthony Hopkins describing the reasons that he had to get away from his birthplace: it was not, he said, that there was any-thing wrong with Wales, but that he felt he had to escape 'the agony of my empty mind'. There are those who say that the bliss of nescient unbeing would be nirvana, but for me there needs to be something to think about, which means something to think with. In this I am approving the sentiments at the end of E. Nesbit's 1905 poem 'The Things That Matter', in which an old lady regrets not the impending loss of life, but the silly squandering of all the useful things she knows:

> O God, you made me like to know,
> You kept the things straight in my head,
> Please God, if you can make it so,
> Let me know *something* when I'm dead.[38]

I could not be experiencing nirvana if I could not know that I was experiencing it, in which case all the old trouble would simply kick in again. I do not think there is any thinking, even the most gossa-mer grade of reverie, that is not at least implicitly a working through of implications and consequences, and therefore a kind of reason-ing. So, not *cogito ergo sum*, but *cogito ut sim*, not 'I think, therefore I am', but 'I think in order that I may be' (unlike Portuguese, Latin is lamentably lacking in a future perfect subjunctive). And in order to think, you need to know things, to have a store of ideas or internal representations. Indeed, it occurs to me that I do not exactly have a store of things that I know, all ready to be retrieved and put on display; rather, it is the function of the thing I call knowing to make this kind of intentionality available to me. To know means to be able to take things as objects of knowing.

To think means to move through knowledge, to move from what you think you know to the discovery of something else you did not know, or at least could not say, not quite. And this work of knowing is the capacity to lose or, what seems to be the same thing, to occupy myself in thought. W. R. Bion (1897–1979) evokes the relationship of the container to the contained in conceiving of this relationship, and one kind of agony or perplexity is certainly that of seeming to be full of thoughts that do not feel exactly as though they are mine (though this is not always a distress and can sometimes even approach a kind of onanism, as in certain kinds of detached reverie).[39] Bion thought that unless there were some containing integument the experience would be distressing and disorientating. But this is really too crude a metaphor, because the containment does not operate like a pillowcase round an otherwise billowing mass but is a containment formed from local stresses and linkages, analogous to the kind of structure described by Buckminster Fuller as 'tensional integrity', or 'tensegrity'. Thinking is often a matter of not knowing the dancer from the dance, the thinker from the thinking, or the thinking from the thought.

This is of some help when it comes to the thing about which I am so intermittently (albeit at those times somewhat morbidly) curious, namely what dying will be like. (I have tried being interested in the question of what it is like to be dead, but I can't wring any sense out of that.) I suppose I need to distinguish dying from the feeling of perhaps being about to die, the plummeting plane prospect. What I mean by dying is the extended confrontation with something that will never be able to revert to or recall itself – a knowing that will never be able to be a knowledge. But there is the knowledge of that predicament, and it is within this knowledge that there will be a knowing that will never be able to be known, that the shadow falls. Beckett imagines a kind of consummation in the coincidence of knower and knowing at the end of his prose text *Ill Seen Ill Said* (1981/2), which may perhaps be read as an attempt to double or complete the dying of the old woman who is observed so closely throughout the text. The text is simultaneously consumed and consummated in its momentary happiness at knowing its own end:

> First last moment. Grant only enough remain to devour all. Moment by glutton moment. Sky earth the whole kit and boodle. Not another crumb of carrion left. No. One moment more. One last. Grace to breathe that void. Know happiness.[40]

There is knowing happiness in the last two words – read by some as an imperative, though an infinitive in French ('Connaître le bonheur'), in apposition with 'Grace to breathe that void/Le temps d'aspirer ce vide' – and then there is the happiness that consists in the prospect of being able to know the end of knowledge. This, of course, is no happiness at all precisely because it can only be prospective, so more a gnawing than a knowing.[41] These words are in fact associated in Beckett. Before the 'gnawing to be gone' that is a refrain in *Worstward Ho* (1983), there is Winnie in *Happy Days* (1961), who wishes 'not to be just babbling away on trust as it were not knowing and something gnawing at me. (Pause for breath.) Doubt.'[42]

Indeed, this apparently unique state of exception, of a knowing never able to coincide with itself, may in fact begin to spread to everything, back up the arm, earlier and earlier, so that, in the end, or in fact of course well before it, it may constitute a kind of general paralysis. For everything I currently know may need to be included in the register of the irretrievable, of knowing that can never double itself as knowledge. One expedient, not wholly satisfactory, is to try to externalize my knowledge, in the form of writing, or some other form of record. But even that is not the knowing, just the indication of it. All my efforts at knowing things are doubled by the effort of trying to establish, articulate and thereby coincide with what I know, lest all my knowing get swallowed up in the abyss of things I have never succeeded in knowing that I know. The division between the final frame and the blackout, between the last, the very last act of knowing that will never be able to know itself, in fact potentially fissures all my knowing. So in a sense I do know death, or know that the promised end of knowledge is insinuated always and everywhere in my knowing. Naturally, I am performing these recondite pleasures, or, more certainly perhaps, I am feeling them as I formulate these sentences and (same word really) sentiments. Thinking can derive from the dread of nescience a kind of gratification, seeming to promise that knowing can reach beyond itself even into the heart of unknowing. Often this will draw on the resources of subjunctive knowing, the pseudo-knowledge or quasi-knowledge of imagining and dreaming.

PSEUDO-KNOWING

Literary writing can provide some clues about epistemopathy, both as symptom and diagnosis. It used to be that literature was thought of as the framing of certain kinds of truth in pleasing or sonorously self-certifying ways, as for example in the seeming statement of knowledge about knowledge that concludes Keats's 'Ode on a Grecian Urn' (1819): "'Beauty is truth, truth beauty,"' – that is all / Ye know on earth, and all ye need to know.' If one could imagine a prize awarded for utterances that crammed into a restricted space as many dubious and unearned predications as possible, this couplet would surely bear away the bay. Self-evidently, beauty is not always even true, let alone truth itself; and it is equally obvious that truth is very far from always being beautiful (isn't it in fact generally supposed to be 'stark', 'plain', 'unvarnished' or 'gritty'?). Even if these wild allegations were, for the sake of argument, allowed to count as knowledge, we obviously, as regards 'all ye know', know a multitude of other things apart from them (much more satisfying and useful things at that) which it would consequently seem insane to abandon as unnecessary ('all ye need to know') now that we are in possession of the euphonious but egregiously false twaddle earlier enounced. I trowel things on in this way in order, I hope, to demonstrate how bizarrely beside the point it would actually be to take these assertions seriously, though it has taken quite a long time for critics to explain to us and each other why this is a deeply flawed, or at least unprofitable, way of reading such lines, and indeed of reading literature as such.

At the beginning of the twentieth century a formative perplexity certainly seems to arise as to the kind of knowledge that might be embodied in literature. For much of the nineteenth century the relation between literature and knowledge continued to be thought of as a natural and self-evident one. The correspondence still seems quite casually to be assumed in the titles of any number of nineteenth-century works: Samuel Bailey's *Questions in Political Economy, Politics, Morals, Metaphysics, Polite Literature and Other Branches of Knowledge*

(1823), for example, or the *New London Magazine*, which began publication in 1837 with the subtitle *A Melange of Literature, Science, the Fine Arts, and General Knowledge*. By the end of the nineteenth century it was starting no longer to be obvious that arranging words rhythmically and making up stories should be thought to be part of the universe of learning or the store of human knowledge. It would become important, if literature was to be taught in universities, for it to be put on some kind of respectable academic footing and for some kind of argument to be made out for the sort of knowledge that literary writing and reading might represent.

One of the most influential reformulations of the noetic claims of literature is in the work of I. A. Richards. In *Science and Poetry* (1926), Richards influentially asserts that 'misunderstanding and underestimation of poetry is mainly due to overestimation of the thought in it ... It is never what a poem *says* which matters, but what it *is*.'[43] And what a poem, or indeed any literary artefact is, for Richards, is an 'extraordinarily intricate concourse of impulses', and the words which are employed '*as a means of ordering, controlling and consolidating* the whole experience' (*SP*, 26). This understanding of the work performed by literary writing is made necessary by the decline of what Richards calls the 'Magical View' of the world, along with the huge and accelerating growth in 'genuine knowledge' (*SP*, 52), that is, exact and certain scientific knowledge. This knowledge, so abundant and self-evidently powerful, also dissolves man's supposition that

> his feelings, his attitudes, and his conduct spring from his knowledge. That as far as it could it would be wise for him to organize himself in this way, with knowledge as the foundation on which should rest feeling, attitude, and behaviour. (*SP*, 51)

What literature can supply instead is a knowledge built on what Richards calls the 'pseudo-statement' (*SP*, 56), defined as 'a form of words which is justified entirely by its effect in releasing or organizing our impulses and attitudes', as opposed to a statement, which 'is justified by its truth, *i.e.* its correspondence, in a highly technical sense, with that to which it points' (*SP*, 59). Literature is part of the way out of the contemporary impasse that arises from the knowledge that merely factual knowledge will not essentially do for many purposes:

The remedy, since there is no prospect of our gaining adequate knowledge, and since indeed it is fairly clear that genuine knowledge cannot serve us here and can only increase our practical control of Nature, is to cut our pseudo-statements free from belief, and yet retain them, in this released state, as the main instruments by which we order our attitudes to one another and to the world. (*SP*, 61)

Richards's view that literature provides a kind of as-if knowledge – a performative and experimental cognitive play-space – along with his sense that the organization of feeling is an important component in this, is perhaps not too far from one form of what I am calling epistemopathy. But Richards is not only more confident than I am about being able to separate the claims of literary pseudo-knowledge from exact knowledge, he is also much more sanguine – desperately, even deliriously so – about the redeeming possibilities of such knowledge. In my view, the operations of what we might call epistemofantasia, the reinvestment of Richards's Magical View of the world in the fusion of magical and scientific thinking, are much more widely diffused than he suspects, and certainly not concentrated in literature or art.

There are of course many different things we can mean by knowing. The point of epistemology is to take care of distinguishing these usages, often in order to set many of them aside as unsuitable for philosophical attention – knowing that and knowing how, knowing as having familiarity with, knowing as understanding, knowing as experiencing, knowing as having information about. The aim, in part, of epistemopathy (in the sense here of epistemopathic investigation rather than epistemopathic symptoms) is to be able to register the compacts, confusions and conspiracies between the different ways in which we might feel we know, and the ways we might feel about how and what we know. For the epistemologist, gossip and *idée fixe* have their coat pegs a great distance away from those of religious conviction or experimental data: in the affect-space of epistemopathy they may find themselves jostled in absurd or disturbing proximity. The effect of being surrounded by so many different media of information and experience, along with the institutional modes of knowing and making known they seem to encode, is to multiply both the ways in which we feel we may feel we know things and the occasions of this miscibility. Rather than offering a distinctive and alternative literary mode of knowing, glowing with the glamour or pathos of resistance (one of the things we pretend we know about literary texts is that they are always putting up a fight against something wicked), literary texts may be a venue, albeit neither invariantly nor uniquely, for these convergences and maladjustments. Epistemopathy in modern literature, for example, often expresses itself in the effort to negotiate between the realms of knowledge (embodied in knowing agents) and information (processed in media and machineries). The mediating object is sometimes the literary work itself, which may seem to partake of both the action of thinking and the condition of the database.

The writing and reading of literature are not the only ways in which epistemopathic impulses and postures are rehearsed, though they do provide a rich and varied field of play for them. Literary writings and readings will accordingly have a part to play in the discussions that follow, just as the epistemopathic hypothesis may reciprocally help to make more sense of the relation between literature and knowledge, which has for so long been governed unhelpfully by the idealizing dream of literature as a special way of articulating or transfiguring knowledge rather than a way of encouraging and isolating for attention comportments toward it. Literature can help with knowledge-fantasy not because it is a particular kind of knowledge but because it allows for knowing fantasy. But we should avoid succumbing to the epistemopathic temptation to attribute a special status or destiny to literary writing and reading in this respect. It is one of the uninspected assumptions of those working in certain disciplines, especially in the arts, that they should have to pretend to believe in the special, salvific mission in human history of whatever their area of selective attention happens to be. The difficulty with this is that so many of the forms of the as-if knowledge that I. A. Richards thought might belong essentially or *in excelsis* to poetry, or literature, are also palpably and compellingly at work in many other areas of personal and social existence: for instance, and to look no further than those given attention in the chapters that follow, in intellectual ambition and *folie de sagesse*, sexual curiosity, counterfeit and confidence-tricks, the keeping and broaching of secrets, arguing, quibbling, riddling and quizzing behaviours, the history of idiot-suppression and -sanctification, the actual and imaginary architectures of knowledge, the mythonoesis of artificial intelligence and the projection of our economic and political futures. All of these stage different ways of playing out and working through the human relation to the knowledge that defines us, while remaining so puzzlingly beyond our ken.

1

WILL TO
KNOWLEDGE

According to Aristotle, all humans desire knowledge. But they have not always and with equal vehemence desired to know about that desire to know. This chapter will consider the complex feelings engendered by the idea of the desire to know, or, as it has also been seen, the love of knowledge, will to knowledge or knowledge drive. The difficulty, but also, for that reason, the seductive excitement of this question comes from the complex ambivalence of the value accorded to knowledge and knowledge-desire.

One must assume that the mixed capacity to know – mixed because it cannot really be regarded as a single faculty but must involve a compound of curiosity, speculation, the impulse to experiment, memory and explanation, among other faculties – would have evolved originally as a means to know the world outside humans. Carried to a certain point, knowledge allows one to recognize that there are things in experience that resist and, indeed, are indifferent to us. Early in human evolution practical knowledge must have produced the conception of the object, of what, etymologically, we come up against, and what is thrown up against us. Knowledge allows us to inhabit or be at home in more of the world, but a necessary prelude to that may be the estranging of the world, in the development of the intuition that the world might be otherwise, or might be made so.

But this also made reflection possible – that is, the capacity to treat as objects not only the things of the world, but also our pictures of and ideas about them. Objects must be imageable to be objects, but this then objectifies images. Subjectivity must have come into being simultaneously with what Michel Serres calls the 'transcendental objective', that is, the idea of an object that resists and transcends thinking requiring a reflexive recognition of the act and fact of the thinking.[1] The impediment and the overcoming of knowledge seem to have been born at a stroke, the subject subjected to the objectification it brings about, in what Serres describes as

> a rapid vortex, in which the transcendental constitution of the object by the subject would be fueled, as though feeding back, by the symmetrical constitution of the subject by the object, in lightning-fast semi-cycles and ceaselessly repeated.[2]

FORBIDDING

The Christian myth of the Fall twins knowledge and will. It offers a false, perhaps even satanically devious temptation to believe that it might be possible for humans to exist without a knowledge of good and evil. That might have been possible if only God had not intro-duced the interdiction against eating the forbidden fruit, but once he has, Adam and Eve already know something of good and evil – they must at least have a strong inkling that knowing about good and evil may itself be evil.

For human beings, or at least the kind who have found the story of the Fall compelling, knowledge seems often to be associated with the wilful overcoming of limit. Even acknowledging and obeying the prohibition must imply some intimation of the abstractly bad things that might arise from ignoring it. I cannot imagine what it would be like to imagine a limit without somehow imagining going beyond it. Every thinking of a limit must involve some 'but what if' surpass-ing of it. If it is forbidden to seek to know about good and evil, it is presumably because such seeking to know is a kind of evil. But if it is evil to seek to know about good and evil, is it also, and already, a bit evil to know that? So forbidding the knowledge of good and evil in itself begins to imply or impart that knowledge. Oddly, the God of Genesis does not seem to mind about the doing of evil nearly as much as wanting to know about it. Is it evil to do evil unawares, or is it just the knowing that is evil?

John Milton's *Paradise Lost* (1667/74) adds another turn of the screw, for Milton has Satan, in the form of the serpent, not only tempt Eve to eat from the tree but also show her where it is. This has far-reaching implications. In Genesis 3:3, Eve seems to have been informed which of the trees in the orchard is forbidden to them: 'of the fruit of the tree which is in the midst of the garden, God hath said, Ye shall not eat of it, neither shall ye touch it, lest ye die'. We must assume that it is apparent what 'the tree which is in the midst of the garden' means and that this is not some kind of geometrical guessing-game. But in Milton's poem, extraordinarily, Eve asks Satan for directions to the tree, meaning that she may not know its actual location:

> But say, where grows the tree, from hence how far?
> For many are the Trees of God that grow
> In Paradise, and various, yet unknown
> To us, in such abundance lies our choice.[3]

Now, there is an enormous difference between forbidding access to a specific, known tree and forbidding access to a specific tree that exists somewhere in the garden, without divulging which one it is. The first is an injunction, the second is a conundrum, having something like the following form: 'Somewhere in this garden, there is a tree, the fruit whereof ye definitely may not eat; your task, should you choose to accept it, is to find out which one, without in the process eating from it.' This may be the merest logical wrinkle in a story that is far from being free of other, much larger forms of incoherence. But, significantly, it is of a piece with the essential problem for foreknowledge, which requires the compacting of the two functions of the English word *will* in that whatever will (turn out to) happen will have to be what God wills (intends) to happen, in that special, self-fulfilling way that characterizes God's will. Either God knows already that Adam and Eve are not going to be up to the task of remaining innocent of knowledge – which seems like a sneakily self-pleasuring way for a deity to behave – or he does not know, in which case one must begin to wonder who is really in charge of things around here, since he no longer seems much like an omniscient deity. Perhaps God's omnipotence includes the power to limit his own knowledge, like the child who plays 'eeny, meeny, miny, mo' or covers her eyes and counts to ten. Again, epistemic hide-and-seek of this kind seems anticipatorily anthropomorphic in a God. Or perhaps He knows, but genuinely does not know that he knows? (So God has an *unconscious* now?) God says in Genesis that Adam and Eve have become like gods (what gods?

there are *other gods*?) as a result of eating the fruit, which, in the cognitive gulfs and quandaries it opens up, might be taken as a kind of
'welcome to my world'.

These are ancient objections, and the point of this schoolboy
diversion is not to reveal triumphantly the fact that there might be
inconsistencies in the Creation story. Barrel-fishing is a cheap temptation we should resist in such large and solemn matters. Any story
involving a Creator who is simultaneously omniscient and non-
mischievous is going to have its work cut out to explain how things
could ever have gone otherwise than swimmingly in history. There can
either be a Creator or there can be history; that is, put more simply,
the possibility of there being some story to be told about how things
come about. But a story about an increate Creator himself creating history is always going to run into trouble (fortunately, however,
since trouble is exactly what stories trade in and are designed to deal
with). As soon as it becomes possible for anything to go wrong with
the divine plan, it must have been defective from the start, which is
not usually thought to be a design feature of divine plans. This allows
one to wonder if the point of all origin myths might not be to pose
just these kinds of insoluble riddle, offering as a stimulus to head-
scratching and exam questions a fairy-tale pseudo-knowledge that
is bound never to be enough. Not all creation myths depend on the
problem of knowledge as the Eden story does; but, though this element may look just like an extra bit of bungling on the part of the
collective author of the story of the Fall – since it means that the story
will be bound to have itself to disobey the interdiction on knowledge
that it narrates – it is surely also the source of much of its productiv-
ity. What is more, and most to my present purpose, it will make both
interdiction and the will to disobedience created through prohibition
intrinsic to the understanding of what it is to know, that necessary
mediation between being and doing. Henceforth, knowing will always
have a relation to wanting, and especially wanting to know.

WILLING

Knowledge, we know, we believe, we tell ourselves, is power. It is not
hard to recognize the ways in which, as Francis Bacon puts it in *The
New Organon* (1620), 'those two goals of man, knowledge and power,
a pair of twins, are really come to the same thing.'[4] This must for

many centuries have been something that was too obvious to be of any interest. If I know that deadly nightshade is poisonous, it gives me an obvious advantage over somebody who does not. The more I know of the habits of gazelle, the greater my chances of killing them for food. Gerolamo Cardano provided the first systematic treatment of probability in around 1564 in his *Liber de ludo aleae* (Book of Games of Chance), but refrained from publishing the book during his lifetime, presumably because, being, among many other areas of accomplishment, a highly successful gambler, he relied on his knowledge to maintain his income. Practical knowledge, the knowledge of how to do something, obviously and tautologically implies the power to do it, other things being equal; knowing how to sew is an intrinsic part of the capacity for sewing, since it is the kind of thing I am exceedingly unlikely to find myself doing by accident (even if somebody, somewhere, probably must have). It may perhaps only have been when knowledge began to grow and become abstracted from these immediate purposes that the relation between knowledge and power began to be interesting enough to be reflected and remarked on. Indeed, it may very well be that knowledge and power begin to be twinned just at the point at which mediations become ever more numerous and subdivided. Blackmail provides a good example: my knowledge of somebody's adultery or iniquitous tampering with the market will only be powerful as a result of the cooperation of many other conditions (the possibility of shame, the premium on preserving reputation, the existence of regulatory frameworks and so on). That is, it is perhaps only when know-how is no longer straightforwardly and in itself 'being able to do' that there is a point in affirming their essential identity.

But this complexity opens up another prospect. Why do we so rarely acknowledge that knowledge is also weakness? For knowledge informs us not only of what we may do, but what we will never be able to do, and should tell us that the ratio of the latter to the former is very large indeed. Knowledge informs us of limits as well as potentials, including the limits on knowledge itself; until I know I cannot know everything, I cannot really be said to know anything much. As I suggested in the Introduction, the ultimate knowledge, the one we struggle against and yet that humans take most pride in knowing, thinking themselves unique among animals in this respect, is the knowledge of our own death. This is perhaps the only sure and certain knowledge, but it is also the knowledge of an unpassable limit to knowledge; we become human in the ultimate humiliation of this knowledge, the unappeasable intuition of what we will never be able to know of ourselves. Knowledge must know the necessity of this ultimate nescience.

Perhaps under these circumstances we might begin to wonder whether the phrase *knowledge is power* in fact contains a kind of fingers-crossed predictive wish within its predication: would that knowledge were power, and always power, and only power, for ever and ever. When the power of knowledge becomes simultaneously greater and more circumstantial, along with the consequences of mistaken knowledge, a certain will to power is summoned up in asserting the simple identity of power and knowledge.

What we know as the will to power is composite, since the will in the will to power must always have arrogated power to itself in advance, otherwise what would you be willing with? It is not easy to imagine any kind of willing that would not give and give itself to a kind of power. For humans, willing is an assertion of power in the first place, and so all willing of any kind, directed towards any object whatever, is a will to power. So willpower, or a power to will, always cooperates with a will to power. Could there ever be a will to weakness that would not be paradoxical, that is, that could itself sufficiently and successfully will weakness, while yet succeeding in weakening its own will to weakness or resisting the self-empowerment that always seems to be part of willing? Chapter Six will look at some of the ways in which unknowing has been imagined and desired, but all of them involve the assertion or assumption of some kind of positive power in that desire for unknowing.

If we can accept that knowledge implies and is impelled by a will to power, this relation can also be inverted; not only does all knowing involve power, all power must also require and desire knowledge. If I am to exercise my will, I must know what it is that I want. As we have come to realize, this is not always a straightforward matter, and so much so that the struggle to ascertain what I in fact want may be an essential part of the operations of will. I can be wilful as a way of being determined to find out what I in fact want, or, often, don't. If I unknowingly do some other person's will, or am impelled by an obsessive-compulsive drive that, in the way of such drives, both is and is not mine, or if I feel myself to be doing the bidding of some impersonal kind of Will, then my failure to know my will means that I cannot be said really to exercise it. The will to will must include a will to knowledge of my will.

If there is a will or a drive to know, what kind of drive or will is it? When we ask about a drive in this way, we are often asking what the drive accomplishes or ensures. Here, the implied infinitive *to* points to a finite object or objects: a drive to eat or to copulate accomplishes survival, enabling an organism to persist in being rather than expiring. A drive may be thought of as a kind of exteriorized will, a will that wills itself through installing a surrogate or mirroring will in me. I want the things I want in order that a higher, or at least a less apparent, will may be accomplished, the will-to-being as such. This miniaturized will module is not only installed and at work in me but also, in a sense, is me, using consciousness for its purposes just as it uses hunger and pleasure and pain.

Perhaps, though, things work the other way round entirely; perhaps the idea of the Will, promoted into a capitalized abstraction – the generalized Will that in a sense simply wills that there must be willing, the Will that always requires there to be surrogate wills and acts of willing to accomplish its purpose – is a back-formation, a projection outwards and backwards from these local, lower-case wills or acts of willing. Perhaps, that is, the idea of the Will is a knowledge effect that can only ever be inferred and can never be immediately known.

The fact that Will seems to require this doubling, in which Will accomplishes its purposes through a secondary or substitute will that strives to fulfil what it takes to be its own purposes, can also make possible a hiatus in which the local will can refuse to do the bidding of the general Will. Anorexics, suicides and other kinds of serial self-harmers, along with perhaps every form of nay-saying ascesis, seem to represent a will to refuse the general Will that would otherwise assert itself through their impulse to self-care. The problem for every ascetic of this kind is that they may never be able to be sure that they are in fact effecting the dissidence they seem to assert in their action. Will, even and especially in the form of Will refusal, can never be sure that it is not in fact accomplishing the purposes of Will. For what does the Will want if not assertion of self, thymotic power, striving itself? No more extreme performance of this uncertainty can be imagined than the effort to unsaying in Samuel Beckett's *The*

Unnamable (1953/8), the vehemence of which comes from its attempt to embody 'the little murmur of unconsenting man, to murmur what it is their humanity stifles'.[5] Nobody can quote that phrase approvingly, as I among many others have done, without sentimental approval of the 'humanity' that the sentence says is actually doing the stifling, of whatever it is that the murmur is trying to murmur.

In English, the distinction between declarative knowing (knowing that, in relation to facts and events) and procedural knowing (knowing how to do things) is elided by the use of 'knowing' to refer to both operations. But the older word *ken* – which survives in Scottish and is related both to German *kennen* and to English *can*, as well as to *con*, meaning to study or learn – testifies to the link felt between knowing and being able. But perhaps the most important feature of knowledge is that it represents an assertion-through-acquiescence. As Francis Bacon promises in his *New Organon*:

> man is nature's agent and interpreter; he does and understands only as much as he has observed of the order of Nature in work or by inference; he does not know and cannot do more. No strength exists that can interrupt or break the chain of causes; and nature is conquered only by obedience.[6]

Conquering through obedience is more common than we might think. Bacon's Latin phrase translated above as 'nature is conquered only through obedience' is 'neque natura aliter quam parendo vincitur', where *parendo* is the future passive participle of *pareo*, I appear, or arrive on command, so literally something like 'being made to appear', or 'being summoned'. To say *I will* is to be willing to will the appearance on stage, as required, of my will. It is an interesting quirk of English that, if will asserts itself through many of our utterances, especially those involving some kind of imperative, our language seems to make it awkward to assert the will directly. The will seems to prefer to do its work through speech rather than in it. If I say, 'you will do as I say', the force of my will dissimulates itself through the use of an apparently simple future tense that is actually straining to make itself into a declaration of what is to come. Something similar operates through the complicated force of the now increasingly antique *shall*: 'Thou shalt not kill' and 'You shall go to the ball' both convey, without directly articulating, the force of their obligation or necessity. If I say 'I will' or 'I am willing', I assert that I agree to some set of conditions which I have not myself proposed or originated. If I speak as a sovereign or empress, I may be grand enough to affirm that 'It is my will that', but in such imperious kinds of utterance I once again distance myself from, and cannot precisely coincide with, the imperative to which I give utterance.

SCHOPENHAUER, NIETZSCHE

The predicaments contrived and striven against (contrived, really, in order to be striven against) in Beckett's *The Unnamable* are as a forensic dramatization of some of the possibilities outlined in the philosophy of Arthur Schopenhauer, which may be regarded as the origin of many modern conceptions of the relations between will and knowledge. Schopenhauer's argument is crystallized in section 27 of the first volume of his *The World as Will and Representation* (1819). Here, Schopenhauer explains how it is that the world as an idea or representation for knowledge arises as an expression of that which seems alien or opposed to it, 'a blind urge and a striving devoid of knowledge in the whole of organic nature'.[7] Since, in different kinds of individual being, will tends to objectify itself, it eventually produces something like consciousness, as a maximizing or refinement of the forces that, at a lower level, express themselves through instinct and result in the differentiation of different organs and organisms:

> Thus movement consequent on motives and, because of this, knowledge, here become necessary; and hence knowledge enters as an expedient, μηχανή, required at this stage of the will's objectification for the preservation of the individual and the propagation of the species. It appears represented by the brain or a larger ganglion, just as every other effort or determination of the self-objectifying will is represented by an organ, in other words, is manifested for the representation as an organ. (*WWR*, 1150)

But the brain is not one organ among others, for it is the organ that allows the world to come into being, not as mere blind striving but as representation or idea, a world that may be known.

But with this expedient, with this μηχανή, the *world as representation* now stands out at one stroke with all its forms, object and subject, time, space, plurality, and causality. The world now shows its second side; hitherto mere *will*, it is now at the same time *representation*, object of the knowing subject. The will, which hitherto followed its tendency in the dark with extreme certainty and infallibility, has at this stage kindled a light for itself. (*WWR*, 1150)

Initially, systems of perception and consciousness work as the agents of the will of which they are the externalization or mechanical expedient. But then perception begins to have knowledge of its own workings – 'the light of knowledge penetrates into the workshop of the blindly operating will, and illuminates the vegetative functions of the human organism', a process that Schopenhauer explains (not all that illuminatingly) with the words: 'I refer to magnetic clairvoyance' (*WWR*, 1151). Instinct gives way to deliberation, which introduces for the first time the possibility of error and uncertainty. But it also introduces a fundamental rift in being, between the two realms of will and representation:

Thus knowledge in general, rational knowledge as well as mere knowledge from perception, proceeds originally from the will itself, belongs to the inner being of the higher grades of the will's objectifications as a mere μηχανή, a means for preserving the individual and the species, just like any organ of the body. Therefore, destined originally to serve the will for the achievement of its aims, knowledge remains almost throughout entirely subordinate to its service; this is the case with all animals and almost all men. (*WWR*, 1152)

Schopenhauer then opens up the prospect of a different function for knowledge. First of all, 'in the case of individual persons, knowledge can withdraw from this subjection, throw off its yoke, and, free from all the aims of the will, exist purely for itself, simply as a clear mirror of the world; and this is the source of art' (*WWR*, 1152). Second,

if this kind of knowledge reacts on the will, it can bring about the will's self-elimination, in other words, and indeed the innermost resignation. This is the ultimate goal, and indeed the innermost nature of all virtues and holiness, and is salvation from the world. (*WWR*, 1152)

This opens up the possibility for a new kind of striving in things: consciousness may henceforth, guided by the knowledge that had come about in order to maximize striving, strive to free itself from striving. At times, Schopenhauer seems to believe that knowledge can lever itself completely clear of the operations of the will, for example in the workings of genius:

> For genius to appear in an individual, it is as if a measure of the power of knowledge must have fallen to his lot far exceeding that required for the service of an individual will; and this superfluity of knowledge having become free, now becomes the subject purified of will, the clear mirror of the inner nature of the world. (*WWR*, 1186)

But by the end of the first volume of *The World as Will and Representation* Schopenhauer seems to have moved to a position in which to free oneself from the operations of will would also mean to free oneself from all knowledge, since knowledge, or 'the world as representation', is 'the objectivity of the will', and 'the world is the self-knowledge of the will' (*WWR*, 1410). So there can be no positive knowledge of the state of being that Schopenhauer wishes to represent as beyond will:

> If, however, it should be absolutely insisted on that somehow a positive knowledge is to be acquired of what philosophy can express only negatively as denial of the will, nothing would be left but to refer to that state which is experienced by all who have attained to complete denial of the will, and which is denoted by the names ecstasy, rapture, illumination, union with God, and so on. But such a state cannot really be called knowledge, since it no longer has the form of subject and object; moreover, it is accessible only to one's own experience that cannot be further communicated. (*WWR*, 1410)

Schopenhauer seems uncertain about the relation between will and knowledge, since knowledge is both the objectification of will and yet also the route to the negation of will – which must also mean the negation of all knowledge: 'No will: no representation, no world' (*WWR*, 1411). Perhaps the will to knowledge must always participate in this paradox, that it is always in and of the world of striving even as it strives to go beyond it (and insofar as it continues to strive, must fail to go beyond it).

Schopenhauer's most influential, and irritable, follower is Friedrich Nietzsche. Though he finds much to approve in Schopenhauer's derivation of knowledge from will, Nietzsche cannot bring himself to approve of Schopenhauer's drive to use knowledge to outwit the machinations of will through self-abnegation. Where Schopenhauer regards life as hugely overrated, Nietzsche wishes to find a way to continue to affirm life while going beyond knowledge as traditionally understood. To this end, he calls for '*a merely empirical epistemology*', in which there is 'neither "intellect", nor reason, nor thought, nor consciousness, nor soul, nor will, nor truth'.[8] For Nietzsche knowledge is power, not in the uplifting sense that knowledge gives you the freedom to do things that you would otherwise be powerless to do, to release yourself from chains that you had not realized had you in bondage, but in the sense that knowledge has as its object 'not "to know", but to schematize, to impose as much regularity and form upon chaos as our practical needs require' (*WP*, 299). The most urgent and incessant need for any organism is to create regularity:

> The development of 'reason' is nothing but a process of arrangement and invention which generates similarity and equality, the same process which every sense impression undergoes. No pre-existing 'idea' is at work here, but rather utilitarian considerations which dictate that things are predictable and manageable for us only when we see them rendered approximate and equal. (*WP*, 299)

On such a view abstract knowledge is always a fantasy, since the entire work of knowing is to be understood as the fulfilment of desire. It is Darwinian in its mixture of ardent striving and the coldness of simple utility, and reads abstraction as the precipitate of a kind of striving for persistence in being (which need not know itself as such and, indeed, might often work better if it doesn't). Knowledge is nature red in pen and ink. At the same time, it is itself an abstraction, because that striving is an outcome rather than a formative impulse, so that nothing really wants all this wanting, which is just the sort of thing that there would have to be in order for there to be something rather than nothing, homogeneous forms and self-subsisting sameness rather than constant differentiation.

This is not a will to knowledge so much as a will that bends knowledge to its own interests; its aim is therefore not so much truth as tractability; the distortion, as Beckett puts it, of perception into intelligibility.[9] Nietzsche continues,

> In order for a given species to preserve itself – to grow in power – it must capture in its conception of reality enough of what is uniform and predictable that a scheme of behaviour can be constructed on that basis. The *utility of preservation*, and not some abstract theoretical need to be undeceived, stands as the reason for the development of the sensory organs ... they develop so that their mode of observation is sufficient to preserve us. In other words, the *extent* of the desire for knowledge depends upon the extent to which the *will to power* grows in the species; a species grasps so much of reality *in order to master it, in order to take it into service.* (*WP*, 287; ellipsis in original)

The operations of knowledge, and even of logical thought, involve what Nietzsche calls 'appropriation', by which he means a proportioning or making equivalent of the world and its knower:

> The fundamental inclination to *equate* things and see *them as equivalent* is modified and held in check by considerations of benefit and harm, by considerations of *success*. It adjusts itself so that it can be satisfied to a lesser degree without at the same time denying life and endangering the organism. This process corresponds entirely with that external and mechanical process (of which it is symbol) by which protoplasm constantly assimilates what it appropriates, and arranges it according to its own forms and series. (*WP*, 297)

This association between knowledge and colonizing appropriation means that it is much harder to escape colonialism than one thinks, since colonialism will succumb only to a greater and more encompassing form of intellectual occupation. So in once colonized societies the space of feeling and opinion will often be kept saturated by the thought of the colonial past. When the physical earth has been entirely colonized, the only space still available is the space of thought. No decolonization is imaginable that does not aim to colonize the space of feeling and opinion, leaving no space unoccupied. No theory escapes the desire to colonize, or is possible without it. What theory does not aim to go forth and multiply? What theory can ever aim to be self-limiting or make provision to put a stop to itself? Pollution appropriates, as Michel Serres has demonstrated, but not so much as cleanliness (does one not 'mop up' resistance?).[10] Why is the opposite of dirt not an object but a quality: cleanness, as though matter had been displaced by idea? Nothing is more colonial than the emptying of space, whether through eviction or the decontamination of the sign, for all colonists require the fantasy of *terra nullius*.

Nietzsche's broadly utilitarian view of the function of knowledge means that '[I]t is improbable that our "knowledge" goes much further than what is absolutely necessary for the preservation of life' (*WP*, 293). One might see this as a subordination of knowing to the subject, a way of asserting the powers of the 'I' over the 'it', even over the 'it' which seems to bring about the 'I'. As we have seen, Schopenhauer promises that 'knowledge can withdraw from this subjection, throw off its yoke, and, free from all the aims of the will, exist purely for itself,' and even, in a further refinement, 'if this kind of knowledge reacts on the will, it can bring about the will's self-elimination' (*WWR*, 1,152). But for Nietzsche even consciousness itself is a kind of strategy or utilitarian makeshift. Hence, he writes: '*Consciousness extends only so far as it is useful*' (*WP*, 295). So, for Nietzsche, there is not a subject which has power, nor power exercised in the interests of a subject; rather, there is a subject formed through the will to power. So, for Nietzsche, there can be no knowledge of will, for willing is the action that produces the phantasm of will. If there is no knowledge, but only willing-to-knowledge, there can equally be no straightforwardly knowable will:

> The logico-metaphysical assumptions, the belief in substance, accident, attribute, etc., derive their persuasiveness from our habit of regarding all our actions as the consequence of our

willing them – so that the ego, as substance, is not assimilated to the multiplicity of changes. *But there is no such thing as will.* (*WP*, 290)

This makes the critique of the operations of the power–knowledge coupling less straightforward than it is sometimes taken to be. Perhaps the most sustained deployment of Nietzsche's arguments about the relations between power and knowledge is that undertaken by Michel Foucault. In a 1977 interview entitled 'Truth and Power', Foucault seems ringingly to endorse a Nietzschean perspective on truth, arguing that what is important is not to try to separate truth from ideology or error, but rather to track the workings of truth-effects:

> There is a battle 'for truth', or at least 'around truth' – it being understood once again that by truth I do not mean 'the ensemble of truths which are to be discovered and accepted', but rather 'the ensemble of rules according to which the true and the false are separated and specific effects of power attached to the true', it being understood also that it's not a matter of a battle 'on behalf' of the truth, but of a battle about the status of truth and the economic and political role it plays.[11]

What matters now will not be whether things are true, but whether knowledges are 'hegemonic' or 'subjugated'. Foucault signs all this with the name of Nietzsche, as the originator of the investigation not of truth but of what might be called 'truthing':

> It's not a matter of emancipating truth from every system of power (which would be a chimera, for truth is already power) but of detaching the power of truth from the forms of hegemony, social, economic and cultural, within which it operates at the present time.
> The political question, to sum up, is not error, illusion, alienated consciousness or ideology; it is truth itself. Hence the importance of Nietzsche.[12]

But it is hard simply to recruit Nietzsche for this kind of purpose. For Nietzsche there would be no remission from the exercise of power in the turn to minor forms of truth-power, as though it were a matter of engineering some kind of balance or proportional representation of truth-power. That is to say, the knowledge of the workings of knowledge-power confers no immunity from those workings, or ethical principle by which to negotiate power. It may be this that accounts for the wary fatigue with which Foucault signs off another interview from this period: 'Nowadays I prefer to remain silent about Nietzsche . . . The only valid tribute to thought such as Nietzsche's is precisely to use it, to deform it, to make it groan and protest.'[13] Although in a sense all knowledge is utility for Nietzsche, there is no very useful knowledge as traditionally understood to be had about that process: for Nietzsche, it is never possible knowingly to use the knowledge of power-knowledge, because power-knowledge is always making use of you.

Nietzsche's rather perverse originality lies in the fact that he seeks to affirm knowledge apart from truth. Unlike Schopenhauer he does not wish to purge or overcome knowledge's will to power, but rather to enable it to assert itself in ways that do not seek to reduce what he sees as the essentially unknowable complexity of the world (but how does he know?) to rational order. What in another writer would compromise the argument about knowledge becomes frankly assumed as a principle of strength, in that, as Rex Welshon puts it:

> Nietzsche links the possession of knowledge with what are blandly called affective states. Whether that state is sweetness, pleasure, feeling superior, passion, daring, gay laughter, or strength, it is clear that knowledge is anything but the dispassionate pursuit of algorithms of justification or precise formulations of thought experiments.[14]

Knowing about knowledge is for Nietzsche a matter of feeling rather than cognition. This is what enables him to affirm the necessity of perspective over truth. There can, he insists, be no absolute truths, or any ways of knowing the world that are not the expression of the needs and interests of some particular embodied form: '*It is our needs which interpret the world*: our impulses with their sympathies and antipathies' (*WP*, 288). This does not mean that Nietzsche does not believe or trust in knowledge, though it does mean that he does not trust in knowledge understood as objectivity, or the cancellation of competing perspectives. In a certain sense, trust in knowledge is the only thing in which Nietzsche has trust, rather than trust in its object of truth:

> In so far as the word 'knowledge' has any meaning at all, the world is knowable. It may however be interpreted differently; it has no meaning hidden behind it, but rather innumerable meanings which can be assigned to it. Hence 'perspectivism'. (*WP*, 287)

A 'perspective' implies for Nietzsche much more than a way of seeing, which one might vary as one shifts back and forth searching for the best angle from which to take a photograph. My angle on things simply is the way the world is for me. But even this is no simple fact. A way of seeing is a way of being, understood as a kind of ambition to take – or make – the world, an ambition to have the world be in a certain way. And this is precisely what allows Nietzsche to continue to put his trust in acts of knowing. Knowledge, considered as something absolute and positive, does not exist, or exists only as a timorous illusion. But seen from the viewpoint of what Nietzsche incessantly, mysteriously and tediously refers to as the strong or lordly, knowing might be said to be all there is, since knowing is the willing of being into existence. This is why Nietzsche can accept, in a kind of Baconian mastery through servitude, that the work of his own life is the expression of a will to knowledge. At the beginning of *On the Genealogy of Morality*, Nietzsche proclaims the unity of all the thoughts he has had on the subject of life, power, knowledge and, well, everything:

> The *fact* that I still stick to them today, and that they themselves in the meantime have stuck together increasingly firmly, even growing into one another and growing into one, makes me all the more blithely confident that from the first, they did not arise in me individually, randomly or sporadically but as stemming from a single root, from a fundamental will to knowledge deep inside me which took control, speaking more and more clearly and making ever clearer demands.[15]

And yet at other times Nietzsche wants to keep ahead of, or aside from, the statement of propositional facts or truths. The only knowledge he will allow is a knowledge in the making. This may be the reason that the topic of knowledge seems to be treated in such a hit-and-run way through Nietzsche's work, as though he were trying to avoid consolidating the force of his arguments into something formal like an epistemology (though many have striven to bully his writings about knowledge into what a recent, hopeful commentator calls 'a hard-core epistemological program'[16]). The question of knowledge is always at work in Nietzsche, but he aims to prevent it resulting in any kind of completed and self-identical epistemological statement. Nietzsche's struggle is not so much to find a way of articulating this joyful knowing as to find a way to prevent it decaying into some lifeless condition of mere knowledge. It is to deploy and defend epistemopathy against the relapse into epistemology. To be 'a joyful epistemologist who practices a *fröhliche Wissenschaft* [gay science]',[17] requires one not just to tolerate multiple and changeable perspectives, as though to effect a kind of averaging out or optimization, but to inhabit and undergo them:

> Finally, as knowers, let us not be ungrateful towards such resolute reversals of familiar perspectives and valuations with which the mind has raged against itself for far too long, apparently to wicked and useless effect: to see differently, and to *want* to see differently to that degree, is no small discipline and preparation of the intellect for its future 'objectivity' – the latter understood not as 'contemplation [*Anschauung*] without interest' (which is, as such, a non-concept and an absurdity), but as *having in our power* the ability to engage and disengage our 'pros' and 'cons': we can use the difference in perspectives and affective interpretations for knowledge.[18]

This is the sense in which power can become strength for Nietzsche: 'to eliminate the will completely and turn off all the emotions without exception, assuming we could: well? would that not mean to *castrate* the intellect?'[19]

If there is something undoubtedly powerful in Nietzsche's refusal to separate knowing from the work of being and feeling – powerful because it enables us to notice and speak of so much of the passion of knowing that tends to get bleached out by the customary epistemological rhetorics – there is also something infuriatingly feeble in the way in which he considers strength and weakness. For there is nothing here of the jubilant, multifarious, life-embracing vitality that Nietzsche insists belongs to the aristocratic spirit. Instead, it is wearily monotonous in its Wagnerian assertiveness and contemptuous crushing of littleness underfoot. Nietzsche's assertion of the fundamentally healthy self-assertion of the powerful (an odd prejudice that seems to be particularly strongly developed in delicate invalids like Nietzsche and D. H. Lawrence) is itself rather feeble, precisely because it seems so wilful and fitfully fevering. It would be possible to keep faith with Nietzsche's insights into the way in which knowing is indeed to be seen as a form of life, while yet allowing for a much more various – and properly Darwinian – understanding of the multiplicity of forms of life. Reducing the complexity of its forms to strength or weakness is just the kind of weak evasion that might be thought obnoxious, in just the way, and in fact for some of the reasons, that Nietzsche finds democracy and feminism obnoxious. What is intolerable about Nietzsche's understanding of the will to know is not in fact that it is mistaken or wrong, but that, given the resources he offers us for thinking about the life of knowing, it is so dreary and lifeless. (The Old English *dreor*, blood, from which *dreary* derives, should be a hint to us about how dull bloodiness always becomes.) In the blaring madness of his knowledge, Nietzsche helpfully fails to be as interesting as he might help us to be.

The interaction of strength and weakness in what we might now call complexity – or, following Peter Sloterdijk, 'immunological'[20] thinking (the science of immunology was being developed on Nietzsche's doorstep at almost exactly the moment that he was framing his philosophy) – finds strength not in joy but in weakness; and finds joy not in huffing, puffing, strutting and fretting but in multiplying the forms of living. In an era in which we are having to train for the cunning stunt of assuming power over our own power, and *Kraft* is beginning, clumsily, to learn to be crafty, perhaps the best way of responding to Nietzsche's work is to deploy the strength of his arguments – including his ideas about the relation between argument and strength – for the case against him. This might be a good moment for me to come clean about the fact that the sneaky, sinuous, democratic arts of *ressentiment* that Nietzsche finds so nauseating have always seemed to me not only much cleverer than the boot and bomb, but also probably much more worth betting on in the long run (the good thing about betting on the long run is that it gives you an interest in ensuring there is one, so you can collect your winnings). Indeed, even Nietzsche cannot conceal a certain grudging admiration on occasion for the insidiously subtle ruses of the slave. The versatile life of viruses is a good indication that once the legion weak get smart, there is little defence except to get smarter still.

FAUST

If the name of Nietzsche recurs in this book, it is because he both diagnoses and so handsomely demonstrates the madness of knowledge. The taut relation between explication and exemplification is a feature also of the figure who, if Nietzsche provides the philosophical framework for understanding the will to knowledge, has supplied its dramatic embodiment: Faust.

At the beginning of Christopher Marlowe's *Doctor Faustus* (1604), Faustus runs through the curriculum of traditional inquiry, rejecting in turn the disciplines of logic, medicine, law and divinity. In each case, Faustus seeks to go beyond the 'end' of the discipline in question: 'Is to dispute well, logic's chiefest end? / Affords this art no greater miracle?'[21] Marlowe's play dramatizes an antinomy that runs through all the versions of the Faust legend. There are two Fausts, which do not equate to the good and bad angels which traditionally embody the orthodox and diabolical sides of his nature. Rather, they embody two modes of knowledge. One Faust is the vulgar materialist for whom knowledge is a means to finite worldly pleasures and powers. The other is the idealist philosopher who craves absolute knowledge of all things. The first Faust desires, or thinks he desires, objects of knowledge; the second desires the experience of pure knowing, without or beyond objects. As Faustus says to Valdes and Cornelius, who have set him on the path to magic arts in the A-text of the play,

> your words have won me at the last,
> To practise magic and concealèd arts.
> Yet not your words only, but mine own fantasy,
> That will receive no object.[22]

'That will receive no object' means 'that will tolerate no objection', but seems also to imply a physical sense of the word as that which knowledge is thrown up against, or which brings it up short.

The mediating principle between the two conceptions of knowledge is magic, for both are driven by a kind of magical thinking, though of different kinds. For the first, knowledge is a magical shortcut to power and action. It is a purely technical knowledge, of nuts-and-bolts procedures that will close the gap between desire and its fulfilment. It obeys mechanical, or in fact pseudo-mechanical, laws, even if they are laws that knowledge in fact privily gives to itself. Its magic is one of incantations and rituals, spells and magic circles. For the second, knowledge itself is magically transfigured into a self-sufficient principle, and thus is thought of as a pure power in itself independent of any accessory benefits that may arise from it. For the first, knowledge is finite, because it is never more than the knowledge of finite objects. For the second, knowledge is infinite, because it is not to be mistaken for the mere knowledge *of* other things. It imagines knowledge as beyond all such earthly constraints of consequence and congruity. The first mode assumes that knowing can know itself; the second wishes knowledge always to remain beyond its own powers of knowing.

Faust's longing is for limitless knowledge, for a knowledge that would open up the infinite. But knowledge is limited in that it can only ever be potential: it must be objectified and instrumentalized in order to actualize and make good its power. Hence the turn to magic as a means of omnipotizing thought. And yet that very actualization is another kind of limit, in that it is a relapse from the infinite power of possibility. Power put into practice is *no longer power*, which consists essentially not in the performance of an act but in the possibility of that performance, or the demonstration through it of what else might yet be possible. Action is finite and finitizing: power is infinitive, since it will need always to take the form of the *power to* effect some action or other. Knowledge is proved in the power to act but dissipates its power if and when it does. So the power of knowledge is proved by that which proves that proof is impossible for it. Faust's damnation lies not in all the devil and hell business, but in the betrayal into action. This is why Faust's knowledge must be imagined as absolutely, rather than specifically, powerful, and so must be directed to this open future. More than knowledge, Faust must desire the desire of knowledge.

This duality mimics the double attitude towards magic entertained within orthodox Christianity. On the one hand, the Church is founded on the principle of miracles, like those performed by Christ during his life and through him in the Resurrection. On the other hand, any kind of magic wrought by humans must be regarded as demonic, or fraudulent, or, following the logic that viewed Satan as the great counterfeiter, both at once. Miracle is essential to the conception of divine power. Magic is its corrupt imitation. Faust seems to oscillate between the magical and the miraculous in his attitudes towards knowledge.

The second Faust, he of the self-sufficiency of knowledge, finds it almost impossible to avoid collapsing back into the first. He scorns the formulaic jingles of established philosophy – 'A pretty case of paltry legacies . . . nothing but external trash – / Too servile and illiberal for me' – but is enchanted by just the same kind of word-magic: 'These metaphysics of magicians / And necromantic books are heavenly, / Lines, circles, signs, letters, and characters'.[23] In the peculiar kind of 'slapstick tragedy' that Marlowe contrives,[24] the poltergeist and pantomime magic that occupies the middle sections of the play are designed, or at least extravagantly permitted, to be as tedious as they seem, as they enact the smoke and mirrors of seeming itself.

This is not just a difficulty for Marlowe's Faustus, but the recurrent tension between finite and infinite knowledge within and across the whole Faust myth, in all its literary embodiments by Marlowe, Goethe, Mann, Valéry and others. In this it reproduces the problem that orthodox Christianity had with divine or saintly miracles, which had to be protected from the idea that they had anything to do with mere magical trickery. It is not therefore surprising that Trithemius (1462–1516) should record that a travelling scholar-magician who styled himself 'Georgius Sabellicus, Faust Junior', and who has been identified by some as the historical original of the Faust of legend, claimed to be able to perform by magical means the miracles credited to Christ: 'quod Christi Saluatoris miracula non sint miranda, se quoque omnia facere posse quae Christus fecit quoties et quandocunque uelit', 'that Christ the Saviour's marvels are not miracles, and he himself could do what Christ did, whenever and as often as he pleased'.[25] The opposition between miracle and magic maps on to the problem of 'the impossibility of distinguishing clearly between the permissible search for truth and wisdom, and the intolerable practice of black magic', which is in a sense as much a problem for Faust as for the Church.[26]

We might even see the operations of magic as equivalent to theatre or even literature itself. François Ost and Laurent van Eynde, the editors of a volume of essays entitled *Faust, ou les frontières du savoir* (2003), see the Faust legend as not just putting the will to knowledge into literary form but also as

> a specifically literary reflection on the possibility of knowledge – a reflection in which the form itself is put into perspective and interrogated. Faust invites literature to excavate its own relations to science and knowledge.[27]

But they also maintain that, since 'literature here appropriates knowledge and so in effect compounds with it', literature may also be regarded as having 'a genuinely epistemological function'.[28] Ost and Eynde see literature as a means for knowledge to investigate itself from the outside, with the Faust legend as central to that enterprise precisely because of the fact that in it the literary and the epistemological are always combined such that

> theoretical knowledge interrogates itself not in the discursive forms that are proper to it, but in terms which are precisely those that are most often presented as subversive of knowledge: the forms of the imagination.[29]

But, as in the work of Nietzsche, this can be read the other way round. The Faust legend is not just a dramatization of the will to knowledge; it is a dramatization of the necessity of drama – projection, performance, phantasmagoria – in that willing of knowledge. This will make it very hard to determine whether this is epistemology or epistemopathy, knowledge of the will to knowledge or the demonstration of its workings. All versions of the Faust story invite us to participate in pseudo- or floridly storied quasi-knowledge, which may give us the queasily sinking feeling that we may not be able to do without that quasi-ness in any act of knowing. The Faust story is the narration of the fact that knowledge needs and breeds story, the story that must betray it.

SPENGLER

Oswald Spengler dispenses with the narrative of Faust in designating the culture of the West 'Faustian' in his vast civilizational history *The Decline of the West*, which appeared in the years following the First World War. Spengler characterizes as Faustian the culture that others would characterize as modern, though he locates its beginnings much earlier, in the ninth or tenth century. The 'world-feeling' which governs Faustian culture is taken up with a dynamic reaching forward into a space conceived not – as in classical or 'Apollonian' culture, the latter term borrowed from Nietzsche's *The Birth of Tragedy* – as fixed and finite, but as open and infinite. Spengler finds this feeling for the infinite to be notably prevalent in mathematics:

> At the moment exactly corresponding to that at which (*c.* 540) the Classical Soul in the person of Pythagoras discovered its own proper Apollinian [*sic*] number, the measurable magnitude, the Western soul in the persons of Descartes and his generation (Pascal, Fermat, Desargues) discovered a notion of number that was the child of a passionate *Faustian* tendency towards the infinite. Number as *pure magnitude* inherent in the material presentness of things is paralleled by numbers as *pure relation*, and if we may characterize the Classical 'world', the cosmos, as being based on a deep need of visible limits and composed accordingly as a sum of material things, so we may say that our world-picture is an actualizing of an infinite space in which things visible appear very nearly as realities of a lower order, limited in the presence of the illimitable.[30]

This is no inert or abstract preoccupation, for the infinite is experienced by the 'mighty phenomenon of the Faustian soul' as a passionate striving 'to transcend every optical limitation' (*DW*, 198), an appetitive traction that is found in many different dimensions:

> The will-to-power (to use Nietzsche's great formula) that from the earliest Gothic of the Eddas, the Cathedrals and Crusades, and even from the old conquering Goths and Vikings, has distinguished the attitude of the Northern soul to its world, appears also in the sense-transcending energy, the *dynamic* of

Western number. In the Apollinian mathematic the intellect is the servant of the eye, in the Faustian its master. (DW, 88)

Spenglerian Faustianism is characterized by a 'direction-energy which has an eye only for the most distant horizons' (DW, 174). The sense of infinitely distant horizons means that the Faustian soul can never feel at home in the physical world, indeed that *infinite solitude is felt as the home of the Faustian soul'* (DW, 86). Spengler identifies 'a Faustian craving – to be *alone* with endless space' (DW, 241), later identified with 'The mad Lear between fool and reckless outcast on the heath, in the night and the storm, the unutterably lonely ego lost in space – here is the Faustian life-feeling!' (DW, 326).

Given that 'in the world as seen by the Faustian's eyes, everything is motion with an aim' (DW, 343), this extended space is also in fact urgently temporal: 'The Apollinian form-language reveals only the become, the Faustian shows above all a becoming' (DW, 266). Spengler finds the tension between self and space expressed in the spires of Gothic architecture, in the music of the violin, in portraiture, even in grammatical structure, in what Spengler described as 'that transformation of the verb which decisively differentiated our tongues from the Classical tongues and therefore our soul from the Classical soul' (DW, 302), manifesting in language the new 'mythical entity' (DW, 302) of the Will:

> This 'ego habeo factum', the insertion of the auxiliaries 'have' and 'be' between a doer and a deed, in lieu of the 'feci' which expresses activated body, replaces the world of bodies by one of functions between centres of force, the static syntax by a dynamic. And this 'I' and 'Thou' is the key to Gothic portraiture. A Hellenistic portrait is the type of an attitude – a confession it is not, either to the creator of it or to the understanding spectator. But our portraits depict something *sui generis*, once occurring and never recurring, a life-history expressed in a moment, a world-centre for which everything else is world-around, exactly as the grammatical subject 'I' becomes the centre of force in the Faustian sentence. (DW, 263)

Scientific and intellectual history are of course also an expression of Faustian culture, and the Faustian '*Will-Culture*' (DW, 308) involves a powerful drive to transcendent knowledge and the capacity it can give – for example through 'the characteristically Faustian discovery of the telescope' (*DW*, 330) – to exercise power at a distance:

> The very word 'discovery' has something bluntly un-Classical in it. Classical man took good care not to take the cover, the material wrapping, off anything cosmic, but to do *just this* is the most characteristic impulse of a Faustian nature. The discoveries of the New World, the circulation of the blood, and the Copernican universe were achieved almost simultaneously and, at bottom, are completely equivalent; and the discovery of gunpowder (that is, the *long-range* weapon and of printing (the *long-range* script) were little earlier. (*DW*, 278)

But despite choosing Faust as his cultural emblem – or perhaps, given Faust's dissatisfaction with traditional knowledge, because of it – Spengler shares Nietzsche's ambivalence about knowledge. The will to knowledge mirrors and enables the imperial extension of power in space:

> The bent of the Faustian Culture, therefore, was overpoweringly towards extension, political, economic or spiritual. It overrode all geographical-material bounds. It sought – without any practical object, merely for the Symbol's own sake – to reach North Pole and South Pole. It ended by transforming the entire surface of the globe into a single colonial and economic system. Every thinker from Meister Eckhardt [*sic*] to Kant willed to subject the 'phenomenal' world to the asserted domination of the cognizing ego, and every leader from Otto the Great to Napoleon did it. (*DW*, 335–6)

And yet Faustian culture is also characterized by an internal distance between prophetic spirit and ordinary citizen, and between expert and layman, a distance unknown in the classical world in which, as Spengler improbably claims, *'everyone knows everything'* (*DW*, 328–9). This is also the harbinger of decadence, in which knowledge and power begin to take mechanical and externalized forms rather than acting as a spiritual principle. In his final chapter, entitled 'Faustian and Apollinian Nature-Knowledge', Spengler explicates

European science, typified in physics, as both the fulfilment and the beginning of the end of the Faustian dynamic:

> its mission as a historical phenomenon has been to transform the Faustian Nature-feeling into an intellectual knowledge, the faith-forms of springtime into the machine-forms of exact science ... [in] *the mechanical and extensional re-ideation of the idea of immortality and world-soul*. (DW, 417–18)

Spengler distinguishes between two modes of knowledge, that he calls 'nature-knowledge' and 'man-knowledge'. Both constitute what he calls a 'morphology', a term which he further divides into the systematic – which follows out mechanical and extended relations – and the physiognomic, which takes as its focus *'history and life and all that bears the sign of direction and destiny'* (DW, 100). Scientific knowledge need not necessarily be systematic, though, for in fact 'in every science, and in the aim no less than in the content of it, man tells the story of himself. Scientific experience is spiritual self-knowledge' (DW, 100). In this sense, science may be seen as mythical rather than epistemological:

> If, then. Nature-knowledge is a subtle kind of self-knowledge – Nature understood as picture, as mirror of man – the attempt to solve the motion-problem is an attempt of knowledge to get on the track of its own secret, its own Destiny ...
> ... If we turn back from Nature-feeling become form to Nature-knowledge become system, we know God or the gods as the origin of the images by which the intellect seeks to make the world-around comprehensible to itself. (DW, 389, 411)

Scientific knowledge can in fact be understood as mythical, that is, expressive of different kinds of world-soul, or physiognomy; the putting of time into science via the theory of entropy is an expression of Faustian spirit, of its mythology: 'What the myth of Götterdämmerung signified of old, the irreligious form of it, the theory of Entropy, signifies to-day – *world's end as completion of an inwardly necessary evolution*' (DW, 423–4).

Here, the claim that knowledge figures its own end mythically seems to enact Spengler's own myth of knowledge-as-myth. Spengler projects his own intellectual ambition to mythologize scientific knowledge into his own story, as the final stage of Faustian knowledge, which will be to understand and articulate itself as Spengler here understands and articulates it:

> But before the curtain falls, there is one more task for the historical Faustian spirit, a task not yet specified, hitherto not even imagined as possible. There has still to be written a *morphology of the exact sciences*, which shall discover how all laws, concepts and theories inwardly hang together as forms and what they have meant as such in the life-course of the Faustian Culture. The re-treatment of theoretical physics, of chemistry, of mathematics as a sum of symbols – this will be the definitive conquest of the mechanical world-aspect by an intuitive, once more religious, world-outlook, a last master-effort of physiognomic to break down even systematic and to absorb it, as expression and symbol, into its own domain. (*DW*, 425)

Faustian wisdom attempts just the same kind of generalization of knowledge systems as Spengler's own analysis does. The final paragraph of Spengler's text creates a kind of symphonic integration of his own analysis with the analytic systems which he analyses:

> The final issue to which the Faustian wisdom tends – though it is only in the highest moments that it has seen it – is the dissolution of all knowledge into a vast system of morphological relationships. Dynamics and Analysis are in respect of meaning, form-language and substance, identical with Romanesque ornament, Gothic cathedrals, Christian-German dogma and the dynastic state. One and the same world-feeling speaks in all of them. They were born with, and they aged with, the Faustian Culture, and they present that Culture in the world of day and space as a historical drama. The uniting of the several scientific aspects into one will bear all the marks of the great art of counterpoint. *An infinitesimal music of the boundless world-space* – that is the deep unresting longing of this soul, as the orderly statuesque and Euclidean Cosmos was the satisfaction of the Classical.

That – formulated by a logical necessity of Faustian reason as a dynamic-imperative causality, then developed into a dictatorial, hard-working, world-transforming science – is the grand legacy of the Faustian soul to the souls of Cultures yet to be, a bequest of immensely transcendent forms that the heirs will possibly ignore. And then, weary after its striving, the Western science returns to its spiritual home. (DW, 427–8)

The decline of the Faustian world-feeling is visible in the very extension of the principle of knowledge as power, in 'the *comparative morphology of knowledge forms* [which] is a domain which Western thought has still to attack' (DW, 60). But this self-knowledge betrays itself, insofar as it represents an attempt to reduce the sense of historical destiny to mere conceptual knowledge:

Acquired knowledge, scientific insight, definition, are all powerless. Nay more, the very attempt to grasp them epistemologically defeats its own object. For without the inward certainty that destiny is something entirely intractable to critical thought, we cannot perceive the world of becoming at all. Cognition, judgment, and the establishment of *causal* connexions within the known (i.e., between things, properties, and positions that have been distinguished) are one and the same, and he who approaches history in the spirit of *judgment* will only find 'data.' (DW, 139)

The Decline of the West figures an internal struggle on Spengler's own part between conceptual knowledge and the feeling of the culture-soul which mirrors the internal struggles of the West's own Faustianism. But perhaps what is most Faustian is the conjuring act, or action-at-a-distance, of the kind of civilizational analysis that Spengler practises. The Faustian desire to reach into lonely infinities is a mirror image of Spengler's command over the immensity of history. 'To call the Faustian Culture a *Will-Culture* is only another way of expressing the eminently historical disposition of its soul', he avers, replicating that effort of historical will as he represents it (DW, 308–9).

Faust embodies the aspiration to what in Germany is called *Geisteswissenschaft*. No more compelling example can be imagined of the operations of magical thinking than the 'spirit-knowledge' practised by Spengler, and the fantasy it enacts of the scholar-magus who, like Yeats's Irish Airman, 'balanced all, brought all to mind'.[31] It is not charlatanry exactly, for Spengler has a genuinely imposing range of cultural reference. He represents his kind of research as attainable by 'confident cool-headed experts', but his Olympian assessment of the rise and fall of civilizations, including, now, that of the West, is as engorged by the will to power as any excitably self-interested programme of historical destiny could be.[32] The aspiration to capture all of this, an effort driven and governed almost entirely by the rhetoric of synecdoche, in which the thrust of a column, the tint of a landscape, are made to stand for the whole 'spirit' of a civilization, in the convergence of accident and archetype, is a whisker away from delusion.

It is a thoroughly Nietzschean procedure, and it is not surprising that in a lecture given to mark what would have been Nietzsche's eightieth birthday, in October 1924, the year after the appearance of the second volume of *The Decline of the West*, Spengler should have used the figure of Nietzsche as a touchstone for the kind of alienated knowledge he fantasized. His Nietzsche is in fact a kind of late Faust:

> His frightful loneliness stands as a symbol over against Goethe's cheerful gregariousness. One of these great men gave shape to existing things; the other brooded over nonexisting things. One of them worked for a prevailing form; the other against a prevailing formlessness. (*sEss*, 181)

Though Nietzsche did not belong to his time, his very unbelonging and untimeliness is a kind of historical signature. Indeed, 'The inability to feel "at home" in one's own time – that is a German curse' (*sEss*, 182). In the Nietzsche who, Spengler tells us, 'possessed the superior vision that allowed him to peer into the heart of whole cultures as if they were organic, living individuals' (*sEss*, 190) and who was the first to appreciate that 'every historical fact is the expression of a spiritual stimulus, that cultures, epochs, estates, and races have a soul like that of individuals' (*sEss*, 191), Spengler himself finds the ideal enactment of the kind of prophetic history at which he, too, aimed. Spengler identifies the tension in Nietzsche between knowledge and something like experience, a tension he described in his own project: 'A thousand years of historical thought and research have spread out before us a vast treasure, not of knowledge, for that is relatively unimportant, but of experience' (*sEss*, 145). On the one hand, for Nietzsche, 'the goal of life was knowledge, and the goal of history became for him the development of intelligence' (*sEss*, *192*). At the same time, this could not be for Nietzsche a mere theme for knowledge; his 'science' must be understood, or felt as a 'vision':

> Following this presentation of the physiognomy of the ages of history, a science of which he was and will always be the creator, he reached to the outer limits of his vision to describe the symbols of a future, his future, which he needed in order to be cleansed of the residue of contemporary thought. (*sEss*, 192–3)

But this is part of what Spengler believed was 'truly novel in my approach, an idea that had to be expressed and made accessible to life after the entire nineteenth century had striven towards it: Faustian man's *conscious* relation to history' (*sEss*, 144). In the person of Faust (Nietzsche, Spengler), history is able to become historical. The knowledge of the historical operations of the Will is what enables the identification of history and the historian, at once concealing himself and dissolving himself into that Will, with the fantasy of knowledge as the mediator:

> His ultimate understanding of real history was that the Will to Power is stronger than all doctrines and principles, and that it has always made and forever will make history, no matter what others may prove or preach against it. (*sEss*, 194)

The Will cannot be known or analysed, so Nietzsche

> did not concern himself with the conceptual analysis of 'will'; to him the most important thing was the image of active, creative, destructive Will in history. The 'concept' of will gave way to the 'aspect' of will. He did not teach, he simply pointed matters out. (*sEss*, 194)

The epistemic identification of history and historian, through the fantasy of the historical will, creates a constant oscillation between thought and action, action given its meaning by thought, thought becoming action through its very act of withdrawal:

Precisely because all action was foreign to him, because he knew only how to think, Nietzsche understood the fundamental essence of the active life better than any great active personality in the world. But the more he understood, the more shyly he withdrew from contact with action. In this way his Romantic destiny reached fulfillment. (*SEss*, 195–6)

Spengler's account of Nietzsche collapses objectivity and subjectivity: the Superman remakes himself in the pure self-overcoming of thought, the thought of pure action:

Deed and thought, reality and ideal, success and redemption, strength and goodness – these are forces that will never come to terms with one another. Yet in historical reality it is not the ideal, goodness, or morality that prevails – their kingdom is not of this world – but rather decisiveness, energy, presence of mind, practical talent. This fact cannot be gotten rid of with laments and moral condemnations. Man is *thus*, life is *thus*, history is *thus*. (*SEss*, 195)

The irony therefore is that all this stern praise of deed over thought should itself be the merest, would-be mightiest deed of thought.

THINKING CURE

The will to power over knowledge has often enough been impregnated with a desire for power over others through knowledge. But that must mingle with the desire for power over one's own desire for power. There is, it seems, a certain, limited will to know the powerful force of desire and demand that is at work in the fantasy of one's own knowledge, but this must coexist with the desire to keep it dark, making the effort to know the will to knowledge an occulted and imperfect affair.

This chapter has focused on the dominative exercise of the will. But willing is broader than this desire for domination or appropriation. As observed earlier, in declaring ourselves to be willing we signal a contrasting state of readiness, consent or even acquiescence. In English, willingness can often therefore signal a willingness to suspend one's will. 'God willing', or, as I still remember people saying,

'D. V.' (*Deo volente*), indicates a surrender of one's will to that of the Deity, who seems to be willing to V. almost anything. Taken in this more expanded sense, willingness can be regarded as a kind of meta-feeling with regard to knowledge – a preparedness to feel, or to know, in the sense of the word *know* we employ when we mean to experience or undergo. This kind of wanting to know may not be merely appetitive, or may be an appetite for what will enlarge our range of feelings rather than what will secure and deepen a state of satisfaction. Curiosity is not just itself a powerful state of feeling in human beings, it is a powerful disposition to know, as well as merely know of, other states of feeling. In this, it is a desire for exposure as well as imposition or appropriation.

Humans value knowledge highly, so highly as to define themselves in relation to it. Our relation to the world we inhabit is one formed not only through necessity but also through curiosity. We are assuredly not the only animal possessed of curiosity, and a willingness to explore one's environment as well as merely inhabiting it doubtless provides advantages of various kinds to different species, making them adaptable and maximizing their opportunities for survival and flourishing. But curiosity seems to have a particularly developed form in human beings, who will often subordinate other needs to that of exploration and who, through language, have evolved the capacity to model their world in representation, allowing for acts of mental as well as physical exploration, wondering as well as wandering.

Freud and others have been at pains to make out a sexual libido at the root of the desire for knowing. One of the reasons for the split between Freud and Jung is Jung's belief that the sexual drive is only one form of 'psychic energy':

> All psychological phenomena can be considered as manifestations of energy, in the same way that all physical phenomena have been understood as energic manifestations ever since Robert Mayer discovered the law of the conservation of energy. Subjectively and psychologically, this energy is conceived as *desire*. I call it *libido*, using the word in its original sense, which is by no means only sexual.[33]

It is not often that I find myself agreeing with Jung against Freud, but on this question I am minded to accept a broader conception of libido than that of the sexual. Jung also postulated 'a hypothetical fundamental striving which I designate *libido*', once again insisting that 'in accordance with the classical usage of the word, libido does not have an exclusively sexual connotation', and suggesting as alternatives 'interest', Bergsonian *élan vital* and Greek ὁρμή, *hormé*, glossed as 'force, attack, press, impetuosity, violence, urgency, zeal'.[34] William McDougall carries forward Jung's idea in his 'hormic psychology', in which, according to A. A. Roback, '[c]onation, and not cognition, is at the root of all animal activity'.[35] But McDougall continued to distinguish cognition, affect and conation – or knowledge, feeling and striving – even if he could also sometimes acknowledge 'the constant participation, even in our most simple and apparently purely cognitive or intellectual processes, of the conative or affective features of our mental life'.[36]

It seems to me that the linkage of the cognitive and the conative is more than adventitious. For human beings, cognition is conation. We need not follow McDougall all the way, or perhaps even very far at all, in his account of the pre-eminence of striving, impulse or goal-directed behaviour, to admit this convergence. Knowing is inseparable from wanting to know, and wanting to know is more encompassing than any of the particular things about which one may want to know. Sexual curiosity provides a target or channel for a libido of knowing, but what Freud calls the *Wissentrieb* (drive to knowing) is both broader and more primary than the sexual libido. This surely makes a great deal of evolutionary sense. Young primates need to know about knowing much earlier than they need to feel sexual desire and attachment.

It may well be that the curiosity displayed by human beings, like that of primates, rodents and other creatures, confers some kind of survival value in developing flexibility and adaptiveness. It is perhaps an expansion into the field of behaviour of the immunological principle that a biological system needs to be exposed to just enough of a potential threat to be able to protect itself against it. But humans are distinguished from other animals in the particular way in which curiosity may be vital to their survival. For curiosity binds humans into a community of mind, by which I mean not just any kind of collective consciousness but a collective consciousness *of the fact of* consciousness; noetic collectivity. This apprehension is at once collective and individuating. The test of whether a child has developed a theory of mind is whether they can show that they know that others do not know what they know. The child without a theory of mind assumes that the contents of its mind will be shared by everybody: the theory of mind is the understanding that everybody has a mind of their own, that, precisely because it is a mind rather like my mind, may not be easy to read or know. You can have biological existence without a theory of mind, but little of what for a human being can be called life. Curiosity in humans must always in part be a drive to know what other people may think or know. Curiosity might occasionally kill the cat, but in humans it is a non-negotiable necessity for survival, not least because of the human capacity to conceal knowledge.

The word that Freud often used in relation to sexual and bodily matters was curiosity (*Neugierde* or *Wissbegierde*), and it is the form of knowledge that Freud most commonly thought of as libidinized. It is a favourite notion of Freud's, who often in his letters says that he is himself 'curious' about various ideas or problems. He was, of course, incurably curious (we will see that the words are related) about sexual matters in particular, but also about sexual curiosity itself. In '"Civilized" Sexual Morality and Modern Nervous Illness' (1908), he ascribed women's intellectual inferiority to the systematic suppression of their sexual curiosity in early life:

> Their upbringing forbids their concerning themselves intel-
> lectually with sexual problems though they nevertheless feel
> extremely curious about them, and frightens them by con-
> demning such curiosity [*Wißbegierde*] as unwomanly and a sign
> of a sinful disposition. In this way they are scared away from
> any form of thinking, and knowledge loses its value for them.[37]

Freud wrote of the patient he called Little Hans in 'Analysis of a Phobia in a Five-year-old Boy' that '[t]hirst for knowledge seems to be inseparable from sexual curiosity [*Wißbegierde und sexuelle Neugierde scheinen untrennbar voneinander zu sein*]' (SE, X, 8; GW, VII, 246). Curiosity is part of Freud's own rhetorical mechanism of dis-cretion and revelation. At one point in *The Interpretation of Dreams* Freud hints at a sexual interpretation of a woman's dream of a visit to a butcher's shop, in which he himself was disguised as the butcher: 'We need not enquire now into the full meaning of the dream. So much is quite clear: it had a meaning and that meaning was far from innocent' (*SE*, IV, 184). A footnote adds: 'If anyone is curious to know, I may add [*Für Wissbegierige bemerke ich*] that the dream concealed a phantasy of my behaving in an improper and sexually provocative manner, and of the patient putting up a defence against my conduct' (*SE*, IV, 184 n.1; *GW*, II, 191). Often Freud's curiosity coincides with that of his patients, for example in the account in *The Psychopathology of Everyday Life* of a thirteen-year-old boy whom he persuaded to act out his castration anxiety:

> I was going on the assumption that he must have had sexual experiences and be tormented by sexual questions, which was likely enough at his age; but I refrained from helping him with explanations as I wished to put my hypotheses once again to the test. I was therefore naturally curious [*neugierig*] as to the way in which he would bring out what I was looking for. (*SE*, VI, 197; *GW*, IV, 220)

'Wißbegierig' is also the word that Freud applies gratefully to the 'wider circle of educated and curious-minded readers' whose continued interest in *The Interpretation of Dreams* had persuaded him to return to the book to produce a second edition (*SE*, IV, xxiv). Freud's case studies are written in such a way as to arouse the reader's curiosity in just the same way as Freud's own, for example in this description from the analysis of Dora in the *Fragment of an Analysis of a Case of Hysteria*:

> At this point a certain suspicion of mine became a certainty. The use of '*Bahnhof*' ['station'; literally, 'railway-court'] and '*Friedkof*' ['cemetery'; literally, 'peace-court'] to represent the female genitals was striking enough in itself, but it also served to direct my awakened curiosity [*geschärfte Aufmerksamkeit*] to the similarly formed '*Vorhof*' ['vestibulum'; literally, 'fore-court'] – an anatomical term for a particular region of the female genitals. (*SE*, VII, 98; *GW*, V, 261)

In fact, what Freud's curiosity is awakened to is Dora's own curiosity:

> This might have been no more than mistaken ingenuity. But now, with the addition of 'nymphs' visible in the background

of a 'thick wood', no further doubts could be entertained. Here was a symbolic geography of sex! 'Nymphae', as is known to physicians though not to lay men (and even by the former the term is not very commonly used), is the name given to the labia minora, which lie in the background of the 'thick wood' of the pubic hair. But any one who employed such technical names as 'vestibulum' and 'nymphae' must have derived his knowledge from books, and not from popular ones either, but from anatomical text-books or from an encyclopaedia – the common refuge of youth when it is devoured by sexual curiosity. (*SE*, VII, 98)

Freud's revelation produces from Dora (who seems to be following closely) an extra bit of dream memory: that *'she went calmly to her room, and began reading a big book that lay on her writing-table'* (*SE*, VII, 99). Freud's analysis remarkably runs together knowledge and sexual desire, making reading – and reading of the very technical kind of language deployed by physicians like Freud – equivalent to sexual assertion:

> The emphasis here was upon the two details 'calmly' and 'big' in connection with 'book'. I asked whether the book was in encyclopaedia *format*, and she said it was. Now children never read about forbidden subjects in an encyclopaedia *calmly*. They do it in fear and trembling, with an uneasy look over their shoulder to see if some one may not be coming. Parents are very much in the way while reading of this kind is going on. But this uncomfortable situation had been radically improved, thanks to the dream's power of fulfilling wishes. Dora's father was dead, and the others had already gone to the cemetery. She might calmly read whatever she chose. Did not this mean that one of her motives for revenge was a revolt against her parents' constraint? If her father was dead she could read or love as she pleased. (*SE*, VII, 99)

So there are three partners in the work of desirous deciphering, looking excitedly over each other's shoulders: Dora, Freud and Freud's reader (unless of course there are four, to include the critic who, as now, reads this work of reading).

The English word *curiosity* exhibits a curious incontinence, in being applied both to its action and its object. We call something that evokes curiosity curious, or 'a curiosity', as though it might be curling over into curiosity about itself. Conversely, it is our curiosity about them that makes things seem curious. The fact that curiosity seems to shuttle between subject and object perhaps enacts something of the mental shuttling involved in the action of being curious, for which, curiously enough, there is no simple verb in English.

The earliest meaning of the English word *curious* is 'careful', in the sense of taking care, being studious, attentive or solicitous. It derives from Latin *cura*, meaning care, carefulness, thought, but also, more sombrely, anxiety, concern, trouble or sorrow. To bestow care in this Latin sense is also, as in English, to take pains. It is related to the English words *cure*, *curate* (as noun and verb), *sinecure* and *secure*, this last a contraction of *sine cura*, without care (though the OED rules firmly that, etymologically, English *care* is 'in no way related to Latina *cura*'). The Roman author Gaius Julius Hyginus (64 BCE–17 CE) includes in his *Fabulae* the story of Cura, who, crossing a river, moulds a figure out of its clay. She asks Jupiter to give it spirit, which he does, but a dispute then arises between them as to which of their names the creature should bear. Saturn adjudicates the dispute, ruling that Jupiter should receive the creature's spirit after death, and that Tellus (or Earth) should have its body after death, but that, since Cura first fashioned it, it would be possessed by Cura (Care) as long as it is alive: 'cura quoniam eum finxit, quamdiu vixerit, cura eum possideat'.[38] Heidegger quotes the story alongside an extract from Seneca's 124th Letter to Lucilius, in which he declares that, where God is perfect in his nature, man is perfected by care ('unius bonum natura perficit, dei scilicet, alterius cura, hominis'), *cura* being translated by Richard M. Gummere as 'pains and study'.[39] Heidegger uses these two sources to support his argument that an essential feature of human existence is care, which he usually renders as 'Sorge', conveying the sense of worry or concern, but also uses the Latin term *cura*:

> Man's *perfectio* – his transformation into that which he can
> be in Being-free for his ownmost possibilities (projection) –
> is 'accomplished' by 'care'. But with equal primordiality 'care'
> determines what is basically specific in this entity, according
> to which it has been surrendered to the world of its concern

(thrownness). In the 'double meaning' of 'care', what we have in view is a *single* basic state in its essentially twofold structure of thrown projection.[40]

Psychologists after Freud have also begun to pay more systematic attention to the workings of curiosity, and have conducted some interesting investigations into aspects of it. It seems important to recognize that curiosity may in fact only be one form in which human beings are motivated to try to know things. To take only one example: a great deal of academic and other kinds of research is concerned less with the effort to answer a question than to form or secure an argument. This may be regarded as regrettable, but it is nevertheless an important part of the epistemopathic landscape. In particular, it may seem to provide an important temporal extension to the work done by knowing and the investment in it, beyond simpler kinds of satisfaction. Such curiosity, as Edmund Burke observed, is 'the most superficial of all the affections; it changes its object perpetually; it has an appetite which is very sharp, but very easily satisfied; and it has always an appearance of giddiness, restlessness and anxiety'.[41] In fact, Burke goes on immediately to draw the conclusion that

> the occurrences of life, by the time we come to know it a little, would be incapable of affecting the mind with any other sensations than those of loathing and weariness, if many things were not adapted to affect the mind by means of other powers besides novelty in them, and of other passions besides curiosity in ourselves.[42]

In fact there are good reasons to think that the model in which curiosity intemperately and unpredictably flares up and is just as quickly extinguished by the filling of the gap in our knowledge – a favourite example is the curiosity aroused by seeing somebody from the back and wondering what their face looks like – covers only a small part of the spectrum of curiosity. For one thing, there appears at least in some people to be a tendency to seek out circumstances in which curiosity is both aroused and sustained, whether by detective stories or by the kind of speculations about the dances of bees engaged in by Beckett's Moran in his novel *Molloy* (1951/5): 'And I said, with rapture, Here is something I can study all my life, and never understand.'[43] This is certainly a strong motivation for my own current interest in the affective work of knowing. There may also be a quantitative component to this, in that the more one knows about a topic, the more opportunities for curiosity may open up. The evolutionist who responds to the creationist's taunt that there is a missing link by providing an example of an intermediary species, will always fail to put an end to the argument, or to the evolutionist's curiosity, by opening up two further missing links on either side of it.

Let us return to this intriguing link between curiosity and care. Curiosity in our modern sense may seem to have dwindled into a rather minor or itchily frivolous impulse. But its history has also included an idea of carefulness and taking care or, in the rather ceremonious expression employed by the OED, 'bestowing care or pains'. This idea contrasts markedly with the giddy light-mindedness of the curiosity that flits from one object to another, being doused as rapidly as it flickers up into life. This idea survives in the words derived from *cura*. The word 'procure' is nowadays close to acquire, but this is a narrowing of a broader sense of to administer, arrange, provide for or cause to be done. The legal term *procurator* preserves an accessory sense of to petition or beg for. Until the middle of the sixteenth century, to procure was also used in the specific sense of to treat medically: a 1425 translation of Guy de Chauliac's *Grande Chirurgerie* described how physicians 'procured al wondes with vnguentz & with swete emplasteres'.[44] The word 'accurate' now means precise or correct but is an adaptation of Latin *adcurare*, to take care of, or perform an action with diligent care; it could also mean to attend carefully to the needs of a guest. To cure and its lost intensifier *recure* means to bring about recovery, but to cure originally meant to care for. This usage survives in the idea of 'curing' substances or foodstuffs (tobacco, rubber or glue) for the purposes of preservation; since the beginning of the twentieth century it has meant to harden substances like concrete.

In these usages, we might see the carelessness or self-gratification of curiosity being protected against, through an action of devotion rather than indulgence, preservation rather than appropriation. Curiosity as care immunizes its object from the debasement of let-me-see curiosity. These alternatives are perhaps always still alive in the impulse to know. Freud is probably right to discern something sadistic or destructive in the drive to know, in which knowing can mean consuming. There is a sense in which once one knows something, and it can no longer stimulate our curiosity, it no longer has any interest or value for us. But there is another kind of drive to knowledge, or a contrasting strain in it, which seeks to preserve the object of knowledge from hasty consumption. It is as though curiosity must curate, must have a care for its own preservation, in order that its object may survive. 'What will survive of us is love', Philip Larkin half-suggests, but there may also be a need to ensure that the things for which we care can survive our love.[45]

Epistemopathy will harden into epistemopathology only when will is able entirely to eschew willingness. The will to know can mean being willing to encounter ways of caring, being willing for knowledge to matter. The chapters that follow will meet with different forms of this mattering. The first is the way in which the care for, or curious lusting after knowledge has seemed to some to be a sickness susceptible of self-cure.

2

KNOW THYSELF

We are beyond our own ken, our selves unknown to ourselves, we would-be knowers. And with good reason. We have never gone looking for ourselves – so how is it supposed that we should one day find ourselves?

Friedrich Nietzsche, *The Genealogy of Morality*

The previous chapter showed clearly that the will to knowledge has not always been seen as a simple and unproblematic impulse towards the good, nature-fulfilling thing that knowledge is taken to be. Indeed we might say that wherever the desire to know has been the object rather than the simple occasioning of inquiry, it has tended to be seen as a dangerous snare, delusion or impediment to true knowledge. But the fact that only knowledge can bring this to light, so that the desire to know is both subject and object of the diagnosis, makes for the irritant ambivalence just evoked. If the excessive care for knowledge is a kind of malady, it has often seemed that the only sovereign remedy is knowledge itself; and only the knowing physician can heal himself of the malady of knowing.

This act of reflecting on reflection, the inward inflection of knowledge, marks the beginning of the kind of activity we think of as philosophical. The maxim 'Know thyself' was particularly prominent in Greek religion and thought and, according to Pausanias (*c.* 110–*c.* 180 CE), was inscribed in the forecourt of the Temple of Apollo at Delphi.[1] It features repeatedly in Plato's dialogues, for example at the beginning of *Phaedrus*, where Socrates declines to speculate about the origins of the myth of Boreas:

But I, Phaedrus, think such explanations are very pretty in
general, but are the inventions of a very clever and laborious
and not altogether enviable man, for no other reason than
because after this he must explain the forms of the Centaurs,
and then that of the Chimaera, and there presses in upon
him a whole crowd of such creatures, Gorgons and Pegas,
and multitudes of strange, inconceivable, portentous natures.[2]

Socrates proposes to start elsewhere, with understanding of his
own nature. But almost straight away the mythographic explanations he has brushed aside – explanations that seem mythological
in their very proliferation – start to enter into his own project of
self-investigation:

I am not yet able, as the Delphic inscription has it, to know
myself; so it seems to me ridiculous, when I do not yet know
that, to investigate irrelevant things. And so I dismiss these
matters and accepting the customary belief about them, as I
was saying just now, I investigate not these things, but myself,
to know whether I am a monster more complicated and more
furious than Typhon or a gentler and simpler creature, to
whom a divine and quiet lot is given by nature.[3]

So Socrates does not quite turn away from the fanciful investigation of the products of the fancy, since his cool and sober
investigation of himself may reveal him to be quite as complicated
(πολυπλοκώτερον, *polyplokoteron*) as Typhon, the earth-born monster with a hundred snake heads, and therefore one of the 'strange,
inconceivable, portentous natures' characteristic of myth. Just as
mythographic discourse may become mythological, so the effort to
distinguish myth from knowledge must allow for the possibility of
coming upon one's own mythical monstrosity.

Socrates' intention is to cultivate self-knowledge in preference
to knowledge about myths and fantasies, but his remarks leave it
moot whether myths and fantasies belong to the world or to the self.
The injunction to self-knowledge has often encountered this paradox, which makes it unclear whether knowing is to be regarded as
on the side of the knower or the known. Sir John Davies's *Nosce
Teipsum* (1599), a poetic disquisition on how the soul's immortality

may be known, begins with a poem 'Of Humane Knowledge', which denounces the ambition to worldly knowledge that the Christian story of the Fall had made conventional:

Why did my parents send me to the Schooles
That I with knowledge might enrich my mind?
Since the *desire to know* first made men fools,
And did corrupt the root of all mankind.[4]

The poem is written, as Davies's editor Alexander Grosart believes, for the benefit of 'wits and virtuosoes' as an 'antidote against the poison they have sucked in from Lucretius and Hobbes'.[5] Davies acquired a reputation among his early readers for being able to compose a poetry of thought that was able to keep reason and rhetoric in balance. Noting that Davies gives us 'hard arguments interwoven with the pliant materials of fancy' in ways that are comparable to the metaphysical poets who were his contemporaries, Grosart nevertheless affirms that '*he* argues like a hard thinker, and *they*, for the most part, like madmen.'[6] T. S. Eliot thought that Davies 'had that strange gift, so rarely bestowed, for turning thought into feeling . . . Thought is not exploited for the sake of feeling, it is pursued for its own sake; and the feeling is a kind of by-product, though a by-product worth far more than the thought.'[7] A century after Eliot, James Sanderson also finds Davies's conclusions 'both logically and rhetorically congruent'.[8]

But the first part of *Nosce Teipsum* seems to put this smooth complementarity under some strain. Its opening poem, 'Of Humane Knowledge', sets out to explain how the Fall has clouded the clarity of the knowledge imparted in Eden. Adam and Eve, originally almost 'intellectual angels', are corrupted, we read, by the whisperings of the '*Spirit of Lyes*', who arouses in them 'A curious *wish*, which did corrupt their *will*'.[9] The corruption of their will involves them in the desire to know 'ill', a desire which, Davies quibbles, is already and immediately the illness of their will: 'Ill they desir'd to know, and ill they did'.[10] It seems that, as soon as will becomes wilful, or something other than the will not to know, it grows, and does, ill. There is something in the milling of these terms – wish, will and illness – that suggests a temporary intellectual hazing-over of the issues. Davies's conventional doctrine, heavily dependent on sixteenth-century sources, is that a knowledge of the soul will redeem the clouded and imperfect knowledge governed by sensory knowledge and worldly will.[11] But he is unable to explain how this can be except by positing a special power of self-inspection and self-knowing in the soul that has nothing in it of desire or sensory imperfection, that is, by an act of pure I-think-I-can stipulation. The only hope for redeeming knowledge lies in turning inward, rather than outward, even though, like Socrates, who may be briefly recalled here, Davies recoils from the sight of the monsters that may turn out to inhabit the self:

> For euen at first reflection she espies,
> Such strange *chimeraes*, and such monsters there;
> Such toys, such *antikes*, and such vanities,
> As she retires, and shrinkes for shame and feare.[12]

Indeed, even as Davies is advocating the priority of self-knowledge over outward knowledge, he blurts out the inconvenient origin of the injunction to 'Know Thyself':

> For how may we to others' things attaine,
> When none of vs his owne soule vnderstands?
> For which the Diuell mockes our curious braine,
> When, *'Know thy selfe'* his oracle commands.[13]

An editorial note of Grosart's reproduces a manuscript comment made at this juncture by one 'Bishop Hacket' in his 1599 copy of the poem: 'Oraculum Appollonis [f]uit Diabolicum' – 'the oracle of Apollo was diabolical'.[14] Others, too, have been made a little queasy by the provenance of the Delphic injunction to self-knowledge. The eighteenth-century preacher Philip Skelton writes:

> We are told, that 'know thyself' was written in capital letters over the gate of Apollo's temple at Delphos. Wise as the words are in themselves, they were placed in that situation, for surely no man, who had the sense to know himself, would have gone in to worship, as a god, a thing far inferior to himself, made by some other man out of a block of wood or stone; or to inquire about futurity of a woman, half distracted by noxious fumes of a cavern, on the mouth of which she sat, and from whence she belched out the windy injections of her scurvy

god in bad verses, and fanatic equivocations, for which they were amply paid by the superstition of their stupid votaries.[15]

Fulke Greville's *Treatie of Humane Learninge* (1633) articulates a much more conservative argument about the reining in of the will to knowledge which seems to avoid the problem of how to immunize self-knowledge against fantasy. And yet it is assailed by a kind of self-division in which the will to knowledge is simultaneously curbed and yet in the process made appetitively self-exceeding. Greville begins by evoking just such a will to omnipotence:

> The minde of man is this worlds true dimension,
> And knowledge is the measure of the minde;
> And as the minde, in her vast comprehension,
> Containes more worlds, then all the world can finde:
>   Soe knowledge doth it selfe farr more extende,
>   Then all the mindes of men can comprehende.[16]

Knowledge goes so far beyond the powers of its human vehicles as to approach to the infinite condition of God, here identified with a kind of maximal condition of knowledge:

> A climinge height it is, without a head,
> Deapth without bottome, way without an ende,
> A circle with noe line invyroned;
> Not comprehended, all it comprehends;
>   Worth infinite, yet satisfies noe minde,
>   Till it that infinite of the godhead finde.[17]

With these exulting words, the poem enters a tangle from which it will spend almost a thousand lines trying to extricate itself. Unlike Davies, who sees the cure for fallen knowledge in the self-illumining apprehension of the soul's immortality, Greville seeks to chasten and contain the incontinent power he here evokes, which is simultaneously 'without a head' (either in the sense of a final limit, or in the sense of a brain to contain it) and yet for that reason approaches godhead. Greville quickly turns that vaulting power of being uncomprehendable into self-incomprehension: 'noe man knowes his owne unknoing minde.'[18] But the very will to restrain not only the desire for knowledge but also knowledge's own desire must itself be a self-transcending force, one that substitutes the omnipotence fantasy of reaching a divinely all-comprehending condition with the omnipotence fantasy of being able to see the limits and liabilities of knowledge from a godly condition beyond it. Late in the poem, Greville includes poetry and music in his list of intellectual accomplishments that are to be held in their place by religious obedience. These, he freely asserts, are to be regarded as helpful ornamentation, since 'if the matter be in nature vile, / How can it be made pretious by a stile?'[19] Greville writes poetically against poetry and on the side of true knowledge, seeing it as no more than 'a harmony to move, and please, / If studied for it selfe, disease of mind'.[20] But the question that cannot easily be articulated here is whether this poem meets its own self-chastening conditions, or itself approaches that 'disease of mind' in which sensory pleasure corrupts thought.

The paradox of a kind of knowledge that led to foolishness was commonly articulated in the Renaissance and is illustrated in the emblematic image of the Fool's Cap Map of the World. There are two versions of this map, both of which show the head of a fool with cap and bells enclosing, in place of a face, a map of the world. The earlier of the two versions, produced by Jean de Gourmont around 1575, is headed 'CONGNOIS TOY TOY-MESME: L'homme peut mieux paruenir / Que sa cognoissance acquerir' – 'Know Yourself: Man can reach further by acquiring self-knowledge'. On the band of the fool's cap are the words 'O TESTE DIGNE DE PVRGATION' – 'O head deserving purgation' – and the image is surrounded by various mottos attesting to the vanity of worldly ambition, chief among them the desire for knowledge of the world. A later version of the print, a copper-plate engraving probably made in Antwerp in the late 1580s, in which the map-face is stretched out into an ellipsis, as though to give it an inane grin, gives Latin versions of the French captions.

Anne Chapple convincingly characterizes the attraction that the Fool's Cap Map may have had for Robert Burton, who describes it in some detail in the preface to his *Anatomy of Melancholy* (1621–38).[21] For Chapple, the map seems to illustrate, at least in its captions, the kind of universal folly that Burton saw in the world around him, as when he writes:

thou shalt soone perceive that all the world is mad, that it is melancholy, dotes: that it is (which *Epichthonius Cosmopolites* expressed not many yeeres since in a Map) made like a Fooles head (with that Motto, *Caput Helleboro dignum*), a crased head, *cavea stultorum*, a Fooles paradise, or as *Apollonius*, a common prison of Gulles, Cheaters, Flatterers, &c. & needs to be reformed.[22]

Yet Chapple does not note what seems to be the most salient fact about the map, which is that its title, 'Nosce te ipsum', seems to condemn itself, or at least the folly of the knowledge that would attempt a picture of the whole world. The map offers a mocking picture, not only of the world but of the mapping of the world in the 'crased head' of externally directed knowledge. For all the fact that maps embodied the power of modern forms of knowledge, maps like this, as Richard Hedgerson has shown,

> instead of doing the work of modernity . . . were made to mock that very project and all those who had devoted themselves to it . . . Like Burton, early modern viewers would have seen not so much a map in a trickster's head as the world in the head of a fool.[23]

Ayesha Ramachandran sees in this image evidence of a project of mediation between the local and the global, despite the paradox of its reciprocal encapsulations, with the world including the head that includes it suggesting that

> to understand the world as a thing made by human ingenuity and imagination is to reconceive the relation of the knowing human self and the world at large. No longer is the self merely subordinate to the world; it simultaneously creates the very world of which it was also a part.[24]

The later, Latin version of the map renders 'O teste digne de purgation' as 'Ô caput elleboro dignum' – 'O head deserving of hellebore'. The beautiful, winter-flowering hellebore flower is very toxic, with a capacity to induce vertigo, inflammation, tinnitus and stupor, and is said to have been the poison that caused the death of Alexander the Great. But, if it was capable of disordering the senses, it was also regarded as a purgative cure for delirium. The first-century CE

Greek botanist Pedanius Dioscorides explains its alternative name of melampodium, which derives from a tale in which the mad daughters of Proteus are purged and cured by the plant as administered by a goatherd called Melampus.[25] Dioscorides also claims that it was sprinkled round houses in order to preserve them from evil spirits and that if an eagle sees you digging it, it will cause your death.[26] Hellebore was also associated with witchcraft, being useful for summoning demons, creating invisibility when thrown into the air in powdered form, and being a component in flying ointments used to grease broomsticks to make them aeronautical or, somewhat more probably, to induce the hallucination of flight. The saturnine, satanic and melancholic associations of hellebore perhaps derive largely from its dark appearance and preferred growing environment, especially in the form of black hellebore, *Helleborus niger*, which has a dramatically dark flower and grows best in shady conditions. Hellebore is in fact pictured in the frontispiece of Burton's *Anatomy of Melancholy* as one of two plants (borage being the other) which are able '*To cleare the Braine of misty fogges*'.[27] It is evoked throughout the text, as it was proverbially through the seventeenth century, as a treatment for various kinds of madness, in phrases such as '*Helleborum edere* [eat hellebore] ... spoken to men which are very melancholike, or be wilde brained', or 'Mad and Frantick beyond the Cure of Hellebore'.[28] It certainly seems to have been known to be violent in its operations: 'Who hath not horror of the torments which both the Hellebores bring to the body?' writes Timothy Bright.[29] Thomas Blount tells us that it was used as a kind of smart drug: 'the Sophisters of old were wont to Purge themselves with *Hellebore*, when they would dispute best.'[30]

And yet the fantasy-purging plant also sometimes had a rather fantastic reputation. Leonardo Di Capua writes that

> of *Ellebore* and many other Plants there is such a number
> of Fables reported as well by the same *Theophrastus*, as by
> *Dioscorides* and *Pliny*, that if I would relate them one by one,
> I should scarce come to an end.[31]

Burton evokes the helleborus in particular as a therapy for the madness of knowledge itself, the various accents and exponents of which Burton excoriates in a typically dizzily self-exemplifying passage of mad scholarly elaboration (or deliriation, as he calls it):

Of philosophers and Schollers, *priscae sapientiae dictatores* [the speakers of ancient wisdom], I have already spoken in generall terms, those superintendents of wit and learning, men above men, those refined men, Minions of the Muses ... These acute and subtile Sophisters, so much honored, have as much need of Hellebor as others ... *Democritus*, that common flouter of folly, was ridiculous himselfe, barking *Menippus*, scoffing *Lucian*, satyricall *Lucilius, Petronius, Varro, Persius, &c.*, may be censured with the rest, *Loripedem rectus derideat, Aethiopem albus* [Let the straight-legged mock the bandy, the white mock the black]. *Bale, Erasmus, Hospinian, Vives, Kemnisius*, explode as a vast ocean of *Obs* and *Sols* [objections and solutions], Schoole divinity. A labyrinth of intricable questions, unprofitable contentions, *incredibilem delirationem*, one calls it ... What shall become of humanity? *Ars stulta*, what can she plead? what can her followers say for themselves? Much learning, *cere-diminuit-brum* [shrink-the-brain], hath cract their skonce, and taken such root, that *tribus Anticyris caput insanabile* [a head incurable by three Anticyras], Hellebor it selfe can doe no good.[32]

We may perhaps see the desire for knowledge as itself just such a kill-and-cure *pharmakon*. Burton in fact ends his long preface to the reader recommending that the whole world be sent for dosing to Anticyra, the region (often thought in fact to be two Aegean islands, the Anticyrae) in which helleborus is produced.

Nunc opus est (tanta est insania) transeat omnis
Mundus in Anticyras, gramen in Helleborum.

Now (so much does madness prevail), all the world must be
Sent to Anticyra, to graze on Hellebore.[33]

But hellebore is an image of Burton's *Anatomy of Melancholy* itself, a madly exorbitant project of auto-analysis and cure from madness, a paradox which is not lost on Burton:

We accuse others of madnesse, of folly, and are the veriest dizards our selves. For it is a great signe and property of a foole (which Eccl. 10:3 points at) out of pride and selfe-conceit, to insult, vilifie, condemne, censure, and call other men Fooles.[34]

PSYCHOANALYSIS

Burton's work may be seen as a sustained work of self-cure through an act of analysis, in which reason defeats madness by bringing its resources to bear on itself. The inheritor of this tradition is the project of what became known as psychoanalysis.

There have been many arguments about the status of psycho-analytic knowledge – whether it has any right to be thought of as a science, whether it is fraudulent or self-deluding, whether it is capable of leading us to any kind of reliable truth regarding human con-sciousness and experience. The history of worries and doubts about the knowledge claims made by psychoanalysis and the response of different forms of psychoanalysis to them have been very well reviewed by Stephen Frosh in his *For and Against Psychoanalysis*.[35] These are broadly epistemological concerns that address the knowl-edge claims made by psychoanalysis. Less attention has been paid directly to the feeling for knowledge in psychoanalysis, that is, to the particular meaning and value that the idea of knowledge has for the subject of psychoanalysis, for the psychoanalyst and for the readers and writers of psychoanalytic theory. The remainder of this chapter will accordingly consider not what kind of knowledge psychoanaly-sis may offer, but the kinds of investment in knowledge made in and through psychoanalysis.

Psychoanalysis, at least in its English-speaking forms, has a spe-cial name for this investment: cathexis. Since in this chapter I am about to undertake an investigation of the cathexis of knowledge in psychoanalysis, a word or two on the history on the history of this word may not be amiss. The word that James Strachey translates with 'cathexis' is the common German word *Besetzung*, which has the principal meaning of occupation – a place at a table or a lava-tory cubicle is said to be *besetzt*, and *Besetzung* is the word used for an occupying garrison. Strachey seems not only to have switched the linguistic register of Freud's *Besetzung* with his invention of cathexis, but, in his usage of the word, also to have added or intensified the idea of some projective force, amplifying the idea of occupation (close to the English idea of a preoccupation) with the idea of investment or charging. Cathexis thus becomes as much the idea of directing energy at some object as the idea of binding or capturing that object. This question of how to convey the idea of a process as well as the state that results from that process is an explicit preoccupation of the long letter Strachey wrote to Ernest Jones about his proposed translation on 27 November 1921. '[I]t seems evident', he wrote,

> that what distinguishes an object that is besetzt from one that is not is essentially that there is some dynamic process going on in it. The 'charge', in fact, seems almost to be the 'charging process'; the 'cathect' and the 'cathexis' refer, from different points of view, to the same fact.[36]

As Peter Hoffer observes, the meaning of Strachey's term 'is essentially oxymoronic . . . [since] *Besetzung* denotes an action that is simultaneously static and dynamic'.[37]

This makes the word 'cathexis' a venue for the very processes it describes, the word itself becoming the target of a process of projection or investment. Strachey proposed that using a neologism rather than a familiar English word to correspond to the familiar German *besetzen/Besetzung* would force the reader to work to make out its meaning for himself, its very neutrality making it easy for it to receive various kinds of semantic charge. This is even more powerfully the case because of the fact that the word is designed to sound like a specialist term from a technical or scientific lexicon. It is a word of art, or knowing-word, a *mot-supposé-savoir*. It is therefore subject to something like the same investment of expectation and attribution of power as it is intended to name, and whatever use we might make of the idea of cathexis to understand the objects or exercise of knowing is already being made use of in the idea of cathexis itself. In both cases the meaning is not so much inherent as projected or invested in the object. Other examples of these knowing-words in Anglophone psychoanalysis include *ego* and *id* for the homely German *Ich* and *Es*, and may even include little verbal tics like the picky habit of spelling 'fantasy' with an erudite initial 'ph' to signal the Greek origins of the word. Psychoanalysis is not alone in projecting an image of its dignity and seriousness through specialist, apparently technical language.

But the question of knowledge at the outset of psychoanalysis was not principally a philosophical question; rather it was a medical one.

Psychoanalysis offers treatment and cure not through pharmacology or physical therapy but through the development of understanding. Of course, philosophy has long thought of itself as the cure for various kinds of malady of thought, or the means to a kind of intellectual health. Conversely, the practice of care and cure has depended upon more or less explicit theories, meaning that being to some degree in the know about the nature of your illness and the reasons for cure, or at least trusting that your doctor knows what he is doing, has been an important part of whatever cures have been more than coincidentally successful. So important have medical knowledges been to the experience of medical care that we might say the arrival of real medicine can be dated only from the moment when it is no longer necessary for the patient to know what the physician knows. Only for about 150 years have we had medical treatments that work whether patients know anything about them or not.

Nevertheless, the importance of knowledge has remained undiminished in certain aspects and areas of medical practice. As the placebo and nocebo effects demonstrate, the expectation that the physician, pharmacist or *somebody* knows *something* remains very potent. It may not even be necessary to hide from the patient the knowledge that they are swallowing sugar pills, just as long as you assure them that 'we know that' the placebo effect can be very powerful in such cases. An engineer friend of mine uses homeopathic remedies, not because she has any belief in their physical effectiveness but because she knows it is just the sort of thing her body will believe in. Nowhere is this framework of supposition, trust and expectation more emphatically present than in the case of psychoanalysis. If what are called 'conventional' models of therapy depend on the fact that I don't need to know how they work, then 'alternative' therapies seem to depend heavily on various kinds of theory, which are often surprisingly crude in the mechanisms they posit. Almost from its beginnings psychoanalysis has been a distinctive mixture of philosophy and clinical practice. Psychoanalysis became known as the 'talking cure', but might just as well be known as the 'thinking cure', so important in it are the processes of interpretation, recognition and understanding signalled in the word 'analysis'. Understanding the nature of your illness may not be much immediate help in recovering from typhoid or cancer, but since the assumption of psychoanalysis is that all the maladies in its sphere of competence – and perhaps well beyond it

– arise from maladjustments of the conscious and unconscious mind, treatment and cure depend entirely on processes of understanding, in both doctor and patient. If the development of conventional medicine has depended upon a medical epistemology which concerns itself with how knowledge of physiological processes can be reliably derived and demonstrated, psychoanalysis may be regarded as a kind of epistemological medicine which offers not only cure through understanding but also a cure for defective understanding itself. There are even some, like Adam Phillips, who would prefer to see the idea of psychoanalysis as physic discreetly retired in favour of psychoanalysis as pedagogy or philosophy:

> I think psychoanalysis is better seen as entering the nineteenth century debate about education; rather than, in one way or another, as a contribution to medicine. Psychoanalysis, whatever else it is, is an enquiry, an opportunity to explore the ways in which people inform each other.[38]

Freud, too, recognized that psychoanalysis occupied a 'middle position between medicine and philosophy', though he did not claim this as a conspicuous advantage.[39] Not only this, experiences of knowing have been at the forefront of psychoanalytic reflections about illness and its own processes. Psychoanalysis both asserts and assails the doctor's knowledge, as Ernst Simmel remarked in the course of a discussion on 'lay analysis' in 1927:

> The narcissistic disillusion which acceptance of psychoanalysis means for civilised humanity is specially painful for the physician. It deprives him of the aureole belonging to the bygone wizard and medicine-man; it wrests from him the mantle of 'omnipotence and omniscience' he wore in unconscious pride, and condemns him to the modesty of 'the wise man who knows how inadequate all his wisdom is'.[40]

Academic standing remains very important to psychoanalysts. Almost the only authors nowadays who insist on signing themselves 'PhD' are authors of dubious diet books, purveyors of conspiracy theories and psychoanalysts. Psychoanalysis has at various times made the investigation of problems of knowledge central to its clinical enterprise, even as it has also struggled internally and externally with the question of the nature and status of its own knowledge, with the will to believe in the courage and rigour of its investigation of the nature of willing and believing – and has also, as is the way with such things, luxuriated in the struggle. It is strange, but perhaps not entirely unexpected, that psychoanalysis should not only provide so many resources for thinking about the psychopathologies of knowledge but should also seem so much like an arena in which they may breed and fever.

OMNIPOTENCE

The question of the power of knowledge is everywhere to the fore in psychoanalysis: in its theoretical content, in its operations and in its own understanding of itself. The power of knowledge means that wanting to know is always shadowed with wanting to be one who knows. To be one who knows is to have great power, even if that power (like all power really) is largely a matter of projection and assumption (I think I can assume that you will assume I have the power that comes from knowledge, while all the time suspecting that you, or I, may not). One of the unexpected difficulties with the power of knowing, one that psychoanalysis was early, if not exactly first, to recognize, is that it can sometimes seem to go beyond the power of the one who knows. As observed in my Introduction, Freud defined what he called magical thinking as 'omnipotence of thoughts' (*SE*, XIII, 84).[41] In Freud's original usage, this phrase refers to the belief of the patient known as the 'Rat Man' that his hostile thoughts and wishes could have injurious effects upon their objects. In his 1909 case history, Freud interprets this as more than just a delusion, for, in a sense, his patient was recognizing the power which his unconscious impulses exercised over himself, precisely by being unknowable and so ungovernable:

> [H]e became convinced of the omnipotence of his love and of his hatred. Without denying the omnipotence of love we may point out that both these instances were concerned with death, and we may adopt the obvious explanation that, like other obsessional neurotics, our patient was compelled to overestimate the effects of his hostile feelings upon the external world, because a large part of their internal, mental

effects escaped his conscious knowledge. His love – or rather his hatred – was in truth overpowering; it was precisely they that created the obsessional thoughts, of which he could not understand the origin and against which he strove in vain to defend himself. (*SE*, X, 233–4)

Freud returned to the idea of omnipotence of thoughts (at once a particular form of omnipotence and of course the only form there could ever be) in the paper 'Animism, Magic and Omnipotence of Thoughts' which appeared in the journal *Imago* in 1912 and would be incorporated in *Totem and Taboo* of the following year. The effort of psychoanalysis is to try to give you power over the power of your thoughts, through giving you knowledge of your own psychological constitution. Freud connects obsessional neurosis, characterized by 'the reality not of experience but of thought' and 'the overvaluation of mental processes as compared with reality' (*SE*, XIII, 86, 87), with the principle of magic operational in primitive humans, which is based on 'mistaking an ideal connection for a real one' (*SE*, XIII, 79). Freud finds the origin of magical thinking in a sexualization of thought (whether expressed or repressed) that he calls 'libidinal hypercathexis of thinking' (*libidinöser Überbesetzung des Denkens*, GW, IX, 109). 'Primitive men and neurotics, as we have seen, attach a high valuation – in our eyes an over-valuation – to psychical acts,' he wrote, this being explained by the fact that 'in primitive men the process of thinking is still to a great extent sexualized. This is the origin of their belief in the omnipotence of thoughts, their unshakable confidence in the possibility of controlling the world' (*SE*, XIII, 89). In the case of modern neurotics the surviving force of this sexualization of thoughts is amplified by the repression of sexual thoughts, which itself produces 'a further sexualization of their thinking processes'. The result of this 'libidinal hypercathexis of thinking' is 'intellectual narcissism and the omnipotence of thoughts' (*SE*, XIII, 89–90).

The topic of omnipotence seems to have caused Freud some difficulty during the later months of 1912 when he was preoccupied with writing 'Animism, Magic and Omnipotence of Thoughts'. Indeed, in a letter to Sándor Ferenczi of 30 December there is a suggestion that the topic may have reached deep into his sense of his own motivations: 'I have just been totally omnipotence [*sic*], totally a savage. That's the way one must keep it if one wants to get done with something.'[42] Freud does not say that he has himself felt omnipotent, but that he has been *all omnipotence* – 'Ich war eben ganz Allmacht, ganz Wilder' – as though to inundate himself in the fantasy of omnipotence were important for the completion of any difficult intellectual work.[43] I think that many writers would agree that a high and probably unreasonable level of confidence in the power and significance of what one is writing is often necessary to carry it through. Freud does not in fact exactly say that a sense of omnipotence is important to get the work done, but rather important if one wants to 'get done with' the work ('wenn man mit etwas fertig werden will'), implying being able to leave it behind, rather than necessarily to fulfil it.[44] Without that omnipotence fantasy, perhaps, there would just be knowledge, which might in turn imply the impossibility of having done.

In writing of the patient he called the Rat Man, Freud is surprisingly inclined to grant omnipotence to what he rather sweetly calls 'Liebe':

> It is impossible to deny that in their case a piece of mental work has been performed which, in spite of its horrifying result, is the equivalent of an idealization of the instinct. The omnipotence of love is perhaps never more strongly proved than in such of its aberrations as these. The highest and the lowest are always closest to each other in the sphere of sexuality: 'vom Himmel durch die Welt zur Hölle.' (*SE*, VII, 161–2)

The quotation from Goethe's *Faust* is the end of the 'Prelude in the Theatre', in which the Theatre Manager is urging his interlocutors to use all the resources of the theatre to convey the immensity of human experience:

> *So schreitet in dem engen Bretterhaus*
> *Den ganzen Kreis der Schöpfung aus*
> *Und wandelt mit bedächt'ger Schnelle,*
> *Vom Himmel durch die Welt zur Hölle!*

> So pace out across our narrow stage
> the whole circle of creation,
> and wander, with thoughtful speed,
> from heaven through the world to hell.[45]

Freud's quotation implies that it is not so much in the 'sphere of sexuality' (simply *in der Sexualität* in Freud's German, *GW*, 5.61), as on the staging of it in the theatre of knowledge that the high and the low are brought together. But, of course, in making this conventional-sounding romantic concession Freud is in fact indirectly affirming his own foundational conviction of the power of sexuality, on which psychoanalytic theory depends. The fervour with which Freud defended the necessity of the sexual theory to Jung in 1910 gives an indication of what was at stake in it:

> I can still recall vividly how Freud said to me, 'My dear Jung, promise me never to abandon the sexual theory. That is the most essential thing of all. You see, we must make a dogma of it, an unshakable bulwark.' He said that to me with great emotion, in the tone of a father saying, 'And promise me this one thing, my dear son: that you will go to church every Sunday.' In some astonishment I asked him, 'A bulwark – against what?' To which he replied, 'Against the black tide of mud' – and here he hesitated for a moment, then added – 'of occultism.'[46]

Jung saw in this not a well-founded scientific judgement but 'a personal power drive'.[47] Freud turns his face against the kind of magical thinking involved in 'occultism' (the parapsychology in which Jung would increasingly be interested), but depends himself upon an alternative principle of occultism which might be described not as hidden knowledge but the knowledge of what is hidden from knowledge, or what knowledge itself might be thought to hide (the force of repressed or occulted sexuality). Jung's view was that the force of this had occult effects on Freud himself, and he remarks that for Freud 'sexuality was a sort of *numinosum*' and that 'the sexual theory was just as occult' as religion and parapsychology.[48]

Here, there seems to be a move away from the idea of an omnipotence applied to the practical effect of certain thoughts, and towards the idea of the overmastering power of thinking in general. This kind of omnipotence of thought may be seen as the phantasmal perfection of the will to know, naming the aspiration to a condition of omniscience and the hallucination of that omniscience that the aspiration in part allows. Ferenczi anticipated some of Freud's comments about the omnipotence fantasies in neurotics in an essay of 1913, 'Stages in the Development of a Sense of Reality'. Obsessional patients, Ferenczi observes,

> admit to us that they cannot help being convinced of the omnipotence of their thoughts, feelings, and wishes, good and bad. However enlightened they may be, however much their academic knowledge and their reason may strive to the contrary, they have the feeling that their wishes in some inexplicable way get realised.[49]

Ferenczi thought that this condition was a lingering of the actual condition of omnipotence experienced by the child in the womb, in which every wish is realized. It is hard to understand, though, how one could really have a sense of omnipotence without being aware of it: for that, one would have not only to be ignorant of the limits to your power, but also to be cognizant of it as a power rather than just as a condition of your existence. But the child in the womb and the obsessional patient are not alone in aspiring to omnipotence, it seems, for Ferenczi assures us immediately: 'Of the truth of this state of affairs any analyst can convince himself as often as he likes' (FC, 214). Ferenczi thought that the child goes through a transitional period, the *'period of magic thoughts and magic words'* (FC, 230), in which, possessed of speech and able to articulate its needs, the child nevertheless believes itself to still exercise a kind of telepathic power over its human environment.

Ferenczi tends not to twin omnipotence with omniscience as others do. In fact, we should remember that the obsessional patient's omnipotence fantasies are severely limited by the sense that his wishes operate in some inscrutable way against his wishes. But there is a strong sense of something like the analyst's omniscience, even if it is transferred to the patient, in the explication of the phenomenon of transference:

> One need only be a physician to become the object of this kind of transference; the mystical part played in the sexual phantasy of the child by the doctor, who knows all forbidden things, who may look at and touch everything that is concealed, is an obvious determining factor in unconscious

fancying, and therefore also in the transference occurring in a subsequent neurosis. (*FC*, 41)

This may be thought of as a substitute omnipotence, one that arises from

> a time when the ego has already long adjusted itself to the increasingly complicated conditions of reality, has passed through the stages of magic gestures and words, and has already almost attained the knowledge of the omnipotence of natural forces. (*FC*, 234)

But Ferenczi's far-reaching essay nevertheless ends with a passage of ambitious speculation about the relations between the ontogenetic history of the individual and the phylogenetic history of the race, with the suggestion that the trauma of birth may be paralleled by the ice age:

> It is perhaps allowable to venture the surmise that it was the geological changes in the surface of the earth, with their catastrophic consequences for primitive man, that compelled repression of favourite habits and thus 'development.' Such catastrophes may have been the sites of repression in the history of racial development, and the temporal localization and intensity of such catastrophes may have decided the character and the neuroses of the race. According to a remark of Professor Freud's, racial character is the precipitate of racial history. Having ventured so far beyond the knowable, we have no reason to shrink before the last analogy and from bringing the great step in individual repression, the latency period, into connection with the last and greatest catastrophe that smote our primitive ancestors (at a time when there were certainly human beings on the earth), *i.e.* with the misery of the glacial period, which we still faithfully recapitulate in our individual life. (*FC*, 237)

Ferenczi immediately recognizes the possible overreach in this fantasy:

> The impetuous curiosity to know everything that has just seduced me into enchanted vistas of the past, and led me

to bridge over the yet unknowable by the help of analogies, brings me back to the starting-point of these considerations: to the theme of the acme and decline of the feeling of omnipotence. Science has to repudiate this illusion, or at least always to know when she is entering the field of hypotheses and fancies. In fairy-tales, on the contrary, phantasies of omnipotence are and remain the dominating ones. (FC, 238)

Ferenczi recognizes that he has been seduced by a sort of scientific fantasy, and pulls himself back from it, telling us that science must know when it has entered fantasy. But the contrast between fairy tales and scientific fantasies is not as clear as it might be, since fairy tales are also known to be fantasy. Knowledge may indeed, in such circumstances, allow rather than discredit the work of fantasy. Especially when it comes to the knowledge of beginnings, and even more with the beginnings of knowledge itself, omnipotence and impotence can be closely twinned. In fact, although omniscience and omnipotence seem to be logically equivalent, there are grave difficulties involved in both being and knowing yourself to be omnipotent, as opposed to merely very powerful indeed, since knowing yourself to be omnipotent would in fact tend to limit your power, by separating you from it. The internal self-division involved in knowledge will always be able to introduce a flaw in the absolute self-identity required for real omnipotence.

The American psychoanalyst Bertram D. Lewin devoted a number of essays to the desire for knowledge. In an essay on education, he asks that we recognize the importance of the infantile fantasy of omniscience and the desire to restore it:

> there exists a very widespread fantasy that heaven lay about us in our infancy and that then we were omnipotent and omniscient. The world and our knowledge of it was intuitively a priori graspable, finite, though unbounded. When we are proved otherwise than omnipotent and omniscient, there is resentment, followed by an effort through magical, real, or part-magical part-real, means to restore and to repair the gaps and lesions in this primal feeling.[50]

In an earlier essay Lewin describes some of the workings of efforts to reinstate the sense of omniscience, concluding that in many persons a repression is perceived narcissistically as a blow to their omniscience, which they try to repair through real or magical means. It also happens that later any insult to narcissism, whether in the field of knowledge or in other fields, evokes as a response an assertion of omniscience or a setting into play of the investigatory impulse in an attempt to recapture the sense of omniscient perfection.[51]

Lewin suggests that the quality of feeling attaching to belief, which he defines as 'a partial omniscience', derives from this desire to reinstate omniscience:

> it is quite probable that such phrases as 'all men hold these truths to be self-evident', or philosophical systems of knowledge which begin with an appeal to the self-evident, or those which predicate a surer and higher non-empirical knowledge, owe their emotional appeal to their harmony with the unconscious trust in the original narcissistically orientated conviction that everything is known and that what is true is self-evident.[52]

There are neurotic, obsessional and delusional ways of repairing this loss – but, if all goes well, or better than can be expected, there are also more sublimated ways, and Lewin sees the scientific method of Copernicus, Darwin and Freud as efforts to repair the omniscience that their very theories had maimed.[53] Lewin's essay was given as a lecture at the Chicago Institute for Psychoanalysis in November 1957, to mark its 25th anniversary. Though Lewin draws somewhat grandiose parallels between the rise of psychoanalysis and other episodes in European intellectual history, his view is that 'The psychoanalytic institutes are too young to take on or to feel the responsibilities of omniscience.'[54] On the contrary, it seems very likely that the will to knowledge, and perhaps also the fantasy of omniscience, seems to be a pervasive and defining fantasy within, amid and around psychoanalytic knowledge.

Like other kinds of knowledge, omniscience must always be supposed, imagined or assumed, so it is often a kind of omnipotence by proxy. Nowhere is this more the case than in the apparently defining and governing assumption of psychoanalysis that there are no accidents in unconscious life – that things that seem trivial, inattentive, arbitrary or coincidental are in fact determined in various ways. I cannot find any statement in the works included in the Standard Edition of Freud's works that corresponds to the view that there are no accidents, though it is routinely affirmed that Freud maintained this. What can be demonstrated is that, in *The Psychopathology of Everyday Life* in particular, Freud had a very strong predisposition to see many apparently 'chance actions' as in fact 'symptomatic'. He begins section XII on 'Determinism, Belief in Chance and Superstition' with the statement that 'If we give way to the view that a part of our psychical functioning cannot be explained by purposive ideas, we are failing to appreciate the extent of determination in mental life' (*SE*, VI, 240). He then goes on to demonstrate, as he believes, the impossibility of choosing a number at random. To do this, he gives the example of a chance remark made in a letter to Wilhelm Fliess while he was proof-correcting *The Interpretation of Dreams* that he did not intend to make any more corrections to the book 'even if it contains 2,467 mistakes' (*SE*, VI, 242). Freud then reproduces the analysis he immediately conducted of this number, in order to bear out his judgement that 'nothing in the mind is arbitrary or undetermined' (*SE*, VI, 242; *Nun gibt es aber nichts Willkürliches, Undeterminiertes im Psychischen*, *GW*, 4.270). As is often the case, the analysis turns on Freud's anxiety over his own intellectual achievements and ambitions, here measured against those of a certain General of his acquaintance about whose retirement he had read. Though Freud is fully aware of the strong predisposition to superstition (German *Aberglaube*, or 'over-belief') to be found in many human beings – and indeed notes that 'in these unconscious thought-operations with numbers I find I have a tendency to superstition, whose origin for long remained unknown to me' (*SE*, VI, 250) – he does not seem to fully embrace the suggestion that what he may be detecting is itself an unconscious will to coherence in the analyst.

What this seems to promise or assume is not actual omnipotence but the prospect of absolute determinability; not so much the omnipotence of thought, as the thought of such omnipotence. Everything means and so everything matters. A very good example of this principle is furnished by symptomatic readings of difficulty in learning, by Melanie Klein and others. The source text for this way of thinking about learning may well be Klein's essay of 1923 'The Role of the School in Libidinal Development'. Here she records the feelings that young children told her they had for numbers and letters, and remorselessly translates them into their sado-phantasmal corporeal equivalents – nowhere with more mad calm than in the explication of the inhibition that a child called Fritz had in performing division sums, which Klein believes had its origin in a fantasy of mutilating the body of the mother:

> He then related (also in connection with a previously elab-
> orated phantasy) that actually every child wants to have a bit
> of his mother, who is to be cut in four pieces; he depicted
> quite exactly how she screamed and had paper stuffed in her
> mouth so that she could not scream, and what kind of faces
> she made, etc. . . . He continued that every child then took
> the piece of the mother that it wanted, and agreed that the
> cut-up mother was then also eaten.[55]

Klein's view is that the inhibition which Fritz had unconsciously imposed on these violent fantasies accounted for his failure to understand how long division works: 'It now appeared also that he always confused the remainder with the quotient in division, and always wrote it in the wrong place, because in his mind it was bleeding pieces of flesh with which he was unconsciously dealing' (*LGR*, 70). It seems alarming rather than reassuring that Klein's explanations to Fritz of what he was really thinking about 'completely removed his inhibition with regard to division' (*LGR*, 70). Might it not be a useful thing to inhibit impulses to tear other people's bodies apart?

The peculiar and unexamined assumption here is that, were it not for this kind of inhibition, long division would come perfectly naturally to children. It seems as though, for many early psycho-analysts, there could be, as it were, no simple kinds of difficulty for human beings when it comes to learning. Difficulty must be construed as inhibition, on the seeming principle that everything can and should be fully knowable unless there is some knowable reason why not. This is a magical view precisely because it does not seem to allow for any kind of accident or exception (people with little experience of machinery tend to regard such perfect functioning as 'purely mechanical'). There is a magical logic to the idea that there is never any magic, for it gives omnipotence to the thought that makes out the universal reasons for things, or universally makes out the reasons for them. As Ernest Gellner has observed, psychoanalytic rationality '[i]ndulges wholeheartedly in the sense of a tight determination of things, as do many primitive thought-systems'.[56] Indeed, psychoanalytic thinking resembles in this the kind of thinking it regularly subjects to analysis, having

> a marked similarity to a certain kind of paranoia, in which the sufferer sees all events as menacing or significant, and credits himself with the intuitive power of reading their significance. In this form of paranoia, our pattern-seeking sense of causation seems to be come overactive, unrelenting and compulsive.[57]

THE FIRST, GRAND PROBLEM OF LIFE

The explicit concern with knowledge seeking is in fact a rather minor preoccupation in Freud's thinking. In the work of subsequent psychoanalysts, especially Melanie Klein and W. R. Bion, the question of knowledge has come to be a much larger and more explicit preoccupation. And yet the question of knowledge is at the heart of what would become the defining structure in Freudian psychoanalysis, and therefore the centre of its knowledge claims, namely the Oedipus complex. Oedipus is important for Freud and later psychoanalysts not just because of the fact that Oedipus acts out the desire to sleep with his mother and kill his father but because, in Sophocles' version of the myth, he is so concerned with knowing what he has done, or rather, who has done it. The Oedipus story is not just a dramatization of desire, it is also a dramatization of the desire to know about the nature and consequences of that desire.

The Oedipus myth is also a story that asks the question that seems to be at the heart of all the versions of the drive for knowledge treated in psychoanalysis, namely 'Where do I come from?' Freud first directed attention at this question in a paper on the 'Sexual Theories of Children' of 1908. This was followed by a section entitled 'The Sexual Researches of Children', which was added in 1915 to the *Three Essays on the Theory of Sexuality* (1905), in which Freud's curiosity about the origins of sexual feeling and awareness in children maps on to the child's own curiosity about such matters. Others following him have often assumed that the inquiry into origins is also the original and defining curiosity of the child. The fact that the first object of infantile curiosity seems to concern sexuality allows Freud, somewhat oddly perhaps, to assume that it is in fact an expression of sexual libido, whatever that is supposed to be. (Is it self-evident that a curiosity about the sexual workings of the body is necessarily to be regarded as involving sexual feeling, as Freud and others usually take it to be?)

Freud acknowledges at the beginning of 'On the Sexual Theories of Children' that his own researches are subject to the same difficulty as the child's, namely that they are dependent on recollection and report, rather than contemporaneous witness (*SE*, IX, 209). It is striking that Freud uses language that seems designed to establish the parity between the child and the researcher into the origins of sexuality: the child engages in 'researches' and develops 'theories'. The 'first, grand problem of life', Freud claims, is the question "*where do babies come from?*" – a question which, there can be no doubt, first ran "Where did this particular intruding baby come from?" (*SE*, IX, 212). This can be read both as the first big problem that one encounters in the course of a life, and the big problem that relates to life, or its origin. Freud says that we should hear the echoes of this primal riddle about priority 'in innumerable riddles of myth and legend' (*SE*, IX, 212), and indeed, in an open letter on the question of sexual education published in the previous year, he had made it clear that he had in mind specifically 'the riddle which the Theban Sphinx set to Oedipus' (*SE*, IX, 135). In order to account for the myths of origin that the child will be offered or may devise for itself, Freud must devise and depend on some origin myths of his own. Where the child toils at the riddle of where babies come from, Freud broods on the question of where knowledge about babies comes from; and in a sense these come to seem like equivalent questions. Rachel Bowlby notes a similar analogy 'between children's enlightenment and the knowledge claimed for psychoanalysis itself, which enlightens the world in relation to children's sexuality and the sexual aspect of neurotic illness in adults'.[58]

However, Freud is not willing to allow the origin of the knowledge instinct to be spontaneous, and therefore mysterious. Rather, he insists, it is prompted by anxious self-interest on the part of the elder child (who seems in this respect to stand for all children) when a new baby arrives: 'The loss of his parents' care, which he actually experiences or justly fears, and the presentment that from now on he must for evermore share all his possessions with the newcomer, have the effect of awaking his emotions and sharpening his capacities for thought' (SE, IX, 212). The story Freud tells is one of bafflement and disappointment. Fobbed off with fatuous drivel about storks or gooseberry bushes, the child may well begin to mistrust adult authority or reliability regarding such questions and start to develop some theories of his own. Ultimately, however, the child will probably have to abandon his inquiries as inconclusive. But from this point on, Freud thinks, the sense that the knowledge he seeks is in some sense inaccessible or forbidden will account for the characteristic emotional tonality attaching to knowledge, which combines fear, fascination and a curious kind of doubtful despair:

> It is not hard to guess that the lack of success of his intellectual efforts makes it easier for him to reject and forget them. This brooding and doubting, however, becomes the prototype of all later intellectual work directed towards the solution of problems, and the first failure has a crippling effect on the child's whole future. (SE, IX, 218–19)

Freud added a digested form of this essay to his *Three Essays on the Theory of Sexuality* when it was reprinted in 1915, in which he describes 'a permanent injury to the instinct for knowledge' (SE, VII, 197). This is intriguing given that this first, unsolved mystery might seem to be so productive of later investigations, including, of course, Freud's own. Freud insists on the private nature of these inquiries. The fable of the stork is received, writes Freud with amusing terseness, 'with deep, though mostly silent, mistrust', and 'The sexual researches of these early years of childhood are always carried out in solitude' (SE, VII, 197). The drive to know therefore occurs as a result of a withdrawal of confidence, a breaking of the continuity between child and world. In this sense, it may indeed qualify as something like the origin of separate existence, meaning that there is not only epistemic injury at the origin, but also a kind of origination in the injury: sexual researches 'constitute a first step towards taking an independent attitude in the world, and imply a high degree of alienation of the child from the people in his environment who formerly enjoyed his complete confidence' (SE, VII, 197).

Freud does not here register the very considerable power that many children discover inheres in the very social act of framing questions, not least in the fact that it guarantees just the kind of parental attention that is of such importance for children coping with a newborn rival. The only sign that Freud gives of awareness about this social dimension of questioning is a letter he quotes from Lili (*SE*, IX, 136), a motherless eleven-year-old girl:

Dear Aunt Mali,

Will you please be so kind as to tell me how you got Christel and Paul. You must know because you are married. We were arguing about it yesterday evening and we want to know the truth. We have nobody else to ask. When are you coming to Salzburg? You know, Aunt Mali, we simply can't understand how the stork brings babies. Trudel thought the stork brings them in a shirt. We want to know as well if the stork gets them out of the pond and why one never sees babies in ponds. And will you please tell me, too, how one knows beforehand when one is going to have one. Write and tell me everything about it.

With thousands of greetings and kisses from us all,
Your inquisitive niece, Lili

There is something of Lewis Carroll's Alice in the determination with which Lili pursues her enquiry, and in the fact that it is not pursued by secret brooding at all, but in an affectionate but insistent and formal written petition, one that seems confident of the justice of its demands. Despite Freud's support for candour in speaking to children on such matters, it is hard to imagine the optimistic, rational courage of this letter leading to the grim outcome he lays out: 'I do not believe that this touching letter brought the two sisters the enlightenment they wanted. Later on the writer of it fell ill of the neurosis that arises from unanswered unconscious questions – of obsessional brooding', and added in a dark, dismissive footnote of 1924, 'After some years, however, her obsessional brooding gave way to a dementia praecox' (*SE*, IX, 136).

Julia Kristeva points to the extraordinary and rather magical power that children realize can be exercised through the asking of questions, which she calls a 'pleasurable trance'. Part of the pleasure

surely comes from the fact that children realize that a question subjects the one interrogated to a demand for some kind of answer
that is hard to resist. There is a cautious jubilation in this, just as
there seems to be an intoxication in entering into a strange world of
question and answer that is simultaneously less real and yet, for that
very reason more powerful, than the world of physical reality: 'Still
straddling the border between the flesh of the world and the kingdom of language, the child knows with a hallucinatory knowledge
that all identity – object, person, himself, the adult's response – is
a constructible-deconstructible chimera.'[59] Freud's questions about
children's questions themselves seem to straddle the force of bodily
need and the powers derived from language, both of which can claim
priority in the question of what comes first.

There is another aspect of the child's inquiry into the origin of
life, though one on which Freud lays little emphasis. As Sophie de
Mijolla-Mellor has observed, the inquiry into where a baby sibling
has come from may be tied to a deeper and more troubling inquiry
with a more personal resonance. The question 'where was the intrusive
sibling when it was not here yet?' may lead to the more perplexing
questions 'where was I when I was not here yet?' and 'where will I be
when I am no longer here?' In its grandeur and reach, thinking must
confront and encompass its own nonbeing: omnipotence must confront ultimate impotence, with knowledge being on the side both of
absolute strength and absolute debility. The coming of knowledge
must also come up against its own overcoming in the knowledge that
knowing must come to an end just as it has had a beginning. Mijolla-
Mellor sees this as creating a kind of 'identity-castration', which is
the 'real point of departure of a need for causality to re-establish the
meaning that has been dissolved'.[60] At least at the time of writing
The Interpretation of Dreams, Freud appears not to have believed that
children had a conception of death:

> a child's idea of being 'dead' has nothing much in common
> with ours apart from the word. Children know nothing of
> the horrors of corruption, of freezing in the ice-cold grave,
> of the terrors of eternal nothingness – ideas which grown-up
> people find it so hard to tolerate, as is proved by all the myths
> of a future life. The fear of death has no meaning to a child.
> (*SE*, IV, 254)

Liran Razinsky sees this as a systematic repression of the knowledge of death in psychoanalysis, despite Freud's celebrated treatment of the death drive in *Beyond the Pleasure Principle*. As she argues,

> Even if we accept the Freudian claim that everything essential is already shaped in childhood, and that conscious thought and knowledge are never to be counted among crucial things, what are we to do with newly acquired knowledge of finitude? Can one really suppose we are indifferent to it, that the knowledge has no independent influence on our minds and lives? We know of our own finitude. This is significant knowledge, worthy of being theoretically and clinically considered. Failing to account for it is a problem that should have troubled everyone involved in psychoanalysis.[61]

If I have not been here forever then omniscience must include the knowledge of the fact of my transience. The most important role for omniscience is the knowledge of nonbeing – where I was when I was not here, where I will be when I am here no longer. The knowledge of unbeing is both a defeat of knowledge, an admission of the unknowable, and a fantasized apotheosis of the defeat of unbeing through knowledge which can qualify, or be constituted in fantasy as, a kind of immortality. This may be why nobody really dreams very seriously of the immortality of the body any more (though in a sense it is obvious that the elements of my physical being, if not perhaps their local and temporary arrangement in me, are indeed immortal already). What we dream of is living on as a mode of knowing – through the survival of Freudian psychoanalysis, perhaps, or even in its historic rebuttal.

The partiality of the omnipotence theory lies in the fact that knowledge can never be wholly one's own. To know must always be to know the limit of one's knowledge. Not only can you never know everything, but everything you can know testifies to the necessity of that limit. To say that you want to know for yourself is to recognize that ordinarily the source of one's knowledge is others. The others who keep you in being in their continued attention are the proof that you yourself are gone for good. To know is simultaneously to build a continuity between yourself and the world that knows and to bind yourself into the abyss of your absence from the world. It is to make yourself continuous with that discontinuity.

The questions of where things, including especially things like questions, come from, and what sorts of things can be thought to be 'established causes', will continue to nag at Freud. In particular, he will remain uncertain as to whether the drive to know is to be regarded as having the same original force as other 'self-seeking' drives, or the same power to originate (brooding or breeding) as they do. Freud's strange conception of the primal injury or impotence effected at the beginning of knowing seems to stand in contrast to ideas of the primal omnipotence of thoughts. But perhaps the two may come together in the theories of Mary Chadwick and Melanie Klein, in which the desire for knowledge is brought firmly together with a will to power.

In a pair of essays published by Chadwick in 1925 and 1926, the relations between power and knowledge are recast in terms specifically of sexual potency. Chadwick builds on the Freudian suggestion that the drive to knowledge is a sublimation of the infantile curiosity about sexual and procreative matters to suggest that what this drive sublimates in the male child is more particularly the wish to bear a child. Knowledge represents the penis (Chadwick enjoys pointing out the relation between curiosity and nosiness, and the curious fantasy of 'seeing with the nose'), but is more specifically a renunciation of the desire for the mother, because of the dread of being without a penis that she seems to embody. 'The child falls back, as it were, upon the gratification of the component instinct *curiosity*, in the pursuit of knowledge.'[62] Chadwick emphasizes a theme that has more recently come to the fore in feminist epistemology, that knowledge of life-processes embodies the essential function of knowledge as a substitute for the giving of life:

> Man would like to be the controller of life and of childbirth, in the same way that he wishes to control all the other forces of nature. Indeed, his desire to do so is but the outcome of the primitive desire to have the child of his own, and if he cannot, to be in complete command of the one who can.[63]

This accounts for the particular prominence in Chadwick's essay of the question of contraceptive knowledge for women, since to control life is also to be able to destroy it. Thought and knowledge could not only inhibit life, it could also generate it. In her book *Difficulties of*

Child Development (1928), Chadwick alludes to Nietzsche's reference to himself in *Beyond Good and Evil* as 'the parturient woman with his thoughts (books) as his offspring', and records children's theories that depend upon the idea that children might in fact be the products of thinking alone, for example that:

> If one kissed one's pillow and wished very hard one would find a baby under it in the morning, or that the two parents, thinking of the baby they would like to have, produced it; which theory was elaborated by one little girl from the saying of her family, meaning a long while ago, 'before you were born or thought of.' She was always disappointed that they had not thought of her as a boy, and not a girl, being quite convinced that this mistake was due to some error or want of due precaution on their part; that they had been careless and had not given the matter enough thought.[64]

The charming error of this little girl, which suggests that one must concentrate hard in order to ensure a good 'conception', has in fact been common in human history. Something like this view was suggested by Empedocles, who suggested that imagination could impress a particular form on the fertilized seed, a view generalized in the Renaissance belief in the powers of maternal imagination to form and deform the foetus.[65] We may see in this argument another version of the suggestion that the will to knowledge may enact in a particularly intense way the performative self-contradiction of a will to unwilling, or a will that strives against Will. In Chadwick's case, and more generally in the psychoanalytic discourse on the question of knowledge, there seems to be a conspicuous overdetermination by the question of the generative potency of psychoanalytic curiosity and knowledge themselves. Chadwick's account of the male homosexual enclaves in which knowledge has been concentrated through history might seem to apply as much to the institutions of psychoanalysis as to those of knowledge and education more generally. There might seem to be a relation in particular to the fact that Chadwick identifies the neurotic complement to the successful sublimation represented by knowledge in the 'unsuccessful perversion' known as 'folie de doute', 'doubting mania' or *Grübelsucht*.[66] The condition was also known as 'metaphysical delirium'.[67] The combination of obsessive doubt as to the givenness of appearances with the exorbitant certainty of interpretation might often be said to be a feature of psychoanalytic reasoning and method.

Chadwick never developed her ideas about the desire for knowledge systematically, but the theme recurs in her later writing about child development, especially in relation to young girls. In her book *Adolescent Girlhood* (1932) she argues that the inhibition of girls' early curiosity, especially about sexual matters, produces difficulties in learning and efforts to overcompensate: '[I]t is not uncommon for children to put many unconscious symbolic values upon this subject of Knowledge as a sign of superiority.'[68] In one case history, published in the same year as her paper on the origin of the desire for knowledge, Chadwick describes her conversations with a young girl who had developed a habit of stealing. The history is rich in details concerning the child's fantasies and speculations about babies, and seems to centre around her jealousy of the rights and entitlements of her older brother, her wish to displace him from the scene and the power that having knowledge of the origin of babies would give her. Details about her such as the fact that the girl's mother would subject her to severe beatings are casually interspersed with playful remarks about cutting off a leg that had got infected, as though they were entirely equivalent. Chadwick does not seem to feel that these regular beatings need to be interpreted, despite the fact that they are severe enough for the child's headmistress to keep her at school overnight lest the mother 'did her grievous bodily harm'.[69] The girl's desire for knowledge seems to be related to a desire to arrest the processes of growth, in herself and others:

> The child's ambition to be a kindergarten teacher showed how closely connected the idea of the baby and knowledge had become; it was as well an identification with the teacher she had met when first she went to school after the birth of the sister. She wanted to be wise and know more than others, to be able to answer their questions. Her pupils were never to exceed the age of five years, the age she was when she asked questions that were never answered, when her mother deserted her for B. and she had felt her inferiority so keenly. To possess the knowledge whence the baby had come was second in importance to possessing the baby; her desire to attain these things, *baby, knowledge, penis*, became so

overwhelming that, like the little boy who wanted the wall-flowers, she 'couldn't help taking' something which symbolized the coveted objects.[70]

The most important way in which the feeling for knowledge, as opposed to ideas about the nature of the knowledge drive, is mediated is through the distinctive mode of free indirect style by which speech and knowing are distributed in the narration of the case history. Chadwick's style of narration seems to record much less intervention than is usual at this stage. And she published in *Zeitschrift für psycho-analytische Pädagogik* in 1929 a fragment concerning her conversations with a little girl she met in the zoo. These little sketches were an occasional feature of the journal, but Chadwick's has a teasingly cryptic quality. The narration is carefully level in tone, with no interpretation offered of its principal elements, which seem to circulate eating, speaking and understanding in anagrammatic equivalence. Chadwick relates her conversation with the little girl who comes every day to the zoo to pursue her favourite occupation, which is

> to work out what each animal liked to eat and what they did not like, and especially those which could be fed safely, which ones were greedy and the dangerous ones who would bite your finger by snapping after the offered food.[71]

The child's researches seem to be equivalent to her schoolwork, perhaps precisely because they have put schoolwork at risk:

> Once during that summer a monkey had bitten her fingernail badly and she had been bandaged in the First Aid Centre. She had had to wear a sling and it had held her back quite a lot in her school work, since it was just before her exams. ('IZG', 235)

The little girl has her own kind of greediness when it comes to finding out what foods animals like: 'She was always in a hurry and hated it when the animals took a long time to decide whether they should take the food or not' ('IZG', 235). She instinctively understands the need of the animals to hide from observation, especially when they are moulting or shedding their skin, even though her need to see all the animals eating in their different ways is compulsive:

Every animal had to be seen eating, the lizards and marsh creatures fed with flowers, the penguins eating their fish, and then we had to run to see the polar bear's legs, as he plunged into his pool and dived for his lunch that had been thrown in. ('IZG', 236)

Seeing and knowing seem themselves to be a kind of hunger for the little girl, who is herself, of course, under observation (the piece is published in a series entitled 'Beobachtungen an Kindern', 'Observations of Children'), even if she is also confidently directing the process, in contrast to the shyly retiring animals: 'She drew my attention to her Irish eyes, as a sign of her nationality, deliberately so that I should not overlook them. They were really her most beautiful feature and she was altogether a strikingly beautiful girl' ('IZG', 236).

The strange climax of the story is the child's account of her own hunger, which has led to her eating a brown paper bag, after her bad-tempered nurse – who is, interjects Chadwick, 'perhaps as wild as the baboon' ('IZG', 235) – has punished her for disobedience by giving her nothing to eat. The nurse herself seems to have no interest in food, preferring to gorge on cigarettes, once making herself ill by smoking an entire pack all at once. The little girl has also made herself ill, by eating a whole pack of chocolates, though that was not because of excess, she explains, but because they were 'bad'.

The whole thing reads much more like a modernist short story than a psychoanalytic case study. It seems to hold in suspension different kinds of hunger and different kinds of knowledge: the hunger for knowledge and knowledge about hunger. Chadwick had written in her *Difficulties in Child Development* (1928) of phantasies of eating and being eaten in young children, which she connected to curiosity about the process of birth and death:

Being swallowed by a monster therefore, is an attempt to solve the dual problem of life and death. Where did we come from? Whither do we go? Out of a hole somewhere, and we are put into another hole when we die. The child first grasps the idea from observation that it is possible for a baby to be inside the mother, but the next difficulty is, how did it get out? And the last of all, how did it get in?[72]

Even as she protested against the exclusive structures of the psychoanalytic establishment, Chadwick maintained her adherence to Freudian argument and method. There are hints from what H.D. (Hilda Doolittle, 1886–1961) wrote about her discontinued analysis with Mary Chadwick as compared with her later, more satisfactory analysis with Freud, that Chadwick exercised plenty of her own kind of authority in and over psychoanalytic knowledge and process. H.D. wrote to her friend Bryher (Annie Winnifred Ellerman) of her analysis with Freud: 'Once in a while I drag out a dream, and he gets ME to interpret it (how marvelously a comment on Chaddie who told me in so many words, to keep right off the psycho-analytical grass).'[73] H.D. also wrote of Chadwick's 'sadism' and said of her that 'You swank about your own work and run down everyone else (Freud included if you are Chaddie, but C. carries it too far).'[74]

BEARING KNOWLEDGE: KLEIN AND BION

Melanie Klein took Mary Chadwick's arguments about the rivalry between the envious, male will to know and the generative life of the female body and intensified them, filling out the Freudian idea that the desire for knowledge is inflected by specifically sexual knowledge with a full-blown claim about an 'epistemic drive' which is almost entirely characterized by the sadistic desire to appropriate, consume and destroy. Klein used her analysis of children to generate new forms and methods of psychoanalytic understanding, and a complete, rival school of analysis. The analysis of children was crucial to the reorientation that Klein effected in psychoanalytic thinking, making the relation to the breast rather than to the penis crucial, and shifting attention from the Oedipus conflict to the more archaic and more luridly violent impulses that characterized the pre-Oedipal stages of development.

Where the focus for Freud had been on desire and the pleasure principle, Klein's focus is on rage and the desire to destroy. Acknowledging but hugely elaborating the arguments of Chadwick's 1925 essay about the boy's envious desire for a child of his own (*LGR*, 191), Klein described in 'Early Stages of the Oedipus Conflict' a 'feminine stage' in boys in which the fear of the loss of the penis is accompanied by a greedy desire for 'the organs of conception, pregnancy and parturition, which the boy assumes to exist in the mother', along with 'the vagina and the breasts, the fountain of milk, which are coveted as organs of receptivity and bounty from the time when the libidinal position is purely oral' (LGR, 190). Just as the boy wishes to colonize the organs of female parturition, so Klein aims to steal back the apparatus of Freudian analysis by representing it as having its origin in an assault on the female body, founded on 'the amalgamation of the desire for a child with the epistemophilic impulse' (LGR, 190–91). Where Freudian psychoanalysis mimics the boy's 'displacement on to the intellectual plane' through its assumption of '"knowing better"' (LGR, 191), Klein forces a desublimating recognition of the primitive, bodily impulses at work in the boy, rendering him simultaneously subordinate and violent.

Some of that envy seems to have to do with the enraging capacity to turn the body into an object of knowledge through psychoanalytic explication. Calmly and, as it were, unflinchingly, though there is often something lubricious in the very levelness of her explication, Klein made out from her child analyses a series of horrifyingly savage and irrational, if also quite often for that reason rather ludicrous, desires. The interplay between the ecstatic and the systematic, *sparagmos* (dismemberment) and reparation, will describe the whole curve of Klein's career, but is also at work at a stylistic level in all of her writing, which wants both to be orgiastically elbow-deep in imaginary inner organs and to retain an analytically antiseptic distance. The distance between the matter and manner of Klein's theory and her equanimity in the face of the desperate, murderous impulses she describes can, accordingly, at times seem both psychopathic and comic themselves:

> The child expects to find within the mother (*a*) the father's penis, (*b*) excrement, and (*c*) children, and these things it equates with edible substances. According to the child's earliest phantasies (or 'sexual theories') of parental coitus, the father's penis (or his whole body) becomes incorporated in the mother during the act. Thus the child's sadistic attacks have for their object both father and mother, who are in phantasy bitten, torn, cut, or stamped to bits. (LGR, 219)

It may perhaps be that this coolness is necessitated by the prominence of the question of knowing in her analysis. Where sexual curiosity had been an occasional and ancillary topic of interest for Freud, what Klein described as the epistemic drive was at the centre of her thinking. Children were inhibited from learning, Klein believed, because they were paralysed by anxiety at their own sadistic impulses. The most developed example of this is to be found in the case of Dick, a boy whose analysis is described in the essay 'Symbol-Formation in Ego Development' of 1930. Dick's internal, unconscious defences against his own sadistic impulses towards his mother's body, we are to understand, 'had resulted in the cessation of the phantasies and the standstill of symbol-formation. Dick's further development had come to grief because he could not bring into phantasy the sadistic relation to the mother's body' (*LGR*, 224). Klein's assumption is that being given the chance to act out his 'epistemophilic and aggressive impulses' (*LGR*, 227) meant that he could establish a symbolic relation to the world and therefore begin to develop intellectually.

The epistemic drive was not merely prompted by self-interest, as it had been for Freud; it was at the centre of a life-and-death struggle for ownership of and control over the maternal body. It is hard to know how to separate the explication of Freudian epistemic envy from the Kleinian envy of Freudian process. Where the child is concerned with evacuation, Klein is engaged in a single-minded project of injection, in her determination to discover murderous violence everywhere in the child's fantasy life. One can understand the need for as studied a neutrality as possible given the news she was bringing, lest she lay herself open to the accusation of a kind of epistemic rape of her child subjects. Nevertheless, it is hard to read of the interpretations she offered of childish games and dreaming, in which preschool children are calmly informed that what they are really acting out in their play is their desire to capture the treasure of faeces from their mothers' bodies by ripping her open with their teeth, without a certain kind of queasiness.

Seemingly, Klein's own analytic behaviour is supposed to be regarded as entirely immune from the sadism of the epistemic drive. Yet when she writes about the techniques of child analysis, which she was prepared to take much further than adherents of the adult talking cure like Anna Freud, the appetite for penetration of the child's imaginary depths becomes clear:

> If one approaches child analysis with an open mind one will discover ways and means of probing to the deepest depths.

And then, from the results of the procedure one will realize what is the child's *true nature* and will perceive that there is no need to impose any restriction on the analysis, either as to the depth to which it may penetrate or the method by which it may work. (*LGR*, 142)

Klein seems to regard children as something like human beings in a primordial condition, which gives her confidence that she can 'expect to establish a true analytic situation and to carry through a complete analysis which should penetrate to the deeper layers of the mind' (*LGR*, 143). Where Freud had depended upon decoding the complex material involved in speaking and listening, Klein hopes, through a technique that involves symbolic play, to cut out the anxiety-driven resistance that is characteristic of verbal expression. Believing that children 'are very much more under the sway of their Ucs [Unconscious]', Klein assumes that symbolic representation of fantasy through the playthings she provides will be both more indirect than in words – because, she argues, 'symbolic representation in general, as being to some extent removed from the subject's own person – is less invested with anxiety than is confession by word of mouth' (*LGR*, 149) – and yet also more immediate, which is to say (though she does not herself say it), more immediately available to be interpreted by the analyst.

The essential question regarding the *Wissentrieb* or drive to knowledge is whether knowledge, and the humans who are its bearers, may be regarded as a part of nature. If knowledge is impelled by a natural drive, then humans may *be*, but may never fully know their being, since there will always be something unconscious in that work of becoming conscious – id will never fully yield to ego. If knowledge is not merely the expression of will, then humans may perhaps be able to know without having to be. In the first case, being will continue to escape or transcend knowing in that it will determine it; in the second, knowing will be able to escape and transcend mere being. Perhaps this can be reduced to the question of whether knowing can fully know itself, or, put in psychoanalytic terms, whether consciousness can become fully cognizant of the unconscious.

Rachel Blass suggests that Freud arrived at a view of knowledge as driven by the principle of Eros, that is, the desire for unity between mind and nature:

The desire to know, the desire to grasp reality as it is, may be understood as a kind of striving towards unity that would be very consistent with Freud's view of Eros. Our intellect is moved by a desire for unity, which is intimately tied to the sexual drive but is not identical with it. In our minds, we grasp the unity of the world and the laws that govern it, and through that grasp our minds unite with the world.[75]

This erotics of knowledge is offered as an overcoming of the conflict that Blass makes out in Freud's essay on Leonardo of 1910, in which Freud appears not to be able to reconcile Leonardo's 'insatiable and indefatigable thirst for knowledge' (*SE*, XI, 74) – *unersättlichen und unermüdlichen Forscherdranges* (*GW*, VIII, 140) – with the coolness of a knowledge that would seem to stand clear of such impulses to longing and satisfaction. Freud in fact quotes Leonardo's view that knowledge is beyond the principles both of love and hate, pleasure principle and death drive: 'Nessuna cosa si può amare nè odiare, se prima non si ha cognition di quella' (*SE*, XI, 72). Freud offers an interestingly casual, or perhaps rather overworked, translation of these words: 'That is to say: One has no right to love or hate anything if one has not acquired a thorough knowledge of its nature' (*SE*, XI, 72) – *Man hat kein Recht, etwas zu lieben oder zu hassen, wenn man sich nicht eine gründliche Erkenntnis seines Wesens verschafft hat* (*GW*, VIII, 139). Where the Italian sentence maintains a studiously passive mode throughout, suggesting a translation like 'Nothing can be loved or hated without there first being knowledge of it', Freud's rendering injects the urgency of agency, justification and the question of completeness. That is, the translation raises the very question that is at issue in Freud's essay, the question of who or what knowledge is, and who or what, *Es* or *Ich*, id or ego, is driving the drive.

Blass sees the essay on Leonardo as dramatizing the problem of 'how we are to reconcile Leonardo's passionate desire for knowledge with the Freudian idea that knowledge can emerge only from a dispassionate stance' ('DK', 1267). She sees in this a gap in Freud's understanding of knowledge in general, which she identifies as Freud's own 'struggle with the passion to know' ('DK', 1266). In essence, Freud's problem is how to understand what knowledge might be for. If Freudian theory is to be trusted, then we must be suspicious of the claims of knowledge to be disinterested and so self-directing and self-sufficient. But if that is true, then what kind of knowledge claim would psychoanalysis itself be entitled to make? What is psychoanalysis's cathexis of knowledge?

Blass assumes that 'Eros, the universal life instinct that seeks to unite all things, to bind them together, may manifest itself in a personal way without the danger of distortion through personal need (since the working of Eros per se stands beyond such needs)' ('DK', 1270). This seems like a strange kind of eros, an erotics of knowing which must nevertheless be held to be immune from the force of personal desire. Why, one wonders, would such an epistemic erotics not be subject to all the arguments that psychoanalysis is so good at making – that, indeed, one might almost say psychoanalysis exists to make? Why might one refrain from asking the psychoanalytic question of this psychoanalytic answer, namely, what makes this knowledge rather than desire?

And what drives these questions about the drive to knowledge? Blass writes that, for Freud, 'Our intellect is moved by a desire for unity' ('DK', 1269). What is more, this has a particular application to psychoanalytic knowledge, which provides a certain idealized fulfilment of this unity of logos and longing: 'psychoanalytic self-knowledge is, according to Freud, a most immediate expression of our human participation in the universal desire to know, that is, to encounter that which lies beyond us' ('DK', 1272). But there is another kind of desire that may be at work in the drive to or longing for knowledge. Freud finds the evidence of Leonardo's inhibition in his dilatoriness and incapacity to complete works. But he does not see in this any kind of unsteadiness or lack of purpose, finding instead 'a quite extraordinary profundity, a wealth of possibilities between which a decision can only be reached with hesitation, demands which can hardly be satisfied' (*SE*, XI, 67). Is this then the desire for unity, growth, persistence in being, completion, eros? Or is it the desire for discontinuity, incompletion, ongoingness, thanatos? Is there a desire for a knowledge, a knowledge that would bring desire to an end, or a desire for the desire of knowledge? Is knowledge the ruse of desire, a way for knowledge to remain a desire rather than a desired, a way for desire to remain in being, unsated, insatiable? In other words, might the 'Lebenslust' (life-instinct) of the 'Forschertrieb' (drive to investigation; *GW*, VIII, 140) in fact be intertwined with the force of thanatos, or the drive to death, which aims both to lunge and linger, to hurry and tarry to its end? The *Forschertrieb*, or 'instinct for research' as Strachey renders it (SE, XI, 70), seems as though it is an accessory to the *Wissentrieb*, investigation having knowledge as its consummating end. But things may be the other way round: the idea of an end may provide the means for the instinct for research, the instinct to put off knowledge to maintain itself in being. And, in all of this, the question of who or what is driving the drive, is both pressing and impossible to hold on to.

Psychoanalysis depends upon its 'discovery', or at least the proclamation of its discovery, of the unconscious or, in German, the *Unbewusste*, unknown, in human life. Its capacity to make known the unknown depends on what seems like an assumption of omnipotence. But the beginning of the urge to know is also the beginning of the urge to know what cannot be known, what one is when one is not. The knowledge of the 'first, grand problem of life' is also a knowledge that is twinned with death.

So the question of knowledge exerts an unconscious force on psychoanalysis, the very form of knowing that depends on the claim to bring the unconscious to knowledge. More and more contemporary psychoanalytic writing seems to focus on the process of analysis itself as the scene of knowledge and inquiry, rather than as a means of generating knowledge about the patient's experience outside analysis. This increasing self-reference focuses attention on actions, processes and fantasies of knowing, which are held to be what is occurring in the analytic session. This in its turn may be the reason that the question of knowing has come to the fore in psychoanalytic theory and writing. The relatively simple understanding of psychoanalysis as a movement from unconscious desire to conscious knowledge on the part of analyst and patient has given way to a much more complex and elaborated drama, in which patient and analyst perform a set of fantasies about who knows what, when and how. This generates a state of abstracted knowledge-without-a-knower, in which the *sujet-supposé-savoir* neither resides nor comes to rest in any one position in particular. The subject becomes a scenography. In the processes of transference and countertransference, patient and analyst do not so much act out the growth of knowledge as transact it, in an exchange of knowledge suppositions. Psychoanalytic process becomes the performance of a theory of mind, through a series of attributive or second-order knowings – me knowing that you know and do not know, you knowing what I do and do not know about what you know. One might see such scenarios as a retreat from the bad faith of the supposed subject of authoritative knowledge in psychoanalysis. But it might be possible as well to see this willing away of the psychoanalytic will to know as another kind of bad faith, not of assumption but of disavowal, a refusal to accept the responsibility of the subject-supposed-to-know, which nevertheless retains much of its privilege and prestige.

If psychoanalysis seems to be becoming ever softer, less authoritarian and more participatory in its attitude towards its own knowledge, we might be permitted a certain suspicion about this solicitation to participate. The most characteristic mode of psychoanalytic knowledge is attribution. Not only psychological states and impulses but whole reasoning structures ('dynamics') are attributed to patients. What the psychoanalyst knows is what the patient wishes not to know that they know. What is explicated is not just a way of feeling but a way of knowing. The unlikely thing here is not the content of unconscious fantasy, extreme though it may seem, but its organization and form as a kind of perverse rationality, the mirror and rival of psychoanalytic rationality. The patient is not simply made a passive object of knowledge, but is made the epistemic accomplice of the analyst. There is an equivalent in the 'If I were a horse' style of reasoning characteristic of much nineteenth-century anthropology, as criticized notably by Wittgenstein in his comments on James Frazer's *Golden Bough* (1890). Wittgenstein writes that:

> Frazer's account of the magical and religious views of mankind is unsatisfactory: it makes these views look like *errors* ... The very idea of wanting to explain a practice – for example, the killing of the priest-king – seems wrong to me. All that Frazer does is to make them plausible to people who think as he does. It is very remarkable that in the final analysis all these practices are presented as, so to speak, pieces of stupidity. But it will never be plausible to say that mankind does all that out of sheer stupidity ... Frazer cannot imagine a priest who is not basically a present-day English person with the same stupidity and dullness.[76]

As we have seen, there is a particular rhetorical tonality to much psychoanalytic writing, in which much depends on the distance opened and maintained between a cool, knowingly technical language and the raging, chaotic, orgiastic impulses it describes. We have seen that this is most especially true of the writing of Melanie Klein. The aim seems always to be, even when what are being explicated are blind and savage mechanisms of lust and envy, to articulate the reasoning engine, the *logos* of the psychological.

Perhaps we might see in this something of the attributive logic attributed to the fetishist who, according to Freudian theory, finds the thought that there could be a living being without a penis so intolerable that he assiduously supplies penis-substitutes in fantasy wherever he can (in the Medusa, in the form of a writhing plethora of penis-substitutes in her snaky hair, just, as it were, in case). Perhaps the analyst here defends themselves against the suspicion that there may be nothing there to explicate in the patient by the insistence that there must always be thought to be thought about, knowledge, albeit of a defective kind, to be known. Indeed, this may account for the distinctive character of the idea of the unconscious itself – as a defence against the idea that there could be a patient who genuinely does not know, as opposed to just not knowing what they know. It appears here that psychoanalytic knowledge allows for an exultance in its anxiety. There is nothing, no vileness, horror or mad absurdity that cannot be known; and knowledge can be defended against the charge that it may have originated the madness it claims to bring to light, first by its very extremity, which seems as far away as possible from the coolly appraising and unflustered rationality of psychoanalysis, and second by the fact that what is being brought to light by analysis are nevertheless indeed ideas – a form of knowledge, if admittedly of a perverse kind. This might explain the attraction of psychoanalysts to the more florid forms of mental illness and in particular the elaborate and bottomlessly interesting forms of systematic psychotic delusion – despite the fact that psychoanalysis has been even less successful in treating this kind of illness than any other. Indeed, psychoanalysis is not only drawn to delusional psychosis as opposed to workaday forms of 'neurosis' – neurosis, depression, phobia, obsessive compulsion – but it is likely to find the evidence of psychosis wherever it can, for example in the *dementia praecox*, or premature madness, that was deployed as a term to describe almost any kind of mental disorder in young people, including children. Indeed, the attraction of child analysis, as we have seen, may very well have been that it seemed to offer up a rich field of psychotic delusion ready-made and unconcealed. Psychoanalysis might sometimes seem guilty of finding cognitive distortion wherever it looks, but perhaps it is just as guilty of *pangnosticism*, seeing the illogic and ill logic of cognitive defect everywhere. Thinking, it seems, is really man's malady. Perhaps this is another aspect of the refusal of accident and the determination to find determination everywhere that is so marked a feature of psychoanalytic reasoning and its lucid madness.

John Farrell suggests that

it is the allure, the charisma of psychoanalysis that needs to be explained, not the imaginary resistance it evokes. And there seems no better way to explain this allure than to recognize its profound appeal to the mind's sense of what should be.[77]

There are indeed striking rhymes between the system building of the paranoid schizophrenic and the systematic rationality of psychoanalysis – for example in their shared preoccupation with machines and mechanisms.[78] Part of this appeal lies in the power of the principle of unsuspected complexity. We have become so used to the revelation that almost everything in the structure of the physical world is unimaginably more intricate than we might think that complexity itself can come to seem like a guarantee of plausibility. Indeed, the more incredible the complexity, the more reasonable it may seem, and the more potent the desire to believe it to be true, in part as a complement to our own wish to believe in our capacity to see through and beyond appearances. This resembles the Tertullianic formula for faith in the unlikely sequence of events constituting the story of the incarnation and resurrection of Christ: *credo quia absurdum*. Or, as people, more commonly, though no more intelligibly, seem to say: *you couldn't make it up*, usually applied to exactly the kinds of thing that people most characteristically and compulsively do.

The knowledge that explains everything, that creates unity everywhere and abolishes every discontinuity nevertheless encounters the problem of the discontinuity it must itself introduce into things. The early Kleinian view of knowing suggests that it will be inseparable from a will to sadistic and envious assault. To know is never just to acquaint oneself with something: it is always to intervene in a scene that one both constitutes and transforms by coming to know it. By comparison the work of W. R. Bion draws out the idea of knowing as toleration rather than destruction or appropriation. It moves more emphatically than almost any other psychoanalytic theory, but still following a pattern established by Freud, Klein and Lacan, building from a particular therapeutic intervention into a complete world view with an epistemology at its core.

In his book *Attention and Interpretation* (1970), Bion added to the three principles he had previously distinguished as L (Love), H (Hate) and K (Knowledge), the principle O, where O signifies something like the complete reality of a given experience, undistorted by any perspective. Increasingly, Bion saw the role of analyst as being not to interpret, but to embody; not to know, but to become:

> O does not fall in the domain of knowledge or learning save incidentally; it can be 'become'. But it cannot be 'known'. . . the psychoanalyst can know what the patient says, does, and appears to be, but cannot know the O of which the patient is an evolution: he can only 'be' it.[79]

It is a kind of dream of omniscience and epistemic omnipotence (the more omniscient you are, the less you need to do – indeed, the less it is possible for you to do, given your necessary foreknowledge of your own actions). This omnipotent dream of omniscience can be seen as the reverse of Bion's doctrine of the 'attack on linking', in which a psychotic patient assaults in fantasy everything that threatens to produce ambivalence in its turn – including, in particular, language – by joining together dissimilar things, this ambivalence producing anxiety.[80] At its limit the attack on linking atomizes everything to produce an inert world in which there can be no pain because nothing has anything to do with anything else. Knowledge is, of course, the mode of linking that causes most anxiety and that requires most in the way of toleration of ambivalence. If the attack on linking were an attempt to dissolve all possibility of connection in the effort to evade knowledge, the condition of inclusiveness that Bion called O would subsume all knowledge in a kind of maximization of potential through negative capability. O would be an omniscience without the guilty action of knowing.

In his work of the 1950s Bion had focused not on emotional difficulties in his patients but on difficulties with thinking, and had proposed that the role of the analyst was to help replace the psychotic condition of 'thoughts that have no thinker' with the idea that one might generate a stabilizing mental container for otherwise wild and unassimilable thought fragments.[81] In this, the analyst would fulfil the function of what he called the 'reverie' of the mother, which offered to the child a kind of safe and stabilizing screen or haven for its disconnected and incontinent ideas.[82] This has often seemed to me to be a very helpful way to think of conversations one might have with students or colleagues about ideas which they are having difficulty in integrating or organizing.

In his later work during the 1960s and '70s, Bion imagined that container made infinitely elastic, to the point of comprehensiveness – a container that would itself be uncontainable and that would once again dissolve the thinker, but this time into ubiquity. One of the characters who speaks in the first volume of Bion's *The Dream*, the first volume of his *Memoir of the Future*, declares:

> I am thought searching for a thinker to give birth to me. I shall destroy the thinker when I find him . . . I am the thought without a thinker and the abstract thought which has destroyed its thinker Newtonwise, the container that loves its content to destruction; the content that explodes its possessive container.[83]

This prospect represents a certain will to will-less knowledge, a knowledge that would be purged of all privative and subtractive operations of the will. It is impossible to give any instance or idea of what kind of thing this knowledge could either be, or be knowledge of, since it is in fact entirely projective and consists only in the will for there to be such a thing, or the dream that there could be.

Freud used the term 'metapsychology' to refer to more general kinds of speculation about the fundamental conditions of psychological experience that went beyond the clinical details of individual pathology and treatment. Both in Freud's work and in later usage, the term has come to refer to theories about the nature of psychology as such, especially as these may seem to move into the place previously occupied by metaphysics. We may say that psychoanalysis has moved ever closer to metapsychology in a slightly more restricted sense, becoming increasingly self-addressing and self-referring, practising and perfecting a knowledge that has no objects of which it might articulate knowledge save for its own theories and process. In this way it has moved from the pursuit of knowledge – which requires and creates investigable objects of understanding – to the production of knowledge-feeling, the apparatus and sensation of knowing in which there is nothing to be known but this sensation itself (though it is perfectly able to project a range of 'as-if' objects equipped with their simulacral resistances and particularities). It will feel just like it seems knowing ought to feel, delivering the same consequences, complications, impediments, involvements and elations.

In its growing preoccupation with the conditions of its own knowledge, psychoanalysis needs to repair its own breached sense of, or wish for, omniscience. This problem is an intense one since psychoanalysis as theory weakens the possibility of omniscience, showing it to be the effect of locked or egotistical striving and the expression of a will to power that psychoanalysis as practice tends towards. The only possible compromise involves emptying omniscience of the pathological will to know, with all its drive to self-assertion and to absolute comprehensiveness and coherence – the 'world-filling exhaustiveness' that Ernest Gellner has argued characterizes psychoanalytic thinking.[84] The problem is that this will-less, nondesiring knowledge suffuses the idea of knowledge with fantasy just as the will to omniscience had. Psychoanalysis has been vulnerable to two kinds of error or malady of thought in relation to its own knowledge: the first is a dogmatic mistaking of a narrow and drastically fixated set of perspectives for a total explanation of human development, behaviour and distress; the other is the belief in the possibility that such a theory would be the gateway to an escape from every kind of limit or exclusion of knowledge: a mode of knowing self-cured of all the ills of knowledge.

3
SECRECY

I n a letter to *The Independent* (1 October 2007), Richard Dawkins complained about the teaching of theology, on the grounds that there could be no knowledge of something that does not exist:

> We who doubt that 'theology' is a subject at all, or who com-
> pare it with the study of leprechauns, are eagerly hoping to
> be proved wrong . . . But as for theology itself, defined as
> 'the organised body of knowledge dealing with the nature,
> attributes, and governance of God', a positive case now needs
> to be made that it has any real content at all, and that it has
> any place in today's universities.[1]

The pressure implicitly put on the word 'logos' here – theology as literally the 'knowledge of God' – may suggest some interesting difficulties. It is not that *logos* means truth or knowledge, but rather that the way it means truth or knowledge has been so strongly implicated in, one might say incriminated by, its religious understandings, and those religious understandings are characteristically wrapped in mystery and ideas of secret knowledge. I am tempted to think that in one sense theologians are right: the idea of God is caught up in the machinations of the notion of *logos* itself.

Peter Sloterdijk has said that religion has never really existed, as it is simply a vehicle for human projects of self-transformation through discipline.[2] Knowledge is a leading part, and perhaps the leading part, of this ascetology.[3] Knowledge of God seems to promise God-like knowledge. Hence the extreme ambivalence relating to knowledge in much Christian teaching, in which knowledge can be both duty and sin. This is why epistemic ascesis involves both self-denying devotion to study and the devotion to the denial of knowledge. God is the name for the libido of knowing that may not speak its own name. So, if in a limited sense it certainly seems that theology has nothing to do with knowledge of things that really exist in the world (rather than in human heads and loins), in a broader sense there may be something theological in all knowledge.

The most theological thing about knowledge is its assumption and cultivation of mystery. It would be tempting to sexualize this, reducing the knowledge of God to a repressed knowledge of sexual themes and feelings. Wilhelm Reich is among those psychoanalysts who have explicated mysticism as the sign and effect of repressed or deflected desire.[4] But sexual desire may itself be a deflection. As I argued in Chapter Two, this would be to displace into the objects of knowledge a libido that more properly, or at least primarily, attaches to and is expressed through knowledge itself. The objects of knowledge can be seen as the mediate occasions of knowledge's own autocathexis. Of course, there must always be an object for knowledge since a knowledge that is not a knowledge of something, or of nothing else than of itself, might seem meaningless. But whatever particular object it may be, it will always fulfil the generic function of being an object-for-knowledge, a proof of knowing. Religion is as much a carrier of the knowledge drive as sexuality. In his 'On Narcissism' (1914), Freud described this alternation between a focus on the object and a focus on the self as the alternation between 'object-libido' and 'ego-libido'.[5] We might borrow this to distinguish between libido-for (objects of desire like sexual pleasure, food, power, status) and libido-in (the desire of desiring, the desire of being and remaining in the condition of desire, and the knowing of knowing).

The cultivation of mystery in knowledge is an effect of this autocathexis, which gives knowledge its ascetological form. In one sense the drive to know likes to think of itself as without limit – this instanced in the story invented by E. M. Cioran (1911–1995) that, when he was asked why he was learning a new tune on the flute as the hemlock was being prepared for him Socrates replied, 'To know this tune before dying'. Cioran declares grandly that the reply is 'the sole serious justification of any desire to know, whether exercised on the brink of death or at any other moment of existence', but this

view does not take account of the fact that there is a certain inhibition, or perhaps rather deferral, that is also bound up in the drive
to knowledge.[6] Sloterdijk's 'ascetology' seems the right term because
of the ascesis, the schooled self-denial in every operation of logos.
Knowledge gives power, and therefore pleasure, because it makes the
world available as object. But for there to be an object I must subject
myself to it. Knowledge of an object gives a subjecthood in abeyance,
the subjecthood that comes from the conjuncture of being 'not-able'
and 'being-able-not-to' be. The subject retreats and yet asserts itself
in that very retreat.

As a legal term, abeyance, in the OED's definition, is 'the position
of waiting for or temporarily being without a claimant or owner'.
The Norman French word *abeiaunce* may be influenced by *abeance*,
to desire or long for, itself a modification of *abayer*, to yawn or gape,
from which we derive canine *baying* and the condition of being *at
bay*. But the gaping of *abayer* also signifies a longing desire, as does
English *yawning*, which is kin to *yearning*, probably from the idea
of gaping wide in order to consume – from Germanic *ger-* or *yere*,
to long for – as though a kind of nothing were always hungering to
be filled or annihilated with something. Indeed, until the end of the
seventeenth century one could be said to 'yawn after' something. As
the nightingale says in *The Owl and the Nightingale*, 'Þe gost . . . ȝeoneþ
after more & more' (The spirit . . . yearns for more and more).[7] In
knowing, the knower gapes, occupying the chasm in its own knowing.
Knowing is a gnawing.

I must also separate myself from my self-gratification at the fact
that I make myself a subject in the act of projecting, and even abasing
myself before, an object. I must keep myself apart even from the gratifying feeling of having been able to keep myself at bay. This necessary,
and necessarily secret, schism between the object of knowledge and
the powerful gratification that knowing it gives to the knower is the
root of the mysticism that is always at work in knowledge.

The mystical signifies both that which is hidden and the deliberate obscurity in which it is kept, as in the example from *The Kalender
of Shepeherdes* (1506): 'You blynde folke derked in the clowde / Of
ygnoraunt fumes thycke and mystycall'.[8] The OED is slightly uneasy
about including this quotation with other examples of the word 'mystical', as it feels that 'the sense may be rather "imparting obscurity"'
than 'imbued with obscurity', perhaps 'suggesting an independent

derivation'. But this imparting of obscurity (an oddly oxymoronic phrase, since mystery would seem to resist any imparting) may have always to be a part of giving witness to the hidden. To designate something as secret is always in part to keep it secret even in its breaching.

There are two kinds of secrets: secrets whose secrecy is public, and secrets whose secrecy is itself a secret. Greek μύστης, *mystes*, is built on the root μύειν, *muein*, which means to close the lips or eyes (and perhaps, suggests the *OED*, under 'mystery', 'of imitative origin', thus keeping mum or stumm), so a *mystes* is 'one who keeps silence'. A craft or profession involving special practical knowledge was also known as a mystery. The *OED* explains that mystery in this sense of an office or occupation is an 'altered form of classical Latin *ministerium* MINISTRY n. by confusion with *mystērium* MYSTERY n.', though the confusion exerts force. Perhaps Coleridge knew or guessed this relationship in the opening line of his 1798 poem 'Frost at Midnight': 'The frost performs its secret ministry' – unless it was, as it often enough is, the secret minstrelsy of the unsounded chime between ministry and mystery that ministered to him.[9] The *OED*'s clarification makes it clear that it is the confusion that is, secretly, most telling, for there is something mysterious in every ministry and something administered in every mystery. There may even be an overlay of 'mastery' in some uses of the word 'mistery' to mean skill or special technique. This in turn may have exerted its own influence on the word 'mister', which was formed on the model of 'master' but may also suggest the mastery of a trade or mystery.

Now, everything I know is a secret to me, as a condition of my being said to know it. I was once part of a group of vacation students working as labourers on a building site who were assigned to the demolishing of a lowish brick wall. Not having ourselves graduated from the school of anything like hard knocks, we enquired of our foreman what the approved technique was for knocking down a wall. After a slight hesitation, and perhaps beginning to suspect that no good was going to come from trying to answer the question, he replied that his usual method was to 'make a hole in the middle and [miming the growing hole with two hands] ... enlarge it'. This sounds plausible to a theoretical intelligence, though as soon as you try to put it into practice it in fact turns out to be both inefficient and rather dangerous.

The point is that to be a skilled practitioner involves having internalized your knowledge of how and what to do to the point where it is no longer easily abstractable from the doing or knowing of it. This is not only true of the kinds of knowing signalled by German *kennen* and French *connaître*, procedural and implicit *knowing how* as opposed to explicit and declarative *knowing that*, as they are conventionally distinguished. Because even if I know *that* something (that all prime numbers are odd, that Paris is on the Seine), and know *that* I know it, in a way that I can make fully explicit, I still don't know how I know it any more than I know how to play an F-sharp minor chord or a forward defensive. If you know something, you no longer quite know how you know it – and indeed that seems to be the aim and outcome of gaining knowledge. If I do not know something, I have instead to have the knowledge of how to ascertain it – who to ask, where to look, and so on. So to know something is to be able to keep its secret, or to keep a large part of the knowing secret from yourself.

This constitutive secrecy seems borne out by the fact that if you ever ask someone 'how do you know?' the answer is so often evasive or beside the point. How do I know the Amazon is the longest river in the world? I read it in a book (or thought I did, since the Nile is actually the longest river, though I am comforted to read that there are ways of measuring that give the prize to the Amazon). How do you know what depth of rawlplug to insert? I have found that putting too long a rawlplug into a cavity wall makes for wobbly insecurity. But these are answers to the question 'why are you confident that your knowledge is correct?', not to the question 'how do you know?' Even an answer having the form 'I studied Latin for eight years and was put in detention every time I made a mistake with the fourth declension, so have it always at my fingertips' only describes some putative process where one has learned or come to know something, and does not go very far to explaining how knowing works or what it feels like.

The final words of the following paragraph from James Joyce's *A Portrait of the Artist as a Young Man* (1916) have always struck me as mysterious.

Eileen had long thin cool white hands too because she was a girl. They were like ivory; only soft. That was the meaning of *Tower of Ivory* but protestants could not understand it and made fun of it. One day he had stood beside her looking into the hotel grounds. A waiter was running up a trail of bunting on the flagstaff and a fox terrier was scampering to and fro on the sunny lawn. She had put her hand into his pocket where his hand was and he had felt how cool and thin and soft her hand was. She had said that pockets were funny things to have: and then all of a sudden she had broken away and had run laughing down the sloping curve of the path. Her fair hair had streamed out behind her like gold in the sun. *Tower of Ivory. House of Gold.* By thinking of things you could understand them.[10]

The mystery of the final statement about understanding through thinking about things does not lie in the fact that there are things that still in fact escape the young Stephen, though perhaps not to the reader – especially if they have read *Ulysses* and connect it with the description of the barmaid Lydia Douce ministering manually to the beer-pull: 'On the smooth jutting beerpull laid Lydia hand, lightly, plumply . . . slid so smoothly, slowly down, a cool firm white enamel baton protruding through their sliding ring'.[11] It is mysterious because it is true that there actually is an understanding for the young Stephen, though, precisely to the degree that we see more than he does, it is a kind of understanding that itself passes, or passes beneath, understanding.

I remember very vividly lying in bed at the age of six or seven, or whenever one learns times tables, and discovering the astonishing fact that you can learn things simply by saying them repeatedly, whether out loud or inwardly. I am still amazed at why this might seem such an obvious and uninterestingly self-evident fact about learning. We nowadays regard such a form of rote learning, defined by the OED as learning in 'a mechanical or repetitious manner . . . acquired by memorization without proper understanding or reflection', as a crude and unsatisfactory affair. But how does it happen that simply repeating something such that I can safely forget that I know it can be so effective and long-lasting as a way of coming to know things?

Of course, my own professional mystery, or one part of it, is here in operation: the technique of making a mystery play out of a series of historical usages. I am here bringing to light a set of hidden affinities and, in the process of bringing to light, suggesting a kind of paradoxical entanglement, without clear beginning or end, in which I both do and do not have a part. The one who professes must also conceal. Saying this also suggests that I may have an interest in imparting mystery to knowing precisely as part of my not entirely public pleasure in it – a pleasure I am here making public, but only in part, in order to ensure the accessory pleasure of keeping some of it secret.

It is not surprising that Freud should have found so much that was uncanny about the word uncanny. It is not just that there is something thrillingly uncanny about the uncertainty of the idea of the uncanny; it is that there is something uncanny about *knowing* it, especially since the primary reference of the word is to knowing itself. This is actually more true of the English word 'uncanny' than it is of German *unheimlich*. Heimlichkeit – homeliness, familiarity – becomes unheimlich through an intensification of the link between the familiar and the privacy or withdrawn nature of the family home. The uncanny therefore has to do with the kind of family secret with which psychoanalysis concerns itself. As Freud observes,

> the word '*heimlich*' is not unambiguous, but belongs to two sets of ideas, which, without being contradictory, are yet very different: on the one hand it means what is familiar and agreeable, and on the other, what is concealed and kept out of sight.[12]

Strachey appends to his translation a note explaining that, according to the OED, 'a similar ambiguity attaches to the Northern English "canny", which may mean not only 'cosy' but also 'endowed with occult or magical powers'.[13] Both reversible words involve a kind of privacy that may become suspiciously secretive, and a familiarity that may become strange; but the ambivalence in the English word largely does without the associations with home and family that come to light in the German, the emphasis being more directly on the ambivalence of knowing. Many of the epistemological associations of the word 'can' have passed across to other words, like *con* meaning to learn or study and *cunning*, along with the derivatives of *ken*. This may be the reason that *canny* comes to signify an allegedly Hibernian quality of being 'close', 'tight' or 'careful', especially in matters of money. *Can*, which has shrunk to the condition of a modal verb in English, is associated with power, skill or ability. *Can* and *ken* had become sufficiently distinct by 1530 for John Palsgrave to record the phrase 'I can konne more by herte in a daye than he can in a weke.'[14] In English, there is the suspicion that knowing can become the kind of cunning that makes one unknowable, untrustworthy or uncanny. This skewing of sense happened quite slowly. Cunning originally meant learning, wisdom or erudition. As late as 1533 it was possible to refer to 'great vertues, and great gyftes of god, as chastyte, lyberalytye, pacyence sobernesse, temperaunce, connynge, & suche other'.[15] By 1612, Francis Bacon could begin his essay 'Of Cunning' with the words 'We take cunning for a sinister or crooked wisdom.'[16]

We live in a world of specialized knowledges, and many of us are still defined, as academics in particular are, by disciplines, or 'learninghoods' as they might antilatinically be called. A craft (compare German *Kraft*) signifies a power or force, but craft follows the pattern of many knowledge words in moving towards a condition of suspicious inwardness: as conning becomes cunning, so craft becomes crafty, via the idea of occult art or magic (from about 1220, a *craft* could mean a spell or enchantment). A craft means a discipline, or special branch of skill or knowledge; but such branches have a way of turning into defensive mysteries, ways of declaring that are simultaneously ways of keeping dark. Knowledge or craft communities are secret societies, by which of course is not necessarily meant a society the existence of which is secret, but a society known to be organized around certain kinds of private or withdrawn knowledge; known, that is, to cohere around shared knowledge which is available to the members of that community and relatively unknown to others.

Human societies depend upon communication, and what is communicated is very often some kind of knowledge, whether in the form of news or of know-how, and whether social, technical, personal or religious. But we may say that, in a more pervasive sense, human societies come into being through, and come to depend upon, the structured inhibition of certain kinds of communication, through the construction and maintenance of secrets and secrecy. Human societies are systems of communication, but those systems are closed, or only semi-permeable, rather than purely open, so that knowledge is restricted as well as in circulation. There can be no communication without a channel, and a channel is a way of aiming, streaming, tuning in, and so tuning out.[17] The most basic form of privative human community and interrecognition is through the secret of language. You become a human being through internalizing the metaknowledge of how to speak and therefore convey knowledge; but the first thing a child comes to know about this medium for transmitting knowledge is that it is also a way of keeping things secret. The advent of the child's 'theory of mind' involves the functional awareness of the principle of background secrecy that is veined through every making-common; becoming aware that you may have something in your mind that I do not have in mine makes me aware that everything in my mind is a secret unless and until I make it known to you.

Indeed, all languages are secrecy machines, because you have to know them to speak them, meaning that there will always be those for whom the language is unintelligible. Even a tribe that was completely unaware of a larger world in which there were other humans speaking other languages (and one must doubt whether there have ever been many human groups of this kind) will nevertheless have internal outsiders in the form of children, who pass into the secret of the group's language; older people, or others subject to illness or injury who may pass into muteness or incommunicability; along with other non-human beings, most particularly animals, who are only partially privy to human language. What are called initiation ceremonies beat out passages in time (beat out musically and often corporeally) by means of spatial passages, *initiation* signifying literally a going-in (from Latin *ineo*). Many such ceremonies involve a passage into a hidden place (interior places, like the interior of the body, being the bodily image of the secret), which may imply or perform a kind of rebirth through re-entry. But the real 'place' into which one enters is the imaginary place of the secret knowledge, which one can in English strangely be said to be 'in on'. Such a second birth will not be bodily, but noetic; it will be a birth into symbolic knowledge, which signifies both knowledge contained in symbols and the power symbolized in knowledge itself. A secret is that which is separated – from *se-*, aside, apart and *cernere*, to distinguish, sift or separate. The odd fact that the verb to *secrete* means to give out, or *excrete*, typically from a body, and therefore seemingly become less secret, derives from the fact that fluids secreted from the body, like milk, or bile, were thought to have been separated out from the blood. From the late sixteenth century onwards English began to mark a difference between being *discreet* – that is, showing discretion, caution, tact or prudence, especially in matters of social management or communication and in particular being regarded as trustworthy enough to keep confidences – and being *discrete*, in the technical sense of being physically separated, detached or distinct; *discrete* therefore being the opposite of *concrete*. The distinction itself is a discreet one, that is set to music in Emily Dickinson's evocation of the first, solitary bird heard singing in spring:

> With specimens of Song,
> As if for you to choose –
> Discretion in the interval
> With gay delays he goes.[18]

'Discretion' allows one to think both of the separated flurries of song as the bird dashes from twig to twig and of the musical intervals and 'gay delays' within each fluttering cascade of notes, the bird thereby both hurrying on and holding back the surmise of spring. It almost allows as well internal allusion to the dash, that characteristic hiccupping interval within and between Dickinson's own lines that precedes the word 'Discretion', offering a choice between differences.

Not only are there no societies without secrets, there is, somewhat more surprisingly, no secrecy without society. Eurasian jays seem to prefer to cache their food stores in out-of-sight locations when in the presence of other birds of their species; when caching unobserved, or 'in private', they will be more likely to choose readily visible locations.[19] There must be at least two persons and three discursive positions with any secret. There must, that is, be the one who has or keeps the secret and those from whom it is kept. The latter category may include all other subjects whatever, living, dead or as yet unborn, but it is much more likely to include some and exclude others. And to have a secret is also to effect a more subtle kind of division within oneself, between the open and the secret, the tellable and the untellable. For the best way to keep a secret is to keep it in part from yourself – hence the rise of the principle of 'plausible deniability' in cryptography. This self-secreting can never be total, however, for you must for safety's sake be in the know about what is not to be known. You can partly keep a secret from yourself, but you cannot do it wholly unawares, since that would no longer qualify as a secret, but rather a simple hiatus in your knowledge. That is, you can only keep something secret that you know, and know is a secret. But you can never be sure that you know something before you have articulated it in some way, if only to yourself, that would make the secret shareable and transmissible. You must at least have confided what you know, as something known, in order to be able to keep it secret. You can only keep a confidence you can lose.

There are two kinds of secrets, with two kinds of cohering effect. One is the differentiated secret, which produces a space set apart in which one group is privy to knowledge to which another, usually larger group, is not. Usually both parties have a formal knowledge of the existence of the division. The stratification resulting from the boundaries between insides and outsides can become very complex indeed, with members of a society being members of many different kinds of secrecy-formations. A scale model of this is provided by the distribution of disciplines in an academic institution. Here the secret knowledge of each discipline consisted much more in ways of doing things than in simple information, which is usually not held apart from general scrutiny in any way. This will often take the form of the coded secrecy preserved in specialized sublanguages, meaning that it is not necessarily knowledge that is secret but the means of exchanging it. As Alex Posecznik remarks, 'much of scholarly work is about secrets. Members of nearly all academic disciplines engage in oblique theoretical debates that are so wrapped up in obscure jargon that it is challenging for a layperson to figure out.'[20]

In all of this, the fact of the secret cannot itself be a secret. Social trust can be embodied in an institution such as the British Secret Intelligence Service, previously MI6, the existence of which was not officially acknowledged until 1994, though knowledge of it was widely circulated and enjoyed in film, fiction and rumour. It currently occupies a £150 million building of exhibitionist grandeur designed by Terry Farrell, in Vauxhall, London. With its steep terracing and blank exterior, it seems to many observers to combine the features of a sci-fi military-industrial mechanism with the suggestion of a Maya pyramid or Middle Eastern temple. That is, it brazenly advertises its secretness, and even advertises the fact of that advertisement. It has frequently been shown to be under attack in successive recent James Bond films, and was actually attacked by a rocket, probably launched by Irish republican dissidents, in 2000. The website of the SIS announces, with winning, if weird, candour, 'At the Secret Intelligence Service (SIS) – otherwise known as MI6 – our mission is clear. We work secretly overseas, developing foreign contacts and gathering intelligence that helps to make the UK safer and more prosperous.'[21]

Distinct from the differentiated secret is the general secret, which usually takes the form of some sacred object or subject which the community keeps a secret not just from outsiders, but from itself. No society can be completely open, because all societies are organized around some notion or other of the sacred, and the sacred is usually in some way or another secreted, in the sense of set apart – either because it is holy or because it is accursed, as in the Latin word *sacer*, which can mean both. Democratic societies are suspicious of secrecy. But in the sorts of societies that think of themselves as secular, or beyond ideas of the sacred, the very idea of openness – the idea of free speech, or free expression, for example – can itself move into the place of the sacred, as, in certain circumstances, can the idea of the secular. The sense in which the sacred is secret is that it may not, or sometimes simply need not, be inquired into, or subject to scrutiny, and so is known to be unknowable.

So a society based on candour and accountability will need secret institutions pledged to defend those values. At the heart of most democratic arrangements is the secret vote, a ceremony that formalizes the arrangements adopted by the Eurasian jay. The metaphor that has become usual to describe the purging of secrets, *transparency*, seems secretly to acknowledge this complexity. To be sure, if there are no obstructions to your seeing how I act, as if I were standing naked in front of a glass window, I would not be able to keep any secrets from you. But if I were myself transparent, then you would see nothing at all of me, and would not even know I was there. You can only see something that blocks your view of something else. So perhaps the very idea of transparency is itself, in this somewhat dubious sense, transparent.

The cohering effect of secrets – of secrets that must be kept without needing to be known, or '[k]nowledge of the *that*, not of the *what*', in Georg Simmel's phrase – does not seem to extend to the kind of secret societies which attempt to keep the very fact of their existence secret.[22] Such groups deny that intricate latticing of the known and the unknown that is characteristic of socially binding secrets. This can make truly secret societies, which do not wish their existence to be known or acknowledged, seem socially very threatening (though of course only if and when their existence is, in fact, suspected). It is by definition hard to be sure where and when such societies arose, though it is commonly claimed that they have great longevity. It seems likely, however, that many of them actually have their origin during periods of increased exchange and connectivity in human society, from which they represent an attempt at secession, even as that act of secession is itself a communicative act. Simmel notes of the English court that 'the actual court cabals, the secret whisperings, the organized intrigues, do not spring up under despotism, but only after the king has constitutional advisers, when the government is to that extent a system open to view' ('ss', 468 n.2). Certainly the period known as the Enlightenment was particularly exercised (excited, fascinated and appalled) by the idea of secret societies, such as the Hell-fire Clubs largely populated by roistering young aristocrats.[23]

One of the most prominent of these Enlightenment secret societies was the Illuminati, a group of rationalist thinkers established in 1776 by Adam Weishaupt in Bavaria. The Illuminati aimed at the gradual overthrow of all forms of despotic Church and State power, and the establishment of a free and fair order of things founded upon principles of morality and rational justice. They counted among their members at one time Goethe and Herder, and became prominent enough to be banned, along with the Freemasons, with whom they allied themselves. So, by a singular but frequently seen paradox, those pledged to the shining of the light of rational deliberation into the dark places of superstition and obscurantism were committed to means that seemed to require them to act under conditions of murky concealment. One of the most influential contemporary denunciations of the Illuminati was John Robison's *Proofs of a Conspiracy against All the Religions and Governments of Europe* (1797), which laid out the connections between the Illuminati and the Freemasons, alleged that the French Revolution had been directed and overseen by members of the secret society, and warned that 'this Association still exists, still works in secret, and that its emissaries are endeavoring to propagate their detestable doctrines among us.'[24] The paradox of the Masons' strangely public secrecy, and vice versa, was not lost on Robison:

> The inquisitive are always prying and teazing, and this is the only point on which a Brother is at liberty to speak. He will therefore do it with affectionate zeal, till perhaps he has heated his own fancy a little, and overlooks the inconsistency of this universal beneficence and philanthropy with the

exclusive and monopolizing spirit of an Association, which not only confines its benevolence to its own Members (like any other charitable association) but hoards up in its bosom inestimable secrets, whose natural tendency, they say, is to form the heart to this generous and kind conduct, and inspire us with love to all mankind. The profane world cannot see the beneficence of concealing from public view a principle or a motive which so powerfully induces a Mason to be good and kind. The Brother says that publicity would rob it of its force, and we must take him at his word: and our curiosity is so much the more excited to learn what are the secrets which have so singular a quality.[25]

The pleasurable dread evoked by the idea of a secret society of this kind impelled many revivals and scandalizing revelations which continue to this day. The need to believe in the Illuminati means that there is no need for anything like them actually to exist, or even have existed. They have become the template for the many secret conspiracies, political, military, psychological and spiritual, that have accompanied the growth and complexity of communications and have produced a second-order semi-secret confraternity of writers and readers who believe themselves to be in the know about the great, propagating Concealment.[26]

Even in societies without very much specialized division of labour and function, secret knowledge has an important role. The passage from one condition of life to another, most particularly the transition to adulthood, often involves entry into a community of knowledge, through the passing on of secrets. There are minor ways of being let in to restricted knowledge even in complex societies: when you start a new job, one of the first things to happen may be that you get a password for the IT system, or are told the door-lock code.

Many forms of initiatory secret knowledge involve questions of generation and of gender. In many societies, one passes into the possession of secret knowledge as part of becoming an adult, which means becoming a male or female. We may suggest that there really is no secret of generation or gender other than the public fact of it being a secret, for it is possession or not of the secret knowledge that maintains the gender distinction. The secret that the secret conceals is that it, like we ourselves perhaps, comes out of nowhere, that is, that there is no secret, or that the idea of the secret is both self-generative and generative of gender. The OED suggests, in an etymological note to its entry for *can*, that the root which gives words like gnosis and know 'was originally related to the Aryan *gen-* (with by-forms *gnā-*, *gnō-*), to bring forth, produce'. The most generalized form of secrecy both within and across different societies is sexual knowledge, or knowledge of generative process itself, the knowledge of how human beings come about. The fact that individuals experience being born without ever being able to know it for themselves makes the society itself the bearer, carrier and keeper of the secret that each individual in the society will be let into, of the conditions of their own being, on the condition that they enter into the symbolic understanding that ensures that they can never again be what they know about their own coming-into-being.

Secrets must be kept, because secrets are things we want to know. We want to know them, of course, mostly because others want to keep them. We might even say that secrets themselves are a wanting-to-know, or even a wanting-to-be-known, no matter what their content. It is part of the definition of a secret that it would constitute the resistance to some pressure to reveal it. You seem to have to want to know a secret, and if I find myself not being curious about a secret, what I am really doing is denying its status as a secret. Secrets carve out the lines of force, flow and impediment in wanting-to-know and the wanting of knowing. Secrets, or the omissions and voluntary inhibitions of knowledge, provide the libidinal force that structures the whole field of human knowledge. The essential and ultimate knowledge is often held to be sexual, which, as we have seen, for Freud accounted for the sexual investment in curiosity and research, and the excitement of concealment and revelation. But secrets may not need to borrow their libidinal power vicariously from specifically sexual knowledge, for the conjoined desire to know and to withhold knowledge, to disseminate and contain, seem to be amply possessed on their own of libidinal and libidinizing force. Indeed, the difficulty for most humans of separating sexual desire from forms of imaginary representation implies that sexual desire needs the structuring force of secret knowledge and the revelation of secrets. To kiss and tell is to betray the secret into which one enters in every sexual encounter. It is not so much that secrets are sexualized, as that sexuality is *secretized*. There may be good reason to associate this with Michel Foucault's arguments for the strong association of modern sexuality with the paradoxical interplay of sexuality and secrecy. In the first volume of his *History of Sexuality*, which first appeared in French as *La Volonté de savoir* (The Will to Knowledge), Foucault insists that 'what is peculiar to modern societies is not that they consigned sex to a shadow existence, but that they dedicated themselves to speaking of it *ad infinitum* as the secret.'[27] Sexuality is both a form of secret knowledge and an allegory of the libidinal force exercised by the process whereby the open and the concealed are integrated in modern life, obeying the principle that, as Michael Taussig puts it, the '*secret . . . has to be spoken so as to preserve it*'.[28]

Knowledge and desire are linked in an economic relationship. And secrets are not only essential to economic life, secrecy is the central principle of the economics of knowledge as such. Secrecy performs a function parallel to that of scarcity in classical economics, motivating the cycles of poverty and plenty and what Beckett refers to as the 'quantum of wantum' in knowledge.[29] Late in his life Simmel would articulate his confidence in the power of knowledge to encompass more and more of its own non-knowledge: 'That we ourselves know our knowing and not-knowing, and that we again know this more embracing knowledge, and its infinite potential – this is the real infinity of the mind's vital movement.'[30] But in his earlier 1906 essay on secrecy, he is less confident of the telic movement of mind, seeing instead a kind of homeostatic equilibrium between the known and the unknown:

> throughout the form of secrecy there occurs a permanent in- and out-flow of content, in which what is originally open becomes secret, and what was originally concealed throws off its mystery. Thus we might arrive at the paradoxical idea that, under otherwise like circumstances, human associations require a definite ratio of secrecy which merely changes its objects; letting go of one, it seizes another, and in the course of this exchange it keeps its quantum unvaried. ('ss', 467–8)

The competitive desire for knowledge is often represented as the drive to unravel secrets and solve riddles, as though the unknown were being deliberately withheld from us. Secrecy drives and arises from the desire on the one hand to concentrate knowledge-capital, thereby limiting its free circulation, and on the other to be open

always to the broaching of new epistemic markets, thereby trans-
ferring assets from the debit (secret) column to the credit (public)
column. Secrecy at once increases security and exposes one to risk.

The ratio between the public and the private is changed by the
growth and spread of public and official histories, which prompted
the appearance of what became known as 'secret histories'. The name
first appeared as the title of a book by the historian Procopius of
Caesarea (*c.* 500–*c.* 554), who wrote a number of histories of the wars
of the Roman general Belisarius and the Emperor Justinian. Towards
the end of his life, Procopius composed an account of the scandalous
behaviour of Belisarius and his wife Theodora, which he introduced
nervously to his readers:

> I find myself stammering and shrinking as far from it as
> possible, as I weigh the chances that such things are now to
> be written by me as will seem neither credible nor probable
> to men of a later generation; and especially when the mighty
> stream of time renders the story somewhat ancient, I fear lest
> I shall earn the reputation of being even a narrator of myths
> and shall be ranked among the tragic poets. But I shall not
> flinch from the immensity of my task, basing my confidence
> on the fact that my account will not be without the support
> of witnesses. For the men of the present day, being witnesses
> possessing full knowledge of the events in question, will be
> competent guarantors to pass on to future ages their belief
> in my good faith in dealing with the facts.[31]

The work was mentioned in the entry on Procopius in the *Suda*,
a tenth-century encyclopaedia, where it is referred to under the title
Anekdota, meaning 'unpublished things' (from Greek ἀν, *an*, un- or
non-, + ἔκδοτ-ος, *ekdotos*, published), but remained unknown until
the discovery in the 1620s of a fourteenth-century manuscript in the
Vatican library. This was published with a commentary and a Latin
translation, which gave the work the title *Arcana Historia* or *Secret
History*, by Nicolas Alemannus in Lyon in 1623. A French translation
appeared in 1669 and then an anonymous English translation bearing the title *The Secret History of the Court of the Emperor Justinian* in
1674. This translation followed the two previous versions in expurgat-
ing most of Chapter Nine, which deals in colourful detail with the

early life as a prostitute and showgirl of Justinian's wife Theodora, most notably the story that she performed naked on stage with geese trained to pick barley seeds from her vagina. We read only that she 'exercised a profession that cannot with modesty be named; nay, the Devil so wrought with her, that there was not a place in the whole Empire where Theodora had not left the marks of her immodesty'.[32]

These translations of Procopius' book prompted an outpouring of secret histories of many different kinds, possibly because of the parallels with contemporary British politics – powerful royal mistresses, mercenary military leaders, the suspicion of debauchery in high places.[33] As Melinda Rabb suggests:

> Here was a paradigm of heroic action transformed into a mock-heroic world of fools and knaves. Here also was a narrator whose 'doubleness' as both a respectable public agent and as an irreverent clandestine saboteur served as a paradigm for ironic narration.[34]

The secret history represented a reaction against orthodox or accredited forms of public history. It articulated the perspectives of marginalized groups, especially women, it suggested a historically new sense of the necessary partiality of all official history, and demonstrated an impulse to bring to light alternative or excluded experiences and perspectives. At the same time it must be doubted that many of the secrets allegedly disclosed in works that advertised themselves as secret histories were in fact unknown, or even unavailable in print. Rather, they require what Rebecca Bullard has described as 'a rhetorical rather than a positivist approach to the motif of revelation'.[35] That is, they are a way of playing with the idea of making known.

The genre of secret history began to recede during the nineteenth century, partly as a result of the absorption into official history of many of the perspectives characteristic of secret history. Surprisingly, perhaps, the secret history was part of the invention of privacy, as a general right and expectation. As privacy became part of the fabric of social life – reflected and encouraged above all by the development of the realist novel which insisted at once that everybody had a private life, not just marquises and prime ministers, and on the publicly attested and accepted fact of that private life – so secrecy and revelation became less charged. Many of the meanings of the word 'privy'

– possessing esoteric knowledge, carried out by stealth, concealed or hidden, recondite – became obsolete or archaic. Eventually the word dwindled to the naming, with mock ceremony, of the lavatory, place of the most universal but mundane human function exercised in private. John Pudney was able to report in 1954 that '[t]he fact is the word has come down in the world, a victim to the flushing closet.'[36] The word that once had a sense of regal luxury about it at a time when 'most of England went about its business in the open' has come itself to denote 'a place of easement outdoors'.[37] The open secret of plumbing generalizes privacy, making the privy seem archaic. Any mention of the abstract British institution of government the Privy Council is likely to be associated with the comic recalling of the superintending of the monarch's private functions, especially those signalled in the office of the Groom of the Stool. Indeed, we might say that the institution of plumbing, which enables every citizen access to a private means of disposing of their bodily waste, is the most telling example of the generalization of privacy. Increasingly, the word 'private' moved into the places occupied by *privy* in naming the *private parts*, for example, a usage, at once dry and coy, characteristic of courtroom testimony. It signalled a much more everyday and bureaucratic division between the public and private spheres, especially in the naming of occupations and what were essentially public functions, like private investigators and private companies. Privacy is now thought of not as a condition but a right, that is, to be made as much a part of the fabric of social life as possible. As the idea of private life grew more general and extensive, so the gap between the public and private lives of those in high places became less dramatic. This lowering of excitement and absorption of secret history into official history was also mirrored in the fortunes of the word 'anecdote', which by the end of the eighteenth century had ceased to be used in the plural as a synonym for a secret history and had come to mean simply the story, usually amusing, of a detached incident – often, though not necessarily, concerning a public personage. Secrets became part of the tissue of everyday life.

At the same time, the extension of the availability of secrecy has made it possible to generalize the effects of the publicizing of secrets. The guerilla war from below waged by spies and inside informants during the seventeenth and eighteenth centuries started to seem like a war from above, or rather, perhaps, from all sides, practised by publishing media. In an essay in the *Harvard Law Review* of

1890 that may be said to have inaugurated the modern understanding of the right to privacy, Samuel D. Warren and Louis D. Brandeis identified two important and seemingly contrasting preconditions for the legal protection of privacy. One is '[t]he intense intellectual and emotional life, and the heightening of sensations which came with the advance of civilization'.[38] The other is the abstract fact of the growth and invasiveness of different forms of publishing media, which threatened the privacy not just of the powerful, but of ordinary citizens: 'Instantaneous photographs and newspaper enterprise have invaded the sacred precincts of private and domestic life; and numerous mechanical devices threaten to make good the prediction that "what is whispered in the closet shall be proclaimed from the house-tops".'[39] Privacy, like secrecy, is part of a complex interchange between objective structures and subjective processes, the systems which allow for the exchange of information, and the affective force of that knowledge-feeling. Warren and Brandeis justify the right to privacy in epistemopathic terms, as the protection of, and against, 'sensations', the word that increasingly connects private feeling and public representation:

> The intensity and complexity of life, attendant upon advancing civilization, have rendered necessary some retreat from the world, and man, under the refining influence of culture, has become more sensitive to publicity, so that solitude and privacy have become more essential to the individual; but modern enterprise and invention have, through invasions upon his privacy, subjected him to mental pain and distress, far greater than could be inflicted by mere bodily injury.[40]

In fact, the easier and less restricted access to different media became, the more privacy and publicity existed as a war of all against all. Individuals were at risk, not just from invasion from outside, but from their own curiosity and cupidity. New divisions were spawned: the idea of 'the public' was distinguished, usually positively, against 'publicity'. Privacy marked off what was confidential but not secret; secrets were what the powerful and iniquitous had. And yet, secrecy was also increasingly produced rather than discovered: any incursion into the private by the public transformed the merely unmarked into the secret.

The most important function of the secret in media-saturated society and, one might even say, the secret function of secrecy, is to keep the secret alive in, through and beyond its revelation. The power possessed by the holder of a secret or, in the case of blackmail, by its discoverer, is the threat of discovery. The revealed secret both consummates the force of the secret and dissolves it. A society depends upon the making and breaking of secrets both to structure time and to keep it under tension: time needs structure, the changeable relation between its elements, and the variation of speed and slowness to maintain tension, to stop it being just one damned, indistinguishable thing after another. But structure needs to be threaded with temporality too, lest it become a pure and inert net of relations. The question this bequeaths for the secret-consuming society is how to keep intact the cake it wants to keep consuming. The problem with breaking a story is that the story's cover is thereby broken.

One way to keep the flame fed is by the creation of an imaginary well of infinitude, borrowing the exponential powers of the epidemic. The form it takes is well illustrated by the accusations of sustained sexual harassment and assault made against Harvey Weinstein in October 2017. That Weinstein's behaviour seems to have been appalling and deplorable has everything and nothing to do with the metanoietic functioning of the scandal. It has everything to do with it, because it provides the fuel and the cohering force for the revelations. To fail to deplore what had been revealed with sufficient vehemence, or to suggest that anything might possibly be a more serious subject, or even one of equal seriousness for the media to attend to (hurricanes, the flight of refugees, environmental threat), was to suggest one was secretly party to it. But the nature of the offence was also nothing to do with it, in that the aim of a process such as this is to move towards formal autonomy from its occasion, in accordance with the principle articulated earlier in this chapter that the object of an object of knowledge is to become an object-for-knowledge. What matters is that the revelations should be able to be sustained indefinitely, without surrendering any of their alleged 'shock' or their power to recharge indefinitely the sense of offence that must be inseparable from it. So the violent force of the 'outing' of Weinstein, the natural tendency of which is towards redundancy and exhaustion, as the appalling begins to pall, must be recruited to the creation of a looming suspicion that what we now know is both vaster than anything that could previously have been imagined and yet also horrifyingly negligible compared with what (we are now increasingly sure) remains to be brought to light. The effect of this is to reverse the valency of every new revelation, which thereby becomes the confirmation not of what we know, but of what we can be sure we do not yet know; knowledge of the *that* outstripping knowledge of the *what*.

Once the story can go no deeper in Hollywood, the way is then clear for collateral spread, with revelations of a similar nature relating to other semi-closed worlds, like that of Westminster in the UK. Where will it all end? The building up of this secrecy-reserve, which ensures the continuing possibility that the full story has yet to be told, has proved to be an indispensable part of the aetiology of many scandals or catastrophes. The shared expectation that only full disclosure will purge the evil and make it impossible for such abuses of power ever to happen again – that it will bring closure, allow us to move on, be cleansed and safe, and so on – makes it possible for the scandal to enter its final white-dwarf condition. Nevertheless, there is a continuing suspicion that not everything has yet been hauled into the light, such that, after a decent interval, it will always be open to some boldly unintimidated investigator to poke the embers into life on our behalf, revealing that the dying back of the story was not due to any abatement of our righteous desire for seek-and-destroy extirpation, but to a cover-up, whitewash or premature burial of the permanently undead secret. The death of the accused used sometimes to mark the end of such cycles, but recent cases like those of Jimmy Savile and Edward Heath show that death can in fact become a mode of suspended (re-)animation, a slinking away from the public eye into the grave suggesting a cowardly attempt to escape justice. And in all these sacred rites of concealment and revelation we must keep decently under wraps the predictability both of the offence and of the cycle of exposure, the recognition that this is always what is enacted in the passion-play cycle of secrecy and scandal. The celebrity plays an important role in this, since celebrities exist very largely in order to have secret lives that may be subject to exposure. A large standing reserve of celebrities increases the probability of their being able to be detected behaving culpably, or at least shameably. Besides which, the advantage of a celebrity is that they do not need to have transgressed, since their inaugural offence is to hide from us behind their glamour, meaning they must be stripped, often simply by being reduced to their humiliating (thin, fat, pregnant, old) corporeality. The secret knowledge that our open, airy, transparent society may depend upon the brewing up of noxious secrets to blow up is not to be inquired into – except, perhaps, in the form of another purgeable secret.

There is, in every discovery or revelation, a fantasy of a force to which the discoverers or revealers are mere accessories. Truth, we sometimes assure ourselves, will out. A great deal lies latent in this phrase from Shakespeare's *The Merchant of Venice* (Act II, Scene 2). Its very compression suggests the core idea that truth is not a condition or state of affairs but a force, a force that presses from concealment to revelation, and on its own account; hence it is not that truth will be found out, made out, worked out, pulled out, but, rather, that truth will achieve exteriority through its own impetus or will to exteriority, as though 'out' were a reflexive verb, implying the necessity for truth to 'out itself'. Truth, the phrase assures us, not only has, but *is* this force or self-outering, or uttering. The will to truth projects itself into the world as Truth's will to be. The force of this idea imparts a distinctive tonality to thinking about truth. It seems a strange and puzzling idea to us that the truth of things might be a merely contingent, adjectival condition, and not a substantive thing. Truth is the name, the noun, that arises from a thing being taken or assumed to be true. All manner of things are true: truth is almost infinite and therefore trivial and indifferent. Yet it seems scandalously insufficient for things simply, flatly, indifferently to be the case, without intent or implication. This does not seem right to us, since we want truth to be and to have force, the force we force onto it. It is not enough for being simply to be, there must be a truth of that being separate from and beyond it, a 'having-to-be' which is the 'needing-to-be-known', of that being.

ESOTERICISM

As I have been suggesting in the last few pages, one of the striking features of modern esotericism is its strange alliance with densely mediated society. In such a society the secrets that previously formed the substance of esotericism are now loudly available and everywhere proclaimed. Ours has become an era of open-source esotericism. Esotericism denotes an increase in circulation rather than a withdrawal from it. The contrast between the esoteric and esotericism parallels the contrast between the primitive and primitivism, often incautiously conflated. Primitive people cannot by definition be primitivist, since the primitivist is one who looks back fondly on the condition of the primitive, so as soon as you are primitivist you have lost your chance of being primitive. The esoteric is possible in a world with limited publicity, and so with loose connectivity, which is incapable of knowing everything about itself, or capable of not knowing everything. Esotericism, by analogy with primitivism, belongs to a world in which everything is known and knowable as what it is, or is felt it should be. The existence of esoteric traditions indicates traditions set apart from each other; esotericism indicates the nesting of traditions within each other. The esoteric implies a distributed social field; esotericism implies a field *formed* of distributions, of entanglements and reciprocal entailments.

The word 'esoterism' is first used in the 1820s in French and in 1846 in English, indicating the emergence of a kind of general category of the exceptive or set apart. There is a distinction to be made between the esoteric and the merely hidden. There are many intellectual traditions that have been at different periods little known-about, passed over or simply forgotten. There may be no conscious effort at concealment involved here, nor need such traditions necessarily have been kept secret. Ignored, passed over or forgotten does not mean concealed. But since the nineteenth century the increasing prestige given to unofficial or marginal kinds of knowledge has meant that esoteric traditions are much more likely to be thought of as suppressed from the outside than concealed on the inside – that is, the product of historical outcasts or members of an underclass rather than aristocratic elites, or a subterranean rather than superior Other. Thinking of knowledge as a unified field purges contingency and accident, making the esoteric something pushed away from visibility rather than preserved from prying eyes.

One might say that the status of secret knowledge changes markedly during the period that came to be known as the Enlightenment. Previously, knowledge that was secret was believed to be so because it was powerful – for example, because it involved magical power. Military and intelligence secrets might be modern equivalents here. But the Enlightenment emphasis on the values of explicitness and communication gave increasing power to secrecy itself. Previously, power was kept secret; increasingly, secrecy, especially known secrecy, was in itself power. In fact, of course, the power of magic must have rested largely on the unbroached secret, or at the very least the secret suspicion, that it did not in fact possess any of the power attributed to it. It would have been apparent to the devisors of spellbooks and grimoires that the most powerful forms of magic – cloaks of invisibility, flying ointments, spells for raising demons or the dead – depended entirely on belief or suggestion. The most closely guarded secret was that there was nothing in them but the apparatus of secrecy.

Another mode of hiddenness is latency. This is the view that esoteric kinds of knowledge are so because they are connected by certain currents of thought that are held to contradict mainstream or official modes of thinking, and so must have been silenced or pushed into the margins. Many histories of esotericism attempt to account for it in terms of the specific content of different traditions – the emphasis on ideas of living nature, for example, or similarly 'holistic' ideas.[41] But, rather than attempting to spell out the content of secret traditions, we would do better to focus on its formal or functional nature – that is, the force of the idea of the secret, rather than the secrets being kept. And indeed, the history of modern esotericism tends towards syncretism, which implies a move from the idea of isolated pockets of secrecy to the idea of a general and interconnected underground current of secrecy, which is usually identical with mainstream ideas, such as the interconnection of humans and nature.

A common preoccupation in the eighteenth century was the idea that religions had an exoteric and an esoteric face. The exoteric face consisted of the doctrines and rituals prescribed for the populace; the esoteric side of religion was secret or mystical and consisted of doctrines that could not be disclosed to the people but were jealously guarded by an elite priestly class. There were some favoured locations for the operation of this secret doctrine. Jan Assmann has argued that ancient Egypt provided the prototype for this idea of what is known as the double doctrine. The claim, made powerfully by Ralph Cudworth in his *The True Intellectual System of the Universe* (1678), is that there is an ancient and universal understanding of monotheism that is dissimulated through polytheistic systems designed to distract and pacify the population.[42] Exposures of this duality, in which an esoteric doctrine was hidden behind a public and popular set of practices and institutions, became common through the Enlightenment. This allowed for a mimetic duality to arise, as scholars were able to break through the obfuscation with the light of their scholarship while harbouring their own semi-secret knowledge of the systems of secret knowledge of the past (albeit hidden behind the veil of footnotes and specialized abstraction rather than actual rites of initiation). Thus began the long history of Egypt as the place of mystery, the myth of Egypt as the source of mythology. Indeed, one can say that Egypt became a locus of a whole idea of time, an unhistorical Ancientness, providing a well of secret understanding that can never be fully explicated and so can never run dry.

The secret harboured by many secret societies is simply that of their existence, though they may also often have a set of shared beliefs or purposes which are also clandestine. But some esoteric groups do in fact double this secrecy with their guardianship of certain kinds of secret knowledge, knowledge which must be preserved yet also interdicted. This doubling is given a further iteration still in the case of the tradition known (though not in fact by most Gnostics themselves) as Gnosticism. Indeed, as its name suggests, the question of knowledge is at the heart of Gnostic doctrine, for Gnostics affirmed the existence of a God who consisted of a principle of pure knowledge, and was thus far remote from the fallen world of matter, thought to have been produced by a secondary emanation from the Godhead, the Demiurge, itself prompted by the figure of Sophia, or Wisdom. According to the account given by Irenaeus (130–202) in his *Adversus haereses* (Against the Heretics), the Demiurge of the Gnostics worked in a condition of nescience, thereby affirming the absolute exteriority of the created world to divine knowledge:

> the Demiurge imagined that he created all these things of himself, while he in reality made them in conjunction with the productive power of Achamoth [Sophia]. He formed the heavens, yet was ignorant of the heavens; he fashioned man, yet knew not man; he brought to light the earth, yet had no acquaintance with the earth; and, in like manner, they declare that he was ignorant of the forms of all that he made, and knew not even of the existence of his own mother, but imagined that he himself was all things.[43]

But Gnostics also believed in the possibility of redemption through access to the divine spark of divine knowledge and therefore 'the *self-empowerment of the knowing subject*'.[44] The heretical, secret knowledge harboured in Gnostic tradition is that of the identity of divinity and knowledge. In such a tradition, the knowledge of the divine moves toward and finally merges with the divinity of knowledge itself. Such knowledge is cosmic and yet, of course, only available to the few in whom the divine spark survives or can be awakened. One can understand how the keeping of secrets might have contributed to the cathecting of the idea of knowledge and especially that of knowledge that is unknown to others.

During the nineteenth century and after there was a growing academic interest in the secret knowledges and mystery cults of the past. The most prominent among these were the Eleusinian mysteries of ancient Greece that were connected with the worship of Demeter at Eleusis. The secret of the mysteries was kept by the thousands of initiates to whom it was vouchsafed for many centuries before the sanctuary was closed down by the Emperor Theodosius in 392 CE, but it seems clear that it would have involved some ritual or symbolic representation of the three stages of the story of Demeter and Persephone: the abduction of Persephone by Hades; the agonized search of her mother, Demeter, for her daughter; and the final rescue of Persephone from Hades (though, having eaten four pomegranate pips while in the underworld, her return could not be permanent and she had to return for the four months of each winter).

From the late eighteenth century onwards the explication of the Eleusinian mysteries came to stand synecdochically for the scholarly enterprise of mythography, or comparative mythology, which became a highly influential form of scholarly mystery. One of the earliest explications of the mysteries was provided by Thomas Taylor in his *The Eleusinian and Bacchic Mysteries: A Dissertation* of 1790. Taylor was a Nonconformist who established himself as a radical proponent of Greek philosophy and paganism against religious orthodoxy – he is said once to have sacrificed a bull to Zeus at his home in Walworth, London – and seems to have had an impact on Blake, Shelley and other Romantic writers.[45] Though he did not attend a university – as a Nonconformist neither Oxford nor Cambridge were open to him – he set out to wrest academic authority for himself through a programme of self-directed classical researches and translations of Greek texts. His own uncertain relation to knowledge is enacted through his discussion of the mysteries of Eleusis. *The Eleusinian and Bacchic Mysteries* begins with an assertion of the dignity of the secret meaning which he will make out, thereby asserting his mastery of the mystery over that of the cloistered Oxbridge classicists: '[T]he secret meaning of the Eleusinian and Bacchic Mysteries is unfolded, from authority the most respectable, and from a philosophy of all others the most venerable and august'.[46] His Platonic argument is that the secret rituals at Eleusis, which enacted the descent of Persephone into Hades and her return in the spring, were elaborate allegories of the relation of spirit to matter:

> I shall endeavour to prove, that, as the shews of the lesser
> mysteries occultly signified the miseries of the soul while in
> subjection to body, so those of the greater obscurely intimated,
> by mystic and splendid visions, the felicity of the soul both
> here and hereafter, when purified from the defilements of a
> material nature, and constantly elevated to the realities of
> intellectual vision.[47]

In the absence of any records or testimonies of what was enacted in the Eleusinian ceremonies, Taylor relies heavily on a reading of Book VI of Virgil's *Aeneid*, suggesting that the descent into hell of Aeneas is a narrative reworking of the enactment within the rites at Eleusis of the capture and corruption of the pure soul in the trammels of bodily matter. The soul is conceived principally as intellect, 'falling into generation, and ascending from thence into the intelligible world, and becoming perfectly converted to her divine and intellectual part'.[48] Taylor thereby allows for the identification of his own allegorical readings, which may be seen as freeing the soul of the ritual's meaning from its material veiling in mythical narrative, with the workings of this divine intellect. Taylor defends the dignity of the Eleusinian wisdom against the readings of Christian commentators, ancient and modern, who suspected that indecency and licentious behaviour occurred as part of the mythic celebration of fertility. In maintaining the philosophical dignity of the mysteries, Taylor effects a tacit identification of the Platonic knowledge he unfolds with the mystical knowledge of the Eleusinian initiate. In the usual pattern, the secret is both withdrawn, yet also ubiquitous and sempiternal:

> its respectability is no more lessened by its concealment, than
> the value of a diamond, when secluded from the light. And

as to the philosophy, by whose assistance these mysteries are developed, it is coeval with the universe itself; and however its continuity may be broken by opposing systems, it will make its appearance at different periods of time, as long as the sun himself shall continue to illuminate the world.[49]

Later artistic evocations of Eleusis and the mythical personages associated with it – such as by Swinburne, Tennyson, Pater and D. G. Rossetti – would follow Taylor in his abandonment of any attempt to see the Eleusinian mysteries as presaging Christianity, and value instead the sensory power of a kind of pagan wisdom.[50] The knowledge of myth which was developed in the nineteenth-century sciences of comparative mythology thereby becomes itself mythified as a knowledge against knowledge, a knowledge infused with the sacred energies of the generative body.

A remarkable confederacy began thereby to grow up between academic and popular knowledge. Scholarly investigations of Eleusis leaked sideways and downwards during the nineteenth and twentieth centuries into more popular and public forms of esotericism, encouraged by the fantasy of a kind of popular wisdom able to access traditions of thought that both mimic and resist mainstream academic knowledge. Much of the force of the idea of the Eleusinian mysteries has to do with the sense that secrecy must equate in some way with sex, if only in the sublimated form of 'fertility ritual', which since the eighteenth century had been a code that allowed for the secret commerce between academic knowledge and pornography (being able to read Greek or Latin was essential for anybody in search of pornography until well into the nineteenth century). The sexualizing of religion is the not-so-secret principle that seems to impel many of the awed revelations made by pseudoacademic occultists. They would often draw on Frazer's *The Golden Bough*, which suggested to many, especially those who resisted the temptation of reading it, a delicious commerce of academic knowledge with themes of sex and death.

The most preposterously inflated rhetorical economics of secrecy are to be found in H. P. Blavatsky's *The Secret Doctrine*, the two-volume *summa* issued in 1888 of the occult ideas and beliefs that underlie Theosophy, the philosophy she had invented with Henry Steele Olcott in the mid-1870s. Blavatsky sings the by now conventional song that the world's religions and mystical philosophies are all just fragments of a more original and encompassing secret wisdom embodied in a vast hidden archive of sacred texts largely unknown to Western scholarship, which at one point she claims includes every sacred text ever written:

> The members of several esoteric schools – the seat of which is beyond the Himalayas, and whose ramifications may be found in China, Japan, India, Tibet, and even in Syria, besides South America – claim to have in their possession the sum total of sacred and philosophical works in MSS. and type: all the works, in fact, that have ever been written, in whatever language or characters, since the art of writing began; from the ideographic hieroglyphs down to the alphabet of Cadmus and the Devanagari.[51]

These texts are hidden away in underground crypts and caverns cut out of the rock. Blavatsky allows us tantalizing glimpses of their miraculous, mysterious survival:

> Beyond the Western Tsay-dam, in the solitary passes of Kuen-lun there are several such hiding-places. Along the ridge of Altyn-Toga, whose soil no European foot has ever trodden so far, there exists a certain hamlet, lost in a deep gorge. It is a small cluster of houses, a hamlet rather than a monastery, with a poor-looking temple in it, with one old lama, a hermit, living near by to watch it. Pilgrims say that the subterranean galleries and halls under it contain a collection of books, the number of which, according to the accounts given, is too large to find room even in the British Museum. (*SD*, I, xxiv)

We are assured that infinite pains have been taken to conceal the secret wisdom both safe and yet hidden from the light of common day. Though Blavatsky hints at the 'tremendous occult powers, the abuse of which would cause incalculable evil to humanity' embodied in this wisdom, it is never made at all clear what these powers are and what the evil might be (*SD*, I, xxxv). As such, it is hard to understand why it continues to be necessary to keep it secret in the face of what might seem like the most pressing need for the spread of its enlightening influence, and especially since Blavatsky intends anyway to lay the doctrine out for us across over a thousand pages:

The world of to-day, in its mad career towards the unknown
– which it is too ready to confound with the unknowable,
whenever the problem eludes the grasp of the physicist – is
rapidly progressing on the reverse, material plane of spirituality. It has now become a vast arena – a true valley of discord
and of eternal strife – a necropolis, wherein lie buried the
highest and the most holy aspirations of our Spirit-Soul. That
soul becomes with every new generation more paralyzed and
atrophied. (*SD*, I, xxii)

What is more, the principles of the wisdom that Blavatsky laboriously
and at enormous length unfolds, though they were originally revealed
to her by spiritual adepts or mahatmas, is in fact spelled out in prodigious numbers of texts, and attested to through thousands of years of
religious and occult doctrine spread across every people in the world,
not to mention extraterrestrial regions. Throughout Blavatsky's writing, the hidden-away and bruited-abroad, the rare and the abundantly,
blazingly apparent, compound bizarrely.

Not only is the secret itself ubiquitous, ubiquity is exactly what
the secret amounts to. Blavatsky aims to bring to explicitness the
secret doctrine of 'the universally diffused religion of the ancient and
prehistoric world' (*SD*, I, xxxiv). The secret of the secret doctrine is
that everything is everywhere One, the principle of Theosophy being
that '[e]soteric philosophy reconciles all religions, strips every one of
its outward, human garments, and shows the root of each to be identical with that of every other great religion' (*SD*, I, xx). Everything is
concealed, and yet nothing is kept apart from anything else in the
universal syncretic collapse of Blavatsky's system.

This most important form of the refusal, or overcoming, of division is the denial of the difference between cosmos and gnosis such
that 'the impersonal reality pervading the Kosmos is the pure nou-
menon of thought' (*SD*, I, 14–15). In common with many of the occult
doctrines explicated in rivalry with scientific knowledge, the essential
principle of the secret doctrine is that the universe is everywhere conscious – and indeed essentially consists of consciousness – though it
is also in constant evolution towards that condition of spiritualized
matter that it already essentially is. As the thought that announces
the omnitude of thought, this makes the doctrine pleasingly tauto-
logical. The apparent vastness of reach of the doctrine is designed to

dissimulate its essential self-magnifying, yet self-consuming 'I AM THAT I AM'. The secret of the secret doctrine is that it is a knowledge with no objects of its knowledge, with the image and emanation of knowing brooding voluptuously on its fantasy of itself. This makes all the contradictions and approximations of which sceptical commentators have accused it beside the point. The point is that nothing can or need stand in the way of the fantasy of superlative Knowledge. In the words of W. B. Yeats, a sometime intoxicatee of Blavatsky, 'mirror on mirror mirrored is all the show'.[52]

The dual economy of the unfolding nonsecret depends upon the fact that *The Secret Doctrine* is so massive, mimicking the accretive form of many of the explications of myth and ritual, but especially Frazer's endlessly augmented *The Golden Bough*, which many readers read, or at least sipped at, in parallel with Blavatsky. The lesson of the essential oneness of the universe requires seemingly endless complications, detours and delays, through which we can be shown that in fact all roads lead relentlessly back to the essential truth:

> the Occult teaching says, 'Nothing is created, but is only transformed. Nothing can manifest itself in this universe – from a globe down to a vague, rapid thought – that was not in the universe already; everything on the subjective plane is an eternal IS; as everything on the objective plane is an ever becoming – because transitory.' (SD, I, 570)

It is a miraculous pastiche of philosophical thought and argument that succeeds so well in hiding its performance from itself that it actually comes a tissue-paper's width away from being what it pretends to be. For its simulation seems indeed to demonstrate that it is possible for there to be something like a world formed of pure thought.

The dual economy of simplicity and multiplicity extends beyond the text of *The Secret Doctrine* into the Theosophy for which it provides the template. For here, too, as in many secret societies, there is a huge, hierarchical apparatus of internal differentiation, with different levels of spiritual apprenticeship and progressive enlightenment. As Georg Simmel argues, it is the fact of organization itself that matters, the proof of the creation of a society, not through slow and accidental historical growth but by conscious design: 'We may observe, even in school classes, how small, closely attached groups of comrades, through the mere formal fact that they form a special group, come to consider themselves an elite, compared with the rest who are unorganized' ('ss', 486). The real secret of the secret society is that it is able to create a kind of unity that is unavailable to merely accidental associations: 'The secret society must seek to create among the categories peculiar to itself, a species of life-totality' ('ss', 481). Theosophy goes further than the Freemasonry which it resembles in bringing together the two contradictory pulls of religious affiliation, the centripetal-esoteric drive to secrecy, distinction and apartness, and the centrifugal-exoteric drive to exhibition and missionary expansion. The knowledge that everything is One must attain to the condition of a universal secret, the secret kept by all from all. In this it negotiates the antinomy of every monotheism, as identified by Peter Sloterdijk: 'There can be no universalism without set-theoretical paradoxes: one can only invite everyone if one can be sure that not everyone will come.'[53] The Theosophist idea of a spiritual 'plane' or 'level' mediates this antinomy, allowing for democracy and aristocracy to coexist: for although all are in on the secret, some are more in on it than others.

There is a very complex temporality associated with esotericism. Esotericism always belongs to a past, but that past is always in process of being produced. Indeed, as Ambrose Bierce suggests in the entry for Freemasonry in his *Devil's Dictionary* (1906), esoteric traditions appear to grow backwards from the present:

> Freemasonry: An order with secret rites, grotesque ceremonies and fantastic costumes, which, originating in the reign of Charles ii, among working artisans of London, has been joined successively by the dead of past centuries in unbroken retrogression until now it embraces all the generations of man on the hither side of Adam and is drumming up distinguished recruits among the pre-Creational inhabitants of Chaos and Formless Void.[54]

Such hidden intellectual and religious traditions are not entirely the invention of later ages, and there certainly are secrets to be excavated. But there is a second history of the history of those mysteries, which grow in potency the more they are explicated. The past proves to be an infinitely expanding reservoir of possibility for the attribution and explication of secrets. On the one hand there is a relation of epistemic antagonism, in which what we do not know of the past comes to be regarded not just as the natural and unavoidable decay of knowledge in forgetting, but as the result of suppression, refusal or denial that it is the task of historical analysis to bring forcibly to light. The entire programme of history is reimagined as the unearthing of mysteries, the extorting of confessions. On the other hand, history is imagined as entirely tractable to this action of explication. It may appear as though it requires prodigious acts of intellectual labour to unearth these hidden histories, but, once unearthed, they all have in common the gratification that they offer to the synthesizing intelligence. The secret knowledge is never that things are in fact more complicated and less connected than they seem, that is, that knowledge is less powerful than it might wish to believe. The secret of modern esotericism is always that everything is connected; and very often the secret unearthed is some version of the magical thinking imagined, or desired, in Gnosticism – that is, the secret of the infinite power of mind. Jonathan Black's *Secret History of the World* (2007), for example, thrillingly proposes that 'throughout history an astonishing number of famous people have secretly cultivated the esoteric philosophy and mystical states taught in the ancient societies' and goes on to ask the self-answering question which forms the basis for his book:

> Could the very people who have done most to form today's scientifically oriented and materialistic world view secretly have believed something else? Newton, Kepler, Voltaire, Paine, Washington, Franklin, Tolstoy, Dostoyevsky, Edison, Wilde, Gandhi, Duchamp; could it be true that they were initiated into a secret tradition, taught to believe in the power of mind over matter and that they were able to communicate with incorporeal spirits?[55]

The argument with which Black's book opens is that the universe must have been formed through a divine mental act in which God looks at a reflection of himself. Because the universe is formed from a mental act it seems easy to accommodate it to our own kind of mental activity, affirming that 'the universe is anthropocentric, every single particle of it straining, directed towards humankind.'[56] In a certain sense, the very wildness and absurdity of these formulations, and their sweetly innocent intolerance of any kind of difficulty or contradiction, blurt out the secret conviction behind these syncretic histories: 'Matter is therefore moved by human minds perhaps not to the same extent, but *in the same kind of way* that it is moved by the mind of God.'[57] We might describe this as a benignly paradisiac paranoia, which finds reassurance where the conspiracy theorist and delusional schizophrenic find only a universe of concealment and dread; what they have in common is the vast overestimation of the organizing powers of mind, and the proof in the very fact of organization of the mind's own power to imagine its limitless power.

SECRET FEELING

Secret knowledge has been discussed primarily in terms of its moral or political implications, and therefore in terms of what is to be thought or known about it. But there is perhaps no other kind of knowledge-behaviour or noetic practice that is so intensely charged with feeling of different kinds. Georg Simmel suggestively treats social secrets less in terms of their function than in terms of their affective energy, or rather, perhaps, sees their social function in this affective force. Secrecy activates desire, suspicion, anxiety and fascination, both sealing and breaking social bonds. It 'sets barriers between men, but at the same time offers the seductive temptation to break through the barriers by gossip or confession. This temptation accompanies the psychical life of the secret like an undertone' ('ss', 466). The alternation between concealment and revelation, the 'retentive and the communicative energies' of secrets ('ss', 466), effect the distribution of charge which keeps societies alive and striving as well as coherent:

> The strenuous organizing forms which appear to be the real constructors of society, or to construct society as such, must be continually disturbed, unbalanced, and detached by individualistic and irregular forces, in order that their reaction and development may gain vitality by alternate concession and resistance. ('ss', 448)

Simmel often bases his understanding of the dynamics of secrets on the model of the erotic component in marriage, which he believes loses its vitality and binding force if couples surrender all their secrets: 'Relationships of an intimate character, the formal vehicle of which is psycho-physical proximity, lose the charm, and even the content, of their intimacy, unless the proximity includes, at the same time and alternately, distance and intermission' ('ss', 448).

Is there, we may first wonder, a distinctive spectrum of feeling relating to secrets, or a feeling-tone of secrecy? I think we can say first of all that the feelings associated with secrets are convulsive, in that they involve the tension and discharge associated with sudden reversal. There is a force required and displayed in the disclosure or discovery of secrets, a force which displays itself in rapid and substantial changes in levels of cathexis: what was previously unknown becomes known, and what was previously private is now public. These movements are always experienced as sudden change, whether or not the actual process has been swift. It might seem as though the discharge of secrecy in communication would produce a reduction of tension, with a move towards affective equilibrium. In fact, though, something like the opposite seems to be the case. The unexpected passage or sudden eruption of a secret into publicity produces a sense of imminence – the anxious yet excited expectation of what will come next. The keeping and releasing of secrets concentrates the sense of the temporality of knowing as no other action does.

Perhaps the temporality of the feelings aroused by secret knowledge explains the prevalence of 'secret histories' of all kinds. A secret history is a history of what has been kept secret, but the phrase hints tellingly at the idea that there may be a secretive dynamic in all history-making. If all histories involve the making public of the unknown, then history itself may seem to have the temporal rhythm that seems characteristic of the secret withheld, then discovered. Secrets allow for the feeling of temporality and the temporality of feeling.

This particular complex of secrecy-emotions is intensified by the socially sedimented idea that emotions themselves have the form of secrets that require expression, that is, the passage from a latent to a manifest, or an unknown to a knowable condition. To express a feeling is in itself to protest against secrecy. The essential feeling associated with a discovery or revelation is that we should feel something. To feel nothing at the disclosure of a secret would be to suggest that it had never been a secret at all. This belongs to the class of incitement-feelings: feelings we feel we and others should have, feelings that include the meta-feeling that they should be felt as widely as possible. This may be why we feel the need to pass on a newly communicated secret, maintaining or even accelerating the original impetus of its disclosure. Human beings ordinarily feel the need to communicate feeling much more intensely than the need to communicate knowledge. Seen from this point of view, secrets may perhaps be understood as knowledge experienced as a state of feeling.

To pass on a secret is very often a way of keeping a confidence while breaking it. I am told that in Cambridge, and probably in many other places too, a secret is something you tell only one person at a time. In such a paradoxical passage, the secret is betrayed by being confided, and restriction is prolonged through release. This ambivalence allows for the simultaneous satisfaction of two contradictory impulses, that of affirming community and that of its destruction. It weaves together the secret commerce of love and rage, eros and thanatos, the libido of belonging and the longing to cut loose.

The interplay of eros and thanatos in the oxymoron of public secrets is manifest in the matching interplay of distance and intimacy that is made possible when media and mediation occupy so much of the space of shared public experience. These forms of media allow for the dissemination far and wide of the up-close-and-personal. Knowing-that and knowing-how are braided tightly together in mediations that seem to allow us to be teleproximally present in experiences that we are distant from. The knowledge of intimate secrets seems to allow something like the intimacy of shared knowledge, allowing one to share in the sharing of the secret through its very exposure. It is hard to say quite how it feels to entertain, or be the fraught occasion of, these contrary feelings of warm community and cold aggression, for one both participates in and stands apart from the feelings themselves. Being in the know in this way initiates us into a secret feeling of knowing that must never come to know itself.

4
QUISITION

We look to knowledge to supply certainty and the security from risk and injury it can bring. Among those risks are the risks and injuries arising from the strife with other persons or beings. And yet our relations to knowledge and the acts of thinking that lead to them seem unthinkable without striving and conflict. It may be that understanding what Walter Ong describes as this 'adversativeness' requires the assistance of what he calls 'noobiology', the study of the biological dimensions of human mental or intellectual activity.[1] The most important aspect of our biological constitution for Ong is our apparent inability either to live apart from each other or to live alongside each other without quarrelling. Our knowledge-relations – the relations we have to knowledge, and the relations we form with each other through it – are an important part of the ways in which enmity and contest both endanger and ensure community. This chapter concerns itself with what Ong calls 'the adversative stance in the noetic world, the world of knowledge', that is, the ways in which the workings of knowledge are veined with contention.[2] If we dream of a peace that 'passeth all understanding' (Philippians 4:7), it may be because the work of understanding seems so unlikely ever to let us rest in peace.

It can be hard to be sure what I know about many matters, since I can easily assume that I know things that, on reflection or when put into practice, I turn out not to know very well at all. This may imply that I not only do not know for sure what I know, I also may not really have much understanding in general of what it means to know things. What does it mean, what does it feel like to know things?

How can I secure my sense of being in the know about things? This uncertainty means that human beings and groups have often come to rely upon performative procedures of various kinds which can act as the outward warrant or concrete enactment of knowing. These acts of working out and making manifest are part of the adversative fabric of human society. Perhaps the most important of these ways of performing knowledge – and in the process being able to form an affective relation to it – is the action of questioning, an act which is always in some way demanding. I propose to call this *quisition*.

There are many different modalities of question in human life. Inquisition differs from enquiry. When I enquire what time the park closes or whether the sweater I have picked out suits me, I am seeking information which I did not have prior to receiving the answer. But an inquisition aims not to produce the transmission of information but rather to make known what another knows. An inquisition challenges me to demonstrate that I know something rather than requesting me to impart what I know. Of course, the word 'inquisition' will nowadays summon up the kinds of violent interrogation which are designed to make me confess to crimes or secrets, in religious or legal-political contexts, but I wish to set these aside for the moment. It is said that those setting mathematics examinations in the nineteenth century would sometimes slip in a problem to which there was no known solution, in the hope of flushing one out from a brilliant candidate. But it would be pointless in the kind of encounter I am describing here for there to be the possibility of any discovery or invention.

This procedure of formal questioning and response is important, not just as a method of inquiry but as a way of giving me the sense of what it is to know what I know. We may say that in giving actuality and existence to knowing quisition is a necessary accessory to the understanding we have of what counts as knowing, what knowing feels like, and what we in turn feel about that. Knowing is not a private affair, since it must always involve this circuit of query and demonstration. Indeed, this is so fundamental that I may need to institute this kind of inquiry with myself if I want to know what I know. The one who asks you what you know may provide necessary assistance to you in recognizing what you do or do not know. It is for this reason that questions are asked in order to generate knowledge that one does not already have, or does not know one already has.

The operations of question and answer are so simultaneously ritualized and embedded – while also being extremely volatile and ephemeral – that it is hard to isolate the complex and always shifting relations they institute between persons involved in the practice. Interrogative practices are one of the most important ways in which we demonstrate interest and concern. A student who may find it unbearably difficult to speak up in class can sometimes make their entry safely into this circumstance through the framing of a question, which is formalized enough for them not to feel compromised. It is perhaps only when one is deprived of landmarks with regard to the asking of questions – the who, how and when of questioning – that one realizes how much the fabric of social existence is made up of it. The OED makes it clear the Latin *quaerere*, to search, seek or ask, is active in a large number of words, including quest, conquer, require, exquisite (highly sought out or after) and even perhaps queer.

RIDDLES

One of the most widespread forms of formalized question and answer is the posing of riddles. There does not seem to be any human group in which this practice is entirely unknown. Though it has many different forms, which makes it hard to offer a rigorous definition that would encompass all riddles, there is nevertheless a sufficiently strong family resemblance to make the practice readily recognizable.

A riddle is more than a question: the history of the word suggests that it contains wisdom or advice, for a riddle is a *rede*, or *rätsel*, belonging to a group of Germanic words that encompasses a huge range of reference, signifying advice, expedient, trick, method, plan, understanding, wisdom, thought, teaching, solution, assembly, discussion, agreement or rule. These words are cognate with the word 'read', which could also mean to advise, deliberate, consider, discern or interpret, especially of dreams or riddles. But the advice it offers lies only in a secondary way in the answer that might be forthcoming to the question.

You always know the answer to a riddle – it is a pretty inflexible rule that the answer will always be some object that is already known to you, however outlandish or self-contradictory the attributes are that are assigned to it in the riddle. The difference between a problem and a riddle is that you don't yet know the answer to a problem, whereas a riddle contains its answer in its manner of asking. As Shlomith Cohen observes,

> Riddles seem to carry in them the feeling that the solution *should have been known* . . . When solved, most riddles seem simple and immediately available to the listener. It becomes clear that the elements for solving the riddle were within reach, but beyond awareness.[3]

This makes the enactment of the riddle relation a minor and regulated exercise in mockery and shaming, the most socially cohering of adversative modes. Annikki Kaivola-Bregenhøj notes that many riddles have as their primary aim 'to put the riddlee to shame'.[4] There would be no shame without this sense that one really ought to have been able to guess the answer.

Solving or guessing the answer to a riddle in fact means working out what kind of question it is, and what kind of thing could count as an answer to that kind of question. As Cora Diamond puts it, 'it's only when one has the solution that one knows how to take the question, what it is for it to have an answer'.[5] Getting the answer right means guessing how the question ought to be read. For this reason, riddles do not harbour or impart knowledge of any significance, which is why it would be absurd to say, on hearing the answer to a riddle: 'Oh, I see: so in that case . . .', for there are no consequences to the riddle answer in terms of the answer itself. The answer is folded back wholly into the question, which is itself wholly cancelled by it, no supplementary questions being conceivable or worthwhile. As Emily Dickinson, who is often drawn to the form of the riddle, has it:

> The Riddle we can guess
> We speedily despise –
> Not anything is stale so long
> As Yesterday's surprise – [6]

This is why it is so tempting to make riddles the answer to which is 'a riddle', because in a sense it always is. Galileo's elegant example of this kind of riddle ends by characterizing the paradox of that which ceases to be what it is the moment it becomes clear what it is, and becomes null by gaining a name:

Che se dall'ombre al chiaro lume passo
Tosto l'alma da me sen fugge . . .
E l'esser perdo con la vita, e 'l nome.

When I pass from darkness into clear light,
suddenly my soul flees from me . . .
and, coming to life, I lose my being and my name.[7]

This self-relation or self-consuming nature of the riddle routine makes the Sphinx's riddle to Oedipus wholly appropriate, since it foreshadows just such a tragedy of self-consumption, or incestuous short-circuit, in Oedipus' relation to the mystery of his own beginnings.

In Cora Diamond's words, the particular kind of revelation provided by the answer to a riddle 'isn't a discovery in a space, describable in advance, but a "discovery" of a space'.[8] But this new space that is disclosed is actually a new or not previously apparent dimension of the existing space provided by the question. This is why the answer to a riddle cannot usually be said to be any kind of new knowledge, as opposed to a new conception of existing knowledge. If you have to go to a laboratory or a library to answer a riddle, you may turn out to be going about it the wrong way, looking for something you don't know as opposed to reflecting on what you might not have realized. In Sophocles' *Oedipus Tyrannus* Oedipus tells Creon,

> her riddle was not one for the first comer to explain! It required prophetic skill, and you were exposed as having no knowledge from the birds or from the gods. No, it was I that came, Oedipus who knew nothing, and put a stop to her; I hit the mark by native wit, not by what I learned from birds.[9]

This is what leads Wittgenstein to make his claim that 'the *riddle* does not exist. If a question can be put at all, then it *can* also be answered'. This is because 'For an answer which cannot be expressed the question too cannot be expressed.'[10] Wittgenstein is here referring to the use of the term riddle to refer to questions that we think we know are unanswerable – large and open questions where the terms of the enquiry or the nature of the answer that might be returned are completely open and undetermined, as in a phrase like 'the riddle of the Universe'. But perhaps the kind of question that a riddle poses is always in fact as closed or self-referring as a question can be: 'what kind of question would you say this is?' If one were to pose a riddle that had no solution, one might be taken to be inviting speculation as to the kind of response that might serve to turn the question retrospectively into a riddle, that is, a joke question built around its answer.

This may begin to account for the otherwise rather odd fact that riddles are often also poems, for poems tend to be self-indicating in a way that ordinary discourse is not. The poetic quality of the riddle is a strong clue that you should be paying attention to the rhetorical procedure of the riddle rather than referential matters. This also means that it is hard to be sure if something is a riddle or not, that is, whether its solution will have this self-consuming quality, a quality that comes from transforming or displacing the sense of the original question. This may account for the fact that riddles often occur in contexts that clearly indicate that what are in question are riddles rather than regular questions.

So one of the odd features of riddles is that they often seem to impersonate themselves, that is, they give every appearance of posing a real question which will require thought and ingenuity, as well as quite a lot of experience in riddle-solving, to answer. But in fact the conventions of riddle-posing seem to assume that the solution will always, after a short delay, need to be given by the riddler. To reply, 'Hmm, that really is a teaser. I will need to go away and give it some thought', is usually not in fact an appropriate response, since the point of asking a riddle question is to reduce the riddlee to having to ask for the answer. So the riddler pretends to be asking a question by which the riddlee must pretend to be defeated, since they know they are not really expected to investigate the matter, and indeed to do so would usually be rather unmannerly. Lee Haring suggests that in African riddle practice what matters is not the intellectual action of solving riddles but simply the prestige that comes from knowing plenty of them. This makes the practice of asking and answering riddles 'more like a catechism than a creative enquiry', in which the rule of the game is that the answer is to be learned rather than guessed.[11] So 'knowledge of riddles as wholes entitles the knower, probably in late childhood, to membership in the "society of knowers"', since possession of this kind of knowledge is 'a form of power allied to magic'.[12] The point of a riddle under these circumstances is not guessing the answer, it is knowing the answer. This allows the riddle to act, as it often does, as a social filter, dividing those in the know off from those who do not know. 'The right answer is a password for admission to the group of those who know. Ingenuity in devising alternatives may be commendable, but it doesn't guarantee entry. Only the right answer does.'[13] The riddle allows a play with the idea that there are certain kinds of hidden knowledge to be had about the ostensible subjects of riddles – fish, sky, stones, rivers, chickens and the like – when the knowledge that matters is of the question/answer couplings that riddles are and the riddle-procedures that govern behaviour in relation to them.

By creating a pseudo-knowledge, a knowledge that is not of anything other than how to play at the particular kind of knowing involved in exchanging riddles, riddling enables a play with the very idea of knowledge, in which knowing becomes a kind of socionoetic currency. John Blacking describes the paper-chain of riddle 'purchases' that take place among the Venda people of South Africa:

A asks B a riddle. B does not answer it; instead he 'buys' A's answer by posing another riddle. A answers his own first riddle and then 'buys' the answer to B's riddle by posing another riddle. B then answers his own first riddle and 'buys' the answer to A's second riddle by posing another riddle. The game continues in this fashion, with the burden of question-ing shifting regularly from A to B, until one side or the other is unable to ask any more riddles.[14]

There is a kind of magical power in these riddles. Blacking reports that 'riddles, songs and stories, besides being recreations, are the first taste that Venda children have of magical power, and riddles are perhaps the most significant and powerful of all, since many have a cosmogonic, mystical flavour.'[15] The magic of riddles may in fact also have a great deal to do with the fact that they are a way of asserting and transforming social status – youngest sons needing to hold their own against their stronger siblings were often very good at riddling, though careful not to crow too much over their victories.[16] So, although – or more likely because – riddles have little positive knowledge content, riddle-play nevertheless allows for a noetic agonism that is real enough in terms of the challenges to cohesion posed by the nonsense of riddles. Roger Abrahams argues that 'riddles are fundamentally aggressive in design and purpose', not just because they assume and institute disparities of power and status between riddler and riddlee, but because they also represent an assault on the categories by which things are known.[17] And yet, riddles are also 'just one of the many traditional forms of licensed aggression that, though antisocial in tendency, are not antinormative. They take energies potentially destructive of the community and its values and channel them into harmless, indeed psychologically helpful, creative avenues of expression'.[18]

Literary riddles seem to have acquired a rather different, more elevated reputation. Rafat Borystawski connects the medieval instinct for riddle-reading as essential to the Christian mission to read out the presence of divine truth in creation:

> The search for the truth is the path towards God. This is likened to the ability to find Him and His wisdom everywhere; enlightenment is only possible through answering an all-encompassing riddle, whose answer is the omnipresent God ... The Christian confidence in God's personal participation in the process of creation and the necessity to discern and understand His ubiquitousness in every being, hidden there as part of his divine scheme, might have been, and indeed was, interpreted as resembling a riddle posed by Him to mankind.[19]

And yet the Old English riddles are also to be seen as 'a semantic and poetic play with creation [which] could not ensue without knowledge as such, and without playing with it in the form of a game with what is known'.[20] So, although one may agree that 'the primeval function of riddles was most certainly associated with hidden wisdom', they are also a kind of playing with and, one might say, playing at knowledge.[21] In fact, there seems to be very little in the way of useful knowledge, let alone wisdom, embodied in riddles – the fact that human beings are immobile when young, largely self-propelling as adults and then rather less mobile in old age scarcely seems like a precious and hard-won illumination of the human condition. In fact, whatever wisdom there may be in riddles may largely be reduced to the unsurprising proposition, or, rather, formal enactment of the fact, that things may be understood in surprisingly various ways. Cancelling down even further, one may say that the question asked by every riddle is: how can 1 be 2? And that elementary question of number relates to the game structure in which knowing is distributed unevenly between the two participants in a riddle-posing, the one that may become two, and the two that may become one.

Riddles are actions rather than objects – things for riddling with. They are always discursive events as well as structures, with certain kinds of set-up and a range of prescribed moves or outcomes, among them that of determining just how much deliberation is afforded to the riddlee – 'I'll give you three guesses, do you give up?' This is what makes the fact that Lewis Carroll's Mad Hatter himself turns out not to know the answer to his own riddle, 'Why is a raven like a writing desk?' simultaneously absurd and disturbing.[22]

Riddles are also often jokes. But why? Perhaps it has something to do with their general inconsequentiality, the fact that it is so difficult to do anything with the answer to a riddle other than to 'get' it – 'aha' rather than, or as well as, 'haha'. And yet in myth and folktale the form or event of the riddle, as opposed to its content, will often in fact have extremely serious consequences for the one who answers wrongly. A riddle of this kind is known as a 'neck-riddle' (*Halsrätsel*), or 'capital riddle'.[23] Why does the Sphinx eat you if you fail to guess the answer? Cash machines used to do something that felt similar if you made three unsuccessful attempts to enter your identification number. In fact, it is not just the one who ventures on answering a riddle who is at risk: the Sphinx precipitates herself to her death when Oedipus solves her riddle, just as Rumpelstiltskin bores himself into the earth (or in some versions, splits himself apart) in self-consuming rage, a fate shared by many alien intelligences out-riddled by *Star Trek*'s Captain Kirk. Like the teller of an unsuccessful joke, the perpetrator of an insufficiently obscure riddle may 'die'.

Why should riddle-knowledge be construed as a matter of life and death? Why are riddles such fatal proceedings even when they are entertainments? Roger Abrahams suggests that riddles may be as popular as they are in funeral wakes in Tobago because they play out an exposure to confusion and obscurity which can be reversed through the providing of the solution, and so may suggest an immunological exposure to and recoil from the unknowability of death: 'Perhaps in this wake situation, riddles when given with their solutions suggest sympathetically that the larger riddle also has a solution.'[24]

Here, we need to distinguish between the kind of riddle-practices that are part of social life, and narratives in which riddles feature, for it is these narratives which accord the special jeopardy and power to riddles. They include the account in 1 Kings 10 according to which 'when the queen of Sheba heard of the fame of Solomon concerning the name of the Lord, she came to prove him with hard questions'. Later legends of Solomon turned him into the propounder as well as the solver of riddles and enigmas.[25]

In *The Dinner of the Seven Wise Men*, Plutarch relates that a letter is brought to the Greek sage Bias by the Egyptian king Amasis, asking for help with a high-stakes contest in which he is engaged with a neighbouring ruler:

> The king of the Ethiopians is engaged in a contest in wisdom [σοφίας ἄμιλλαν, *sophias hamillan*] against me. Repeatedly vanquished in all else, he has crowned his efforts by framing an extraordinary and awful demand, bidding me to drink up the ocean. My reward, if I find a solution, is to have many villages and cities of his, and if I do not, I am to withdraw from the towns lying about Elephantine. I beg therefore that you will consider the question, and send back Neiloxenus without delay. And whatever is right for your friends or citizens to receive from us shall meet with no let or hindrance on my part.[26]

The challenge resembles the 'impossible tasks' motif of folktale and ballad, in which girls are required to spin straw into gold, make a cambric shirt without seam or needlework, and so on. As is often the case, the challenge is won with a bit of ridding wit rather than the display of conspicuous knowledge: 'let him tell the Ethiopian to stop the rivers which are now emptying into the ocean depths, while he himself is engaged in drinking up the ocean that now is; for this is the ocean with which the demand is concerned, and not the one which is to be.'[27]

In such narratives, riddles are probative tests and ordeals, ways of deciding other matters of more moment than they are. They are ways of sorting and settling scores, ways of winning and losing. They can lead to triumph and humiliation. They are in a sense divinatory procedures, though they work with rather than towards knowledge, that is, they do not use physical structures (sieves, tea-leaves, the flight of birds) as randomizing mechanisms, but use the distribution of knowledge and ignorance themselves as the randomizing mechanism.

The most notable riddler of all, the Sphinx, is a riddle herself, in that she is a valve or gateway for regulating passage (like Maxwell's demon she is an information-machine). As Eleanor Cook explains, she is like the Griffin in being a creature of indeterminate form, and so well-suited to asking the kinds of questions evoking strangely compounded bodies that characterize riddles.[28] Galileo's riddle sonnet, quoted earlier, the answer to which is 'a riddle', represents the riddle as just this kind of unnamable monstrosity:

> *Mostro son io più strano, e più difforme*
> *Che l'arpìa, la sirena o la chimera;*
> *Nè in terra, in aria, in acqua è alcuna fiera,*
> *Ch'abbia di membra così varie forme*

> I am a monster, stranger and more deformed
> than Harpy, Siren or Chimera.
> Nothing on earth, air or water, nor any beast,
> has members so various in their forms.[29]

That the answer to the Sphinx's riddle is 'Man' suggests a certain rhyme between monstrosity and metamorphic humanity. Giants and monsters guard gates with riddles, and the passage is always from ignorance into awareness as well as from one location to another. The uncertainty of their form makes the riddles they ask performances of the traditional 'What am I?' form of the riddle. The choice seems to be consumption or safe passage; being swallowed or spat out. Riddles are often liminal phenomena which mark places of impediment and passage, or retarding and accelerating. The name of the Sphinx seems to be derived from σφίγγειν (*sphingein*), to draw tight, so her function seems to be the same as that performed by any number of muscular structures that contract and relax in order to let things selectively in and out, most notably in the *sphincter ani*, or anal sphincter, or *sphincter vaginae*, the vaginal sphincter, but also in the larynx. It is tempting to see some relationship between the riddle in the sense of a sieve, which effects a similar kind of sorting, by letting through some items while holding back others. The two different kinds of riddle may well have had some kind of influence on each other, though they do not have any etymological relationship.

Perhaps the reason that the greater part of riddle analysis is as tedious and obsessive as it is, is that it concerns itself with what riddles are rather than what they do, and with riddle in itself rather than with the kinds of things that riddles resemble and relate to. Riddling may be understood as part of the large and diversified work of quisition, the ordering of the work of knowing in terms of interrogation and response which human beings undertake. Riddle analysis is largely incurious about why so many different kinds of human should spend so long asking each other formalized questions.

Riddle-critics of a structuralist bent tend to see them as cognitive procedures, ways of examining and negotiating social meanings. Ella Köngäs Maranda suggests that riddles essentially 'combine the incombinable' and are thus analogous to the institution of marriage, which riddles often accompany.[30] Indeed, she sees riddles as a sort of description of the institution of marriage:

> Riddles can be viewed as the perhaps more specialized language in which a group speaks of its most basic social action, the union of a man and a woman. On the level of social action, this reciprocity – be it between the marrying individuals, as in our present-day Western societies, or between the marrying groups, as in many other societies – constitutes the foundation. It is my contention that this reciprocity 'on the ground' corresponds to a continuous reconciliation of opposites on the less tangible, but equally fundamental, cognitive level.[31]

Ian Hamnett suggests a slightly broader way in which riddles might be seen as a reflection on forms of cognitive ordering: '[R]iddles and riddling may illuminate some of the principles that underlie classification in social action and cognition generally and can, in particular, indicate the role that ambiguities play in the classificatory process.'[32]

But there is another and probably more important function of riddles. We may see riddles not as containing or communicating knowledge, but as sculpting and texturing knowing, giving a particular kind of aetiology and temporal shape to the work of coming-to-know, connecting concealment, questioning and revelation in a kind of rhythm. The fact that both riddles and jokes constitute delay followed by intensification in the discharge of tension is the most important aspect of the relation between the two. In this, riddles are the affective scansion of knowing. Matthew Marino concludes his attempt to argue for the literary quality of the Exeter Book riddles by arguing that Keats's principle of negative capability, which allows one to remain in a condition of uncertainty without the need for fact or rational explanation, 'better explains the rich impulse of the *Exeter Book* riddles'.[33] The point of this claim is to distinguish literary riddles from the kind of open-and-shut case represented by most folk riddles, in which the answer immediately and entirely exhausts the question. But whether literary or not, the tonus of knowing is defined by the quisitive form, the feeling of alloyed gift and demand in the commingling of hanging back and reaching forward, possibility and fact, and the ways of feeling the imminence of knowing and turning its suspension into satisfaction. The literary riddle certainly allows for the play of anticipation and recall to be made more complex and multi-factorial than the oral riddle, but this thickens the temporal tension rather than suspending it or shifting its mode to something else. Ilan Amit's account of the noetic economics of riddle posing and solving highlights the ways in which riddles put knowing into play:

> I know something, which you do not know. I wish to capital-
> ize on it. If I impart my knowledge, I shall lose the knowledge;
> if I do not, you will be unaware that I possess it. I could pose
> a riddle, in the hope of creating in you a sense of deficiency
> and a need to redress it. By posing the riddle, I establish my
> status as a knower. Eventually I will have to surrender my
> knowledge and solve the riddle. If I do not, something else
> might distract your attention, or someone might arrive at the
> solution independently.[34]

The principle to which this experience reduces is that the experience of knowing is always in time rather than on time, for it is either too early – you do not know the answer yet – or too late – you know it already. Question and answer are a way of forcing this ambivalence into a sequential structure, a way of escaping from the ambivalence or irritability of wanting to know, while yet also fulfilling it through the promise of knowledge. Here the thought of time and the time of thought are woven together, and knowing is tempered by time.

Riddles are just one of the many modes of quisition that make up the relation to knowledge. This leads to and is expressed by the tendency to construe the relation between objects of enquiry and the enquiry itself as an interrogative dialogue. When one puzzles about the meaning of life, or the riddle of the universe, one has created an imaginary relation in which the object has been made to pose a 'What am I?' question for the seeker after truth, or the seeker after truth is made to demand (is made of the demand), to know what kind of question it may be thought of as asking of him. Students making the transition from undergraduate to graduate work are sometimes puzzled by the fact that they are required not to answer questions, as though they lay around waiting to be answered, but to invent them, which can often lead to a painful or perplexed kind of recursion: 'what kind of question do you mean?' Research involves not discovery but the invention of things in need of discovery. Academics can often be heard querulously bleating that such and such a view is 'problem-*aa*tic', as though devising problems on which to dwell and with which to deal were not the only thing that makes academic discourse possible, or at least worthwhile.

If the quisitive work of asking and answering is neglected in riddle literature, so too is the cognitive operation that is supposed to intervene between question and answer, that of guessing. What is involved in guessing? Guessing is a strange mixture between deliberation and chance procedure. For Johan Huizinga 'the answer to an enigmatic question is not found by reflection or logical reasoning. It comes quite literally as a sudden *solution* – a loosening of the tie by which the questioner holds you bound.'[35] The feeling of intuition that one may have in forming a guess suggests the belief in a special kind of unknown knowledge, a knowledge that may involve some kind of power or external intervention beyond ordinary thinking. You guess an answer by guessing at it: rather than working out the answer you try to think of a way of putting yourself in the way of it. We still today speak of an 'inspired guess'. To guess in English can mean both to search for an answer and to succeed in forming it: 'how did you guess?' (German distinguishes these two senses of guessing as *raten* and *erraten*). Erratic thought it may be, but it is still a kind of knowledge, or the similitude of one at least. A close relative of the word 'guess' is 'conjecture', a word which in the fourteenth century was much closer to 'conjuration' than it is now. In the rendering of Daniel 2:5 in the Wycliffite Bible, Nebuchadnezzar says to the Chaldeans charged with the expounding of his dreams: '3e shuln shewe to me the sweuen, and the coniecturyng, or menyng therof' (you shall explain the dream and its portending or intent), and as late as 1580 a French–English dictionary could still gloss *devinement* as 'coniecturing, diuination, soothsaying'.[36] In this sense, guessing is a kind of prophecy which aims to tease out the knowledge of the not-yet by forcing it into present existence. As discussed above, this forcing out of truth from indeterminacy is intrinsic to the riddle, which is why riddles only have one answer that will count as correct, even though most riddles are in fact susceptible of many correct answers. A riddle is a device for producing determinacy from indeterminacy; in Huizinga's words, it 'forces the hand of the gods'.[37] Sarah Iles Johnston sees the inter- action of prophecy, riddle and interpretation in the messages of the Greek oracle – which were always delivered in the form of riddling utterances that had themselves to be interpreted – as involving a series of reductions:

> divination, as it played out at Delphi, was not so much a matter of *solving* a problem as it was of *redirecting* a problem out of a world that human enquirers could only imagine into a world in which their actions could have concrete effects.[38]

To understand the most powerful and significant feature of riddling behaviour in human society we need to return to Johan Huizinga, who sees the riddle as forming a link between 'playing and knowing'.[39] Huizinga sees wisdom and frivolity as bound together in the earliest forms of sacred wisdom contest which he believes leave their trace in the paradoxical cosmogonic hymns of the Rigveda and in the riddle contest between Odin and the wise giant Vafþrúðnir in the *Vafþrúðnismál*. Huizinga asserts,

> we must not think of seriousness degenerating into play or of play rising to the level of seriousness. It is rather that civil- ization gradually brings about a certain division between two modes of mental life which we distinguish as play and seri- ousness respectively, but which originally formed a continuous mental medium wherein that civilization arose.[40]

Huizinga sees the origin of human wisdom in 'sacred game'.[41] It may be that knowledge and play have never really fallen apart, though not because we should view the act of playing as sacred, but because it does not seem possible to think knowledge otherwise than through play. Huizinga sees ancient wisdom-games as echoing a world view in which the principle of strife was preeminent. But the games of quisition make knowledge itself part of the agonistic picture it enshrines, so that the knowledge that would capture the contrariety of things is caught up in it. Perhaps the work of quisition helps us see that all knowing is playing at knowing. This is not because all knowledge is pretence or pseudo-knowledge, but because we know nothing of knowledge until and unless we can put it into play, and play it out. Walter Ong makes sense of the intriguing fact that the Latin word for school, *ludus*, also means a game. This should not suggest that school is regarded as a place of unattached pleasure or distraction, but rather that the play activity of school is to be regarded as a preparation for the battles and challenges of life. This is a way of thinking that, according to Ong, was particularly marked through the teaching of Latin, which was central to the creation of a tribal academic culture based upon rigour, threat and assertion.[42] The formation of the distinctively 'agonistic noetic' character of academic life in Europe means that students were not taught in a way that encouraged 'objectivity' (that ferociously contested notion), but 'to take a stand in favor of a thesis or to attack a thesis that someone else defended . . . They learned subjects largely by fighting over them.'[43] Even today, few words bristle with more academic menace, or are less likely to be used in any way that might be characterized as neutral and objective, than the words 'logic' or 'illogical'.

Quisition is one of the ways in which we requisition knowledge, conjure it up in conjecture. Most importantly of all, quisition temporalizes knowledge, stretching knowing out into coming-to-know. Human knowledge is typically ranged against time: it is won from time and allows us to step outside time and command it. And yet knowledge must always be deployed in time too. The play of question and answer seems to enact this play, in the sense of the play of a joint; the extent of variation possible. This may be why knowledge contests so often operate within time limits – the answer must be given by sunset, or within some given period. Indeed, perhaps time is always in fact knowledge's adversary in knowledge contests. To put knowledge into play is to play it out in the time that it hopes to command but must always emerge from and be immersed in. To play is both to suspend and to inhabit time. Playing is the time of thought that always animates and erodes the thought of time.

Many riddle contests seem to involve a contest between wit or wile on the one hand and death, often in the form of being eaten, on the other. Oedipus and the Sphinx is here typical of the set-up. Guile will always tend to win out over force in narrative presumably because narrative is itself formed of contrivance and so disposed to take contrivance's side. But guile is not the opposite of force, rather it is a modality of it and knowledge in the service of force or victory may be regarded as the ruse of force, which dissimulates itself in dissimulation. Nature may move from hard to soft, from force to form, and from physics to information, but that does not make a cyberattack that destroys a financial or healthcare computing system any less lethal. Soft victory can still bring about hard defeat. If knowledge is a kind of playful force, diverting force into ruse, it can often thereby play at being mere play. Playing at knowing may be a knowing play. Indeed, it is very hard to imagine a human relation to knowing that is entirely free of the will to win, even if it dissimulates itself in the seemingly peaceable will to win out over winning and losing themselves.

During the twentieth century, riddles begin to be more and more closely connected with secrecy and obscurity, especially in the fields of art and literature. But both the 'rhetorics of obscurity' which Brian Tucker believes are shared by Romantic literature and psychoanalysis, and the particular kinds of obscurity which Daniel Tiffany shows are characteristic of modern lyric, have an agonistic dimension in the fact that their obscurity is a public act: not an open secret, perhaps, but an openly aggressive challenge to the reader or viewer, accompanied by a demand that they attend to the riddle.[44] Tucker writes of 'a new relationship between language and knowledge, one in which the ideal is no longer communicative clarity but rather noncommunicative obscurity. Resistance, delay, and privation come to be the index of the superior text, figure, or sign.'[45] Such a formulation does not seem to wish to account for its own excitement at the prospect. Epistemologically, the tonality of such a condition is earnest and austere. In epistemopathic terms, the idea of the riddle-text and the riddle-self seem to represent a voluptuous prospect of analytic self-pleasuring.

THE FULL HALF-HOUR

Over the course of the last millennium the structure of quisition that is embodied in the riddle contest has spread and solidified into two different but related forms: on the one hand the structures of knowledge and learning, as characterized by various kinds of formal debate and disquisition; and, on the other, the diverse forms of quiz and puzzle entertainment. These may seem to have little to do with each other, the one being devoted to an ideal of truth-seeking through dialogue, the other being a form of trivial amusement, but both are part of the investment of the idea of knowledge in and as contention.

Formal philosophical disputation has its beginnings in the Socratic dialogues recorded by Plato. Indeed, we may say that the kind of formal, sustained reflection we think of as philosophy begins in contention. This tradition passed from the classical into the Christian world of medieval Europe from around the eleventh century, in the formal disputations that became common ways of investigating matters of religious disagreement and of communicating knowledge in the universities that were then beginning to form in Europe. Not only was the disputation the bearer of knowledge, it became itself the subject of close attention during the early modern period, with the production of prodigious numbers of seventeenth- and eighteenth-century texts devoted to the explication of the *ars disputandi*.[46]

The prefix *dis-* of disputation does complex work. Its primary meaning is to suggest that which pulls in contrary directions, the word being related to Greek *bis*, two, and therefore to the idea of duality. Varro, the Roman historian of language, thought the essential principle of disputation was that of a separation of the pure from the impure, deriving from the arborist's practice of pruning, the principal meaning of Latin *putare* being to purge or purify (the other surviving text of Varro, alongside his *De lingua latina*, is *Rerum rusticarum*, or *Agricultural Topics*):

> *Disputatio* 'discussion' and *computatio* 'reckoning,' from the general idea of *putare*, which means to make *purum* 'clean'; for the ancients used *putum* to mean *purum*. Therefore *putator* 'trimmer', because he makes trees clean; therefore a business account is said *putari* 'to be adjusted,' in which the sum is *pura* 'net.' So also that discourse in which the words are arranged *pure* 'neatly,' that it may not be confused and that it may be transparent of meaning, is said *disputare* 'to discuss' a problem or question.[47]

But *dis-* also develops increasingly the sense of a more generalized movement away from a given condition, as in *dispersal*, along with the intensive idea of something pushed to an extremity or limit, as in *dissolution*. The disputation seems to take both of these directions: it retains something of the bilateral encounter still suggested by the word 'dispute', but also gathers the sense of a complete and formalized examination of all relevant possibilities. Disputation can never be entirely peaceful, but its movement in all possible directions allows it to spread out the thymotic investments in conflict in such a way as to move thought away from the possibility of action. Its function is literally to be more and more beside the point. This history is nicely embodied in the word *dissertation*, nowadays used as an alternative to a thesis, the latter word signifying the taking or occupation of a position, and therefore standing one's ground. But *dissertate* existed in earlier periods as a verb, from *disserere*, *dis* + *serere*, to sow (seeds), distribute or arrange, the *dis-* therefore seeming to mean to spread out or set forth in order, in a kind of saturated propagation. Varro writes that:

> Our word *disserit* is used in a figurative meaning as well as in relation to the fields: for as the kitchen-gardener *disserit* 'distributes' the things of each kind upon his garden plots, so he who does the like in speaking is *disertus* 'skilful.' *Sermo* 'conversation,' I think, is from *series* 'succession,' whence *serta* 'garlands'; and moreover in the case of a garment *sartum* 'patched,' because it is held together.[48]

Thinking in conflict deploys play in order to balance aggression and the will to knowing-power on the one hand and peaceful conversation on the other. Such a view sees thinking as a radiation rather than sharpening to a penetrative point. The point of such exchanges is to keep the issue going, to defer conclusion and keep questions in play.

The disputation became ever more central to the conduct of academic life, with the requirement to dispute in public being prescribed in the statutes of the universities of Paris and Oxford by the thirteenth century.[49] The single most important form of examination for a university degree was the final disputation, in which a student demonstrated his fitness to be a citizen of 'the academic republic'.[50] But it is important to recognize the conspicuous amount of play in their constitution and conduct. Disputations took place in front of active and engaged audiences, which gave a considerable element of theatre to the proceedings. Medieval disputations often took place on feast days and public holidays, especially Lent and Advent, with dignitaries being invited to attend.[51] Disputants with a reputation for skilled and engaging performance would attract attentive audiences who, without any need for jeering, catcalling or applause (though these may indeed have featured at times), would have played their part in the working through of the argument. The disputation was a display of intellection and argument, meaning that proofs and objections were not just deployed but also performed, that is, set out in exemplary fashion as the warrants of their own force. The argument is the proof in practice of arguability.

A disputation is supposed to be a discussion between two or more interlocutors in which each sets out their own views and defends them against those of their opponents. This implies that having views is a straightforward sort of matter compared with the business of knowing which of those views is to be regarded as correct. But does anyone have a clear sense of what it means or feels like to have a view, and how does one know what that is? We act as though we think that opinions are the cause of disagreements; when a moment's honest review will suggest that disagreements are in fact the generator of opinions. This is why disputations can so readily be staged: announced in advance and formally arranged, rather than arising spontaneously out of the clash of already-formed opinions. But it is also the reason that, just as with our questions discussed by modern debating societies or TV programmes, medieval disputations could be quodlibetal, that is, focused on any topic whatever suggested by members of the audience and formally put to the question. Not surprisingly, the capacity of academics to generate a formal disputation from any question at all meant that, like many of the Latin terms associated with the academic discussion, 'quodlibet' came to mean an obscure and minor quibble, a word which it may very well have influenced. Disputations are not ways of coming to know the truth of any kind of matter; they are ways of convincing oneself of the truth that one has certain views that may stand out in specifiable ways from those of others. Disputations are ways of getting to think you know what the things are that you know you think. They are also ways of organizing or disposing those views into regulated patterns, and so conjugating disagreement.

One of the problems for historians aiming to reconstruct disputations is that what we know of them is largely contained either in prescriptions for their conduct, or in written records, often prepared by less than impartial witnesses and sometimes even by one of the participants. It is a difficult matter to construct anything like the experience of the disputations from these proleptic or retrospective representations – it does not matter who is on the committee, as the modern formula has it, what matters is who writes the minutes. And yet it may not be a simple matter to distinguish between the here-and-now oral actuality of the dissertation and the written reconstruction of it. Robin Whelan writes that '[a]s a mode of polemical argumentation, imaginary dialogue is ubiquitous in late antique Christian literature. Disputants were prone to reinvent rivals in the texts they wrote against them.'[52] Actual disputations are inflected by the many imaginary disputations with which the participants will have been familiar. This kind of virtual dialogue would include forms of self-performance in the course of the disputation: 'one's persona was as much a part of polemic (both as a weapon and as the subject of discussion) as one's command of language and biblical expertise.'[53] For the formality of the disputation means that in a certain sense the agon over the question at issue is always shadowed by a secondary agon over the nature and meaning of the disputation itself. This is encouraged by the formal recapitulations and encapsulations of voices that were a feature of the disputation; but the experience of almost any argument will confirm that the struggle for control of the argument – the struggle to establish oneself as the one who sees the terms of the argument most clearly – is a considerable part of its substance.

Perhaps the most important feature of a dispute is that it is promiscuously and compulsively self-propagating. The Latin word *arguare* derives from the Greek ἀργής (*arges*), white, and ἀργός (*argos*), bright, shining or glistening, as of a goose. *Argentum*, the Latin word for silver, preserved in the toponym Argentina, has the same derivation. The mythological hundred-eyed Argos is so called for the brightness of his eyes, and local newspapers borrow the name to signal percipience and keen observation. But argument has come to mean something very different, for an argument is more likely to lead to tangle and deadlock than to clarity and consensus. We rightly say that two people 'get into an argument' for the argument that they form between them quickly consumes them; you can only ever argue your corner if you have first been backed into it by your argument.

It is almost impossible to see the shape of a dispute from inside it. But this is not because none of the participants in an argument are paying attention to it. In fact, the amorphousness of an argument comes precisely from the fact that the participants in it are in fact deeply interested in defining its shape: one might even say that what one is arguing over in an argument is possession of the argument itself, as though the parties were struggling to gain a summit which would give an unbroken view of the whole toiled-over terrain. An argument is a roiling sea of interlocking and reciprocally resiling attributions. All arguments perform in the sense that they 'play at' the arguments they wish to be. Everything depends on how the argument is represented, even though the argument is nothing more than its representations.

There is a difference, of course, between a formal disputation and a spontaneous dispute. But it is a difference within each as well as between them, and a difference that is constitutive of both. The formal disputation is an attempt to provide an external shape for a process which threatens always to burst apart at the seams and is always growing internally from the middle. It may appear that here pure force is contained by form: by the ordering of turn-taking, for example, the fixing of roles or positions like that of proponent, opponent and chair (*praeses*, or president, 'first seat'). But unless there were the force of opposition animating the argument, which we might think of as the force of a desire to displace or depose a position, there could be no positions. There would be no force in these oppositions without a certain implied geometry of enmity. The architecture of adversarial form is both external and immanent to the actual argument. There is form in the force, and force generated from the form.

The Monty Python argument sketch, first broadcast on BBC TV on 2 November 1972, in which a man arrives at an agency wanting to pay to have an argument, demonstrates this principle very well. The absurdity of paying for an argument is that there seems at that point to be no point at issue, and so nothing to argue about. But having nothing to argue about is equivalent to being asked to argue about a quodlibet question, supplied by the audience of a Renaissance disputation. The client's interlocutor skilfully manipulates the formal exchange of civilities into a heated discussion of whether or not the client has already been told whether he is in the right room for an argument and then, by stubbornly and childishly gainsaying everything the client asserts, into the question of what actually constitutes an argument: simple controversion ('saying no all the time') or an honest and deliberative procedure – 'a connected series of statements intended to establish a proposition', as, quoting the OED definition, the hapless client insists. The client feels rooked because he comes up against somebody whose idea of an argument appears to be to contradict everything he says; but in the end is actually lured into just the kind of childish wielding of absolute, all-or-nothing eristic logic aimed at triumph rather than truth against which he has set his face, while his opponent suddenly seems to be the one offering careful and reasonable qualifications to absolute positions:

> MAN: Aha! Well if I didn't pay, why are you arguing . . . got you!
> MR VIBRATING: No you haven't.
> MAN: Yes I have . . . if you're arguing I must have paid.
> MR VIBRATING: Not necessarily. I could be arguing in my spare time.[54]

It is never easy to decide whether a given instance of noetic gaming, or playing at knowledge, is 'playing for real' or 'merely playing', since the oscillation between the two modes are part of what it means for knowledge to be in play.

Many elements of the disputation remain in place both in academic institutions and elsewhere. But it operates in a very different noetic landscape now from that which obtained at the beginning of this millennium. The most important feature of that landscape is the role of evidence in the formulation of knowledge. Medieval and Renaissance disputations depended principally on arguments, largely because at issue were metaphysical matters for which no clinching evidence was ever likely to be forthcoming; there might be new perspectives and interpretations, and these could be dramatic and unexpected, but they depended on the application of reason to an existing body of authoritative knowledge. This means that the really formative antagonism of the early modern period was not between science and religion but, counterintuitively, between science and reason. Ultimately, the dependence on interpretation rather than experiment privileged the agonistic noetic, since it seemed both to depend on and make possible the idea that one might have one's knowledge fully in mind, at one's fingertips or tongue's end. For all the apparent openness of the culture of disputation to putting things to the question, the agonism was fundamentally conservative, a fact that may have something to do with its oral nature, which privileged the here-and-now manipulation of the already known over the development of new ideas. One late guide to disputations asserted quite positively that 'the discovery of new things in truth is not possible' ('veritatis novae inventio . . . esse nequit') in academic disputations.[55] William Clark writes of the disputation that

> It aimed not at the production of new knowledge but rather at the rehearsal of established doctrines. What was produced – oral argument – was consumed on the premises. The disputation did not accumulate and circulate truth. It, rather, disaccumulated or dismantled possible or imagined error.[56]

This confirms Walter Ong's view of the fundamentally defensive nature of disputation:

> The universities remained even more oral [during the Renaissance], filled with disputation and declamation. What was taught, in physics for example, was a set of theses or positions felt as under permanent siege. Peter Ramus (1515–72) thought of his lectures on the various 'arts' (logic, arithmetic, and so on) not as positive explanations of the arts themselves, which were supposed to be limpidly clear because of the 'methodized' way they were presented, but as defences against his adversaries, real or imagined.[57]

Joshua Rodda agrees that the purpose of disputation in the Renaissance was to provide assurance not only of the truth but the verifiability of the truth which, despite its Catholic origins in scholasticism, made disputation as important for Protestants as for Catholics (that is, as long as the outcome could be assured, which was often achieved through the reporting of the disputation, as in the Westminster disputation of 1559 which was designed to show that Catholics had no grounds for complaint from the Acts of Supremacy and Uniformity).[58] Disputation therefore 'was the answer to human error; the means of crossing confessional bounds and testing doctrine by way of common, established authorities'.[59] Renaissance writers commonly followed Varro in deriving *disputation* from the horticultural practice of pruning away dead or diseased branches. The defensive agonistics of disputation mean that it was often engaged in a work of amputation, as error and falsity are pared away from truth; the word 'amputation' seems to have entered English as a Latinate invention, the earliest appearance in print being in 1609, in which it is said of heretical sects that 'The crime of heresy, and schisme doth amputate them (for the most part) from the blessed communion of the CATHOLICK Church.'[60]

The growth of experimental science produced a huge and constantly renewing stock of data which outstripped the capacity of any individual to encompass it. This calmed down many of the charismatic features of the disputation. From now on knowledge could not be produced and made present in the here and now of the disputation but would be forced to operate in textual networks. Gradually, over a number of centuries, the oral disputation has given way to the text of the dissertation. Ku-ming Chang observes that 'The more the dissertation became self-contained as a text, the more its authorship belonged to an individual, and the more it was detached from the experiential and communal form of presentation characteristic of medieval disputation.'[61] The written dissertation can certainly be adversarial, and one might even say that the absence of an interlocutor makes discursive violence much easier. During the late eighteenth century, oral disputations began to give way, earliest of all perhaps in the University of Cambridge, to written examinations as a way of admitting students to degrees, with a transitional phase during which questions would still be dictated to examination candidates. William Clark observes that the apparent cooling of the written mode could in fact involve its own kind of brutality:

> The traditional exam had been heroic oral theatre, analogized by jurists to the three trials of a crowned athlete in Roman law. That heroic theatre, colored by metaphors of blood and ordeal, seems to have hurt few. The modern exam has become a mundane, meritocratic exam associated with sweat and labor, but it can make one nearly 'sick to death'.[62]

Even today, the process of examination for higher degrees in Northern European countries remains highly formalized, with the process, which takes place in front of an audience, being called a 'defence' and examiners still often being called 'opponents'. The practice in the UK is for examiners to interrogate a doctoral candidate *in viva voce*, but in private (though it is still announced as a 'public examination' in Oxford and one is required to wear academic dress for the occasion). And yet the somewhat absurd theatricality of the formal public defence also contains its own self-immunization against threat and terror. In such circumstances, the thesis has often been published, and may already in fact have been passed, and candidates will have had the opportunity to familiarize themselves with the process through attending their contemporaries' defences. By contrast, it is very hard for candidates exposed to the British style of doctoral viva to know what to expect. The participants in a more formal disputation style of viva know, as they perhaps would have known in the medieval university, that they had to put on some kind of show together. The fact of display can be a kind of deterrence of threat.

There is something magical in the process of logical deduction, since it suggests that it may be possible, by simple sorting of propositions, to generate knowledge that has lain hidden but undetected within the fabric or ordinary speech and assumption. The world assumed by deductive reason is simultaneously a closed plenum and infinitely expansible. So the logic of scholastic disputation is really the logic of the riddle, in which seemingly unknown or occult qualities can be explicated by the riddling or sieving of existing elements. It is, following the formulation by Cora Diamond referred to earlier in this chapter, the generation of a new dimension of space from within an existing space, rather than an extension outwards into existing space. This perhaps accounts for the extraordinary powers of persistence of the disputation, traces of which may still be seen in academic examinations all over the world: the disputation apparently allows any topic to be broached and encompassed, in an infinitely elastic method which ensures that nothing need ever change in its essentials.

Interpretation and evidence are complementary, for there must be something to interpret, and no evidence can be self-interpreting. But disputation may be thought of as inclensive, or inwardly self-propagating, through the principle of redundancy and self-reference (leading to the interestingly convoluted condition of being, as popular usage has it, 'up yourself'), while evidence is declensive, in that it permits outwards propagation. The history of the disputation has attracted a lot of attention from scholars in recent years, and there is a great deal of absorbing material to consider during the long history of formal disputation that runs from its Socratic beginnings through to its eventual decline in the eighteenth century. So absorbing is this history that it is easy for those engaged not to recognize its essential quality and function of intellectual absorptiveness. The craziness of the disputation lies in the fact that it failed to resolve anything, and in fact is designed never to. The game relation to knowledge allows the same competitions to be had over and over again, over hundreds of years. If knowledge of the truth were really the aim and outcome of disputation there would be no need for this, since questions could be regarded as able to be settled. But human beings seem more interested in sustaining than settling questions, especially in circumstances where various kinds of faith require to be upheld. What disputations allowed was the feeling of having won though to the truth, through the purgation of error, when their purpose is the deterrence of thought about all the questions that might in fact occur to a rational person – all the things, in fact, about which *non est disputandum*. Disputations exist to perform the idea of reason through a narrative of jeopardy repeatedly confronted and overcome. Knowledge is made to seem to matter through a process that ensures it does not get close to anything that might really matter at all. The institution of the quodlibetal disputation in the thirteenth century was the demonstration of the confidence that the institution of dispute could survive any conceivable challenge, and also the clearest possible demonstration of the phantasmal nature of its operations. The fact that so many thought, and said so openly, that disputation was a frivolous waste of time that served only to inflame pride, envy and contempt, was itself drawn into the immunological play of the disputation. In the end, the only thing that could defeat disputation was people getting bored with it, or more excited by other things: hostility to disputation only fed the libido of quasi-contention.

One might suggest that the culture of formal disputation that became identified with the Schoolmen – who prized what Milton in his *On Education* (1644) decried as 'the scholastic grossness of barbarous ages, that . . . present their young unmatriculated novices at first coming with the most intellective abstractions of logic and metaphysics' – was a kind of excess of structure over content.[63] In fact, it became identified with the intensive focus on the learning of the classical languages, rather than on what they might convey. Lorraine Daston suggests that in the work of Francis Bacon and others in the early seventeenth century the authority of axioms and universal systems gave way to the authority of the 'deracinated particular', which became 'the indubitable core of knowledge'.[64] Facts of this kind which, as Mary Poovey (1998) argues, will increasingly take the form of numbers of various kinds, would from 1630 be called 'data', a word designed to borrow from the authority of Latin, though not in fact used in this sense in Latin.[65]

Modern forms of quisition arose corresponding to the disputation but adapted to the new world of accumulated facts rather than interpretative capacity. The first of these was the examination, which began to take the place of the formal disputation in universities. Though the phrase 'general knowledge' was a common enough pairing from the seventeenth century onwards, it began to be used as a formula in the naming of examination papers at the beginning of the twentieth century.

Early in the eighteenth century the term 'gerund-grinder' starts to be used to refer to a dull pedagogue. The phrase seems to have appeared in print for the first time in 1708, in the dedication to Oswald Dykes's *Moral Reflexions Upon Select British Proverbs*, in which its author described himself as 'a *poor Gerund-Grinder*, or a *Haberdasher of Nouns and Verbs*'.[66] Among the 'Sages and Virtuosoes of all Sects' who attend a dissenters' wedding dinner is 'Cl—s, the walking Gerund-grinder, a noisie wrangling Sophist, whom his Scholars therefore called the *two-edg'd Cutter*'.[67] By the beginning of the nineteenth century, the expression was commonly shortened to 'grinder' and used interchangeably with 'crammer', their particular purpose being to prepare students mechanically for examination. Their first appearance in print is from the mouth of the headstrong young Buckhurst Falconer, who is trying to persuade his father to train up his dunce brother for the church rather than him: "'Put him into the hands of a clever grinder, or crammer, and they would soon cram the necessary portion of latin and greek into him, and they would get him through the university for us readily enough".'[68] Where the Schoolmen had inculcated a kind of dialectical form immaculately empty of fact, it became a received idea during the nineteenth century that children were being tortured by the need to imbibe and emit formless facts – grist rather than Geist.

QUIZ

But the idea of general knowledge passed during the second half of the century from formal examination to the curious kind of entertainment known as the 'quiz'. The origins of the word *quiz* are uncertain, in a way that seems to make it quizzically self-designating. The word seems to have come into circulation during the last two decades of the eighteenth century and to have been applied originally to an oddity or slightly ridiculous eccentric, especially in relation to appearance. A comic poem in the *Britannic Magazine* for 1795 advises, 'A man of fashion – nothing but a *quiz* / I'll tell you what a man of fashion is'.[69] A satirical song by G. S. Carey of 1800 tells us: 'The Quaker's a very queer kind of a quiz, / His back so erect and so prim in his phiz'.[70] The word remained a staple of satirical comic verse, as in Charles Dibdin's *Mirth and Metre* (1807), George Daniel's *Democritus in London* (1852) and the poems of Thomas Hood (1799–1845). Byron was rather fond of the word, which makes for a slangy counterpoint to 'metaphysical' in *Don Juan*:

> But I am apt to grow too metaphysical:
> 'The time is out of joint,' – and so am I;
> I quite forget this poem's merely quizzical,
> And deviate into matters rather dry.[71]

Used as a verb, to quiz meant to ridicule, tease or chaff, in a seeming inversion, for one would probably quiz someone or something you took for a quiz: thus, Don Juan, following a ghostly apparition, 'Pondered upon his visitant or vision, / And whether it ought not to be disclosed, / At risk of being quizzed for superstition'.[72] This encouraged Thomas Moore, in his *Life* of Byron, to remark that 'there is so much of the *quizzible* in all he writes, that I never can put on the proper pathetic face in reading him.'[73] Accordingly, a quiz could be somebody inclined to quiz in this way, rather than its object, as in John Collins's poem from his comic collection *Scripscrapologia* of 1804:

> And so, for Thrift, I turn'd my Coat, a good Turn when
>   we're needy,

And then I got it turn'd again, because it look'd so seedy;
Which, when a Quiz was staring at, says I, 'Don't make
   a Pother'.[74]

The later interrogative meaning of quizzing may be anticipated in the fact that the teasing or ribbing involved in it seemed sometimes to take the form of bewildering questions. An old man complained in these terms in the comic journal *The Quiz* in 1797:

> wherever I appear, I am sure of being accosted by one of these Quizzers, as one of his acquaintance; my confusion, and his effrontery, are the cream of the jest; and I am always left, after a few bamboozling questions, with a loud laugh, and a 'damme he's fairly quizzed'.[75]

Charles Dibdin introduced his comic entertainment *The Quizes, or A Trip to Elysium* in 1793 with a song entitled 'The Etymology of Quiz', which reflects rather sharply on the inversiveness that is a feature of the quiz, in which all that is required to be a quiz is to seem quizzible to a quizzer:

> At this same play of quiz each loses and wins,
> Ins are quizzes to outs and outs quizzes to ins,
> Honest men are all quizzes to rogues, then again,
> All rogues appear quizzes to all honest men,
>
> Beaux are quizzes to slovens, and slovens to beaux,
> Rich to poor, poor to rich, and 'tis thus the world goes.
> In short, every creature to some other is
> The present company excepted a monsterous quiz.[76]

The word vaguely suggests Latin origins, given the many words that end in *-quis* and *-quibus*, along with the *qui* of words like *quod-libetal* and *quibble*. Hamlet muses in the graveyard: 'Why may not that be the skull of a lawyer? Where be his quiddities now, his quillets?' (Act v, Scene 1). The associations with Latin *quis*, 'who', made it a popular choice for anonymous authors (The Doctor of *Doctor Who* would probably qualify as a quiz in early nineteenth-century terms). A satirical letter pretending to be from newspaper editors calling for '"*ready-made news*" for the ensuing summer' in 1809 is signed 'Quiddity Quiz, Humbug Row'.[77] Quiz was also a popular name for racehorses, pet dogs and, oddly, steamships. *The Hamiltoniad*, John Williams's satirical assault of 1804 on Alexander Hamilton, provides for Horace's proverbial 'Vir bonus est quis?', 'who is the good man?' (*Epistulae* 1.16.40), the dog-Latin translation 'The good man's a political *Quiz*'.[78]

The Latin feel of the word *quiz* accords with the fact that it seems to have its origin in the mockery of academic types. It features as part of an undergraduate's slang in Richard Polwhele's 'The Follies of Oxford' (1785), and one of the earliest explanations of its meaning is in a pamphlet entitled *Advice to the Universities of Oxford and Cambridge* (1783), which begins with the claim that it was 'the University, from whence I believe this amphibious creature originally sprung'.[79] The Quiz is described as 'one of those dull, pedantic, spiritless animals, who jog on in the same beaten track, pulled along, as it were, by rules, and frightened, every step he advances, with a continual terror of sconces and impositions'.[80] His leading characteristic is his desire to be taken for a deep and assiduous scholar:

> If he is tired of being in his room all the morning, let him not stir, on any account, within the walls of the college, without a large Greek folio under his arm, appearing to muse, every step he advances, on some intricate point of dispute, or on some subject the most dry and remote from common observation . . . Whilst his room is cleaning out, let him handle his folio again, which should be always ready for that purpose, and march, reading, with slow step, up and down the quadrangle; observing to chuse that part opposite his tutor's window, and to have his book open towards the latter end . . . In his conversation, he should assume the air of a pedant, by studying it long before he attempts to speak, and taking care always to select words the most remote from common use.[81]

It may not be that this sort of academic quirkiness can stand for every kind of quiz at this point in the development of the term, as the author seems to acknowledge, even as he restates the association between the academic and the quizzical. 'What I have said concerning a *Quiz*, may seem to appertain chiefly to the character of a pedant;

but, upon observation, I believe a very great compound of pedantry will always be found in the materials of a *Quiz*.[82] Further evidence of the association of the quiz with academic pedantry is found in a 1794 spoof 'Address to the Freshmen of the University of Cambridge' signed by one 'Quizicus'. It begins by remarking that his audience 'have all heard, and have all ridiculed the idea of a *Quiz*; no doubt but that all of you have been admonished by some *good friend* or other, not to rank yourself in that degraded class'.[83] It then goes on to give a definition of the term, explaining that:

> By a Quiz, according to the original meaning of the word, was meant a rigid disciplinarian, or one, who having attained all the goods of this world he could either expect or wish for, would in defiance of every custom and of all society pursue his one peculiar plan.[84]

The explication then offered of what is said to be the current meaning of the word suggests that it was the equivalent of a swot (this a variant of 'sweat' that would not appear until 1850).

> Now every young man who wishes to attain that for which he was sent by his friends to the university, namely *improvement*, is immediately denominated a Quiz, and is subject to the petty insults of every buck (a species of the human kind so called in Cambridge) he meets with.[85]

The only way for a new student to avoid the accusation of quizicality, explains 'Quizicus', would be for him to fling himself into dissipation and extravagance.

The fortunes of the word *quiz* seem bound up with the popular force of the letter 'z', stigmatized in *King Lear* as 'thou whoreson zed! Thou unnecessary letter' (Act II, Scene 2), because it did not feature in Latin except when it was used to signify words of foreign, especially Greek, origin, thus being suggestive of the outlandish.[86] Z tends to prolong and propagate itself, as in the words that open Samuel Pratt's comic poem 'The Modern Hercules' of 1805: 'Except that muzzy Quiz, an Owl, / A Goose seems Nature's silliest Fowl'.[87] Alexander Rodger's 'A Clerical Canticle' urges: 'Let's try our bit clerical dance, / To quiz and bamboozle the people'.[88] The comic writer

'Momus Medlar' produced a couple of issues of a magazine called *The Quiz-quozian Gazette* in 1813. There seem to have been a number of short-lived comic magazines entitled *Quiz*, and in 1879 *The Times* reported on the prosecution of John Rochfort for intending to publish an 'immoral and indecent publication called *Quiz*'; a newsagent named James Simpson was similarly prosecuted 'for selling obscene papers – *Quiz* and the *London Peep Show*'.[89]

In 1835, a story emerged claiming to account for the origin of the word *quiz*, the stages of development of which have been well-documented by Alex Boese at his Museum of Hoaxes website.[90] The earliest version of the story appeared in the *London and Paris Observer*. Its opening observations raise the stakes extravagantly high:

> Very few words ever took such a run, or was saddled with so many meanings, as this monosyllable: and, however strange the word, 'tis still more strange that not one of our lexicographers, from Bayley to Johnson, ever attempted an explanation, or gave a derivation of it. The reason is very obvious. It is because it has no meaning, nor is it derived from any language in the world, ever known from the Babylonish confusion to this day.[91]

The story then explained that Richard Daly, a Dublin theatre proprietor, laid a bet that he could introduce by the following day 'a word having no meaning, and being derived from no known language'.[92] To win the bet, he sent out all his theatre employees to chalk the word 'quiz' on every door and shop window in town. The piece concludes that 'the circumstance of so strange a word being on every door and window caused much surprise, and ever since, should a strange story be attempted to be passed current, it draws forth the expression – *you are quizzing me*'.[93] The story was reproduced in a slightly compressed form over the initials 'S. T. B.' in *The Mirror of Literature, Amusement, and Instruction* a week later, and appeared again in the *New York Mirror* on 2 May 1835. Of course, this story of a hoax is itself a hoax, or, according to the final definition of the word it offers, a quiz.

And yet there may be something more to this hoax. Ben Zimmer points to evidence that some such phenomenon as that confected in 1835 did in fact occur, namely the appearance of a mysterious word chalked on shutters and doors – the word was not *quiz*, however, but *quoz*.[94] The London newspaper *The World* reported on 15 August 1789 that two gentlemen had bet that 'one of them should fix upon any absurd expression, which should, in a given time, become the *Town Talk*'.[95] The article reports that the campaign began simply by the chalking of the word on doors, but was then elaborated, as 'Future wits and more ingenious heads, improved on the idea, and added various other strokes of humour to the *original* QUOZ'.[96] The paper presents various other examples from other front doors, either authentic or of its own devising. Whether or not they were mystifying at the time, they certainly succeed in being so today:

> Mrs. ABINGDON's *Lodgings – Belinda, Arabella, Araminta*, and youth that is immortal, is all – QUOZ.
> Lady A—R's – A man with *two faces* was once called *Janus*. What shall we call a Lady? – QUOZ.
> Counsellor GARROW's – Give you a bad cause and a cross-examination, and nobody does more than – QUOZ.
> Hon. Mr. ERSKINE's – When you get your *true John* for a Juryman, he believes you are serious and in earnest. But if you lay hold of a line a little beyond that – why then – QUIZ finds out – QUOZ.[97]

A week later, on 22 August, there was an announcement in the same newssheet for a farce at the Haymarket Theatre, London, entitled *Duke and No Duke; or, Trappolin's Vagaries*, which would include a song by John Edwin entitled 'Quoz'.[98] If the quoz rumour was set up as part of the publicity vehicle for the show, it would not be the first time such a campaign was run. The song itself made an appearance on 5 September in the newspaper *The Diary; or, Woodfall's Register*:

> Walk about the town, each time you turn your head, Sir,
> Pop staring in your phiz, is Q, U, O, and Z, Sir:
> Cried, Madam Dip to deary, its monstrous scandaloz
> To write on peoples shutters that shameful, nasty, Quoz . . .
> Tipsy, dizzy, muzzy, sucky, groggy, muddled,
> Bosky, bund as Chloe; mops and brooms, and fuddled,
> Florid, torrid, horrid; stayboz, heyboz, layboz,
> Words with terminations not so good as Quoz . . .

Some may think it French, some may call it Latin,
Some give in this meaning, other will give that in:
Mean it what it will, or sense or *non compos*,
The meaning, I should think – the meaning must be
    – Quoz.[99]

The phrase was even alluded to in the following year by Tom Paine in his *Rights of Man* (1792), which complains that the word 'constitution' is as vague in its meaning and as magical in its performative effect as the word 'quoz' (though for the opposite reason, since the point about the constitution is that it is not written down): 'It has got into circulation like the words *bore* and *quoz*, by being chalked up in the speeches of parliament, as those words were on window-shutters and door-posts.'[100]

These phrases are in fact much more mystifying than the simple appearance of the word 'quoz' might have been. They have a slight air of menace akin to that of the mysterious postcard that recurs through James Joyce's *Ulysses* that reads: 'U.P.: up'.[101] Quoz seems to add to quiz the meaning of bosh, nonsense or nothingness. The reference is entirely performative, naming the act of naming nothing that becomes something through the sheer fact of being multiplied.

At some point during the 1860s, probably in the USA, quizzing made the transition from teasing or twitting to inspecting closely, or interrogating. Perhaps the transition was helped by what was known as the 'quizzing glass', a single, hand-held lens that became popular in the late eighteenth century, often among the kinds of affected men known as 'exquisites'. The quizzing glass seems to be referred to in print for the first time in 1802, in a report in the *European Magazine and London Review* of June 1802, which described a gala in celebration of the peace agreements signed by Napoleon at Ranelagh Gardens, in which the raffle had as prizes 'shawls, parasols, handkerchiefs, quizzing glasses, &c.'[102] In his 1836 *Walker Remodelled: A New Critical Pronouncing Dictionary of the English Language*, B. H. Smart defined 'quiz' as 'something to puzzle; one whom an observer cannot make out, an odd fellow', and 'quizzing' as 'The act of mocking by a narrow examination, or by pretended seriousness of discourse'.[103] He offered the example 'Fitted for quizzing', adding that 'a *quizzing-glass* is an eye-glass'.[104] The phrenologist George Combe wrote in 1839 that many of his friends came to see his large collection of head-casts, 'some to examine, and some to quiz', a phrase that, in contrasting serious examination with ridicule, also associates them.[105] Pretended scrutiny seems to have started to be, or be taken to be, serious examination, and the quiz moved from inspection to inquisition.

The suggestion that is was in the USA that quizzing may have first become questioning rather than teasing is reinforced by the fact that the first use of the word in this sense in *The Times* is in a contribution from their American correspondent dated 29 August 1873, discussing whether President Grant was likely to again be nominated for election in 1876: 'If the newspapers wanted to know whether he would be re-nominated, they ought to quiz the party that elected him.'[106]

The quiz marks the surprising translation of the regime of inquisition embodied in the academic examination into popular culture. The first quizzes and puzzles appeared in newspapers and popular magazines: among their early exponents was Lewis Carroll, who compulsively invented puzzles all through his life, though neither the word *quiz* nor any of its associated forms seems to appear in his published works. Quizzes as popular entertainment then became a mainstay of radio, especially in the USA, where the first radio quiz show, *Professor Quiz*, began in 1936.[107]

Perhaps the quiz is a testing of the possibility not so much of general knowledge as of common knowledge. Human groups are held together not just by customs and institutions but by what they can assume that others in the group know. A shared familiarity with the work of Shakespeare, for example, has given way to micro-knowledges held in common by different generational, ethnic and taste communities. An interest in sport, or a devotion to a particular team, is likely to involve the commitment to absorbing prodigious amounts of information. This kind of knowledge may have the same kind of inclusion and exclusion function as the knowledge of riddles. The use-value of such knowledge is wholly social: its advantage is that one is in the know about certain defining and socially cohering fields of information. Such knowledge is practical-symbolic. It is symbolic because it does not bear directly on the conduct of life – making a living, negotiating the conditions of modern transport, commerce and communication – but symbolizes a particular social affiliation; yet it is also wholly practical, in that such symbolic knowledge-affiliations form much of the weave of modern social existence. The role of the celebrity, for example, seems predominantly to be heard of and known about, and therefore to form part of this fund of common reference and exchange.

The phrase 'common knowledge' has subtly shifted its emphasis. During the nineteenth century the phrase tended to be used to indicate not the range but the level of knowledge, for example to contrast unspecialized with more specialized kinds of knowledge: 'we think it requires no more than a common knowledge of cause and effect, to perceive that elements are now combining, which cannot fail to produce the most serious effects.'[108] Common knowledge was often paired with 'common sense', as in the statement in 1848 that 'What is meant by "good sense" is clear; we understand a vigilant presiding reason, having the common knowledge of the world in greater or less degree under its control.'[109] In 1852, we read that 'Sensible men past forty, who have acquired the common knowledge of dietetics, and are careful to avoid the causes of disease, very illiberally laugh at the Doctor'.[110] In 1867 *Scientific American* could look forward to 'a distant future of greater common knowledge and wealth'.[111]

Common knowledge is now much less likely to refer to un-exceptional or ordinary knowledge than it is to a generally dispersed knowledge, something that 'everybody knows' – often with the implication of a piece of gossip that it might have been better to have kept quiet. It is one of the odd effects of media society that this village way of thinking should in fact have become more rather than less common. Occasionally, the phrase is taken up in ways that suggest a more positive possibility for an ideal of communal knowledge-making, as for example in the Duke University Press journal *Common Knowledge*, which describes its aim as to form 'a new intellectual model, one based on conversation and cooperation rather than on metaphors (adopted from war and sports) of "sides" that one must "take"'. Despite this cooperative ideal, the editors feel obliged to assure its academic readers without delay that '[t]he pages of *Common Knowledge* regularly challenge the ways we think about scholarship and its relevance to humanity' – inviting the readers of *Common Knowledge* to cooperate in seeing cooperativeness as a challenge (presumably to all the unthinkingly pugnacious others who automatically see all academic discourse in terms of challenges).[112]

Quiz shows depend upon a kind of common knowledge that is not held in common as knowledge, or not as knowledge that is useful for anything else than for purposes of demonstration. Its role is to be, that is to stand for, an idea of 'knowledge' in just the same way, perhaps, as *quiz* and *quoz* came to stand as examples of mysterious and puzzling quiddities through their arbitrary vacancy.

This is the reason for one of the principles of the quiz, namely that there can be no question about the right answer. For, if quizzes really concerned matters of knowledge, their answers would always have to be approximate. The governing principles of the quiz are homogeneity and divisibility. The very fact that quizzes seem to allow for questions (and answers) about anything means that all the questions can be thought of as equivalent or precisely commensurable units, measurable in points or graduated cash prizes. And quiz questions can be asked of any category of knowledge just as long as they can be assigned securely to some category or other. Most importantly, even though question and answer are locked together as tightly as riddles and their solutions, those questions and answers must also be absolutely divisible. Quizmasters must pretend to be as nettled as prep-school History teachers by answers that take the form of a question – 'Is it Mary Queen of Scots?' 'Are you asking me or telling me, boy?' Anything other than a clear-cut answer – any probing, reflection, rumination or thinking out loud – is routinely forced into the condition of one: 'Is that your final answer?' 'I must take your first answer.'

Quizzes also mandate an absolute divisibility between right and wrong answers and therefore between winners and losers. In part this is to fulfil the demands of competition, for such all-or-nothing determinations are also required in most other forms of competition – a corner kick must be given one way or the other, a flukey or an easy goal scores exactly the same as a magnificent one, and you can be almost out in cricket only in the sense in which you can be 'a little bit' pregnant. In the world of the quiz, a question is anything for which an unquestionable answer may be supplied. The idea that a quiz might in fact allow for the asking of real questions – that is to say, questions rather than quisitions – seems to open onto the Kafkaesque nightmare of Forced Entertainment's performance *Quizoola!* (first performed 1996), in which members of the company are required over the course of a six-hour or sometimes 24-hour performance session to improvise answers to questions that can vary from the factual (What does an Eskimo look like? Name seven kinds of cheese) to the rhetorical (Who's the daddy? What's your problem with me?) and the metaphysical (Is there a Hell? Where are the dead?). In contrast to the peremptory rule that a blurted-out first answer must be accepted, one of the rules of *Quizoola!* is that an answer may be repeated until a satisfactory response is elicited, where it is not clear or given in advance what will count as satisfactory.

It would be easy to reduplicate the work of quiz shows in distinguishing between real knowledge and the play knowledge of the quiz, blaming it for the weakness of education and the infantile stupidity of the uneducated. In fact, quiz shows have been at pains to distinguish different strata of educational distinction and authority from the beginning. One of the most successful American radio quizzes was *Quiz Kids*, which ran from 1940–53, in which teenage children were given challenging questions to answer and puzzles to solve.[113] A brainy quiz like British TV's *QI*, which has a round smirkingly called General Ignorance, does just this, aiming to humiliate panel members who relapse into popular suppositions about such things as the rotation of water draining from sinks, and even giving extra points for candidates who correctly identify questions to which the answer is 'nobody knows'.

Strong claims have sometimes been made for quiz shows as what Olaf Hoerschelmann calls 'symbolic forms that produce and naturalize discourses on a variety of forms of knowledge'.[114] They are, he argues, 'a unique site where the validity of different forms of knowledge and practice is negotiated and are a central tool for the maintenance or disruption of educational and cultural hierarchies'.[115] It is certainly the case that quiz shows seem to play with the social expectations of the audience, especially in their projection of ordinariness: 'Real people with real emotion, these contestants are individuals whom viewers can briefly know and interact with', Thomas A. DeLong optimistically and undemandingly concludes at the end of his exploration of quiz shows.[116]

Nevertheless, the inquisition fantasy is deeply embedded in our understanding of what knowledge is. One of the bits of folk knowledge that quiz-show aficionados are supposed to have is that the set-up and music for *Mastermind* were designed by its deviser Bill Wright to recreate his experiences of interrogation as a war-time POW.[117] What scenario of truth-extortion can possibly be in the mind of someone who tells you 'I could not for the life of me give you the answer to that'? This opens up the hilarious prospect of the thumbscrews being applied, not to elicit your knowledge of intelligence networks, or your congress with the devil, but the nicknames of Romantic symphonies. The absurdity of the fantasy that your life might some day or in some way depend on your knowledge of bits of trivial and unrelated information seems to permit the fantasy to flourish and to fulfill its obscure need.

An important principle of quizzing is that one should not be able to prepare for it. Of course, there are contestants who dutifully pore over encyclopedias and collections of facts (along with books of quiz-show questions) in preparation for quizzes, but there is a sense in which this is to miss the point: while it may not constitute cheating, it is certainly rather bad form. Quiz shows tend to elicit knowledge that you did not know you had – which is why contestants make such a show of agonizing over questions that they are sure they ought to be able to answer ('Don't tell me . . . I *know* this, I *know* I do'). Quiz shows depend upon the modern experience of having a vast store of contingent and fragmentary bits of information, held in a sort of limbo between knowledge and ignorance, knowledge that hovers just under or on the edge of being known.

The quiz show is also characterized by the extreme tension within it between the pleasure of entertainment and intellectual ordeal. The capacity for shame is very great in quiz shows, especially those that, like the UK's *University Challenge*, seem to provide an opportunity for those who are supposed to be in the know to be shown up as frauds. Why do contestants feel the need so often to apologize for not knowing answers – 'I'm sorry, I just don't know'? This is perhaps related to the shame dynamic of the riddle alluded to earlier in this chapter.

It seems as though the adversarial dimension of knowledge remains an essential part of how knowledge comes to be known through performance. What is performed in the riddle, disputation or quiz is a curious kind of game-like seriousness. This framing of questions, and framing of knowledge as a matter of questions and answers, is a cognitive procedure. But, more importantly, it is a way of behaving in relation to knowledge – one might almost say a way of *behaving* knowledge, recalling the fifteenth-century formation of the word *behave* as the way in which you 'have yourself', in the sense of carrying yourself (a riddle relation if ever there was one), the way in which you comport yourself or give your existence its way of existing.

I began by stripping away prefixes from words like *enquire* and *require* to isolate the manner of knowledge-behaving, the way of giving knowledge a manner, that I called *quisition*. But there is always in fact a kind of requirement, a demand for acquisition, in enquiry. By putting questions to the world we put the world to the question, constituting and constantly reinstituting an agonistic relation in which things are to be made to yield up the meaning of their being. For Heidegger, our relation to ourselves has the same agonistic form: as he argues in *Being and Time*, 'Dasein is ontically distinguished by the fact that, in its very Being, that Being is an *issue* for it' – 'es diesem Seienden in seinem Sein *um* dieses Sein geht' – this in turn glossed by Sartre, who defines consciousness as '*a being such that in its being, its being is in question insofar as this being implies being other than itself*'.[118] The madness of knowledge consists in the belief that the questions are there first, waiting for us to come along and ask them rather than being produced from the act of putting into question. This is more than just the attribution of a certain rhetorical colouring to the work of knowing. It is rather something like an ontological rhetoric, a relationship of torsions or opposed forces that makes it possible to conceive of the question of being at all, since being is the questionable category and the originary object of questioning.

5
IMPOSTURE

The notable abeyance at the heart of knowing – the uncertainty that always attaches to knowing how and whether one knows – means that the possibility of imposture is always active or in wait when it comes to the question of possessing knowledge. Being unsure about the how of knowing erodes one's certainty as to the who. Assumptions about what we can know about what others know are essential to that interlocking of minds that is essential to psychosocial life – in particular through the development of that capacity known to psychologists and philosophers as the 'theory of mind', with the power it implies of making plausible guesses and projections about what others may or may not know, and their relation to what we ourselves know. Indeed, perhaps we rely heavily on that capacity to be able to make judgements about the quality and extent of our own knowledge, as a sort of back-projection from what we assume about the minds of others. Perhaps we begin to get an understanding of what knowing means only by our growing understanding of the nature of others' knowing.

Imposture at once chips away at the intricate and fragile recursivity of shared knowledge – what I can know of what you know of what I know, and so on – and cements it, since everything in fact depends upon the principle of transferred and circulating epistemic credit. It is no mystery that many forms of knowledge-imposture are designed to make financial profits, for assumed and imputed knowledge may be regarded as itself a parallel system of social credit, allowing societies to believe in themselves as systems of belief-investment. I want very much for it to be true that the Vatican had particular difficulties at the beginning of the financial crisis of 2008 in translating into Latin the phrase 'credit crunch', given the close relationship between the ideas of credit and religious credence. This may usefully remind us of the economics of faith, the fact that there is a religious kind of binding in networks of shared belief, and the belief they allow us to share in the shared belief of others. Intelligence is always had and held on credit, on what we may feel entitled to believe about what we and others know of one another's knowledge. The knowledge system is, like the financial system it mirrors and motivates, literally a confidence trick.

The capacity to be wrong about the nature and extent of others' knowledge is increased by the fact that there seems to be a desire to suppose knowledge in others that mirrors the will to know, or the will to be a knower, in ourselves. Indeed, these urges are perhaps affectively linked, since what we want in knowledge is not just the utility and satisfaction that come from particular kinds of cognitive capacity (along with the yield of pleasure that comes from reflection on these capacities), but also the greater social standing and consequent self-esteem that comes from being one of Dante's *color che sanno*, those supposed to know.[1] We need to suppose the existence of knowing others if we are to be able to suppose ourselves to be one of those supposed to know. The fact that all human knowledge is experienced collectively – there can be no secrets on a desert island, since there must be others to keep secrets from – means that we must repose a great deal of confidence in the belief that other people – pilots, cooks, doctors and parents – know what they are doing. In fact, this confidence in others' knowledge is a very large part of what is necessary for human beings to live socially.

The feelings provoked by impostors are accordingly more intense than those provoked by more ordinary forms of fraudulence and deception. The impostor or confidence trickster, who has persuaded us that we know that they know something they do not, or sometimes that they do not know something that they do, has menaced the frail assumptive framework of social life that requires us to trust both in the knowledge of others and in our own knowledge of that knowledge. The jeopardy is all the greater because it may make us recognize how mutable and contingent such second- and third-degree knowledge of knowledge must always be.

At the same time, there can be something fascinating, seductive and even heroic about the figure of the impostor or charlatan. Such figures are often celebrated in histories and biographies which, if not exactly adulatory, seem to enjoin a certain respect for the daring of the impostor, or admiration for the extent of their power.[2] The figure of the charlatan has joined the group of romantic outsiders and seceders from social norms – female thieves, seducers, spirit mediums, vampires, pirates – whose seeming powers of self-fashioning have attracted the star-struck approval of contemporary academics. As we will see, the writers who are most attracted to imposture are often aware of the analogies between their own art and that of their subjects – none more, as we will soon see, than Ben Jonson.

Not all imposture involves the pretence of knowledge, of course. It is the particular kind of trickster known as the charlatan who embodies the kind of imposture that will be the focus of this chapter, namely the fictitious claim to knowledge, skill or special intellectual capacity. But it is difficult to be sure of the status of the charlatan's pretence. The question of intention is very hard to distinguish in the use of the word 'pretend', which up to the seventeenth century could mean seriously to assert, allege or propose (*prae* + *tendere*, to stretch forward) – as *prétendre* still does in French – but which nowadays seems exclusively to suggest dissimulation or deception. The noun *pretence* perhaps makes the transition clearer. A pretence was a claim to property or status, and in 1667 Milton could refer in *Paradise Lost* to 'Spirits that in our just pretences armed / Fell with us from on high'.[3] The Young Pretender ('Bonnie Prince Charlie', Charles Edward Stuart, 1720–1788) was perfectly serious about his claims to the British throne. Fifty years later, the modern sense of a false pretext seems to have been fully established, as evidenced in 1719 in the command given by a mistress to her servant in Eliza Haywood's *Love in Excess*: "'You may get into the drawing room; but if not, make some pretence to stay as near it as you can 'till the ball be over".'[4]

Assuredly, there are persons who knowingly pretend to knowledge for profit, credit or simple gratification. Aristotle defined sophists in just this way, as those who deliberately employ fallacious reasoning. Their form of dialectic, he argues,

> has in view not the man who knows but the man who is ignorant and pretends to know. The man, then, who views general principles in the light of the particular case is a dialectician, while he who only apparently does this is a sophist.[5]

But if it is hard to be absolutely certain that one knows what one thinks one does, or believes whole-heartedly what one believes one does, it is even harder to pretend to anything in a way that holds the pretender rigorously apart from their pretending; the demands of being single-mindedly duplicitous are very exacting. Performance is so much a part of every aspect of human relations, not least in matters of knowledge and learning, where it is absolutely indispensable to be able to rehearse roles and to project oneself into intellectual postures that are not yet, or not fully one's own, that the pretender's success is likely to rest on their capacity to project themselves believingly as well as believably into their role. Successful tricksters must cultivate credulity in themselves to match the credulity of others whom they hope to stimulate. This implies being able to convince oneself, or temporarily to suspend one's disbelief in one's professed belief. Professing, a word that has moved from a religious act to a secular situation, bears the weight of these oscillations. A professor is one who professes, a word that originally meant to declare a faith but which by 1530 already had the implication of insincerity: 'Wolde to God every man that professeth chastyte coude kepe it well'.[6] By the later part of the eighteenth century, the word 'professional' referred not to the making of vows or declarations, but to the following of an occupation, often with the implication of being paid for something for which one ought ideally to have a nonmercenary motive, as in Robert Lowth's reference in 1787 to 'professional mourners, well accomplished in all the discipline of lamentation and woe, and with tears always at command for a reasonable stipend'.[7] Nowadays a professional is one who derives a living from a practice, not one who lives by a particular faith; hence the insult involved in calling somebody a professional saint, or professional victim.

The nineteenth century saw the rise of philosophical charlatans whose aim was not to wheedle fortunes out of their victims or to gain social status, but to build followings and reputations through the elaboration of systems of religious or philosophical belief. The two areas of imposture in which this kind of charlatanry developed were medical and religious, often combined. It may be that the prevalence of imposture in medical and religious matters has to do with the fact that these two areas of knowledge seem to bear on ultimate questions of the life and death of body and soul respectively ('health' and 'holiness' derive from the same root). The need for truth, or at least something like the atmosphere of knowledge, is intense in both areas, putting imposture at a premium. Certainly this fact makes these two forms of imposture liable to the most vigorous, even at times vicious denunciations.

One of the most prominent intellectual charlatans of the late nineteenth century was Helena Petrovna Blavatsky, discussed in Chapter Three, who progressed from being a spirit medium in New York to being the inventor and explicator of the syncretic religious and philosophical system she called Theosophy, a system of hidden wisdom skilfully stitched together from a host of different mystical and religious traditions. Even though her leading motivation was the explication and production of a complex and exalted system of ancient wisdom which would distance itself consciously from the vulgar theatrics of spiritualism, Blavatsky remained addicted to the production of fraudulent occult effects, and was eventually exposed through them. This makes for a complex kind of charlatanry in her and her many followers. It is hard to accuse her of pretending to the abstruse knowledge which she seemed to claim. One might very well say that her understanding of the mystical and oriental ideas she explicated was shallow, but that is a rather different kind of charge. The imposture seems to lie in the fact of seeming to believe her system, or offering the spectacle of belief in it, at least to the extent of persuading others to believe in it. So imposture is often found not in those who pretend to a knowledge possessed by others that they do not have, but rather those who themselves credit an untruth and profit from the credit that others give it. Dickens's Mrs Gradgrind, when asked if she is in pain, replies, 'I think there's a pain somewhere in the room . . . but I couldn't positively say that I've got it.'[8] One might say, paraphrasing Mrs Gradgrind, that there is pretence somewhere in this network of credence, but it is difficult to say quite who, or even what, is doing the pretending, or to whom.

This makes the category of imposture inherently unstable, since only the most fanatically or obsessively convinced believer (convinced in the way a particular kind of charlatan might seem to be) can really be absolutely certain of their knowledge. So there must be an element of pretence not just in the kind of belief in impossible things that Lewis Carroll's Alice declares to be impossible, but in all beliefs. Even in the case of what we take to be indubitable knowledge, there must be positing, postulation and exposition of the truth in question. Things are not known until there are knowers to personate them. This means that many of us may turn out to be charlatans-in-waiting, holding with a sort of willed incuriosity to things we believe we know to be true, which may however turn out to be no such thing. Throughout the history of charlatanism, error, delusion and pretence alternate and combine unpredictably.

Whether or not they believe what they propound, propounding of some kind is essential to the idea of the charlatan, who must always make some kind of show of their knowledge, with a view to luring others into accepting it; a charlatan who kept their wonderful knowledge to themselves would be a contradiction in terms. The word 'charlatan' entered English via French from Italian *ciarlare*, to babble or chatter. 'Wherefore should we rather thinke him a skilfull Phisiition, then a pratling Ciarlatan?' writes Anthony Munday in 1590.[9] Randle Cotgrave's French–English dictionary of 1611 defined a charlatan as 'A Mountebanke, a cousening drug-seller, a pratling quack-salver, a tatler, babler, foolish prater, or commender of trifles'.[10] *Quacksalver*, for a pedlar of false medicines, is current in English somewhat earlier, and one explanation of the word suggests an origin in the early modern Dutch *quacken*, to squawk, quack, croak, chatter, boast.

The interlacing of different kinds of will to knowledge is demonstrated in the behaviour of the victims of gulling in Ben Jonson's *The Alchemist*. (Gull, the common name for the victim of the charlatan, probably derives from the name for an unfledged bird, in particular a gosling, young birds being eager to swallow everything given them.) It is imperative for Subtle, the pretended alchemist in Jonson's play, not only to convince his victims of the extent of his secret knowledge but also to recruit them to his 'project'. Sir Epicure Mammon's cupiditous longing for immeasurable wealth transfers to his own fantasies of esoteric knowledge:

> I have a piece of Jason's fleece, too,
> Which was no other than a book of alchemy,
> Writ in large sheepskin, a good fat ram-vellum.
> Such was Pythagoras' thigh, Pandora's tub,
> And all that fable of Medea's charms,
> The manner of our work: the bulls, our furnace,
> Still breathing fire; our argent-vive, the dragon;
> The dragon's teeth, mercury sublimate,
> That keeps the whiteness, hardness, and the biting;
> And they are gathered into Jason's helm

(Th' alembic) and then sowed in Mars his field,
And thence sublimed so often, till they are fixed.
Both this, th' Hesperian garden, Cadmus' story,
Jove's shower, the boon of Midas, Argus' eyes,
Boccace his Demorgorgon, thousands more,
All abstract riddles of our stone.[11]

Mammon's fantasy-knowledge is not directly of alchemical theory but of the hidden wisdom or occult intimations of alchemical knowledge allegedly sown through mythological writings, suggesting that the golden fleece sought by Jason was in fact a manuscript containing alchemical wisdom. It concerns alchemical allegory, that projective, as-if or what-if knowledge that was so promiscuously commingled with the knowledge of chemical practice. His knowledge projects back into an imagined past a projective vision of an imagined future. The intertwining of allegory and practice in the history of alchemy means that the secret of how to turn base metals into gold, a secret which is often deeply concealed in allegory, may itself be an allegory for the general power of mystical or philosophical knowledge. Secrets are secreted in secrets.

'Projection' is the metaphor that Jonson uses throughout *The Alchemist* for the compounding of knowledge and fantasy. Projection is the final stage of alchemical process, which involves, according to George Ripley's *Compound of Alchemy* (1591), calcination, dissolution, separation, conjunction, putrefaction, congelation, cibation, sublimation, fermentation, exaltation, multiplication and projection. Projection referred literally to the casting or throwing forward into a crucible the stone or metal that it was believed would have the power to transmute ordinary metals into gold. The word was also in use by the early seventeenth century to refer to geometrical projections of three-dimensional objects onto flat surfaces and the forming of schemes, plans or 'projects': in Shakespeare's *Henry IV, Part Two* (Act 1, Scene 3), Bardolph uses the word to describe the vaulting ambition of Hotspur:

> . . . who lined himself with hope,
> Eating the air on promise of supply,
> Flatt'ring himself with project of a power
> Much smaller than the smallest of his thoughts . . .

The mythical projection of the alchemists that will magnify and multiply wealth so prodigiously must always therefore be kept in prospect, as the various projects held out to the cozenors' dupes are kept in the promised future. In Jonson's *Alchemist*, Epicure Mammon associates the powers of alchemical transmutation with a kind of numerical projection:

> But when you see th' effects of the great medicine,
> Of which one part projected on a hundred
> Of Mercury or Venus or the Moon,
> Shall turn it to as many of the Sun;
> Nay, to a thousand, so ad infinitum:
> You will believe me.[12]

In this Mammon seems to follow Ripley's *Compound of Alchemy*, which also makes it clear how allied to the multiplicative imagination of number the idea of projection is: projection enables something like a chain reaction in which not only can base metals be turned into gold, but tiny amounts of the projective material can produce huge increments. Ripley writes,

> Ten if thou multiplie first into ten,
> One hundreth that number maketh sickerly,
> If one hundreth into an hundreth be multiplied, then
> Ten thousand is that number if thou count it wittely,
> Then into as much more ten thousand to multiplie,
> It is a thousand thousand; which multiplied ywis,
> Into as much more a hundreth millions is.
>
> That hundreth millions being multiplyed likewise
> Into ten thousand millions, as I to thee doe say,
> Maketh so great a number I wot not what it is,
> Thy number in Proiection thus multiplye always.[13]

Mammon's ambition is not to have gold to hoard, but to have the means to project his own reputation in munificent good works and projects of redemption: 'my only care is, / Where to get stuff enough now; to proiect on; / This town will not half serve me'.[14] But this makes the desired effect highly unstable and predictable, as intimated in the squabble between the conspirators that opens the play, which looks forward to the disintegration of the plot at the end: as Dol Common complains, they threaten to 'fly out i' the projection'.[15] Knowledge is also sexual knowledge, with which alchemy is libidinously commingled in *The Alchemist*, in which Dol Common must masquerade as Queen of Fairy and as a nobleman's mad sister to lead on the victims of the pretence. The libidinization of knowledge means that knowledge can never be possessed or consummated in the present. As in a psychoanalytic account of sexuality, the desire of knowledge is for the projective prolongation and intensification of desire rather than the physical projection that would satisfy but consume it. Jonson's use of the idea even seems to anticipate a psychological usage that would not develop until the early twentieth century, in which projection refers to the unconscious transfer of feelings or desires on to another person. *The Alchemist* is a hyperprojection of all the overlapping and intersecting projects of the different characters.

Jonson conspicuously makes his play conform to the classical unities of time and place, such that the events are to be imagined as lasting just about as long as they do on the stage and are confined to the space in Lovewit's house with which we are presented. This gives another layer of meaning to the word 'projection', since the real business of the play is in fact to be imagined as happening offstage in Subtle's (imaginary) laboratory. Even the final explosion, which means that, as Face laments, 'all the works / Are flown *in fumo*: every glass is burst. / Furnace, and all rent down', is presumably a fabrication (and explosion was itself a metaphor that was commonly used for laughing an actor off the stage).[16] This constraint intensifies the comic pressure of hurry and concealment, as the beguiled victims are pushed on- and offstage and the beguilers are driven to ever more desperate improvisations. But this very principle of what-you-see-is-what-you-get allows Jonson to practise a kind of imposture of his own. For Lovewit's house seems to be not only a house in which appearances are in play, but something of a playhouse, full of exits and entrances, disguises, substitutions and projections. So it is a kind of allegory of theatricality itself, enabling it both to be and not to be what it is, namely, an imposture, in which the play imposes upon its willing audience, who must be beguiled into believing in this unlikely story of beguilement. For one of the most important functions of the history of imposture and beguilement – of which *The Alchemist* is both a distinguished example and a kind of exposition – is to persuade us to believe in the possibility of others' credulity.

In both *Volpone* and *The Alchemist*, Jonson attended to two areas of intellectual imposture that have often been associated and remain strongly open to imposture today: the medical and the religious. In both cases, the imposture will seem the more dangerous to the degree that, far from simply imposing on the ignorant or credulous, it will induce a relation of reciprocal supposing, in which the believer will do a great deal of the projective work – as in the ventriloquial performance, in which it is in fact the spectator who throws the voice, attributing it to its alternative source, following the hints of the performer. In recent years the decline in the popular authority of science and academic knowledge, and the increasing allure and respectability of what are thought of as competing forms of knowledge, has encouraged the reading of the history of charlatanism in terms of a simple division between 'official' and 'marginal' or 'subjugated' knowledges. The history of medical knowledge in particular provides a rich field of competing theories, in which the 'professionalization hypothesis', or the idea that the history of medicine may always be understood in terms of a conflict between medical professionals and lay or popular traditions, continues to govern the field. Just as, in a certain style of Marxist history in the 1970s and '80s, you could be sure that in whatever place or period one looked the bourgeoisie would always be rising, so in medical history one can be sure to find evidence that doctors and medical institutions are at every moment attempting to cement their professional authority at the expense of alternative and competing beliefs and practices. One of the most emphatic readings of this kind is Piero Gambaccini's *Mountebanks and Medicasters* (2004), a history of Italian medical charlatans. The book offers an indulgent, even affectionate portrait of the charlatan as anti-authoritarian hero:

> While licensed physicians high-handedly prescribed cataclysmic enemas, drastic emetics, exhausting purges and merciless bloodlettings, the charlatans sold simple remedies that all could afford, accompanying them with words of hope and consoling promises. They were not only a throng of fraudulent quacks committed to swindling a gullible and ingenuous rabble; often, theirs was a form of opposition to a false,

arrogant and presumptuous academic medicine. Sometimes, new and courageous ideas were hidden beneath their ironical and clownish postures, a disguised rebellion against orthodox physicians.[17]

In his history of unorthodox medicine, Roy Porter declines to succumb to the rather sentimental division between insiders and outsiders, and the wielders and victims of discursive power. Although quacks are regularly regarded as preying on the credulous and the gullible, there is no simple and asymmetrical distinction between the two sides. What is more, the conditions for what was known as quackery were created not so much by a powerful professional elite jealously attempting to guard and consolidate its power by excoriating outsiders and banishing traditional forms of practice, but rather by the complex market in medical practice that grew up from the late seventeenth century onwards. This produced a three-way colloquy of medical probability, involving not simply the tussle between official and unofficial practitioners but also patients, with their different demands and desires – not least the desire to be made better, but also to know what was making them better (or to feel that they knew). Nicholas Jewson saw in the eighteenth century 'a network of segmental, unregulated patient-practitioner relationships' in which the work of theory was essential to the work of therapy:

> the successful medical innovator was one whose theories offered the patient a recognizable and authentic image of his complaint as he experienced it. At the same time the practitioner sought medical theories which offered him the opportunity to dramatize his special healing powers and thus distinguish him from his ubiquitous rivals.[18]

Drawing out Jewson's insights, Porter argues that:

> the patient's purse power, coupled with an enduring ignorance of internal physiological processes, combined to encourage a proliferation of speculative medical systems; the sick expected to be told what was wrong in explanatory formulations that made sense. Humoral medicine retained its hold, alongside the newer chemical and mechanical models. Some medical

theories privileged the heart, some the blood, others the nerves. Thus regular medicine itself, aided by ignorance and pressurized by patients shopping between rival philosophies, produced a cacophony of explanatory systems . . . patient power was able during the long eighteenth century to impose upon *regular* medicine the terms of existence we nowadays view as typical of *quackery*.[19]

Contemporary prejudices incline academics to counterpose real understanding and the conditions of the market. But quackery and imposture were the effects of a new and expanded discursive market: a market in understanding. Pseudo-medicine is closely allied to inventions and expansions in forms of media, like the printing press and the Internet.

Human beings are singularly ill-equipped to understand what makes a medical treatment effective or beneficial, even when such treatments might seem indubitably to be available. But there were certainly some patients before the nineteenth century who seem to have grasped a truth that many contemporary historians of medicine keep at arm's length, namely that in the absence of any real experimental knowledge or inquiry, pretty much all medicine before the later nineteenth century, from top to bottom and without exception, including wise women, midwives, traditional healers and members of the College of Physicians, was pseudo-medicine. The field of medical history, like the history of theology, is a history of involuntary imposture. Almost everybody concerned in this long history is sure that they know what they are doing and why they are doing it, and is able to give detailed reasons for why their interventions might be effective. But that is precisely the problem. Indeed, we might say that real medicine can only come about at the point at which somebody can admit that they have a treatment that seems to work without their having the faintest idea how or why – and this is why mistaken methods and conclusions can indeed lead to new knowledge. Medical quacks were often called empirics, though this is somewhat odd, for empirics were so called because they relied upon experience and observation rather than academic theory. Yet they too are regarded as pretenders to a kind of knowledge. So it is not that there is no real medical knowledge until the development of epidemiology and bacteriology, it is rather the reverse: that, in the absence of any actual medicine, there was only *physiosophy*, medical knowledge, as far as the eye could see and the dinned-at ear endure.

Jonson's genius was in blending his own linguistic fertility with the prodigality of the knowledge-impostors that he took as his comic subject. For the essential condition for credibility is not plain and honest, four-square and jointed truth, but a certain perverse balance between the fantastic and the probable, which operates, as so much human knowledge has, on the Tertullian principle of *credo quia absurdum*. Every meeting of rationality and the real involves a necessary encounter of the absolute and the contingent, and every truth must operate in circumstances that muddy and complicate. The work of knowledge is precisely a work because it must labour, or at least labour to appear, to overcome complexity through assimilation, rather than through simple denial. The most convincing kinds of knowledge-imposture are therefore the ones that hover on the edge of being the least convincing, precisely because of their sheer excess of circumstance. The various versions of the humoral system, which sees the body as governed by the interaction of four different humours, or bodily fluids – two of them, 'yellow bile' and 'black bile', completely imaginary – offer good evidence for this. The humoral system allows for the reduction of all ailments and distempers to a question of 'imbalance' (one of the most rockily unbalanced principles in all medical thinking), even as it admits of fantastic complexity in the elaboration of its details – indeed, the notion of complexity itself has had considerable impetus imparted to it by the humoral concept of the 'complexion'. This may be why the cosmic and the comic are so closely alloyed in the history of medical imposture. Only theories which are able to orchestrate this tension between essence and excess, rational good sense and absurdity, are likely to be successful.

Supposititious knowledge requires and requisitions the representation of knowledge in the forms of writing that both makes knowledge widely available and severs it from the knower. The medical quackery of the seventeenth century onwards depended upon the increasing availability of medical writing of different kinds. By 1786, it was possible for the anti-quackery campaigner James Adair to include an essay in his book *Medical Cautions* on 'fashionable diseases', which argued that medicine and cure had been taken up into the discourses of publicity and advertisement, instancing the malady of 'spleen'

popular in the early years of the eighteenth century, that exhibited
the effects of social as well as physical contagion:

> The Princess, afterwards Queen Anne, often chagrined and
> insulted in her former station, and perplexed and harrassed
> in the latter, was frequently subject to depression of spirits,
> for which, after the courtly physicians had given it a name,
> they proceeded to prescribe Rawleigh's confection and pearl
> cordial. The circumstance was sufficient to transfer both the
> disease and the remedy to all who had the least pretensions
> to rank with persons of fashion.[20]

A biographical account of Adair from 1848 affirms that, ironically,
he himself succumbed to one of these diseases, for he 'became
hypochondriacal, and died at Harrowgate in 1802'.[21]

An essential part of knowledge-imposture is the claim that the
knowledge in question has come from some authoritative elsewhere.
In Europe, this has usually meant from somewhere in the East; the
precise location shifts at different times. Alchemical knowledge
usually suggests Arabic origins. From the late eighteenth century
onwards, with the development of the idea of the 'mystic East', the
source of knowledge moved to India, Tibet and China. The supposed
knowledge of magic helps to secure the magical status of knowledge
from these mythical locations.

The question that has been asked from the seventeenth century
onwards was not why quacks saw the opportunity to make a living
through fraud and deception, but how and why they should have
succeeded as well as they did (and, roaringly, still do). Roy Porter
suggests that we need to see a division between the alternative medical practices of the seventeenth and eighteenth centuries and those
that began to succeed them from the nineteenth century onwards. It
would be easy to mistake the quackery of the former period as the
development of a set of romantically 'alternative' practices and philosophies of health. Porter cautions us against seeing any such thing.
Despite the mixture of the scientific and the occult or magical in
the way in which quack cures were marketed, there was no call to
radical alternatives in medical thinking: 'Eighteenth-century propri-
etary medicines did not carry primitivist "back to the earth", "back to
nature", purity crusades; quite the reverse, for Georgian empirics and

their nostrums basked in the reflected glory of the Enlightenment.'[22] During the eighteenth century, the alternative practitioner borrowed the authority of a medical practice that had not yet succeeded in establishing itself as entirely and unquestionably authoritative. Increasingly during the nineteenth century more ideologically 'alternative' medical practices developed that rejected established forms of medical authority and borrowed and mimicked the forms of sceptical resistance to established authority that were developing in other fields. By the nineteenth century the quack could draw on the allure of the renegade and the intellectual refuser.

The biggest unanswered question, perhaps because it usually goes entirely unasked, is how quacks could be as inordinately ridiculous as they appeared to be to everybody, and yet so persistent, even ineradicable a presence. When the question is asked, the usual answer is that quacks preyed upon the credulous, the imbecile and the uneducated. The answer, in the short term, seemed to be to subject them and their victims to shaming campaigns of ridicule and in the long term to intensify efforts at education that would immunize the population against them. Neither strategy has ever seemed to work particularly well. We should in fact be struck by the fact that increases in education and awareness regularly provide more rather than fewer opportunities for imposture to thrive. The explanation that Alexander Pope supplied in 1709, in his *Essay on Criticism*, sometimes furnishes an explanation for this:

A *little learning* is a dangerous thing;
Drink deep, or taste not the Pierian spring:
There shallow draughts intoxicate the brain,
And drinking largely sobers us again.[23]

But it is not at all plain or palpable that the deeper the immersion in knowledge the more balanced the knower's temperament becomes. What this ignores is the fact that the increase and expansion of knowledge also diversifies the affective economies of knowledge, constituted and maintained through the many different kinds of sign and performance that elaborate knowledge and make it knowable. The more education there is, the more the idea of knowledge – along with all the ways in which we invest in it, idealizing, scorning, desiring it – becomes autonomous of its actuality. The signs, projections and performances of knowledge are not mere accessories to 'actual' knowledge, ways for people to coin from the credulous (though they are that, as they have always been). They also constitute autonomous knowledge economies, systems of storage, investment, exchange, expenditure and distribution that govern not just facts, information and evidence but also ideas, images and projections of the noetic.

Roy Porter wonders whether the absurd excessiveness of the quack's performance may have been part of the point:

> How are we to assess showmanship such as this? . . . [A]re we witnessing theatricality, astutely carried to the point of self-parody, the cultivation of pure make-believe, accepted as such on both sides? Perhaps it was of the essence of that quack's act that his blarney was known to be baloney. Was, then, getting people to listen, and entertaining them with tall stories, the name of the game? Did some quacks even want to rouse disbelief at the preposterousness of it all, provoking chaffing, catcalls, and heckling?[24]

It seems possible that the excess and absurdity of charlatan public performance may have acted as a kind of permission or passepartout for the pseudo-claims being put into play. Neither belief nor conviction are required for the entry into fantasy-representation to be assured. Indeed, the atmosphere of rivalry and disputatious hostility that characterized the field of sickness and health from the mid-seventeenth century onwards made ridicule a necessary and valuable tactic for quacks themselves, who constantly warned their audiences to beware of quacks and impostors. Quacks might have been represented as parti-coloured fools and poltroons, but the more itinerant forms of charlatan are almost always shown themselves employing fools as part of their warm-up routines.

So the discourse of medical imposture was much more than a bit of discursive decoration or a way of stimulating and smoothing consumer relations. Rather, it was the means of putting medicine into knowledge, inasmuch as this knowledge was carried by and given its form by a diverse field of medical knowledge-representations – representations, that is, not just of what might have been known of medical matters, but also of the supposition of its being known, in different ways, by different claimants to knowledge. There were undoubtedly plenty of people who simply had no time for the claims of quacks and shunned their words and works; yet increasingly there was nobody who did not have to take account of their claims, and the different kinds of authority asserted, promised and denied in the choppily contentious field of medical knowledge. Medical imposture marks the movement of illness from the corporeal into the cognitive. The spread of imposture produced the sense that patients – and not just patients – needed to take responsibility for their illness and health. The many warnings against quacks – and against doctors – amounted to the warning not to 'die from ignorance', as the AIDS campaign slogan from 1986 had it, though there may have been as many who have died from quasi-knowledge.

It can come as little surprise that the period of conspicuous growth in medical imposture also sees the arrival and consolidation of hypochondria in the modern sense. In his *Detector of Quackery*, John Corry claimed that

> Three-fourths of the diseases of the people of London are *ideal*; and many persons contribute to the support of the physician, and pay him liberally for regular attendance, while they labour not under bodily indisposition, but the imaginary ailments of a *mind diseased*.[25]

Hypochondria, which moved over the course of the eighteenth century from being an abdominal disorder to being a 'nervous' disorder characterized by the morbid dread of illness, may be seen, in a period marked by an increase in the knowledge of disease, as the disease of knowledge, in which you do not so much suffer from illness as suffer from the prospect of your suffering. The imposture of the quack induced the anxious, answering imposture of the patient, anxious about how precisely they might fit the medical bill. Some of the explanatory terms invented during the eighteenth century, like 'nervous' and 'bilious', were still on the lips of my parents' generation when I was growing up. In the twentieth century, almost every aspect of life was drawn into systems of medical self-scrutiny. The saliency of words like 'therapy' and 'healing', the latter often employed in a free-floating way unrelated to any particular malady, implied that infirmity was a universal condition rather than an undesirable departure from well-being. Health was increasingly not a condition to which one could be restored, but rather something to be striven for.

By the end of the eighteenth century there was a growing tendency among quacks to develop more elaborate justifications of their remedies. This was the period of the philosophical entertainment in which 'serious' science was put on display in a large range of styles and venues, from the Egyptian Hall in Piccadilly and the many lectures and displays that took place in Assembly Rooms throughout the country, through to the prestigious Royal Institution lectures. Tom Gunning's 'cinema of attraction' of the early twentieth century, in which audiences went to exhibitions not only to see what cinema could show them but 'to see machines demonstrated', was anticipated by a similarly spectacular science of attraction a century earlier.[26] In the case of the X-ray exhibitions that became popular in the 1890s, encouraged by the cheapness of X-ray equipment, these two streams converged.

Conspicuous among these early celebrity charlatans was James Graham, who made his name with the Temple of Health he established in Pall Mall, London, featuring the Celestial Bed which he encouraged couples to hire for the purposes of ensuring pregnancy. By the end of his life, having overstretched himself financially with his West End ventures, he gave himself over to demonstrations of the powers of the 'earth cure', arranging to have himself buried naked in soil taken from Highgate Hill to demonstrate its vivifying influence.

As Roy Porter astutely observes, from the late eighteenth century onwards, quacks 'made the pill-vending side of their trade play second-fiddle in their self-presentations. Above all, this cohort of quacks principally aimed to sell their opinions, backed by the voice of science, scholarship, and authority.'[27] At the same time, medical imposture began to commodify and epistemify gadgetry and technology, most notably through electricity and the various ingenious ways that were developed to apply it to the body.[28] This enabled medical pretenders to present themselves as not less but more up to date than traditional doctors. These developments coexisted with an explosion of alternative medical systems which emphasized the natural curative powers of air, water and, as we have seen, earth. These are only superficially distinct. For the natural remedy was in fact always presented as some kind of system which, for all its naturalness, needed to be explicated and mediated to sufferers by experts and knowledgeable exponents. Technology became technique, which represents a clever and often rather sophisticated internalization of the insult that has often been thrown at practitioners like Mesmer, namely that their systems of treatment had no physiological basis and depended upon the suggestibility of the patient. Mesmerism and the growing understanding of placebo effects made it clear that this suggestibility was indeed a powerful and potentially very useful phenomenon. The placebo depends upon the *noscitur*: the *it is known*.

Charlatanism's move from pills and potions to the production of intellectual systems is anticipated during the eighteenth century by works such as Johann Burkhard Mencken's *De charlataneria eruditorum* (The Charlatanry of the Learned) of 1715. The imposture of quackery is presented here as uncomfortably close to the posturing and pretension which had become characteristic of the intellectual life, itself more and more coextensive with the academic life. Mencken, who was himself a professor of history in Leipzig, enjoyed mocking the vanity, triviality, exhibitionism and love of extravagant titles among scholars:

> Quackery is found . . . not only among physicians but also everywhere among the learned. Believing that they become more god-like in proportion to the amount of applause they receive, they seek it no less eagerly than they suck in the air that they breathe . . . Just as the charlatans on the streets are wont to display their degrees and diplomas, and to arrogate to themselves high-sounding and extraordinary titles, so among presumably better men are found not a few who court rank and position by means of new and impressive titles . . . Who has not heard of those academies in Italy which bedizen themselves with such bizarre and ridiculous designations as the Argonauts, the Seraphs, the Elevated, the Transported, the Parthenians and the Olympians, not to mention the Obscure, the Immature, the Unfruitful, the Obstinate, the Obfuscated, the Indolent, the Sleepy, the Incapable, and the Fantastic?[29]

Imposture is pretended action, but there is one form of action that is particularly powerful in the work of intellectual imposture, namely that of writing. Human beings have seen the possibility for imposture in writing since Plato reported the suspicions of Socrates in his

Phaedrus. For Socrates, writing gives the false impression of being a kind of knowledgeable speech. But, while giving intelligence, writing can never be treated as intelligent, for writing can never know what it is talking about:

> Writing, Phaedrus, has this strange quality, and is very like painting; for the creatures of painting stand like living beings, but if one asks them a question, they preserve a solemn silence. And so it is with written words; you might think they spoke as if they had intelligence, but if you question them, wishing to know about their sayings, they always say only one and the same thing. And every word, when once it is written, is bandied about, alike among those who understand and those who have no interest in it, and it knows not to whom to speak or not to speak. When ill-treated or unjustly reviled it always needs its father to help it; for it has no power to protect or help itself.[30]

For Socrates, writing is in essence a kind of forgery, meaning that one can truthfully write the words 'I am dead' where one can never truthfully say them. Precisely because writing cannot know anything for itself, not being alive as speech is, it allows for a counterfeit life after death in which a writer can appear to live on in his or her (actually its) words. Socrates' doubts persist. There is still a strong presumption that the author of written words ought to know what they meant by them. It can be hard to persuade people that one does not preserve a memory of the intention behind every sentence that one writes. Asked what a particular sentence may mean, the author has to do exactly what any other reader has to do – and can in principle do just as well as the author – namely interpret the text, which is to say, work out what it means, where 'means' means seems to know what it is saying without necessarily knowing that it is saying it. Reading means understanding precisely what kind of imposture is being effected by the writing.

There is a long history of literary forgery as a means of imposture, in which these questions of knowing are attributed and distributed in complex ways. One extended case of this is the history of the myth of *The Three Impostors*. At some point during the eleventh century, reports began to circulate of a text that denounced as impostors the three prophets of monotheism, Moses, Jesus and Muhammad, arguing that their claims to divine inspiration were false and their doctrines therefore without foundation. It is not clear whether the text is accused of lying in its claim that the prophets were liars, or only pretending to lie, nor is it quite clear which would be worse. Many different people were identified as the author of this scandalous but elusive text (and it was scandalous just because of being so elusive, which allowed everyone to imagine its enormity for themselves). The suspects included at various times Frederick II, Averroes (Ibn Rushd), Simone of Tournai, Bernardino Ochino, Campanella and Machiavelli. Many people claimed to have read it, though it was not until the middle of the eighteenth century that a version of the text actually appeared.[31] This was in fact an imposture to the third degree – a tricked-up version of a text falsely believed to claim the falsity of the three Abrahamic religions, or the substantial substitute for an inexistent text. The imposture is caught up in a web of suppositions about knowledge, truth and belief, an imposture that went beyond the need for identifiable impostors.

Imposture is so called because it imposes on people, but in this case the imposition is itself a kind of imposture on the part of those who claimed acquaintance with the text, the diabolical dangerousness of which was in fact a useful way to secure orthodoxy by denouncing the authors of this pretended work and condemning it as itself an imposture. Indeed, the devilish nature of the imposture involved is of a piece with a common view that the power possessed by the devil was not really that of working evil (since everything the devil does has to be by divine permission, otherwise God would not in fact be omnipotent), but the power to counterfeit that power. The first impostor was therefore Satan in Eden, representing to Eve the glories of the knowledge she might gain through disobedience: 'And the serpent said unto the woman, Ye shall not surely die: For God doth know that in the day ye eat thereof, then your eyes shall be opened, and ye shall be as gods, knowing good and evil' (Genesis 3:4–5). Indeed, the story of the Fall in Genesis makes imposture and the access of knowledge inseparable: Adam and Eve both will and will not have the knowledge of good and evil, including the good and evil of knowledge itself.

As written mediation has bulked ever more largely in human history, and as more human beings than ever before have lived their lives through writing and its electronic equivalents, epistemic imposture has become ever more prevalent. Well before the development of what, from around the mid-1950s, began to be referred to as 'artificial intelligence', human beings began to see in writing a sort of autonomous knowing, anticipating and subsequently elaborating Teilhard de Chardin's idea of the *noosphere*. Surprisingly, perhaps, there is as much to be learned about the ways in which we feel about knowledge from this kind of unknowing knowledge or knowerless knowing as there is from the more familiar ways in which knowing is lived and experienced in human persons. This world of apparently spontaneously self-generating texts has increased the sensitivity to questions of the origin and ownership of ideas, particularly in relation to plagiarism.

The topic of plagiarism has generated a great deal of writing, broadly divided into two forms: there are the many technical guides to the ways in which plagiarism is conducted and how it might be detected and guarded against; and there are the explorations of the ethics of plagiarism, some of them uncompromising in their condemnation of the act, others inclined to find ways of explaining or mitigating the charge. What cannot be doubted is that plagiarism is taken very seriously indeed. K. R. St Onge opens his exploration of plagiarism with words that make clear the intensity of feeling attached to it, prompted by the revelations that Senator Joseph Biden had plagiarized a published article for a paper he had written as a student in law school:

> Senator Biden's problems should remind us of how demoralizing and devastating charges of plagiarism can be, of how the verdict is embedded in the charge itself, and how voracious the appetites of accusers and spectators for details of the 'tragic flaw.' But it is not good theatre, or a fair fight. Real people are inflicting real pain. The unhappy reality is that plagiarism, whatever else it is, is an exercise in pure pain: purposely inflicted to inhibit or punish.[32]

The fact that we seem to require the warrant of being able to say or, even better, to write something in order to demonstrate to ourselves that we know it ('I don't know what I think until I see what I say') seems to take us some way to understanding the vehement feelings that cluster round the practice of plagiarism. No doubt, most instances of plagiarism involve the simple desire to get some kind of credit or benefit without engaging in the hard work of thinking and writing. But, if plagiarism is disrespectful of the rights and what we have learned to call the 'intellectual property' of others, it is also the sign of respect, perverse as it may be, for the kind of intellectual authority believed to be exemplified in the plagiarized work. This is especially the case where the plagiarization is more brilliantly written than the work whose ideas it steals.

The easy availability of means for the copying and reproduction of text means that plagiarism appears to have reached epidemic proportions in the academic systems of the world. Of course, the same conditions of accessibility also work in favour of the plagiarism detective – and nowadays some universities employ people full-time in this role. Successful plagiarism actually requires quite a lot of work – or a lot of money to employ people to engage in this work on your behalf. Some of this work, for example in the kind of plagiarism that involves stitching together quotations plausibly from various authors or sources, so resembles the work involved in actually producing original texts that one wonders quite what the motivation might be.

My concern here is with the kind of plagiarism that seems to constitute the imposture of knowledge – not, then, the many kinds of literary or artistic plagiarism that involve the pretence to 'originality' by copying the words of others. The artistic plagiarist tries to appropriate a work as their own; the academic or philosophical plagiarist uses this appropriation to hotwire the credit of being the thinker or knower of what is written. The artistic plagiarist masquerades as an author; the epistemic plagiarist masquerades as an authority. Despite the many arguments that may be had about the nature of originality there is a particular complexity that attaches to the discourse of knowledge, namely that, to the extent that it is in fact knowledge, or knowledge of true matters (and many would agree that you cannot know something that is not true), it can be the subject neither of property nor larceny. This is to say, you can only plagiarize texts, just as you can only infringe the copyright of something that exists in a form capable of being copied. You can plagiarize Newton's *Principia mathematica* but you cannot plagiarize the laws of motion it explicates, precisely because they are (very largely) true, and so, as the phrase has it, 'common knowledge', which it is widely accepted cannot be the subject of plagiarism. Artistic plagiarism is often discussed as though we believed in a Romantic idea of originality which consists in something coming out of nothing. But to plagiarize something that aims to articulate truth, or justified knowledge, is to plagiarize something that is itself a discourse on behalf of something else that, precisely to the degree that it claims to be true, must disclaim ownership or originality.

The reason that knowledge-plagiarism seems to provoke such revulsion is in part the bad faith that it involves. The plagiarist wants, of course, to be one-supposed-to-know, that is, wants to be one to whom what we call 'acknowledgement' or 'credit' is due. This means that they want to enjoy the benefit of the norm that they themselves decline to recognize. Perhaps the strength of this revulsion, and the seriousness of the consequences of being detected in plagiarism, has something to do with the fragility it discloses in the relation between ideas and words – namely, that what we know may largely depend on what we say rather than the other way round. I know what I think and can think about what I know as a result of what I have been able to say or, more particularly, to write. For somebody else to be able simply to use my words jeopardizes not just my right to be credited as the author of my words, but also the right to be able to read back those words as the outcome and guarantee – almost the only ones I really have – that there has been thinking and knowing on my part. To impersonate me by reciting my words without quotation marks is to impersonate the personation that my words, and only my words, gives to my thinking.

The relation here is one that Stanley Cavell has distinguished as the difference between knowing – in all its different senses – and acknowledging. The question of what we can know – for sure, or more approximately – is an epistemological matter; the question of what we are willing to acknowledge is ethical.

> A 'failure to know' might just mean a piece of ignorance, an absence of something, a blank. A 'failure to acknowledge' is the presence of something, a confusion, an indifference, a callousness, an exhaustion, a coldness. Spiritual emptiness is not a blank.[33]

Cavell is here discussing the classical problem of how one knows, or, rather, how one knows whether one can know, the pain of another. His answer is that it does not make any sense even for me to say I

know my own pain (that I might, for example, be more or less certain about it, or even that I might be mistaken about it). Rather I
acknowledge it, in the sense of owning to or bearing witness to it.
This kind of acknowledgement is not too far away from the sense of
confession. This is what seems to make it possible for Cavell to conclude his argument with the words 'To know you are in pain is to
acknowledge it, or to withhold the acknowledgment. – I know your
pain the way you do.'[34]

Does this kind of acknowledgement have anything to do with
the failure to acknowledge that another has a claim to have originated the words I am representing as my own? In a sense it is the
opposite, for it is an appropriation, as though one were to claim the
pain of another as one's own, rather than to fail to recognize it. But
it is an appropriation that does not acknowledge the fact that I have
a relationship of acknowledgement to my words and to the act of
thinking to which they may seem to bear witness: like Prospero saying
of Caliban 'This thing of darkness I acknowledge mine' (*The Tempest*,
Act v, Scene 1), I may need one day to own up to those words. When
I fail to acknowledge another's words as theirs, I steal those words
from them, to be sure – even, sometimes, to the point of putting them
at risk themselves of being accused of imposture. But I also remove
this relationship of responsibility, which always involves the risk that
my own words may nevertheless turn out to be a kind of intellectual
imposture, the making of an unwarranted claim, or the claim to a
knowledge to which I may not have full title. No genuine proposition can be entirely free of this jeopardy, which is paradoxically part
of what we might mean by its authenticity.

In 1978, Pauline Clance and Suzanne Imes published a paper
which suggested that many successful women suffered from feelings
that their success was unearned or due to fluke, and that they were
likely at any point to be exposed as frauds.[35] Pauline Clance herself reported in 1993 that several surveys had 'found no differences
between the sexes in the degree to which they experience impostor
feelings', a finding that has been regularly repeated, but this appears
to be hard for many to accept, and the 'impostor phenomenon' (or, as
it quickly became, 'impostor syndrome') is still regularly put forward
as an explanation for the fact that women do not achieve enough
positions of authority in academic and corporate life.[36] Writing in
2016, Dana Simmons, for example, is still quite sure that impostor

syndrome has been identified as 'a problem specifically experienced by "high-achieving women"'.[37] Specifically, perhaps, but that does not imply exclusively.

Simmons proposes a totalizing explanation of impostor syndrome and a programme for its cure that recommends the acceptance of partial knowledge as opposed to the internalization of the idea of the dominative ideal of total knowledge. But her explication of this situation is itself as domineering as could be imagined:

> The Impostor Syndrome reflects anxiety around partial, situated knowledges. Feelings of imposture reinforce the fantasy of a god's eye, total ideal. When I declare myself an impostor, I imagine a totalizing knowledge and vision, to which I do not have access. This is the vision of mastery, a mastery that is intimately related to legacies of enslavement, exploitation and cooptation ... It is a desire to master and possess. When I attribute this total vision to others, when I apologize for lacking it myself, I associate myself with the Dream of mastery.[38]

Imposture is not an accidental and abstractable feature of the representation of knowledge. Every proposition is a supposition, and every personation of a supposition is an impersonation. It may be that the feeling of imposture is not so much a failure of confidence or assertiveness as a recoil from the fantasy of epistemic self-presence and a demurral from the demand that one seamlessly impersonate the knowledge-claims that one has articulated. In matters of knowledge any assertion is a positing of a subject-supposed-to-know. Only an impostor is capable of the bad faith involved in knowing for sure what, and therefore that, they know. The different kinds of imposture reviewed in this chapter – charlatanry, quackery, forgery, plagiarism – are evidence not of a clear divide between those who know and those who merely pretend to knowledge, but rather of the necessity of a certain kind or degree of impersonation, sometimes even self-impersonation, in any assumption of knowledge. That it is necessary for knowledge always to be enacted means that it is always open to being acted out.

6

UNKNOWING

There are a few categories that stubbornly recur in contumelics, the long history of human mockery and insult. There is sexual insult, encompassing the mocking of the cuckold and the deviant. This often overlaps with the mockery of physical disability or deformity. In previous eras, religious insult would have been much more potent, sometimes overlapping with racial insult, the power of which has been magnified by contemporary deprecation. These categories often combine and overlap, a particularly telling one being 'bugger', which derives from Bulgar, a name given to a set of heretics believed to come from Bulgaria in the eleventh century who were suspected of engaging in forbidden sexual practices. Heresy and sexual perversion were closely linked, the association of religious with sexual irregularity surviving in the idea of the 'missionary position'.[1]

But perhaps the most universal and pervasive category of insult is the mockery of the unintelligent or mentally incapable, whether the stupid or the mad, these two categories so often, and so mysteriously, identified. The impulse to cognitive insult seems so inveterate that words designed specifically to be technical or without value judgements quickly become derogatory – a case in point being 'moron', which met with the approval of the American Association for the Study of the Feeble-Minded in 1910 precisely because at that time it did not have negative overtones, but which has since become the most vehement of jeers. In this respect it follows 'idiot', which in Greek and Latin was a term simply denoting a private individual, and anticipates the fate of 'retard', which was in use among educational psychologists from around 1909 but by the 1960s had passed out of scientific and into popular use.[2]

Perhaps, indeed, the accusation of stupidity is to be regarded as a meta-insult. For the words for stupidity or madness are words which usually indicate a person who is reduced to the condition of an object or category, a signified rather than one capable itself of signifying, and in the use of the word that debasement is actually performed. To be the target of what is rather percipiently called 'abuse' is actually simply to be a utensil, or object of use, as opposed to being a user of language. Epistemic insult therefore puts its object outside the company of language users, though the pain of the insult depends of course upon the target appreciating perfectly well the import of what they are being called.

It is very common for stupidity to be conceived as a kind of insensibility that is imagined to reduce the non-knower or slow learner to some dense, dull, impenetrable and uniformly unresponsive state of matter. Wood and excrement ('shit-for-brains') are favoured items, but so, a little surprisingly, is air (what these states of matter have in common is that they lack sharpness, distinction or individuality). So we have 'blockhead', 'clot' (clod), 'numbskull'; and stupidity as being 'slow', 'dull', 'dim', 'obtuse' and so on. To be blockish, dense or dull-witted, a dolt or a clodpoll, is a form of existence as degraded and undifferentiated as mud. It is to be thick as a brick or two short planks, or, as Falstaff says of Poins, 'His wit's as thick as Tewkesbury mustard; there's no more conceit in him than is in a mallet' (*Henry IV, Part 2*, Act II, Scene 4). Not to know is no longer, or not even yet, to be *Homo sapiens*. To be stupid is to be stunned or senseless, to be not only without knowledge but for that reason without the knowledge of feeling, this being one of the most habitual forms of stupid insensitivity that human beings can display. The play of the word 'sense' between sensible and intelligible allows one to think of being witless as being without being, without the capacity to feel anything at all. John Donne says in his 'True Character of a Dunce' (1622) that

He hath a soule drownd in a lumpe of Flesh, or is a piece of earth that *Prometheus* put not half his proportion of Fire into, a thing that hath neither edge of desire, nor feeling of affection in it, The most dangerous creature for confirming an *Atheist*, who would straight swear, his soul were nothing but the bare temperature of his body.[3]

If there is a powerful set of fantasy desires involved in the idea of possessing knowledge and wisdom, there is a countervailing set of dreads and amusements furnished by the idea of the stupid, and its embodiment in the one-supposed-not-to-know. Indeed, not knowing is more than ignorance. It is seen as witlessness, irrationality, and so comes close to a kind of madness, even to a kind of unbeing. 'Stupid' could actually mean paralysed in the seventeenth century. In fact the unvarying stupidity of the ways in which the stupor or daze of ignorance is conceived, or unable to be conceived as a form of human existence, is remarkable and telling: the imagination of stupidity is as thrombotic as what it imagines, or, in fact, fails to. The 'logic' involved seems to be that only intelligence gives the possibility both of being distinct from the material world and being distinguishable from other beings. To have identity is to be able to be the same (*idem*) as yourself from moment to moment; to be an idiot originally meant to be set apart, as a private individual, but its root is *id*, 'it', as though the idiot were no more than a kind of iterated itness, rather than genuine ex-isting. To be foolish is therefore to be ultimately indistinguishable from the world in general.

Perhaps it is the attribution which is really the mark of our dullness about unknowing, or different modes of knowing, since states of unknowing (infancy, for example, or dementia) can often be accompanied by considerable sprightliness, painfully agitated states of confusion or other kinds of sound and fury. In fact, as we will see through this chapter, knowledge does not always seem quite to know what it is about in its attributions of stupidity.

CUNNING

The two opposite states of matter that signify the stupid, the dense (clods, clots, clowns and so on) and the vacant are mediated through the imagination of the human body, and especially the sexual organs, in particular the female sexual organs. 'Folly' and its many derivatives come from the Latin *follis*, a bag or bellows and, by transference, the stomach. So stupidity is both empty and full, an alternation that is often played out in the play between 'male' and 'female' genital forms.

A fool is a 'lobcock', meaning a limp or hopeless penis, or a 'mouth', from the gaping of the fool, or a 'Tom-cony', from one who has been conned and perhaps also from 'Tom's cunny', the vagina of a prostitute. But at the same time, 'A stiff prick hath no conscience', as an American proverb has it.[4]

Sexual insults often imply the reduction of a human being to a sexual organ or action, which may be regarded as equivalent to the reduction to a merely animal and therefore quasi-material condition. You might think that 'clever dick' would mean almost the same as 'dickhead', though they are, of course, opposites – or not quite, since the former is used ironically to mean a know-all, or somebody who is not as clever as they wish to seem. In this, it resembles the word 'wittol', a modification of late Middle English *cokewold* by the addition of *wete-*, wit, which originally meant a cuckold who knows but who complacently and, for some reason, infuriatingly tolerates his condition. A little collection of contradictory proverbs from the early seventeenth century makes the logic clear: 'P. No greater shame to a man, then to bee a Cuckolde. C. Yes, to be a Wittoll'.[5] From this, the word *witall* was generalized to mean a fool or half-wit, with the *-old* suffix being re-understood as *-all*.

Somewhat surprisingly, the use of 'dick' to mean penis is not recorded in print in this sense until 1891, though it seems scarcely credible that it should not have been in use – for example in military and school contexts – for much longer.[6] Part of the complication of 'dick' is the influence of 'dickens', as in 'what the dickens', to mean devil, which may account for the admiring 'up to dick', which means fly, alert or up to the mark (and which may have exerted some force on 'tricky-dicky', used to refer to Richard Nixon). Also in the phono-semantic vicinity is dick as slang for dictionary, so that to 'swallow the dick' means to use long words without knowing their meaning (though perhaps with the insinuation of a more corporeal sense of dick).[7] The intrigue of word and thing is often at work in bodily idiot-objects. It is true that 'dicky-dido' means idiot, through sing-song pseudo-anagram, and gets transferred in the rugby song 'The Mayor of Bayswater' to the female organ, with its chorus (to the tune of the Welsh song 'The Ash Grove') 'the hairs on her dicky-dido hang down to her knees'.

The links between the penis and stupidity (prick, plonker, pillicock, pillock), though routine, are nevertheless mild and even sometimes rather affectionate or admiring. As many have observed, 'cunt', by contrast, has gone from being a rather quaint and cosy word in English (we are about to see that 'quaint' is in fact at certain points interchangeable with 'cunt') to being the most powerfully demeaning insult. 'Cunt' tends to connote disgust and debasement, but that debasement seems to have a particularly powerful association with the attribution of stupidity, the stupidity of being reduced to an object. The something that is nothing of the fool (sometimes, when they have been fooled, known as a 'bubble') is the nothing that is something of the cunt (or its name).

The lips of the vulva make for the idea of a kind of mindless speech emanating from the female genitals, as for example in the belief whispered among early Christians that the priestess at the Delphic Oracle delivered her prophecies from her privy parts, an idea elaborated into the fantasy that animates Denis Diderot's *Les Bijoux indiscrets* of a magic ring that could set those lips incontinently babbling beyond the will of their owners. The idea that the vagina might just be a vacant if voluble receptacle gives rise to comic exchanges of head and genitals, as in the following characteristically unpleasant 'dumb blonde' joke: 'How do you brainwash a blonde? Give her a douche and shake her upside down.'[8]

There is, however, an intriguing suggestion of knowingness knitted into the history of this word. It is often rendered 'quaint' in earlier uses attested from the thirteenth century, a development of Anglo-Norman *coint*, derived from Latin *cognitus*, knowing, which meant ingenious, skilled, and so also gracious, courteous or refined, especially in speech. A quaint speaker might therefore be defined as one from whose lips the word 'cunt' would be most unlikely to fall. Chaucer makes the relation between the two words perfectly clear in *The Miller's Tale* by actually rhyming the word *queynt* with itself when describing the dalliance between the clerk Nicholas and Alison, the carpenter's wife, as though to signal the two registers of discourse, sensible and sensuous, learned and libidinal, that the word inhabits:

> . . . this hende Nicholas
> Fil with this yonge wyf to rage and pleye,
> Whil that her housbonde was at Oseneye,
> As clerkes ben ful subtile and ful queynte;
> And prively he caughte hire by the queynte.[9]

Like other words signifying wisdom and cleverness, *quaint* could also glide over to the dark side, to signify the curious, the strange, exotic or occult. The word features in Walter Scott's evocation in *Marmion* (1808) of the Lord Gifford, identified with Hugo de Giffard, the 'wizard of Yester', as he is summoned from his underground cavern to help King Alexander beat off the invading Danes:

Lord Gifford, deep beneath the ground,
Heard Alexander's bugle sound,
And tarried not his garb to change,
But, in his wizard habit strange,
Came forth, a quaint and fearful sight;
His mantle lined with fox-skins white;
His high and wrinkled forehead bore
A pointed cap, such as of yore
Clerks say that Pharaoh's Magi wore.[10]

In less approving uses, 'quaint' meant cunning, scheming or full of guile. It therefore resembles the word 'canny', the German equivalent to which, *heimlich*, caught Freud's attention because of its weird inversiveness, which allows it to mean both familiar and suspiciously strange:

among its different shades of meaning the word '*heimlich*' exhibits one which is identical with its opposite, '*unheimlich*'. What is *heimlich* thus comes to be *unheimlich* . . . on the one hand it means what is familiar and agreeable, and on the other, what is concealed and kept out of sight . . . everything is *unheimlich* that ought to have remained secret and hidden but has come to light.[11]

As noted in Chapter Three, the Northern English 'canny' exhibits a matching ambivalence to *heimlich*, meaning both cosy and unsettling, that is, *un*canny. Indeed, the word 'cunt' seems like a participant in the lexical rigmarole, since 'canny' is often aligned with 'cunny', and 'cunt' with 'cunning' and sometimes 'conniving'. An extra link in the intricate daisy-chain of sexualized epistemopathy is provided by the early seventeenth-century adjective 'incony', which conjoins the idea of sexual penetration with the sense of rare, precious, delicate – therefore perhaps recalling 'quaint' in its medieval sense. In Marlowe's *The Jew of Malta*, Ithamore says to the prostitute Bellamira: 'Love me little, love me long. Let music rumble, / Whilst I in thy incony lap do tumble'.[12] In Shakespeare's *Love's Labour's Lost*, Costard calls Moth 'My sweet ounce of man's flesh, my incony Jew!' (Act III, Scene I) and later on employs the word in his relish of the complication he brings about by switching lovers' letters:

> By my soul, a swain, a most simple clown.
> Lord, Lord, how the ladies and I have put him down!
> O' my troth, most sweet jests, most incony vulgar wit,
> When it comes so smoothly off, so obscenely, as it were,
>   so fit! (Act IV, Scene I)

Incony here seems to be a play on 'in the cony' and French *inconnu*, unknown, as well as *uncouth*, from *un-* + Old English *cúð*, past participle of *cunnan*, to know, which generates the Scots *unco*: weird, strange or uncanny. To be caught in the cunt is to be trapped, and therefore to become a sort of silly cunt yourself; but it can also be a cosily womb-like or delicious position.

The links with French *con*, fool, idiot, and also *conning*, in the sense of learning and cognition, also seem to be salient. The link in sound if not in derivation between the cunt and cunning is attested to in a line from the Middle English *Proverbs of Hendyng*, mentioned in ten manuscripts from the late thirteenth century onwards, which is in fact the first recorded appearance of 'cunt' in English: 'ʒeve þi cunte to cunnig and crave affetir wedding [Give your cunt to cleverness and keep your demands for after the wedding]'.[13]

The cunt was often associated with the medieval name for the rabbit, the cunny, coney or cony, probably because it was used, like 'pussy', as an endearment and because of its furry associations; rabbits may not have been introduced into England until the eleventh century, and the word 'coney' is found referring to the fur or skin, possibly imported, a century before the first, early fourteenth-century uses of the word to refer to the animal recorded by the OED. But there is also a suggestive orthographic overlap. 'Coney' is recorded in Anglo-Norman both as *conynge* and *cunil* and in medieval Latin as *cunningus*. Coney-catching means trickery through deceit or, as it was also described, the 'quaint and mysticall form of Foolosophie'.[14]

The phrase was introduced by Robert Greene in two pamphlets published in 1591, to refer principally to trickery through the use of cards.[15]
But the reference to the one duped as a coney must surely have had a
sexual reference and, in any case, quickly gathered one, as in Fluello's
accusation to the titular prostitute Bellafronte in Thomas Dekker and
Thomas Middleton's *The Honest Whore*: 'thou wert yesterday a simple
whore, and now th'art a cunning Conny-catching Baggage to day.'[16]
Coney-catching could work in two directions, signifying both the
catching by means of the coney as well as the catching of it in the
predatory action notoriously recommended by Donald Trump, and
so depending on whether it is the organ or the idiot that is being
caught, as suggested by the title of a seventeenth-century comic pamphlet: *The Cony-catching Bride who After She Was Privately Married in
a Conventicle or Chamber, According to the New Fashion of Marriage, She
Sav'd her Selfe Very Handsomely from Being Coney-caught.*[17]

Coney-catching became associated from the late sixteenth century with canting, a word used for the peculiar sing-song or whining
style of speech of beggars, who were suspected of trickery (the word
'cant' also came to mean a sleight or trick). Ismenus in Beaumont and
Fletcher's *Cupid's Revenge* refers to 'The cunningst, ranckest Rogue
that euer *Canted*'.[18] Canting was also associated with the deceitful
speech of priests, an idea that survives in the modern *cant*. One of the
earliest canting dictionaries defined 'canting-crew' as

> Beggers, Gypsies; also Dissenters in Conventicles, who affect
> a disguised Speech, and disguised Modes of Speaking, and
> distinguish themselves from others by a peculiar Snuffle and
> Tone, as the Shibboleth of their Party; as Gypsies and Beggers
> have their peculiar Jargon; and are known no less by their
> several Tones in Praying, than Beggers are by their whining
> Note in Begging.[19]

Cony is defined in this same dictionary as 'a silly Fellow, *a meer
Cony*, very silly indeed', and Shakespeare's play on 'country matters' in *Hamlet* (Act III, Scene 2) may be at work in the definition
for Cockney, as 'Born within the Sound of Bowbell; (in London)
also one ignorant in Country Matters'.[20] There is no etymological
relation between *canting* and either *cunt* or *cunning*, though there
is a cousin or in-law kinship established by the fact that canting

and coney-catching were so strongly associated, through the many guides to rogues' speech or 'dark tongues' that appeared from the late sixteenth century onwards.[21] The cunt is the ultimate in dubious stupidity, the one-supposed-not-to-know; cant signifies a secret and untrustworthy *inconnu*.

The rabbity associations of 'coney' all derive from Latin *cuniculus*, which meant both a rabbit and, through transference from the rabbit's burrowing behaviour, an underground passage, cavity or canal (*coninges/conyes* is used in 1450 for soldiers who tunnel an underground passage to gain access to a city). In medieval Latin, *cuniculum* also referred to a sewer.[22] The bawdy Novocastrian song 'Geordie's Lost His Penka' centres on the efforts of a boy to retrieve a marble from the drain known as a 'cundy' (from 'conduit') by poking various objects into it (a clothes-prop, the family dog), in each case signalled in the roaring chorus 'And he's rammed it up the cundy'. T. S. Eliot seems to be evoking some of these topographic echoes in a line from his poem 'Gerontion' (1920), which uses seventeenth-century diction to evoke the complexities of historical knowledge, though the associations between the female genitals and a sort of cunning unknowability are not registered even in a recent detailed reading of Eliot's line:[23]

After such knowledge, what forgiveness? Think now
History has many cunning passages, contrived corridors
And issues . . .[24]

One of these cunning passages was Gropecunt Lane, a street name that featured in around twenty English towns and probably indicated a recourse for prostitutes. The earliest recorded version of this name was in Oxford around 1237, abbreviated to Grope Lane in 1312 and then to Grove Street or Magpie Street.[25] There can be little doubt what kind of dealings were signified by this name, especially as Gropecuntlane in Norwich was also recorded in Latin as *turpis vicus*, dirty street or street of shame.[26] Indeed, noting that the earliest appearance of this street name was in Oxford and that the others are concentrated in the kinds of major ecclesiastical cities – London, York, Wells and Northampton – that would have been populated by Oxbridge-educated clerics, Keith Briggs proposes that it may have originated as 'academic slang', suggesting another lamination of the learned and the libidinal.[27]

Passageways connect topography and biology. One of the slang names for a prostitute was a 'road', along with a 'conveniency', and conduits and conduct both suggest the acts and organs of congress: John Cleland offers us in *Fanny Hill* (1748) both female 'conduit' and 'pleasure-conduit pipe'.[28] The association between sexual organs and cunning passages may be at work too in the canting term 'cully' (perhaps echoing French *cul*, arse, or *cullion*, *coglione*, testicle, ultimately from Greek κόλεος, *koleos*, sheath), meaning fool or dupe (and also a prostitute's client). Cully may be overlaid with gully, gullet and groove, furrow.

All of this suggests a certain mixture, resembling that in the word 'uncanny' (and perhaps for that reason having a tincture of the uncanny in it), of knowing and unknowing in relation to the name and nature of the female genitals. One of the prostitutes in the 'Circe' episode of Joyce's *Ulysses* is called 'Cunty Kate'; she pipes up during a mock-scholarly cunning-linguistic discussion with Stephen Dedalus:

BIDDY THE CLAP   Did you hear what the professor said? He's a professor out of the college.
CUNTY KATE   I did. I heard that.
BIDDY THE CLAP   He expresses himself with such marked refinement of phraseology.
CUNTY KATE   Indeed, yes. And at the same time with such apposite trenchancy.[29]

'Cunning stunts', a spoonerism of 'stunning cunts', was the suggestive name of a 1975 album by prog-rock band Caravan and was also taken as the name for an alternative women's theatre company founded by Iris Walton and Jan Dungey that blended circus and cabaret, operating from 1977 to 1982. An empty-headed starlet named Cupid Stunt featured in the BBC Kenny Everett show in the 1980s. The ending of Linda Williams's 2006 poem 'On Not Using the Word "Cunt" in a Poem' indicates that the link between the cunt and cunning can still be counted on: '. . . would you give my poem a date? / Or must I count my kind of cunning out?'[30]

Stupidity and knowingness therefore appear to be bound up with questions of presence and absence, both logical and physiological. Freud reflects on these matters in his short essay 'Medusa's Head' (1922), which suggests that the decapitated head of the Medusa simultaneously expresses the fear of castration and protects against it, since the Medusa's snaky hair acts as a kind of exorbitant, exhibitionist compensation for the ablated penis:

> The hair upon Medusa's head is frequently represented in works of art in the form of snakes, and these once again are derived from the castration complex. It is a remarkable fact that, however frightening they may be in themselves, they nevertheless serve actually as a mitigation of the horror, for they replace the penis, the absence of which is the cause of the horror. This is a confirmation of the technical rule according to which a multiplication of penis symbols signifies castration. (*SE*, XVIII, 273)

Thus the cunt has, or is, cunning, the complication of more-than-seems-to-meet-the-eye (or, *a fortiori*, less). For Freud, discussing the mythical form of the female genitals in the Medusa's head, this is a matter of number, as signalled in his extraordinary offhand remark that 'a multiplication of penis symbols signifies castration' (*SE*, XVIII, 273), an articulation of the principle that, in phallic matters, more is definitely less. Freud remarks during his discussion in 'The Uncanny' of blindness as castration fear (in which the alternation between single eye and plural eyes is also in play) that the language of dreams is similarly 'fond of representing castration by a doubling or multiplication [*Verdopplung oder Vervielfältigung*] of a genital symbol' (*SE*, XVII, 235).[31] This in turn looks back to Freud's suggestions in *The Interpretation of Dreams* that '[i]f one of the ordinary symbols for a penis occurs in a dream doubled or multiplied, it is to be regarded as a warding-off of castration' (*SE*, V, 357), and '[d]reams very often represent castration by the presence of two penis symbols as the defiant expression of an anti-thetical wish' (*SE*, V, 412). The female genitals, hiding, or hiding behind, their screen of hair – so therefore maybe hiding the fact that there is nothing to hide – render undecidable the simple all or nothing, yes/no decision of penis or no-penis. The conundrum of the cunt is how to count it out, whether as singular (vagina) or plural (labia). The phrase which Strachey translates as 'multiplication of penis symbols' is 'Vervielfältigung der Penissymbole',[32] where *Falt* signifies a fold, that simplicity that is itself primally complex (Latin *simplex* does not mean without a fold but rather with only one fold). *Falt* is cognate with 'field' and 'fold', as in 'sheepfold', which is an enclosed plot of ground, a field being both open and marked off.

Bizarrely, this same conundrum of number does not seem often to be in play with regard to the similarly plural image-ensemble of the traditional prick-and-balls. Yet numerical oscillation is present in the uncertainty of what is meant by castration, a word used for various kinds of excision, including in animal husbandry (the removal of a portion of the honey from a hive), horticultural pruning and even literary expurgation, but with removal of the testicles being its root meaning. In psychoanalysis, the fear of testicle loss is transferred to and fixated upon the penis, in an inversion of the process of *Vervielfältigung*, or making-many. The logic is that, of two anatomical multiples, the female and the male genitals, which may be understood in any case as anatomical refoldings or replications one of another, one intimates uncanny complexity and the other stands for (that is, dissimulates) singularity. In both cases, there is a homology between bodily presence and absence and the coupling of the known and the unknown.

The play of exposure and concealment in the Medusa's head corresponds to the play of verbal exposure and concealment in the many euphemisms under which the word 'cunt' has been half-secreted. This perhaps includes Chaucer's *queynt*, which some have seen as the beginnings of a slight squeamishness about the word cunt in polite or courtly usage, and extending through the many sanitized versions of Gropecunt Lane, which lurks underneath many instances in English towns of 'Grape Lane' and 'Grove Passage'. It is there, too, in the not-quite-there ribaldry of cunning stunts, cupid stunts and 'the C-word', the word that lets you see only by hearsay, or the seesaw of C-saying.[33] Seeing, knowing and saying here form a kind of substitutive manifold. The Anna Livia Plurabelle sequence of Joyce's *Finnegans Wake*, a dialogue between two washerwomen on opposite banks of the Liffey which is rendered in the voice of many rivers, is initiated with the words 'Well, you know or don't you kennet or haven't I told you every telling has a taling and that's the he and the she of it'.[34] The river Kennet – named, we can assume, in reference to the many words indicating water-passages – flows together with the Old English and Scots dialect 'kenning' as knowing, just as rivers tend to flow between the conditions of the positive and the negative; 'the Moy changez her minds twixt Cullin and

Conn tween Cunn and Collin', Joyce writes, playing both on hill (*col*) and channel (*cunny*), and the French *cul* and *con*.[35] Earlier in *Finnegans Wake*, Joyce evokes another complex anatomical convolution in his mock-technical account of an auricular radio device called the 'harmonic condenser enginium', which is 'tuned up by twintriodic singulvalvulous pipelines' and 'a meatous conch culpable of cunduncing Naul and Santry'.[36] Like Joyce's river, broadening into a complex delta as its flows out to the sea, the history of the word 'cunt' percolates ideas of knowing and unknowing, wisdom and folly, visibility and concealment, saying and unsayability.

Recent years have seen efforts such as Eve Ensler's *The Vagina Monologues* (1995) that set out to 'reclaim' or revalue the word 'cunt', emphasizing world-begetting fecundity over violence. Reclamation of this kind seems to involve the fantasy of lifting the word up into benignly daylit knowability, unstreaked by hostility and fear. But to detoxify 'cunt' is to remove from it all its powers of intoxication, positive or negative. Even in its purged and happy-clappy modalities, it remains the essential body-word, suspended between sensible and intelligible, pure being and pure knowing. It is a word that seems rankly soaked with corporeality, ready to swallow itself up in pure sensation, and yet still a sign that keeps bodily being just about at bay, as something knowable and nameable. In one sense the cunt is the name for a pure, bestial know-nothing, the nothingness of the body, in that it is identified with a corporeal vacancy, a space scooped out of flesh that is both a secret hollow in the body and the hollowness of the body as such. At the same time, the cunt is the unknown, the concealed, the unspoken, the ineffably intricate. The female genitalia is the absence-connoting organ that produces a suspension of knowledge, for it cannot and must not be known. But it is a nescience that is yet a knowing and a showing of an unknowing that, in its very withdrawal, seems to demand to be both shown and made known.

NINCOMPOOP

As the ongoing history of the word 'cunt' makes plain, knowing is intimately braided with naming. The many words for stupidity divide between cloddish words of Germanic origin indicating elementary states of matter and elaborate words often suggestive of corrupted or mock-Latin. The straightforward way of reading insulting terms like 'nincompoop' and 'ignoramus' would be to see them as a mocking wielding of a learned-sounding term that its target is unlikely to be able to understand, so emphasizing the extent of their ignorance. But terms like this also partly travesty the terms they wield, perhaps in a kind of imitation of the amateurish bungling that one would expect the subject to inflict on them, which then debases the intellectual or spiritual force of the word into the pure matter of sound. 'Ignoramus' derives from a legal judgment made by a grand jury when it found the evidence for an indictment insufficient for it to go to a petty jury. The bill would be returned with the word 'ignoramus' written on it, signifying 'we do not know' or 'we do not recognize it'. To 'give' or 'return' an ignoramus became a common way of signifying that one did not know something, and also, for example in John Stephens's *Satyre in Defence of Common Law and Lawyers* of 1615, and in George Ruggle's play *Ignoramus* – first acted in Latin in 1615, translated into English by Robert Codrington in 1662 – became a satirical name for an obscurantist lawyer, and then started to be used in a general way to signify an ignorant or foolish person.[37]

In this, 'ignoramus' follows the career of the word 'dunce', the origins of which are not specifically Latin, but are certainly scholastic and entrained with the history of religious reformation in England. The word signifies a follower of the Franciscan John Duns Scotus, known as Doctor Subtilis, one of the most formidable and influential religious philosophers of the late thirteenth century. As Richard Chevenix Trench explains, the move away from the highly abstract, nuanced and, as it seemed to many, hairsplitting and logic-chopping style of reasoning took the name of Duns as a touchstone:

> many times an adherent of the old learning would seek to strengthen his position by an appeal to its great doctor, familiarly called Duns; while those who had rejected his authority would contemptuously rejoin, 'Oh, you are a *Dunsman*,' or more briefly, 'You are a *Duns*,' – or, 'This is a piece of *dunsery*;' and inasmuch as the new learning was ever enlisting more and more of the genius and scholarship of the age on its side, the title became more and more a term of scorn.[38]

William Tyndale may have begun the fashion for using 'Dunce' to signify a sophistical hair-splitter:

As the Jews have set up a book of traditions called Talmud, to destroy the sense of the scripture; unto which they give faith, and unto the scripture none at all, be it never so plain, but say it cannot be understood, save by the Talmud: even so have ours set up their Duns, their Thomas, and a thousand like draff, to stablish their lies through falsifying the scripture; and say that it cannot be understood without them, be it never so plain.[39]

Thomas Blount's *Glossographia* defines a 'Rabbinist' as 'one that studies, or is cunning in the works of the *Rabbies*; sometimes used for a Dunce'.[40] So a dunce is not someone who does not understood even elementary concepts, but rather someone who does not understand that they *are* elementary. A dunce was not a complete ignoramus, or rather was so in a particular way. In his 'True Character of a Dunce', Donne describes him not as bereft of knowledge but as deprived of understanding of any knowledge he may have:

> one of the most unprofitable of all Gods creatures, being as he is, a thing put clean besides his right use, made fitt for the cart & the flail, and by mischance Entangled amongst books and papers, a man cannot tel possible what he is now good for, save to move up and down and fill room, or to serv as *Animatum Instrumentum* for others to work withal in base Imployments, or to be a foyl for better witts, or to serve (as They say monsters do) to set out the variety of nature, and Ornament of the Universe; . . . he speaks just what his books or last company said unto him without varying one whit & very seldom understands himself, you may know by his discourse where he was last, for what he read or heard yesterday he now dischargeth his memory or notebook of, not his understanding, for it never came there.[41]

At the beginning of Marlowe's *Dr Faustus*, two scholars enquiring innocently after Faustus's whereabouts are mocked by Wagner, his serving-boy, with a series of elaborate quibbles and qualifications, concluding with 'if you were not dunces, you would never ask me such a question. For is he not *corpus naturale*? And is not that *mobile*? Then, wherefore should you ask me such a question?'[42] This may suggest that Faustus himself is being presented as a kind of dunce in his very ambition and overreach, his tragedy consisting of the fact 'not that he was born a fool but that he studied so diligently to become one'.[43] The idea that a dunce is a quasi- or pseudo-learned fool rather than a straightforward and honest idiot also animates the whole of Pope's caustic mock-epic and epic of mockery the *Dunciad* (1728–43).

The dunce cap, sometimes combined with the traditional ass's ears of the fool, is a humiliation specific to scholastic settings. It is sometimes suggested that the conical form of the dunce cap derives from a wizard's hat, with the suggestion that Duns Scotus himself favoured this headgear because, as alleged by the *Chicago Reader*'s 'The Straight Dope', 'He noted that wizards supposedly wore such things; an apex was considered a symbol of knowledge and the hats were thought to "funnel" knowledge to the wearer.'[44] Perhaps it is the funnel metaphor that makes this explanation puzzling, since funnels usually work the other way round. Surely it would be better for the open end of the cone to be at the top, like a radio dish rather than a lightning conductor? But then what would be the entry point for the concentrating apex?

There are many other kinds of pointy hat worn by humans, often as an icon of distinction or eminence, as for example in the medieval *hennin*, popular among French women, but also sometimes to indicate aggressive intent, as in Prussian military headgear, the form of which survives in British police helmets. The point about hats, and especially large ones, is how fragile their authority can be, given their propensity to fall off, blow away or be sat on. So the hat can easily become an image of the frailty or friability of human intelligence, nowhere more than in the often puzzlingly intricate hat tricks of the clown, which seem to signify a kind of play with one's own head, as parodied and intensified in the hat-exchanging routine in Beckett's *Waiting for Godot*. In James Gillray's satirical etching of 1783 *Apollo and the Muses Inflicting Penance on Dr Pomposo Round Parnassus*, the penitent dunce is Dr Johnson, who is being scourged for reducing the glories of literature to the dryness of literary criticism. Johnson carries a placard which reads: 'For defaming that Genius I could never emulate, by criticism without Judgment', and he wears a dunce cap, in the form of a pyramid rather than a cone, on which are inscribed the names of the poets whose lives he had written, not all of them exactly in the ranks of the Immortals any more: Milton, Otway, Waller, Gray, Shenston, Lyttelton, Gay, Denman, Collins.

The history of the idea of the dunce shows a steady decline from absurd pseudo-sophistication to shameful idiocy. The dunce cap, which is first named in Dickens's *The Old Curiosity Shop* (1841), though sometimes pictured earlier, is probably something of a back-formation belonging, like much of scholastic iconography, to the visual lexicon of how the past was imagined to be at various points.[45] No sophistication remains in the name given by a group of Caltech biologists to the learning-deficient mutation of *Drosophila* dubbed 'dunce', whereby the insect is unable to learn to associate a particular odorant with an electric shock, something normal fruit flies are able to do.[46] Other mutants showing variations of the same learning inability have been heartlessly dubbed 'turnip' and 'rutabaga', or swede.[47]

The blessing or benefit arising from the possession of intelligence is then promoted to a demand, a demand to which one must accede if one is to be regarded as human at all. 'Intelligence is a moral category,' writes Adorno in *Minima Moralia*.[48] To make this claim is to assume and perform the coercive power exercised on and in knowing, and the power of proscription exerted through it. The will to knowledge is more than the desire to be the one supposed to know: it is the desire to be able to denominate and hold in abomination the one supposed to be ignorant.

INSIDE KNOWLEDGE

The most generalized term of abuse directed at the ignorant is 'stupid'. In fact, we can usefully distinguish the stupid from the ignorant. Although there can be something willed and wilful about ignorance, it remains perfectly possible to be ignorant in a non-culpable way, whereas the charge of stupidity always involves an at least implicit charge that the stupid person has committed a sort of offence against sociality, one with wide consequences for which they bear a responsibility. The stupid person is not necessarily, and perhaps not even usually, uninformed, but rather unintelligent – often, it is thought, arrogantly and unrepentantly so. One may say that the stupid person should always have known better, implying, in fact, that the stupid person is not without knowledge, but without the understanding required to interpret or apply what they know. So stupidity is a defect rather than a deficiency of knowledge.

The fact that humans assign themselves the honorific title of *sapiens* makes for a curious attraction to as well as revulsion from the condition of unknowing. Humans are curious about the incurious. In every age and among almost every people there seems to be contempt for the fool or idiot. But the contempt is often associated with fascination, as though there were a suspicion that such persons could be possessed of certain kinds of hidden wisdom, or power in their ignorance. There is, we may perhaps say, something uncanny or not wholly knowable about those who are not in the know. Since to be stupid is not to be fully human, there is often an association between low intelligence and animals: birdbrain, harebrain, ass, coot, goose, nitwit. Some of the words associated with idiocy or foolishness indicate other senses of the alien. An oaf, variant of *aufe* and *ouphe*, refers to an elf's child or changeling left by fairies; a deformed, clumsy or idiot child, a simpleton. A canting dictionary of 1699 defines an oaf as 'a Wise-acre, a Ninny or Fool', where 'wise-acre' is cognate with Middle Dutch *wijsseggher*, wise-sayer, the idea being that a pretender to wisdom is in fact to be regarded with contempt.[49]

The entanglement of knowing and unknowing is suggested by a coinage like agnoiology, which refers to the study of what it is not possible to know. In coining the term, the Scottish idealist philosopher James Frederick Ferrier wrote in 1854 that

> A reasoned and systematic ontology has remained until this day a desideratum in speculative science, because a reasoned and systematic agnoiology has never yet been projected . . . The only way in which a deliverance from this dilemma can be effected is, by admitting our ignorance to the full, and then by instituting a searching inquiry into its nature and character.[50]

Ferrier believed that, since it was only possible to be ignorant of something it might in principle be possible to know, it is in fact a mark of human distinction not to know those things which are in fact unintelligible or self-contradictory. Ignorance is therefore a kind of glorification rather than its humiliating limit, an aspiration embodied in a remarkable oceanic metaphor:

> The agnoiology carries out and completes the work entered on in the epistemology. In the epistemology we beheld only the

backs – the dorsal fins, if we may so speak – of the necessary truths; in the agnoiology we see under them, and all around them. We look upon them – like Horace's first mariner on the swimming sea-monsters – *siccis oculis*, as they turn up their shadowy sides, and gleaming abdomina.[51]

Little wonder that such a condition might come to have an allure of its own, and that foolishness might come to seem close to sanctity and even to a stripped kind of wisdom. To be silly is to be 'sely', 'selig', happy, blessed, fortunate or blissful. In John Skelton's 1522 satirical poem, the eponymous Colin Cloute speaks from, for and perhaps also against such a position of ignorance:

> Say this, and say that,
> His hed is so fat,
> He wotteth neuer what
> Nor wherof he speketh;
> He cryeth and he creketh,
> He pryeth and he peketh,
> He chydes and he chatters,
> He prates and he patters,
> He clytters and he clatters,
> He medles and he smatters,
> He gloses and he flatters;
> Or yf he speake playne,
> Than he lacketh brayne,
> He is but a fole;
> Let hym go to scole,
> On a thre foted stole
> That he may downe syt,
> For he lacketh wyt;
> And yf that he hyt
> The nayle on the hede,
> It standeth in no stede;
> The deuyll, they say, is dede,
> The deuell is dede.[52]

I found when I tried an Internet search for 'prejudice against the ignorant' or 'prejudice against the stupid' it produced page upon page of results intoning earnestly against the ignorance of prejudice, but nothing to the purpose I had tried to articulate. This absence may be telling. Prejudice against the ignorant is, like the equally vile and, well, I almost wrote idiotic, prejudice in favour of the beautiful, one of our great unknown knowns – we think with it so automatically that we find it almost impossible to think about. Lining up instinctively with William Hazlitt (1778–1830) in his declaration that 'Prejudice is the child of ignorance' might imply that we should be on principle (which is to say, by prejudice) opposed to ignorance.[53] This does not necessarily imply that we should be prejudiced against the ignorant, but it is such an engrained habit with us to mistake the bearers of a quality for the quality itself that we find this very difficult to resist. When I eventually found a piece of writing that seemed as though it might answer my purpose, an article by Michael Deacon in the *Daily Telegraph* in 2010 entitled 'Even Stupid People Have Feelings – Let's End this Bigotry', it quickly became clear that its demands for employers to be prevented from discriminating against less intelligent applicants and for parliament to exercise quotas to ensure proper representation of the ignorant were in fact a kind of sniggeringly Swiftean *Modest Proposal*.[54] Indeed, it is almost impossible to find a noncomic investigation of stupidity.

One of the most powerful functions of knowledge is to form and sustain human aggregates. It is impossible to have any social existence as a child without developing the necessary expertise in whatever kinds of shared knowledge are current and approved – films, pop music, fashion, sporting events. The global infantilism that universal media has unleashed depends upon the gossip-glue provided by celebrities whose sociognostic function is to be famous for being famous, or known for being known about. For all our optimistic assumptions about the powers of knowledge to overcome prejudice and spread understanding, shared knowledge has a twisted twin in the hostility and contempt it allows towards those who do not share our knowledge, or have their own forms of shared knowledge to which we are not party. The force of religious inclusion and exclusion is exercised largely through forms of knowledge, since religion is never a matter merely of habitual practices, but also of shared beliefs and doctrines, things taught and so thought to be known. I have never for a micro-second in my life felt the feeblest spasm of religious belief, but I hope I am able to be good-humoured and amicable in the presence of persons of religious faith – whose sanity I would otherwise have to doubt, and who doubtless must sometimes doubt mine – by dint of the long immersion I have had in forms of religious observance, through attendance at a school at which hours were spent praying, singing and the like, and a lifetime teaching literature produced by and for people for whom some form of Christianity was the medium for thinking about almost everything else (sex, money, politics, health, fashion, horticulture and so on). As a consequence, I can sing my part in a soteriological set-to at High Table sociably and with almost no risk of social disgrace, knowing as I do so much of what is held to be known or not.

Almost all nations have ethnic jokes, and the favoured form of ridicule is poking fun at the stupidity of the Irish, Polish, Pakistanis, women, men, or whatever group is to be kept outside the knowing community of self-recognizing deriders. Human beings become and try to remain human through the process of recognition, taken not as the confirmation of what you are, but more literally the reverberation or echolalia of the social cogito, what we suppose each other to know, and the *sujets-supposés-savoir* we suppose each other to be (to suppose being practically the same word as to subject). That is why we so often use words with a noetic cast like 'recognition' and 'acknowledgement' to describe solidarity-effects. What is held in common in a community is its knowledge of what is common knowledge within it, and unknown outside. The idea of acknowledgement has largely positive associations, perhaps because acknowledgement often means accepting the force of another's claims on us, but participating in the heteronoetic aggression of stupidity-jokes also exerts force, in the pressure to acknowledge the demands for affiliation and expatriation they assume and exercise. Making someone or something ludicrous is conducted and continued through a work of community-forming allusion, a literal playing-into the knowledge, and the knowledge about others' knowledge, that acts as solidary cement. There can be no such thing as a society without education, and, reciprocally, you cannot be familiar with anything without being made a member of some family. 'Kin' is cousin to 'ken', to know, make known or acknowledge, but also to conceive, engender or beget. To know is to be in the know, and all knowledge is a kind of inside knowledge.

This is why stupidity is functionally identical with madness, despite the otherwise clear differences between those whose understanding is disordered, and those whose understanding is merely limited. For the one who does not know has the power of deranging the forms of solidary knowing that keep a given community viable, for they may embody the category-chimera of being at once unknowing and human. Knowing is what constitutes *cosa nostra*, our thing, the thing of which we gossip (French *causer*), that gives cause, origin and renewal, the thing with which we make common cause. 'Cause' and 'case' are perhaps from the past participle of *cavere*, to beware, take heed, exercise caution or defend against.

SILLY

This may also explain why the deliberate self-abasement practised by the many different forms of holy fool or knowledge-despising ignoramus can be so paradoxically powerful. The holy fool is particularly identified with Christianity, a religion that comes into being as a reaction against the powerful and pervasive forms of institutionalized knowledge represented by the Graeco-Roman and Judaic traditions. Though Christ is seen in high-level disputation in the Temple, the real potency of Christianity lay in its urging of unlettered or infantile simplicity. Holy fools seem to have had their beginning among the many anchorites and Desert Fathers who withdrew from religious communities to live ascetically austere lives apart. The tradition of the holy fool remains powerful within Christianity all the way through the medieval period to the Reformation, and in Eastern forms of Christianity, especially in Russia, holy fools continued to be potent presences.

It is a very risky strategy, but sacred foolishness can under certain circumstances constitute an alternative community built on epistemic dissidence rather than epistemic conformity. John Saward suggests that:

> Going into the desert expresses a longing to 'unlearn' the sensibility of the age, to be remade in body, mind, and spirit, to become truly and without compromise a new humanity in Christ ... [The holy fool's] vocation would seem to be to recall his brethren to their vocation to be unconformed to the world's wisdom.[55]

We are nowadays surprised and dismayed when politics is made idiotic by being conducted by people who seem to be idiots, or act in idiotic ways. But this might teach us that, insofar as every idiocy in fact has the capacity to be politogenic, and so able to form a polity, there can assuredly be a political idiocy. In order to maintain its political seriousness, such idiocy must also be political in the narrower sense of being conducted strategically or in bad faith. It is necessary, in short, for such idiocy to be 'simulated folly' (PF, 20).

The holy fool phenomenon is given particular potency in societies that are beginning to depend more on knowledge than on power or tradition. Since human societies are constituted through communication, which exacts a considerable cognitive cost, the larger and more complex the society, the more intelligence – both internally in individual persons and externally in systems of impersonal record and communication – is needed to manage and optimize contradictory interests. In such societies, instrumental and calculative reason, with its tendency to create long-term stability, will grow more important than charismatic reason, driven by intensity and effervescence and associated with conflict and convulsion. The institutionalization of religion is an important part of this rationalization. John Saward proposes that '[t]he fool appears most commonly at a time of political tranquillity, when the Church adapts herself to the political *status quo*' (PF, 28). This rationalization may increase opportunities for charismatic recoils against calculation, since the negative potency of the one who ignores or refuses civilized good sense will be greatly increased and can easily change its valence to become a source of positive potency. The tendency for complex rationality to generate different forms of surplus – social, economic and affective – can add unpredictability to social relations. So temperate rationality gives folly a power it could not previously have.

The literature relating to holy fools emphasizes simplicity over sophistication and wisdom over learning. The holy fool is opposed not to knowledge as such, but to the prudential association between knowledge and worldly self-preservation:

> The gospel message of life through self-oblation and sacrificial death cuts clean through the assumptions of the present age. The world lives by the law of the flesh and strives wherever possible to consolidate self. The world believes that power

and glory come through calculating self-preservation. The world can make no sense of the word of the cross, of Christ-wisdom-crucified, and so regards it as 'insanity' (*mōria*, 1 Cor. 1:18ff.). (*PF*, 3)

The other important condition for charismatic folly is the necessary growth of symbolic and communicative media, as part of the push towards rationalization. This term is used, usually of later periods characterized by centralized bureaucracy and the growth of interconnected economic systems, and mostly to suggest the application of homogeneous understandings of what rational action consists of. But rationalization must be understood much more broadly as an integration-through-diversification of the field of social communication. The fool must be more than a wild man or lunatic, whose being is entirely unassimilable to the social order; he, and occasionally she, must be able to instance and inhabit a recognizable category, the category of the non-categorial. The fool's unintelligence must increasingly become intelligible, as a known unknown. The holy fool always exhibits a compounding of the apparently witless and the knowing, if sometimes in the steady resolve with which they keep the secret of their orthodox devotion to the Gospel.

This is what Paul means by the phrase in the first letter to the Corinthians that comes to govern the behaviour and understanding of holy fools, 'fools in Christ'. The phrase is sometimes rendered as 'fool for the sake of Christ', though this seems to take rather a liberty with Paul's Greek; in μωροὶ διὰ Χριστόν, *moroi dia Christon* (1 Corinthians 4:10), the word *dia* signifies through, or by means of. This may mean that the example of the mockery and humiliation endured by Christ enjoins an imitative foolishness, but may also imply that, through the example or agency of Christ, the foolishness is transformed or spiritualized. In either case the foolishness suggests a certain logos of the illogical, a *morosophy*, used to mean both a wise foolishness and a foolish or duncical philosophy – or, to evoke an even rarer cod-learned seventeenth-century term, which seems to appear more often in dictionaries than in ordinary use, a kind of *morology*. As such, it must be seen as an act of communication, a making of a kind of social sense, even, indeed especially, in its apparent hostility to social bonds:

> the holy fool as such is always defined by his relationship to a particular community. Indeed, some of the later fools are monks who leave their monastic community to play the fool in the wider community of the city. In either case holy folly is a social manifestation. (*PF*, 17)

The fool aims for simple detachment, but this detachment can only have meaning in its secession from a world of ever greater connections and communication. In acting as a sign of itself – and the more word-eschewingly corporeal the crazy actions of the holy fool, the more symbolic they become – the detachment from worldliness is bound back into the world, since the world must expand to take note of and encompass it. This then complicates the homonomical drive of the antinoetic fool by linking it to heteronomical pressures. The only consistently holy – that is, whole and self-identical – form of foolishness would need not only to display no care for worldly things, but to display no care for holiness itself, since this constitutes a rational, containing frame for the actions of the holy fool. John Saward has no problem with this doublethink: holy fools, he maintains, 'offer precisely *rational* criteria for distinguishing true folly from false, true wisdom from false' (*PF*, 73), but he buys the serenity of this formula with inattention to all the paradoxes to which the knowing defection from knowledge must give rise. The refusal of worldliness can make no sense, for example, of the fact that the more compelling the gospel, the more successful it may be in enlarging faith and spirituality – perhaps in part precisely through the example given by holy-fool unworldliness, the more worldly God's wisdom must come to seem. Insofar as goodness, truth, justice, mercy, love and faith are all of this world, they will have themselves to be spurned by any right-thinking world-despiser of worldliness. The fool's wisdom can succeed only as long as the goodness of God continues to be unavailing and the world remains wholly and reliably ungodly.

This is to leave aside all the manifold opportunities for masochistic gratification through abasement open to persons of a certain sensibility, sleeping in ditches, wearing dead dogs round one's neck, licking lepers' sores and so forth, though this was another dissimulated complexity of the holy fool that cannot have been lost on intelligent contemporary objectors. The zealotry of the holy fool is essentially an attempt to refuse complexity, not least the complex irony of its own always dawning yet self-disavowing recognition of this fact. As Peter Sloterdijk argues, monotheistic zeal is the effort to outdo God in turning history back and recanting the mistake made in ever making the world.[56] But 'zeal' is from Greek ζῆλος, *zelos*, jealousy or rivalry, and signifies a kind of competitive comparison. The simplicity of the holy fool is always as an absolute minimum duplicitous. It supposes a retreat from the contaminating complexity of the world back to the elementary condition of the child or the idiot – the Greek ἰδιώτης, *idiotes*, signifying, as we have seen earlier in this chapter, a private person or capacity as opposed to office or action in the public sphere, its root related to 'it' as the pure, unmodified thing in itself. But that elementariness must always be a belated and knowing compound, its subtraction of complexity a kind of contract with that from which it marks its distance, the singularity of the fool always also complying with a kind of generic function.

This paradoxical unachievability of knowing ignorance survives beyond religious eras and resurfaces in strikingly similar forms in the agniological ambitions of later periods. The Romantic exaltation of the simplicity of the gentle, childlike idiot is embodied for example in Wordsworth's 'The Idiot Boy' (1798), and sees in mental incapacity the capacity for blissful absorption in the natural world. This faith is enacted in the witless sing-song pleasures of the poem's own jog-along prosody, which doubles the inarticulate burring of the idiot Johnny: 'The owlets hoot, the owlets curr, / And Johnny's lips they burr, burr, burr, / And on he goes beneath the moon'.[57] The poem unfolds a story the purpose of which is to be self-evacuating, since, at the end of the story, we must be shown that the story does not matter as much as the animal pleasures of music and sensation. Sharing her friend Betty's rising apprehension about Johnny and his pony (the latter as good-hearted but hopelessly undependable as Johnny), old Susan Gale, for whom the boy has been endangered, is able in any case to spring from her bed 'As if by magic cured'.[58] The poem sets John's wordless 'burr-ing' against the 'flurry' and the 'hurry' of Betty in her search for him. The choice offered us seems to be 'cunning' (caring about the story) or 'joy', rhymed dinningly over and over with 'boy' and 'Foy', the latter Betty's surname, which merges faith and foolishness. The poem ends with an enactment of the dissolution of reason in rhyme, with Johnny's burbling answer to Betty's questions about what he has been doing all night: '(His very words I give to you,) / The cocks did crow to-whoo,

THE MADNESS OF KNOWLEDGE

to-whoo / And the sun did shine so cold'.[59] But all of the sentimental yield of the poem depends, of course, upon its seemingly unwitting demonstration of the impossibility of the pure, unsullied witlessness it offers, despite the suppression of the first, 'to-whit' part of the conventional poetic formula for owl song, which first appears in print in 1594 in the 'To whit to whoo, the Owle does cry' of a song in John Lyly's comic play *Mother Bombie*.[60] Wit can never be entirely eclipsed in twitter when it is the knowing performance of the unwitting.

The growing power and effectiveness of technical and specialist expertise, along with the increasing economic and cultural centrality of formal education across many different parts of the world, has produced other kinds of reaction against the authority of knowledge. This has sometimes taken the form of a revival of the dynamics of the holy fool. Just as the holy fool's recoil from knowledge took place from within religious belief itself, so reactions to the authority of academic knowledge in the growing epistemocracy that will be described in the final chapter of this book have taken place not from outside but within academic thinking, especially in those areas of the humanities most at threat from technical knowledges. Idiot-figures are the subjects not just of the stigmatizing tracked in Patrick McDonagh's cultural history of idiocy, but also of a kind of antinoetic charisma.[61] However, where an earlier form of Romantic desire for transcendence focused on the saving simplicity of the idiot, modern idiocy is valued for its capacity to introduce complexity. So, as Martin Halliwell concludes in his study of modern images of idiocy,

> If idiocy is often imaged as a kind of empty subjectivity or barren selfhood, it can also be an experience of plenitude, replacing strict identity boundaries with an unruly existence that cannot be delimited by social stigma or reduced to a medical label.[62]

The idiot has a kind of glamour, a word that has undergone a similar corruption as the word 'dunce', since it begins as 'grammar' and, via *gramarye* and 'grimoire', a sorcerer's manual, occult learning or necromancy, becomes, largely through its use by Walter Scott, a word that signifies a delusive enchantment. It thus redeploys something of the magical investment in a mode of knowledge to give a magical potency to that which defeats or goes beyond it.

FANTASIES OF STUPIDITY

Writing in praise of Robert Musil's 'On Stupidity' (1937), Genese Grill concludes that

> we would do well to wonder at the strange topsy-turvydom which declares the stuttering, stammering seers of new worlds, the pioneering founders of new languages and customs, the unseemly actors of themselves the stupid ones, when compared to those who think they already know or who rest comfortably upon the laurels of an already-constructed and controlling system of pre-judgment and assumptions.[63]

There are certainly kinds of innovative thinking that are sometimes called stupid, and certainly kinds of thinking that are based upon prejudice and assumption; but this way of putting the matter certainly sounds more like the latter than the former. We should be patient and attentive when we encounter stammering, but not because every stammer is a tremor of visionary intimation.

The term 'stupidity' seems to have migrated steadily over the last two centuries to the centre of antinoetic discourse, moving into the place once occupied by foolishness and idiocy. The fact that there is no obvious noun for the one characterized as stupid, unlike the fool or idiot – reference to a *stupe* (attested from 1763), 'a stupid' or 'the stupids' as a noun being back-formations – gives it a certain advantage in its loose general applicability. But another advantage comes from the fact that stupidity is part of an expectedly lively complex of word-concepts. To be stupid is to be reduced, as in many other ways of naming witlessness, to a state of mute matter – Latin *stupor* referring to the condition of dullness, numbness or insensibility. But, unlike such conditions, stupor often implies a response to some stimulus. One may be stupid through lethargy but also because one has been stupefied by the kinds of thing we call stupendous, meaning able to cause a state of stupor; this is why Emperor Frederick II was called the *stupor mundi*, the 'wonder of the world', in the *Chronica magna* of Matthew Paris in 1250.[64] So stupor can suggest a kind of astonishment, being turned to stone by some amazing excess or overload, a notion which might recall Freud's comments on the duality (death and arousal) of petrified astonishment by the Medusa's head.

It is not clear what relation there may be between the stupefying family of words and the Latin *stuprum*, meaning rape, fornication or defilement, which yields the words 'stupre' and 'stupration', used until the seventeenth century for rape or ravishment. In the appendix to his etymological dictionary of Latin, reserved for more speculative entries, F.E.J. Valpy refers to J. J. Scaliger's suggestion that *stuprum* derives from *stupeo*, '*ut quod facit ut stupeamus*' – as that which makes us stupefied.[65] Alfred Ernout and Alfred Meillet assure their readers, though without supplying evidence, that *stuprum* is 'certainly from the same radical group to which *stupeo* belongs'.[66] Perhaps the linking conception is that of being passively but ecstatically *rapt*, the past participle of *rapere*, to seize, devour, rape.

Flannery O'Connor opens the door to many of the recent revaluations of stupidity in her remark that 'there's a certain grain of stupidity that the writer of fiction can hardly do without, and this is the quality of having to stare, of not getting the point at once.'[67] Robert Kugelmann enthusiastically amplifies O'Connor's hint, explaining that the poet (a silent promotion here for O'Connor's writer of fiction):

> attends to the mere appearances of things. The desire to transcend the physical world of the here and now ceases to play a role, as one stares, stunned, at what presents itself. If one can stay in the muck of appearances long enough – without abstracting, without categorizing – the thing shows itself. O'Connor states that not only does the thing show itself in its particularity, but the poet simultaneously sees it as a universal: stunned and stilled as the poet is, the thing can begin to reverberate in the depth of the poet's being.[68]

I find it impossible to understand how one sees a particular as a universal while refraining from any kind of categorizing, though I also doubt that Kugelmann means me seriously to try. But what he goes on to say about this mode of open responsiveness, which is intended to duck under the net of knowledge, suggests that there is more to this stupidity than its name might suggest, for it is 'stupidity that knows itself as stupid'.[69] So probably not stupidity in anything like any of its ordinary senses at all, then, if not without a certain kinship with holy folly. This is, like so many of the other epistemic postures and dispositions considered in this book, a kind of playing at stupidity, a quasi-stupidity to match I. A. Richards's poetic quasi-knowledge, met with in Chapter One; a desirous Romantic fantasy of the idiot as mystic. We arrive soon enough at the blending of desire and knowledge:

> This movement to the sheer appearances of things, to the world in its materiality, intoxicates. Stupidity is a desire for earth, for the simple presence of things. And insofar as it is a desire, it 'knows' its goal in some inarticulate way. It knows appearances and materiality. The plunge into the muck is goal-oriented, and this knowing, stupid though it be, is its reflectivity.[70]

Kugelmann is not describing nothing at all here, though what he is describing is not what he seems or claims to be. He is describing the shape of a knowledge-fantasy, the desire for a kind of knowledge that could be made of desire. You cannot simply know the 'simple presence of things', since 'simple presence' is such a sophisticated notion, vastly beyond the capacity of simpletons; but you can know the complex desire for it. We should not be surprised to find that the practice of art, or the attitudes attributed to the artist, have a central role in sustaining this tranquil daydream of a blended knowing and unknowing, since an important function of 'the aesthetic' since the beginning of the nineteenth century has been to harbour and encourage such immoderate fantasies of what certain kinds of mystic knowledge can achieve.

Tony Jasnowski also follows Flannery O'Connor's lead, arguing that it is necessary for writers to press 'beyond the safe realm of logic and reason and into the dangerous province of absurdity and stupidity'.[71] The kind of stupidity he has in mind is rather narrowly defined in the idea of 'virtuous' stupidity, which he explains by telling us that '[t]he virtuously stupid act as if they do not know what *in faith* they do know, but not in *fact*.'[72] This corresponds to 'the authentic stupidity to which Christians are called',[73] making the writer a kind of holy fool, though in fact Jasnowski's definition rules out most of the things that would ordinarily be regarded as any kind of stupidity, and may be reduced to the undramatic suggestion that writers might do well to trust their intuitions, which can often work out well. Since not all that much hangs on whether writers do or do not adopt this strategy, beyond their work working out well for them and their readers or not, it really does not seem as heart-racingly risky a sally into the cognitive wilderness as is here alleged.

Natalie Pollard celebrates in a similar vein the power of certain kinds of unfamiliar or refractory poetry to produce a condition of stupefaction or a bewildering, wordless paralysis in the reader:

> Unable to grasp it and at the same time powerless to leave hold, the poet, reader, scholar are fascinated – gripped, held, and spurred onward – by stupidity ... The study of stupidity in contemporary poetry reminds us of art's enabling capacity to arrest us, and of the courage and intellectual rigour necessary for such a confrontation.[74]

This mixture of demand and delight sounds very stirring indeed, and the pleasure to be had from the contemplation of such possibilities as she proclaims is undeniable. But it must be doubted whether anything like this experience has ever been had by any reader of modern poetry, or indeed by any reader of anything whatever. Being stupefied in the absolute ways described, as opposed to being puzzled, perplexed, intrigued, delighted and all the other interesting but familiar ways in which poetry is experienced, is not something that occurs to readers, it is something that readers are encouraged to say about their reading. It is, in short, a subjunctive rather than subjective experience, one that belongs to the dreamwork of literary-critical let's-pretend knowledge.

Most of the forms of stupidity promoted in recent decades depend upon an extraordinarily, and one must sometimes suspect wilfully, simple-minded understanding of what reason is supposed to be, namely capital-R Reason of an absolute, madly systematic and exceptionless kind, along with an overstated view of what stupidity might be taken to be in relation to this hypostasized notion of absolute Reason. It is certainly possible to hold and hold to an absolute idea of Reason, but that is not the idea that generally prevails. A more sober and for that reason more supple understanding of reason as the attempt to supply good reasons for things, or just 'reasonable' ones, would include a very large number of the things alleged to be reason's outside or adversary in stupidity.

Avital Ronell offers a much more developed account of the powers of stupidity to breach or unbutton the alleged constraints of reason, once again through allegations about the kind of thing that occurs in the writing – and presumably also in some way the reading – of poetry, which she says requires the courage to confront the fact of not knowing:

> Poetic courage consists in embracing the terrible lassitude of mind's enfeeblement, the ability to endure the near facticity of feeblemindedness ... The poet ventures forth undefended, brave, like Wordsworth's Idiot Boy, whose adventure takes him through an unnarratable safety zone where, inexplicably immunized and protected, he has encountered the greatest danger.[75]

This courage points to a particular state of mind or, as Ronell would prefer to personify it, a particular kind of being who cannot be said to be fully in charge of his purpose or process:

> The gesture of traversing peril and running a risk – a risk that does not know and cannot tell where it is going – points in these poems not to a morph of the action hero, quick and present to the task, sure of aim, but to the depleted being, held back by fear or indifference (we are never sure which), a being from the start stupefied, non-present – 'not all there'. No one has been able to account for that which is missing, not there, in poetic origination, but the poets have in their way avowed the secret experience of stupidity. (*SY*, 9)

It would be wilful to deny that at least some poets have had, or have at any rate floated, the view that writing some kinds of poetry can on occasion call for a certain amount of swallow-hard chutzpah, but it seems dogmatic to affirm that it must be true, or even be at issue, in all poetry (if that indeed is what is meant by that succulent locution 'the poets'). The poets seemingly do not know what they need to know – and nor do we – since they keep their avowal of their ignorance a secret, we can surmise, even from themselves. In this kind of argument, unknowing is wielded as knowingly as a noose. And yet, '[s]tupidity is so radically, pervasively inside ... that it is prior to the formation of the subject' (*SY*, 11). In the course of her book, Ronell has many acute things to say about the limits to knowledge, as well

as about the epistemopathic textures involved in writing – the sense
of shame, for example, that can mingle with narcissistic pleasure in
reading what one has written twenty years, or twenty minutes, ago
(SY, 26). What is strange is how all of these realistic, reasonable, if
uneven and intermittent (reasonable because uneven and intermittent) insights into the limits of knowing can be satisfactorily parcelled
up as a thing called 'stupidity', the numinously never-to-be-known
which seems to be perfectly known and magnificently, magisterially
evoked through Beckettian borrowing:

> It is a matter of unrelenting assault and battery on whatever in
> you thinks it can write and live to tell about it. Writing from
> Hölderlin to Pynchon, you to me, brings about a crushing
> blow that comes from someone or something (this is why
> there is something rather than nothing), addressed to you
> but exceeding your grasp. The matter of receiving the blow is
> already beyond your capacity to understand. You don't know
> under whose command you put yourself through it, whom
> you're addressing, or why it must be this way. In a Beckettian
> sense, there's not much else to do but dumbly go on, you can't
> go on, you must go on. The imperative doesn't interrupt the
> wave of stupidity but rides it, relying on stupidity to bring it
> home. (SY, 26)

Ronell writes valuably, interestingly and sometimes even hilari-
ously about the many different ways in which one may not be
completely in charge of what one is doing, especially in writing. What
she does not manage to invoice (though failing to do so is already
of course entirely accounted for on the balance sheet) is the pleasure
and excitement that comes from seeming to identify all of this as
the working of the thing she promotes to metaphysical knowability
in the form of Stupidity. She identifies the impulse for the book in
discovering that she was really bad at learning Tai Chi and hearing
of the death of Gilles Deleuze, who had called for 'a discourse . . .
that interrogated the transcendental principles of stupidity' (SY, 32). It
would be hard to concentrate the same sense of mysterious, ineffable,
all-pervasive potency in a gawky, awkward, tied-together-with-string
notion like 'all-the-different-ways-in-which-we-can-not-quite-be-
sure-of-what-we-are-doing-when-we-think-and-write'. In this, the

wave Ronell is riding, without taking note of it, is the force of a fantasy about a kind of absolute condition of unknowing that has been gathering for centuries. Why should she be expected to take note of it when agniological cathexis is not her subject? I mention it simply because it is mine.

Sianne Ngai offers another variety of redeemed and redemptive stupidity in the form of what she calls 'stuplimity', defined as 'the aesthetic experience in which astonishment is paradoxically united with boredom', and therefore 'the concatenation of awe . . . with what refuses awe'.[76] Ngai assures us that we should not look to the stuplime, unlike the sublime, for anything transcendent or transfiguring, since '[w]hat stuplimity relies on is an anti-auratic, anti-cynical tedium that at times deliberately risks seeming obtuse, as opposed to making claims for spiritual transcendence or ironic distance.'[77] But this suspensive state also allows for that claim that seems to be as compulsory as it is compulsive in the more affirmative kinds of cultural criticism for 'a kind of resistance', a resistance that has to do with a certain kind of amorphous incoherence, a limpness that is thought to cause various kinds of social or discursive machinery to seize up.[78] Artists like Gertrude Stein and Samuel Beckett 'have followed this stuplime path in their confrontations with the systems encompassing them, formulating a resistant stance by growing limp or falling down, among the bits and scraps of linguistic matter'.[79] The resistance of the scattered, mushily nonresistant and the more austere and aristocratic kinds of existential stupidity celebrated by Ronell here share a capacity to outflank knowledge or concept, characterized as they both are by 'a condition of utter receptivity in which difference is perceived (and perhaps even "felt") prior to its qualification or conceptualization'.[80] No such condition of utter receptivity, prior to all conceptualization, is, I submit, actually possible, though it is, of course, well able to be conceived.

For, unlike stupefaction, which may be caused by shock, injury, fatigue or pharmaceuticals, stupidity is not a condition occupied by human beings (even if only human beings could occupy it) but a discursive effect. Stupidity is the horizon assumed by the action of deploying a particular kind of insult, which we might call stupidifaction. Where stupefaction means being stupefied, stupidifaction means being made out to be stupid, or stupidified. It is something done to people, by saying, not something that they are, in being. Stupidity is a medium of social relation, not a condition, and the use of the word, while apparently designating a lack of intelligence, in fact constitutes a mode of intelligibility. As any fule kno, it would be really stupid to call somebody stupid who actually was (and so of course, by the same logic, not *really* stupid at all). Not really meaning it when we call somebody stupid is just what it means to do that. While there are assuredly many aggressive uses of the idea and attribution of stupidity, there is no need to fall into the undemandingly, if gratifyingly simple, knowledge-power equations proposed for example by Dale C. Spencer and Amy Fitzgerald in their study of the legal prosecutions of animals: 'If rationality was to triumph, then social disruptions by the "irrational" or "stupid" must be minimized', meaning that 'if "stupid" animals were going to be held legally responsible for their actions, then certainly "stupid" people would be as well.'[81] The quotation marks do the talking here, since you can only address yourself to somebody stupid, whether pig or poltroon, about their stupidity and its consequences if you assume they are not completely stupid after all.

Turning the stupidity insult into a compliment, as in the recent morosophical tendency to promote stupidity into a redemptive cognitive principle, whether psychological or political, is another allotrope of this discursive compound. The imagination and deployment of the idea of stupidity is part of the densely knitted fabric of epistemophoric affinities, acknowledgements, approaches, abjurings and antagonisms that make up social life. Among those who have attempted to characterize the workings of stupidity as though it were a thing in the world there is a common tendency to conclude that it is in fact to be found everywhere, and so can never be definitively isolated for analysis and extirpation; Ronell, for example, begins her study by asserting that stupidity is 'essentially linked to the inexhaustible' and ends it by evoking its 'irrecuperably improper essence' (*SY*, 3; 277). Stupidity is an elsewhere or otherwise that is always at hand, existing often in the form of dissimulation or citation, as in Flaubert's ironic deployments of novelistic forms of *bêtise*, that snooty French term for vulgar received ideas. As Christopher Prendergast wonders,

> if, as is the case with nearly all Flaubert's heroes and heroines, citational recourse to bookish versions of the world is to be inescapably ensnared in the net of *bêtise*, then what are we to make of the book itself which advances such a claim? ... [I]s

it the case that *all* books, all texts, all orders of discourse are fatally contaminated by the stratagems of *bêtise*?[82]

The pervasive force of stupidity is similarly attested to in Robert Musil's judgement that 'anyone who wants to talk about stupidity, or profitably participate in a conversation about it, must assume about himself that he is not stupid; and he also makes a show of considering himself clever, although doing so is generally regarded as a sign of stupidity!'[83] Musil joins a number of others in identifying a peculiarly pervasive and pernicious kind of 'higher stupidity' or 'intelligent stupidity', which 'participates in the agitation of intellectual life, especially in its inconstancy and lack of results' and which overreaches itself in generalizing on the basis of insufficient knowledge.[84]

None of this – being imprecise, not quite understanding the import of what one is saying, not being as secure in one's knowledge as one wishes or thinks – comes close to being anything like the condition of radical intellectual defect or depletion signalled by stupidity. I will resist the impulse to suggest that this all-or-nothing denunciation of any intellectual debility as stupidity might itself be evidence of stupidity. But it may be evidence of the strange, hypnotic force that the idea of stupidity has, even as one might just as well say that wherever stupidity, as the putatively absolute absence of knowing, is assumed to be, it can never in fact be. Rather, it is something like the imaginary wall against which knowing discourse endlessly bumps up and from which it bounces painlessly back to itself. Stupidity is as much a work of fantasy as knowledge is, acting as it does as the indispensable, imaginary outside to knowledge's gleaming dream of itself.

7
EPISTEMOTOPIA

SCHOOLS OF THOUGHT

I f it is hard to see the trees for the wood when it comes to the architecture of knowledge, it can be similarly difficult to get at the way we think about the actuality of the most formative experience in the lives of most humans in the modern world, namely that of school. It is a very laborious process to tease out references to the experience of schools in psychoanalytic databases, so concerned are psychoanalytic writers with schools as tribal and generational groupings of practitioners – the school of Freud, the Budapest school, the English school and so on. But the physical and social experience of the school programmes and inflects almost every aspect of the human relation to its own processes of learning and knowing. Indeed, in its structures and practice, psychoanalysis is itself a process that extends the schoolroom into all aspects of life. Freud insisted that it is necessary to undergo analysis in order to be able to practise it, this having the effect of making the experience of psychoanalysis an ongoing perpetuation of the examined life. Psychoanalysis continues to perpetuate the experience of school while seemingly never noticing it. The pressure of school-experience passes across into many other areas of sickness and health: it is not just, as Foucault tried to teach us, that the clinic is a disciplinary institution, it is that the discipline of health and sickness itself can become a kind a discipleship. Teaching mature students for thirty years made it plain to me how deeply ingrained and constraining early experiences of school were in students returning to education.

Melanie Klein is one of the few psychoanalytic writers to try to take school experience seriously, most notably in her essay 'The Role of the School in the Libidinal Development of the Child' (1923). But even in this essay, Klein opens up the topic of school experience only to close it off almost immediately. She begins by alluding to the allegedly 'well-known fact' that, 'in the fear of examinations, as in examination-dreams, the anxiety is displaced from something sexual on to something intellectual.'[1] She refers us to Freud's *The Interpretation of Dreams*, though Freud's chapter on examination dreams in that book in fact focuses on their role in managing general forms of anxiety, Freud observing that such dreams are usually of examinations that one has passed rather than failed:

> anxious examination dreams (which, as has been confirmed over and over again, appear when the dreamer has some responsible activity ahead of him next day and is afraid there may be a fiasco) search for some occasion in the past in which great anxiety has turned out to be unjustified and has been contradicted by the event. This, then, would be a very striking instance of the content of a dream being misunderstood by the waking agency. What is regarded as an indignant protest against the dream: 'But I'm a doctor, etc., already!' would in reality be the consolation put forward by the dream, and would accordingly run: 'Don't be afraid of tomorrow! Just think how anxious you were before your Matriculation, and yet nothing happened to you. You're a doctor, etc., already.'[2]

Only at the end of his short chapter does Freud refer to the view of Wilhelm Stekel, with whom he says he agrees, that matriculation dreams occur before some test of sexual maturity.[3]

For Klein, 'school and learning are from the first libidinally determined for everyone, since by its demands school compels a child to sublimate his libidinal instinctual energies.'[4] This simple principle allows school experience to fulfil the function thereafter of the constraining of sexual libido, and school experience thereby to be dissolved into orthodox psychoanalytic symbology. Single-mindedly and almost, it must be said, monomaniacally, Klein reads the objects, persons and actions associated with school as symbolic screens for sexual ideas and feelings. This even extends to the symbolic significance of school furnishings, as in her account of Felix, her thirteen-year-old analysand, for whom, she surmised, standing up meant erection, and falling over the possibility of castration:

> The idea that occurred to him once in school that the master, who, standing in front of the pupils, had leant his back against the desk, should fall down, knock over the desk, break it in and hurt himself in so doing, demonstrated the significance of the teacher as father, and of the desk as mother, and led to his sadistic conception of coitus.[5]

Klein amplifies this sexualized reading in a footnote:

> The maternal significance of dais and also of desk and slate and everything that can be written upon, as well as the penis-meaning of penholder, slate-pencil and chalk, and of everything with which one can write, became so evident for me in this and other analyses and was so constantly confirmed that I consider it to be *typical*.[6]

There would be no point in denying that the schoolroom can ever become the location of sexual fantasy. But the apparatus and architecture of the school are more than a screen for sexual desire. Rather, the school is itself a theatre thronging with different kinds of investments and fantasies, embodying many different kinds of anxiety, comfort, rage, resentment, envy, longing and imaginative opportunity. Perhaps the erotics of school fantasy, when they arise, depend to a large degree upon this prior and primary libidinization of almost everything that is embodied and symbolized by the experience of school. In the example just quoted, for example, there may be rather more to be said about the desk than that it is a figure of the passive female: for example that the desk marks a position in a structured space, sometimes marking an academic position; that if it is a container as well as a support it is a kind of personal camp or nest; and many other considerations too familiar and well-known to be recognized. Later in her essay Klein provides a detailed account of the sexual meanings of the shapes of letters for Felix, concluding that 'the libidinal significance of reading is derived from the symbolic cathexis of the book and the eye.'[7] Klein sees the cathexis as deriving from the displacement of sexual libido, but her analysis surely lets us glimpse a primary cathexis of the objects and actions of writing, a kind of orthographic libido, with no need for the admixture of sexual desire to give it its grain and reach. It may be called a 'symbolic cathexis', not in the sense that the action of writing is a substitute for something else, but rather in the fact that the forming of symbols becomes the scene of a complex kind of pleasure – complex because it is also, of course, a kind of ordeal, for school makes writing inseparable from the idea of work. The physical act of writing involves a literal embodiment of the work of figuring desire, the desire of figuring work, the figuring of desired work.

The school is not in fact merely the kind of vast stage machinery for symbolizing sexual themes that Klein assumes. But the passions it must evoke in children – of terror, exhilaration, ambition, rage, relief, even of boredom (which can certainly take the form of a kind of passion) – do indeed make it a theatre of affect-drenched spatial symbols. In fact, school symbolizes the world, for which it tends to be taken, and perhaps deliberately takes itself, as a scale model. This is why schools can so easily form themselves as, and be taken to be, world-figuring microcosms. The school is the first screen onto which a structured image of the world outside the family can be projected, and which will continue to exert its force throughout life. And, in performing this function, the school provides the first image of the symbolic itself, the first theatre on which the social informing and impassioning of symbols may be acted out. The method which Klein used to disclose the feelings she believed, or at least maintained, were bound up in school experience was that of symbolic play, and thus seems designed both to project and to conceal the central function of the school as a kind of symbolic playground. The school is not only a place of symbols, it is a place of symbolization. As the place where we learn not only how to read symbols but also to form them, it will always symbolize the accession of and into that knowledge.

It should be no surprise that school stories are so perennially popular among children. For the school is a place of story. It not only structures the development of the individual child as a kind of story, an institutionalized structuring of time, it is also generative of story in the personal dream-work whereby experiences of school are assembled and made meaningful for individuals through a patchwork of 'what has happened, what we wish had happened, what happened to others and not to us, what happened but cannot be imagined, and what did not happen at all'.[8]

What is more, the school becomes a kind of cross-temporal reservoir which may receive the back projection of later feelings about knowledge and education in general, whether positive or negative, in the strange, complex mixture pointed to by Deborah Britzman:

> To think the thought of education as a working through of phantasies of education asks a great deal of us since the character of education itself can neither live without reinstituting its own childhood nor leave that which follows from it: the avalanche of complaints, disappointments, narcissistic injuries, and 'queer feelings' that all too often collapse the meaning of education with the classroom and its measures of success and failure and experience and inexperience.[9]

There seems to be a particularly fraught relationship between psychoanalysis and education, given how strongly pedagogic the culture of psychoanalysis is, with its fundamental premise, at least in its classical Freudian variety, that understanding will free one from the dominion of the unconscious. Klein's writing conspicuously leaves out of account the libidinal charge carried by the structure of psychoanalytic analysis and argument themselves – what we might call transference at the level of institution-fantasy. School experience is here being put in its place by the beginnings of what will become the 'school' of Kleinian analysis. Adult thus displaces infant school, school is put to school. Perhaps this is the reason that people like to endow colleges bearing their names. The only way to leave school, it seems, is to leave one to somebody.

I am perhaps both well- and ill-equipped to write of the insistence of the eidos and mythos of school in so many areas of social life, since, as a career academic, I may be said never really to have left school (though who really has, I wonder?). Although my academic life has made it possible for me to travel to a surprisingly large number of places across the world, my professional existence has been located in a tiny number of locations within a triangle about a hundred miles long on each side. I went to school in Christ's Hospital, Horsham, in the middle of Sussex; after a brief recoil to a school in the South Coast town where I grew up, I was a student for six years in Wadham College, Oxford. I taught for 32 years in what was then Birkbeck College, London, and am currently a professor in the University of

Cambridge. My curriculum vitae has indeed, it seems, been nothing but a tricorn course of study. Oxford, Cambridge and London form what is called a 'Golden Triangle', though it is really much more like an equilateral one: a golden triangle is so called not because it contains riches but because the ratio of its hypotenuse to its base is equal to φ (*phi*), the Golden Ratio, which characterizes a line divided such that the ratio of the shorter to the longer section is the same as that of the longer section to the line as a whole. The Golden Ratio 'unifies parts and wholes like no other proportion', so it seems appropriate that it should give its name to the congruence between the actual and the abstract, the geographical and the geometrical – that is, the relation between the realms of reason and reality.[10]

BOOK SPACE

Architecture has often served to externalize and give geometric form to the idea of knowledge. In the classical world, architecture was often employed in mnemotechnics, or the arts of memory. The anonymous *Rhetorica ad herennium* (late 80s BCE) recommended using a well-known sequence of connected places – a street plan, or the layout of a house, say – as a structure to contain and guide the elements of a speech, a technique recommended also by Cicero and Quintilian. The author of the *Rhetorica*, once taken to be Cicero himself, suggests that places (*loci*) can act as frames or settings for images, just as wax tablets or papyrus form the background or support for written letters: 'Nam loci cerae aut cartae simillimi sunt, imagines litteris, dispositio et conlocatio imaginum scripturae.' Harry Caplan, translator of the Loeb edition of this text, translates the word *loci* as 'backgrounds', in order to try to make this point clear: 'For the backgrounds are very much like wax tablet or papyrus, the images like letters, the arrangement and disposition of the images like the script.'[11] But this is to fudge into factitious intelligibility what the author in fact advises. For the point about wax or paper is that they provide an undifferentiated background which allows for letters to be differentiated in the foreground, whereas the author of the *Rhetorica* insists that the loci must themselves be clearly differentiated in the first place (so to speak):

> *Locos appellamus eos, qui breviter, perfecte, insignite aut natura*
> *aut manu sunt absoluti.*

By backgrounds I mean such scenes as are naturally or arti-
ficially set off on a small scale, complete and conspicuous, so
that we can grasp and embrace them easily by the natural
memory. (*RH*, 208–9)

This is why a long row of identical columns is not much use for
mnemonic purposes. If we wish to recall particular forms we will
need to set them in particular places – *locis certis conlocare oportebit*
(*RH*, 208). But this would imply something like a page of writing in
which the letters were slotted into already existing sockets – a literally
pre-scribed surface. Nonsensical though it seems, it also does justice
to how such mnemonic devices feel in operation: it feels as though no
effort has to be made to remember an arrangement which is already
fully apparent to us and ingrained in memory.

The word that the author of the *Rhetorica* uses for furnishing oneself with these images is *inventio*, from *invenire*, which means both to
discover, meet with or come upon and to devise or invent. He offers
us a *thesaurum inventorum*, a 'treasure-house of the ideas supplied
by Invention' (*RH*, 205), showing us *cuiusmodi locos invenire* (*RH*, 208),
'what kind of backgrounds we should invent' (*RH*, 209). The brilliant
mediating definition of *invenire* given by Lewis and Short's dictionary is 'to light upon'. No better understanding of the operations of
fantasy can be imagined than this discovery of what one has oneself
devised in the mediation of the two kinds of memory distinguished
in the *Rhetorica*. As Mary Carruthers has proposed, the idea of an
inventory is also at work in such conceptions of memory, in which
the capacity for improvisation depends on the availability of a store
of memories:

> Having 'inventory' is a requirement for 'invention'. Not only
> does this statement assume that one cannot create ('invent')
> without a memory store ('inventory') to invent from and
> with, but it also assumes that one's memory-store is effec-
> tively 'inventoried', that its matters are in readily-recovered
> 'locations'. Some kind of locational structure is a prerequisite
> for any inventive thinking at all.[12]

In fact, in both its Latin and English usage *locus* already signifies a
place – defined *absolutus*, absolutely, in its own terms – and a position,

defined relatively to other positions in a larger structure of replace-
ments, for example a seat in a theatre, a location in a volume or, as it
may be, a shelf-mark in a library. The first is physical space, the second
is logical space. Locus and logos, place and writing, change places
ceaselessly. The author of the *Rhetorica ad herennium* recommends
commandeering deserted spaces for mnemonic purposes, 'because the
crowding and passing to and fro of people confuse and weaken the
impress of the images, while solitude keeps their outlines sharp' (*RH*,
211). In fact, though, human memory seems to cling more powerfully
to places of habitation, or built spaces, which is to say spaces that are
already strongly impressed with value and coded and that have thus
already begun to move towards the logical relations of signs. Any
human space, whether inhabited or imagined (and perhaps inhabited
simply means imagined, or capable of being imagined, and imagining
a space means in some sense imagining inhabiting it), is 'written' as
a certain set of sequences and relations, and writing is projected in
terms of known spaces.

Books, which are kept in the externally coded and internally
coordinated spaces we know as libraries, also borrow their internal
structures from built spaces, with metaphorical entrances, annexes,
passages, exits and outworks. Philosophical arguments proceed
through an essay or a book but often try to give the impression of
being raised vertically, from their 'foundations' upwards; the term
'premise' still refers both to a place and a philosophical assumption. At
the same time, a book is a volume, a space able to contain. According
to the Byzantine grammarian John Tzetzes, among others, Plato's
Academy was marked at its entrance with the inscription Μηδείς
ἀγεωμέτρητος εἰσίτω μον τήν στέγην, *mèdeis ageômetrètos eisitô mou
tèn stegèn*, 'let no one who is ignorant of geometry enter under this
roof'.[13] These words may apply not just to the specific area of study
they identify but to the conjuncture of physical and abstract space
that is involved in the very idea of a specified place of learning. That
is, the very words themselves represent an overlayering of grammar by
geometry, establishing a metaphorical parallel between ungeometrical
being and being outside the place of knowledge; the imaginary place
where knowledge is paced out in place, that is, geometry.

A library is a collection of books, where collection implies a
gathering together in one place. 'College' is almost the same word,
though both collection and college derive not, as one might hopefully

imagine, from *col* + *legere*, to read together, but *col* + *ligare*, to bind or gather together. (In fact, however, *legere* itself derives from λέγω, *lego*, which includes in its range of significations to pick out or gather up, hence the etymological association between legibility and eligibility, and the relation through the idea of gathering of *legere* and *ligare*.) Thinking and knowing are not easily separable from some idea of concentration in space. A collection brings similarity into alignment with contiguity, as though to recreate an imaginary, ultimately rational universe in which proximity would always signal kinship or relation. Heidegger uses this etymology to justify his argument that Greek philosophy did not originally recognize any distinction between thinking and being:

> What is said of *logos* here corresponds exactly to the authentic meaning of the word 'gathering'. But just as this word denotes both 1) to gather and 2) gatheredness, *logos* here means the gathering gatheredness, that which originally gathers. *Logos* here does not mean sense, or word, or doctrine, and certainly not 'the sense of a doctrine', but instead, the originally gathering gatheredness that constantly holds sway in itself.[14]

There is at least a sort of phenomenological warrant for this in the fact that in English, still, to take thought may be to 'collect' or 'gather' one's thoughts, or even just to collect oneself through taking thought. To collect is to bring or pull together in one place, though that place need not be defined strictly in spatial terms. Indeed, it is to bring together place with meaning, to reduce the many to one, assembly approximating assimilation. This is an anti-Babelian gesture, a Big Crunch that is a move inwards and a move backwards, that promises to restore the imaginary Edenic oneness of things before affiliations were scattered and thinking left home. Nowadays the virtual gathering of electronic connection plays the part previously played by physical collection, and the web-link rather than the bookbinder's thread forms the ligature. In the early years of the World Wide Web, after 1989, the multiplication of these links seemed to be an explosive radiation or propagation outwards into the infinite, self-discovering space of connection. More recently these connections seem to have turned backwards on themselves, creating oppressive 'bubbles' of autistic self-amplification.

The overlaying of physical and imagined space was a feature of written signs from the very beginning. Like our modern 'library', Latin *bibliotheca* signals both a physical structure, whether a building or a bookcase, that contains or binds together a collection of books, and the books themselves, considered as a collection. A library is a self-containing form and a form of self-containment. So it was always possible for a library to exist simply as its own possibility of being assembled. As in the case of the self-signifying theatre of the mind evoked just now, the library is an image of the world gathered together in and for thought, and therefore also of thinking turned in on and enclosing itself. Perhaps any physical embodiment of thinking or learning will tend to function in this way, as a synecdoche for this ideal and absolute homecoming and *mise en abîme*. Perhaps all libraries are in this sense imaginary libraries.

Jorge Luis Borges's 1941 story 'The Library of Babel' is an attempt to imagine a library that would be big enough to contain all other libraries, conceived or conceivable. Borges's narrator reports on the library he inhabits which is also itself a universe, or, rather, the universe itself, made up of an infinite number of hexagonal galleries, each wall of which has five shelves, each containing 32 books, each of which in turn consists of exactly 410 pages, making a total of 39,360 pages and around 1.25 billion letters in each hexagon. The books do not appear to be written in any known language, although there are books in which some intelligible English appears, including one which is 'a mere labyrinth of letters whose penultimate page contains the phrase *O Time thy pyramids*'.[15] The story's narrative is made possible by the history of the growing knowledge of the library among its inhabitants. The cardinal event in the history of that knowledge is the discovery (though it must in fact be merely an hypothesis) that the Library is in fact finite and total, containing, without any gaps or duplicates, every possible arrangement of 1.3 million letters (the number in each book). The library thus contains all that it is possible to express with 25 orthographic symbols (22 letters, comma, full stop and space). Since order is rare in the universe, most of the books in the library are full of combinations of letters that have no meaning in any known language; yet buried among them are all the books that have ever been and could ever be written in human history:

> *All* – the detailed history of the future, the autobiographies of
> the archangels, the faithful catalog of the Library, thousands
> and thousands of false catalogs, the proof of the falsity of
> those false catalogs, a proof of the falsity of the true cata-
> log, the gnostic gospel of Basilides, the commentary on that
> gospel, the commentary on the commentary on that gospel,
> the true story of your death, the translation of every book
> into every language, the interpolations of every book into all
> books, the treatise Bede could have written (but did not) on
> the mythology of the Saxon people, the lost books of Tacitus.[16]

To begin with, the discovery of that omnitude is a source of exultant
joy for the inhabitants of the bibliocosmos:

> When it was announced that the Library contained all books,
> the first reaction was unbounded joy. All men felt themselves
> the possessors of an intact and secret treasure. There was no
> personal problem, no world problem, whose eloquent solution
> did not exist — somewhere in some hexagon. The universe
> was justified; the universe suddenly became congruent with
> the unlimited width and breadth of humankind's hope.[17]

History, and the narrative that we are reading, is made possible by
the growing awareness that the size of the universe means that, though
there are certainly precious books of wisdom in existence, they are lost.
The most inclusive possible library would be like the map on a scale of
1:1 which Borges evokes in his story 'On Exactitude in Science' (1946),
that is, it would in fact be identical with the world, and so offer no
reduction. It seems that, for Borges, if all knowledge involves reduction
and compression, then omniscience would be the same as ignorance.
So the joy at the congruence of world and word gives way to the sense
of absolute desolation, given that everything, including the account
of the library that we are reading, must already have been written:
'Methodical composition distracts me from the present condition of
humanity. The certainty that everything has been written annuls us,
or renders us phantasmal.'[18] Book-space has these two polarities, of
infinite containment and infinite evacuation, as its extreme conditions.

A personal library, the commonest form of collection, is a kind
of cocoon, a way of being at one with yourself or sheltering in your

own vicinity. Personal libraries can certainly function instrumentally, as a way of having a number of texts to hand which one is likely to wish to consult frequently. But they usually do not work in this way, and perhaps less so now than ever. My copy of Lewis and Short's Latin–English dictionary is three steps away from where many of these words have been assembled, but it is much faster for me to type 'legere Lewis and Short' into a search engine if I need to look up a word. Indeed the time it takes for my query to reach my fingers' ends from wherever in my brain it originates seems to be greater than the time the request takes to reach and be returned by the Perseus web server. Space has become speed, or rather, has revealed that it always was. The average speed of physical travel through the congested spaces of London remains today stubbornly at the 10 miles per hour or so that it was at the end of the nineteenth century, but it is only in such congested urban spaces that one can find Wi-Fi connections and libraries with extensive database access readily and openly available. Ubiquity is not itself ubiquitous, but concentrated in certain places.

Libraries are, like all collections, forms of self-authorization and even self-authorship. A library is a kind of second family home into which one adopts oneself. Students occasionally ask me if I have read all the books on my shelves, and I am able to reassure them, 'yes, read and safely forgotten'. Being surrounded by the books I am almost sure I once read, but would have to read again to verify it, is just as soothing as nestling amid well-thumbed old acquaintances. They are an image of *déjà-pensé* rather than of present knowing. The conventional identification between an owner and their books actually means that they can be capable of surviving their owner's dissolution and perhaps are meant to. The very fact that a library is so intimately familiar makes it easily alienable. A fellow of Peterhouse who moved out of his college rooms on retirement was obliged to part with a large number of books for which he no longer had room: shortly afterwards I heard a friend saying to him, 'I saw your books on the second-hand stall in the market, and assumed you must be dead.' Like the inhabitants of the Library of Babel, the owner of a library is both immortalized and spectralized by their library, haunted by the place they haunt. There are many Memorial Libraries, among the most notable the Widener Memorial Library in Harvard, built with a gift from Eleanor Elkins Widener in memorial of her Harvard alumnus son Harry Elkins Widener, himself a book-collector, who died on the Titanic – his mother was also on board but was saved on a lifeboat. The Widener Memorial Room in the library keeps a floating collection of 3,300 of his books intact, a library within a library, with fresh flowers kept near a portrait of Harry following a request made by his mother in 1916.

The library that externalizes my memory in my lifetime may be an intimation in advance of how it may come to be in memory of me. A library is a place, but also a passage. As such it can be a message, even itself a medium of communication, a form of intellectual legacy or commerce. There was a story frequently repeated by ancient writers that Aristotle possessed a magnificent personal library that passed from owner to owner until it finally formed the core of the famed library of Alexandria.[19] Many major world libraries are like the British Library (founded on the collection of Hans Sloane) in having begun as private collections.

Lina Bolzoni has described in detail the operations of a cultural code in the Renaissance in which words and ideas are systematically translated into visual images and enacted through the language of the body, especially in the schematic form of anatomy. Another metaphor employed for ordered thinking in medieval rhetoric was that of a machine; indeed rhetoric itself was often understood and explained through 'rhetoric machines' organized around geometrical structures like grids, squares and wheels.[20] The idea of mnemotechnics is in fact a kind of tautology, since any technics or technique is already a kind of memory-machine, a way of storing up a procedure in a way that can be replayed as desired. The word 'machine' often had a specifically architectural reference, since a *machina* was also a kind of crane or hoist.[21] The idea of physical lifting could also suggest lifting up to view, and a *machina* could refer in Latin both to a platform on which slaves were displayed for sale and to a painter's easel. This idea continues to perform its work in the contemporary metaphor of a particular kind of computing architecture as a 'platform', which has been in use since about 1987. A platform is so named because it is flat or uninclined, like a table or page, that is, a space apt both for calculation (for artillery purposes, for example) and for spectacle – as well as for where strategy and spectacle come together, such as in a field of play. The *machina* was also, in the Greek and Roman theatre, a contrivance for lowering into the theatrical scene the *deus ex machina* to resolve difficulties or bring about denouement.[22] The fact that the *machina* was so strongly associated with theatrical constructions, where what it helped to raise up was both substance and similitude, is of great moment in knowledge's figuring of itself to itself. Every imaginary machinery of mind is a kind of mental scenography which enables the mind to put itself on stage.

Frances Yates describes one of the most curious embodiments of this idea in the 'memory theatre' which was the life's work of the philosopher Giulio Camillo (1480–1544). This was at once an ideal diagram of a well-stocked and perfectly arranged memory and a materialization of it.[23] Camillo was supported financially by Francis I of France. The most detailed reports of Camillo's enterprise are found in the letters to Erasmus of Viglius Zuichemus. His descriptions suggest magical powers for the structure: 'They say that this man has constructed a certain Amphitheatre, a work of wonderful skill, into which whoever is admitted as a spectator, will be able to discourse on any subject no less fluently than Cicero.'[24] A later letter describes entering the structure, which was full of images and wooden boxes:

> He calls this theatre of his by many names, saying now that it is a built or constructed mind and soul, and now that it is a windowed one. He pretends that all things that the human mind can conceive and which we cannot see with the corporeal eye, after being collected together by diligent meditation may be expressed by certain corporeal signs in such a way that the beholder may at once perceive with his eyes everything that is otherwise hidden in the depths of the human mind. And it is because of this corporeal looking that he calls it a theatre.[25]

It appears that the theatre was structured around a series of images, possibly astrological symbols, which were linked to drawers containing books and documents.[26] The theatre was never in fact completed, and perhaps never could have been, since its materialization would always be an intimation of its ideal order.

The most paradoxical form of scholarly theatre is that provided by the study. The Latin *studere* means to strive or apply oneself zealously to something, and as a noun the word 'study' applied originally to a state of mind, as in the expression 'brown study', which first appears in the mid-sixteenth century, meaning a state of gloomy or aimless contemplation. The first appearance of the word in English to mean a particular place to which one would retire for purposes of study is in the account given in Robert of Brunne's *Handlying Synne* (1303) of the music-loving Bishop Robert Grossteste of Lincoln, which tells us that 'Next hys chaumbre, besyde hys stody, / Hys harpers chaumbre was fast þerby'.[27] In its earliest forms, the study would have been modelled on the monastic cell and would have been contained only in institutions and large houses. With the development of forms of domestic privacy during the Renaissance, in particular during the fifteenth century, the study began to become a feature of domestic architecture. It was strongly identified with a particular individual, usually the master of the house, and indeed a study is probably still today the most individualized room in a house; in a large house, a couple who are content to share a bedroom may well have separate studies. When Giovanbattista Grimaldi asked his tutor for advice as to how to lay out the books in the study he was building in his Genoan palace in 1544, he was told that they 'form a complete library, which will ornament first your study, and then, to a much greater degree, your soul'.[28]

The study was the province of a scholar or cleric, and would often have been close to the bedchamber. It was a kind of secularized chapel, a proof of the dedication of its owner to contemplation and selfculture. During the early fifteenth century in Italy the study began to become a feature of the merchant's or lawyer's private house, where it performed the semi-public function of an office. Often it would be located on a mezzanine just off a staircase, accessible to the ground floor but apart from it, where the master of the house might withdraw to meet clients.[29] During the eighteenth century the study also began to be used by physicians and other professionals as a consulting room. Sigmund Freud's consulting room, in his house in Maresfield Gardens, London, is preserved as the study in which he worked and wrote, with bookshelves, desk and antiquities as well as the consulting couch on which patients reclined; it is a materialization of a kind of shared space of contemplation, for patient and physician.

If the function of the study was to provide a new kind of space for private study, it became increasingly public, too, through the many depictions of the study-space that began to appear from the fifteenth century onwards, often depicting saints or Fathers of the Church at work. In the process, the private study became a theatrical space. The commonest subject of such paintings is St Jerome. The accounts of

Jerome's life give no indication of the study that is so often the location of later depictions. Rather, they emphasize either the fact that he lived by the place of Christ's birth in the crib at Bethlehem, or the circumstances of his death, in the cave where he is said to have ended his own long life. The principal emphasis however is on Jerome's dwelling in the wilderness, with the account of his life in Jacobus de Voragine's *The Golden Legend* quoting him as saying: 'I also doubted my proper cell as fearing my conceits and thoughts, wherefore I went and departed wroth, and revenging myself, passed alone through the sharp and thick deserts.' And yet the principal feature of Jerome's life is his devotion to divine scholarship, and 'was all in lessons, all in books, he never rested day ne night but always read or wrote'.[30] So he is usually pictured either in the wilderness, bony, sunburnt and scantily clad, though anomalously furnished with books – as in Pinturicchio's *St Jerome in the Wilderness* (1475–80) or Bellini's *St Jerome Reading in the Countryside* (1480–85) – or in his study. Giovanni Mansueti's *St Jerome in a Landscape* (*c.* 1490) gives a rather cosy compromise between inside and outside, with the saint having laid out his books and emblems, crucifix, cardinal's hat, memento mori skull and hourglass on ledges outside a rather well-appointed little country cottage he seems to have hewn out of the rock.

In paintings and drawings of St Jerome in an interior setting, the study is often depicted in tight close-up, almost as an alcove or architectural cave, cleaving closely around the person of Jerome. In Lorenzo Monaco's depiction, perhaps one of the earliest, from around 1420, Jerome stands in an almost impossibly squashed corner between two shelves, with no suggestion of a desk. Commonly, however, there is in these bookish interiors a suggestion of the wilderness, furnished by the figure of a dozing or cutely romping lion. This is a reference to the animal from whose paw Jerome is said, in a possible blending with the story of Androcles, to have removed a thorn, and which subsequently ran freely in the monastery where Jerome spent his later years. In Niccolò Colantonio's *St Jerome in his Study* (*c.* 1445), wilderness and library are collapsed together, with the lion sitting patiently in Jerome's cluttered study, its paw held out for the saint to remove the thorn. Odorico Pillone commissioned Cesare Vecellio between 1581 and 1594 to paint the fore-edges of three volumes of the *Opera omnia* of Jerome with two images of the saint in his study flanking an image of him at study in the wilderness.

The two most striking innovations in fifteenth-century depictions of Jerome in his study are the importance of the desk – which emphasizes Jerome's role as a translator as he requires a space in which he can read and write concurrently – and the steady crowding of the study with other kinds of furnishings, equipment and ornaments. Perhaps the most extraordinary rendering of this subject is Antonello da Messina's *St Jerome in his Study* (*c.* 1460–75). Jerome is seated in a wooden framework, with neither enclosing walls nor ceiling, in a space that seems to be situated between two long corridors, one ending in a window that looks out on a luminously sunlit scene with a lake, gardens and palatial estate, the other a row of graceful pillars coaxing the eye to a more pastoral version of the same scene. Jerome is separated from the scene which he commands in two dimensions, in that he is physically between these exterior scenes, and also, in the most extraordinary innovation of this painting, in the fact that he is elevated on a kind of dais, reached by a little flight of three steps, at the foot of which his two slippers have been flipped off. We cannot see Jerome's feet beneath his elaborately gathered red robe, but just the hint given by the discarded slippers suggests quiet comfort rather than mortification. Jerome's shelves are filled with books, not neatly stacked upright but opened out, as is common at this early period, but also with jars, pots, boxes, keys hanging on nails and, most suggestive of living space, a hanging towel. The painting suggests openness and closure at once. Jerome appears as though performing on a stage, or even the deck of a ship. Everything is ordered for the eye, spaced out evenly without the least suggestion of clutter. The only thing that appears capable of motion is paper. Even the lion approaching from the right between the slender columns hesitates like a polite courtier in the corridor, as though uncertain whether to intrude. At the centre of the picture is the obliquely sloping line of sight that connects Jerome's eyes to his book, which he holds at a hyperopic distance, a space of attention that seems simultaneously to hold together all the spaced-out elements of the picture. His line of sight continues the line of shadow cast by the light that breaks into this space from where we stand, forming a congruence between our reading of the picture and Jerome's reading of his book. It is as though the space of the book had passed across into all the physical elements that are held open for our view, repeated even in the opened wings of the birds visible through the upper windows.

As noted in Chapter Three, knowledge produces, is drawn to and clings around objects, known things that are not of knowing's own nature, that knowledge is thrown up against, *ob-* + *iacere*. There can be no knowledge without objects, without the genitive relation which makes it knowledge *of* a particular object that we describe as an object *of* knowledge. Objects induce the fantasy of possession. But, following the reflexive logic of much knowledge-feeling, they also provide a mediated form of self-possession by which knowing may come into its own. Objects provide the scenery and the theatrical space in which knowledge may grasp itself; objects of knowledge can furnish the scenery of knowing. If all knowledge objects are architectural in function, giving shape and solidity to knowledge, then specifically architectural objects – walls, foundations, corridors – put on show the grounding and containing structure of architecture. Architecture is therefore both that which contains the scene of thought and is itself *mise en scène*, thrown into the scene. It is both content and container of thinking.

We may suggest that the architecture whereby knowledge imagines itself is all in fact theatrical, that is to say, an architecture that is at once actual and imaginary, the actualizing of the imaginary, and the imagining of the actual. The function of theatrical architecture is to contain itself, to open up a space, or put itself on a stage within which it may imagine itself operating. But that space must always therefore be part of the spectacle, allowing the showing to be shown along with the show. This space mediates the medium it provides. David Hume (1711–1776) provides both example and explication of this principle in his use of the metaphor of the stage to express his idea of the mind as simply the venue for the rapid transit of impressions:

> The mind is a kind of theatre, where several perceptions successively make their appearance; pass, re-pass, glide away, and mingle in an infinite variety of postures and situations. There is properly no *simplicity* in it at one time, nor *identity* in different; whatever natural propension we may have to imagine that simplicity and identity. The comparison of the theatre must not mislead us. They are the successive perceptions only, that constitute the mind; nor have we the most distant notion of the place, where these scenes are represented, or of the materials, of which it is compos'd.[31]

The idea of what has been called the 'Cartesian theatre', in which a sedentary and localized self reviews the passing show of sense impressions played out before it, has been criticized by philosophers of cognition such as Daniel Dennett. But the advantage of the theatrical metaphor is that it allows for the idea of a hypothetical space, which, as Donald Beecher explains, 'is a place of memory and experience, of illusions seeming real, of actors and behind-the-scenes operations, of waking and dreams confused by the fleeting nature of experience'.[32] In this provisional, as-if disposition, 'the self of the *res cogitans* is no longer a matter of ontology but of function and point of view.'[33] The theatre of the mind may not be a good metaphor for what consciousness is, but it is a powerful simulation of how consciousness has often seemed to itself.

Thinking is conducted through 'thinking things' – objects that mediate the nothingness of thought to itself.[34] These things are projective objects: objective in that they stand outside and stabilize the operations of mind, giving them a local habitation, but projective in that they are part of the scenery that the mind projects for itself. Books, libraries, laboratories, lecture rooms and universities are ways for thinking to turn itself inside out. Because thinking is always contained within and reaching beyond its containers, the spaces of thought also provide the scene of its self-exceeding.

Nowhere is the oscillation of space and sign, or, as we have recently begun to call it, of real and virtual space, more apparent than in a library. If a system of relations is always a spatial distribution of elements that orders abstract ideas in relations of distance and proximity, simultaneity and sequence, then a library is an inversion of this, for it is an ordering of physical space in terms of abstract relations. Users of libraries develop kinetic memories for where they will find materials relating to different fields and topics, just as readers of books will have at least the sensation of where on the page, recto or verso, top or bottom, beginning or end of the line, early or late in the book, a particular passage of writing has been encountered. We are accustomed to thinking nowadays that the space of the library has become more abstract and virtual, but thermodynamics and information must always collude. Lisa Jardine, who lived in Bloomsbury a couple of hundred yards from the British Library, once told me that if she really needed a book in a hurry she would get on a train to Cambridge, since the University Library unusually allows readers to fetch their own books from the stacks. This requires skills and stamina for the navigation of much larger and more complex spaces than readers in the Bodleian or British Library need as they sit and wait for their books to be brought by spirits into their magic circle; when I asked for advice about how to use the Cambridge University Library, I was told to 'wear loose clothing'.

It is striking that 'navigation' has become the commonest metaphor for moving through spaces of information, physical or virtual. One navigates the ocean, a space that has little in the way of landmarks, meaning that one must always employ accessory grids of reference – charts, compass bearings and star maps – laid over the featureless seascape in the form of what is often now called 'augmented reality'. The ocean was always already and necessarily logical; unknown, it had to come in under the net of abstract knowledge. It is not surprising that it should now provide the model for contemporary knowledge-space.

ARCHITECTURE

Things that resist keyword searches can be telling. Search for 'university architecture' and you will be provided with an extensive list of university departments of architecture. 'Harvard architecture' will deliver you to accounts of a particular form of computer structure, which is distinguished from von Neumann (or Princeton) architecture. The architecture of knowledge has become very largely an abstract or immaterial affair. And yet, no university can be fully 'open', for it must always represent a concentration of knowledge as well as a means of distributing it. Even when a university has become ubiquitous, beyond the point of having any local habitation, the institution of the university will still harbour the idea of the concentration of knowing in space and place.

Of course, universities like to represent themselves as places where knowledge and knowing are made accessible. The function that is often fulfilled by the embodied architecture of knowledge to be found in universities may be called that of the sequestered open. The university represents a pocket of apartness within an otherwise open field of information exchange, though its function now is not to retard but selectively to accelerate the exchange of knowledge. The economics of the database in principle means that I can read a rare seventeenth-century book anywhere where I can get an Internet connection. But in fact, I need also to have credentials that allow me to log in to the Early English Books Online database, which may require me to be a member of a particular constituency. Seamus Heaney's 'Villanelle for an Anniversary', written to celebrate the 350th anniversary of the founding of Harvard, deploys these opposites of openness and closure, hardness and the softness of spirit. The 'here' of Harvard Yard is a place of layered, spectral coincidences in which the founder, John Harvard, still walks, in a time long before the conquest of the West, the development of atomic physics and the flight to the Moon. Alluding to the ceremony of commencement, which occurs at the point of graduation, or the ending of the beginning of a student's life, Heaney urges the students listening to him read his poem to 'begin again', finding themselves in the footsteps of their founder, still imagined to be walking Harvard Yard, in which both the books and the gates 'stand unbarred'.[35] The poem is a touch sentimental, to be sure, but the syllepsis in which it involves the look back to a time 'where frosts and tests were hard' pleasantly correlates the hard and soft senses in which something may be said to be 'hard'.

A university is a place that is not one. A place of learning is a place that leads to nowhere, or to an atopic plurality. I am deeply irritated by the word 'acadeemia', but it is not a new coinage and aptly evokes the idea of an unfixed region of learning, half place and half idea. If there are not that many groves in universities nowadays, there were indeed olive groves dedicated to Athena in the place known as the Academy founded in 387 BCE, and this bequeaths to all subsequent universities a hint of the open air. We owe the term 'Grove of Academe' to Milton, whose *Paradise Regained* evokes it as part of the withdrawn wisdom of Athens:

> Athens the eye of Greece, Mother of Arts
> And Eloquence, native to famous wits
> Or hospitable, in her sweet recess,
> City or Suburban, studious walks and shades;
> See there the Olive Grove of Academe,
> Plato's retirement, where the Attic Bird
> Trills her thick-warbl'd notes the summer long.[36]

Henry Peacham had in fact employed a similar phrase in his 1612 *Minerva Britanna*, in a poem expressing the longing for retreat from the bustle of London: 'Thy solitaire Academe should be / Some shadie grove, upon the THAMES fair side'.[37]

Since it was first used by Sainte-Beuve in his 1837 poem 'À M. Villemain' in *Pensées d'août*, the idea of an 'ivory tower' has had something to do with this imaginary disposition of place.[38] W. B. Yeats lived from 1921 to 1929 in a fifteenth-century castle he called Thoor Ballylee and which he mythologized in his writing both as a space of retreat from civil conflict and, in its internal spiral staircase, an image of the contemplative mind. The tower acts out a double withdrawal, first of all inwards to a particular concentrated spot, and then upwards, as though to coil away from earthly space itself. For Yeats, the tower and the winding stair were codependent: the stair allowed one to climb the tower, but the tower existed to hold up the stair and deliver it to the open air. The helix makes it possible for enclosure to coexist with, and indeed to consist in, interior movement. As with the burrow described in Gaston Bachelard's *The Poetics of Space* (1958), one does not move in a space but makes space from one's movement. The tower is a vertical igloo, or what Bachelard calls a 'house with cosmic roots'.[39] The towers that once were places of defence or spires of aspiration have been converted into symbols of ascent, the movement away from space into the open dimension of height.

Universities have a fondness for these structures, which sometimes, as with the University of London's Senate House, impractically and overheatingly house libraries. Berkeley's Sather Tower, a campanile whose carillon still plays regularly, houses fossils of animals retrieved from the tar pits of California, as though to figure the transformation of life into stone and then stone into the second life of knowing. When I first visited the University of Pittsburgh I thought the name 'Cathedral of Learning' given to the 160-metre (535-ft) structure that dominates the campus must be an affectionate joke. But that indeed has been its official name since the first class was held in it in 1931. It is in fact only the fourth tallest educational building in the world, after the main building of the Moscow State University, the Mode Gakuen Cocoon Tower in Tokyo (so named because its curved shape, resembling a bud, seed or pair of praying hands, suggests a nurturing structure for those it contains) and the helical Mode Gakuen Spiral Towers in Nagoya.

And yet, at the same time, there is a powerful pull to space and place in thinking about learning and knowing. One 'graduates', one gains 'degrees': one works in a 'field' or has a specialist 'area'. The university often functions as a map of the orders of knowledge. The Bodleian Quadrangle in the University of Oxford distributes the classical subjects of the medieval university around its doors (in my day the *Schola Astronomiae et Rhetoricae* dignified the gents lavatory, but I believe it nowadays gives on to the gift shop). We might say that it is in large part the purpose of university architecture to provide a logokinematic staging of the idea of a university, as a place of approaches, transitions, passages and debouchings, and to project an animated image of the interface between the hard and the soft locations of learning and understandings of place. Even as solid and seemingly imperturbably perdurable a place as the University of Cambridge is to be understood as a kind of Potemkin village, designed to embody precisely the oxymoronic relation between idea and embodiment: the more actual it appears, the more symbolic its solidity seems to be.

The idea that a university might also be a kind of insulator or black box, at once thermodynamic and thaumaturgic, surfaces surprisingly right at the beginning of John Henry Newman's *The Idea of a University* (1852), in which he speaks of the advantage accruing to the Protestant North from their need for physical seclusion:

> Where the sun shines bright, in the warm climate of the south, the natives of the place know little of safeguards against cold and wet. They have, indeed, bleak and piercing blasts; they have chill and pouring rain, but only now and then, for a day or a week; they bear the inconvenience as they best may, but they have not made it an art to repel it; it is not worth their while; the science of calefaction and ventilation is reserved for the north. It is in this way that Catholics stand relatively to Protestants in the science of Education; Protestants depending on human means mainly, are led to make the most of them: their sole resource is to use what they have; 'Knowledge is' their 'power' and nothing else; they are the anxious cultivators of a rugged soil. It is otherwise with us; *funes ceciderunt mihi in præclaris* [Psalms 16:6, 'the boundary lines have fallen for me in pleasant places'].' We have a goodly inheritance.[40]

But the university has become since Newman was writing, and perhaps was already beginning to become while he was writing, a very different kind of institution, with a very different set of spatial relations to its environment. A university used to be a place where knowledge was shored up and defended against erosion and careless destruction. Robert Burton observes that 'some suppose, that a thicke foggy Ayre helps the memory, as in them of *Pisa* in *Italy*; & our *Camden* out of *Plato*, commends the site of *Cambridge*, because it is so neere the Fennes'.[41] In fact William Camden, to whose views Burton alludes, makes a slightly different point about the intellectual advantage of an unhealthy situation:

> Neither is there wanting any thing here, that a man may require in a most flourishing *Vniversity*, were it not that the ayre is somewhat unhealthfull arising as it doth out of a fenny ground hard by. And yet peradventure, they that first founded an University in that place, allowed of *Platoes* iudgement. For, he being of verie excellent & strong constitution of bodie chose out the *Academia*, an unholsome place of *Attica*, for to studie in, that so the superfluous ranknesse of bodie which might overlaie the minde, might bee kept under by the distemperature of the place.[42]

But the university has become something very different from an embodiment of memory. It is more and more a means of passage, a kind of cognitive airport, its inhabitants at any one time constituting a Larkinian 'frail travelling coincidence'.[43] The university has become less a monastery than a kind of factory: less a black box than a transmitter, existing in a complex sociospatial ecology with its apparent outside. Might we in fact begin to consider the university, in its specifically topographic aspects, a pure medium?

The university has become ever more a kind of virtual place. Academics travel much more than your average lawyer or banker, albeit on much cheaper airlines, and increasingly, since its formation in 2002, the enactment of this is in the eduroam data network. Eduroam was originally established under the auspices of TERENA, the Trans-European Research and Education Networking Association, and is now managed by GÉANT, which connects national research and education networks (NRENS) across Europe. Eduroam is principally a distributed authentication system that allows academic users visiting other universities to use their local credentials to access those local systems. The neatness of the eduroam system is that it requires a one-time login: once you have established a link between a particular device and your home institution it will automatically connect you to the local network wherever you may be. No matter what campus you may find yourself in, jetlagged, weary and disorientated, no matter how stubbornly the embedded sound files in your Powerpoint presentation may refuse to play, your phone or laptop will be telling you that you are back home, dunroamin in eduroam. My friend the Birkbeck crystallographer Alan MacKay – discoverer of fivefold symmetry in nature, where it has no right to be – was an early visionary of open access who back in the 1980s was pushing hard for all publicly funded scientists to declare their work in the public domain, and insisting that he was a citizen of no nation state but of what he called the floating Republic of Knowledge. We are seeing some signs of the disembedding of this polity: following the Brexit vote, where the vote to remain was extraordinarily densely concentrated in academic locations, nowhere more than in university towns, there were serious reflections on the possibility of certain places, like Oxford, Cambridge and the City of London, seceding from the planned secession, in the hope of remaining exactly where they were – that is to say, in the nowhere-in-particular of Cognitonia. This was a stubborn, heel-dragging yearning to resist deportation back into the old world of place, the spread-out world of distance and thermodynamics, sweating slaves, foaming horses and snorting locomotives rather than the new stacked world of instantaneities and interpenetrations. The new politics of place seems to offer a choice between position and superimposition, locations and locutions, astronomy and rhetoric.

One of the most concrete embodiments of the extraterrestrial nature of the Floating Republic of Knowledge is the Jet Propulsion Laboratory in Pasadena. The JPL is in fact a department of the California Institute of Technology, though its scale and reach dwarf its parent institution. Visiting the JPL, the mailing address of which is 4800 Oak Grove Drive, Pasadena, but which is in fact located, if that is quite the word, 30 kilometres or so to the north in the town of Flintridge, you can see the next Mars landing vehicle under construction, in a space that is designed to be itself kept under observation. Lest they forget their theatrical function, workers in biosuits labour alongside a life-size mannequin which fulfils their function for when visitors arrive and there is no construction work going on. Mission control communicates with the Curiosity rover on Mars, the mission orbiting Saturn and the Juno spacecraft orbiting Jupiter, along with Voyager 1, launched in September 1977, which left the solar system on 25 August 2012. At 125 Astronomical Units (11.66 billion miles) from the sun, it is the most distant telegnostic object with which human beings are in communication that there has ever been. Confirmation of its position outside the solar system was obtained by measurements that indicated it was in a region characterized by a density of 1.3 electrons per cubic inch.[44] The dramaturgy of celestial information flows is not just for outsiders. When a real-time simulation of data flows up and down from the various transmission stations around the Earth was provided for the public gallery overlooking Mission Control, scientists and technicians demanded one of their own. *The Pulse*, a sculpture by The Studio, the JPL's visual design team in the reception area, shows data flowing downwards and upwards in real-time Lucretian rain.

It is still important to go to particular places in academic life. This was a principle borne in upon me years ago when it was discovered at my previous institution that the largest fieldwork budget by far in the Faculty of Arts had been for years that of the Department of Philosophy. In one sense it is not necessary any more to be, as we still quaintly say in many contexts, 'in residence'. At the same time, the capacity to be ubiquitous or indifferent to place is concentrated in particular places. *Alice's Adventures in Wonderland* seems to belong to the architecture of Oxford, with its peephole gates in castellated exterior walls giving tantalizing glimpses of glowing green lawns. Cambridge seems much too open to the elements for this kind of play of scales – there are many more three-sided courts than in Oxford, where quads are usually enclosed. Carroll's Alice engineers a perpendicular encounter between the cramping, claustrophobic order of three-dimensional space and the abstract orders of number:

> At this moment the King, who had been for some time busily writing in his note-book, cackled out 'Silence!' and read out from his book, 'Rule Forty-two. *All persons more than a mile high to leave the court.*'
> Everybody looked at Alice.

'*I'm* not a mile high,' said Alice.

'You are,' said the King.

'Nearly two miles high,' added the Queen.

'Well, I sha'n't go, at any rate,' said Alice: 'besides, that's not a regular rule: you invented it just now.'

'It's the oldest rule in the book,' said the King.

'Then it ought to be Number One,' said Alice.

The King turned pale, and shut his note-book hastily.

'Consider your verdict,' he said to the jury, in a low, trembling voice.[45]

Like all places of mediation, the university is a mediator of place, or place of holomorphic exchanges, distributions and transmissions. It is not so much a heterotopia, a place apart, or a utopia, a no-place, or even a pantopia, a threshold to everywhere, but a metatopia, a place for the communication and mediate vehiculation of place itself.

Epistemotopia is more than a kind of topography, and one needs more than geometry to come in under the roof of knowledge. It also involves a topopathology, what Bachelard has taught us to see and feel as the poetics of space. Knowledge involves nourishing claustrophilia and oppressive forms of imprisonment, as well as a topophagic appetite for space matched by what the art historian Wilhelm Worringer in 1908 called the 'immense spiritual dread of space' (*Raumscheu*) characteristic he believed of primitive peoples, from which they took refuge in highly patterned abstract art, as the image of the subjection of space to cognition.[46] Space-feeling is governed by a four-term homology which relates the polarities of desire and dread in the case of open space to the polarities of comfort and claustrophobia in experiences of close or closed space. In principle, in this abstract homology the positive desire to explore space as opposed to the defensive dread of being swallowed up by it is in parallel with the polarity between the positive comfort felt in a familiar private space and the negative feeling of constriction or suffocation that such a space may provoke. In either case, there can be a powerful inducement to identify the self with its space or a powerful desire to escape from it, whether inwards or outwards. But this basic schema also allows for compoundings. We have encountered one of these experiences in Chapter Three, in the teleproximity permitted by modern communications, which allows for the sensation of intimate knowledge at a distance.

In general, feelings of arousal seem to lessen as one withdraws into closed or private space, feelings articulated incessantly and in the end rather cloyingly by Bachelard, for whom 'well-being takes us back to the primitiveness of the refuge'.[47] But the crowding together of large numbers of people into a constricted space produces the characteristic state of arousal that Émile Durkheim described as collective effervescence: 'The very act of congregating is an exceptionally powerful stimulant. Once the individuals are gathered together, a sort of electricity is generated from their closeness and quickly launches them to an extraordinary height of exaltation.'[48] One must also take account of mixed or transitional experiences of space, in which nearness and distance come, so to speak, close together. It is as though the crowding of space produces something like a compounding of safety and invasiveness, producing the strange mixture of unity and agitation characteristic of crowds.

There can be no doubt that the madness of knowledge has a spatial dimension; indeed, perhaps it represents the necessary pathos of space in every kind of unreason. For the irrational is that which it tells us it is, beyond measure. There is certainly a *folie de grandeur* in the lust of knowledge for indefinite expansion, to the point where it becomes identical with the world. But this alternates and so even cooperates with a *folie de petitesse*, in which knowledge convinces itself of its capacity to take its own measure. Knowledge is subject to the twin insanity of the desire for infinite self-exceeding and the desire for definite self-inherence, for ubiquity and hiceity, to be everywhere and right here. Knowledge seeks, in the words of Barabas in Marlowe's *The Jew of Malta* as he counts up the wealth he has procured from his global sea trading, 'infinite riches in a little room'.[49] Knowledge has expanded itself through the propagation of its power through space, a power that commands space by reducing it to known, named places: Oxford, Heidelberg, Neptune, Alpha Centauri. But knowledge must incessantly strive for power over its own power, a power that must nevertheless never succeed in locking itself in place.

8

EPISTEMOCRACY

Growth-addicted modern people have great difficulty in recognizing that there can be crises of abundance as well as of scarcity. In the past it was only sovereigns and duchesses who died of surfeit. We may say that human history, like the history of every other organism, has been driven by scarcity and need: indeed, if history involves any kind of development, unfolding or story, it is usually to be understood in terms of the more or less successful struggle to move from scarcity to abundance. This makes it hard for us to see any kind of increase or overcoming of limit, especially the limits imposed by natural conditions or other creatures, as a problem rather than prospering. If we rail against greed, it will typically be on the grounds that it appropriates resources, creating unnecessary need for others, rather than because it might be possible to have too much of something, whether or not anyone else was inconvenienced or suffered injustice. Envy seems to be the engine of a particular understanding of thriving as outdoing. The impulse to seek prosperity in having and being more, and to identify flourishing with growing, seems to be deeply and unshiftably lodged in us.

Nevertheless, there are signs that we may be beginning to understand that abundance can bring problems that do not have to do directly with distributive justice. There is, for example, an absolute health cost to obesity that would be payable even if there were no starvation anywhere. Perhaps our ingrained bias in favour of expansion on every front prevents us from wondering whether there may not be other kinds of dangerous abundance – of choice, of freedom or of opportunities for communication.

What if, for present purposes, an obesity of knowledge, or 'knowledge glut', were to arise that matched and might in its way be as injurious as corporeal obesity?[1] How could we wish for less knowledge, and how would we know how to bring it about? Would we not need to know more in order to decide where to trim or hold back?

It has been a principle of political philosophy since Plato's *Republic* that power should be rationally directed and that those who exercise power should do so on the basis of their knowledge or wisdom. Power and knowledge must be brought ever closer together. Those who, following Michel Foucault, object to the forms which the conjunctures of power and knowledge may take are rarely to be heard demanding the ceding of power to ignorance and prejudice instead. Even those who systematically reject 'Western' scientific secularism in favour of theocracy do not do so out of genuine attachment to ignorance, since religious faith is even more dependent on an ideal of known truth than scientific knowledge. Education has become identified with the powers attributed to the West even by its enemies, like Boko Haram, the name of which means 'The false is forbidden' (*boko* being understood to allude to *ilimin boko*, false (Western) education). It is hard to find anybody with a bad word to say about the prospect of a maximally rational polity, though plenty of complicated argument, if not much in the way of reliable knowledge, about the many different ways in which such a rational polity may be understood and secured. The fact that many utopias seem designed to make us queasy about purely rational schemes cannot help but strengthen certain other forms of assurance. What could be wrong with knowing more rather than less? It should be clear by this point in my argument that part of what might at least go awry is that knowing is rarely fully apprised of the feelings that throb through it and the effects that flow from it. It is easy for knowledge to admit that it does not know everything, but less easy to acknowledge how little it may know about its own operations – especially under conditions of abundance, and more particularly under conditions that forbid the forbidding of any kind of knowledge increase.

Thinkers and intellectuals are typically rather uneasy about their relation to power, resenting the dominion of the unphilosophical but typically unwilling to take on their responsibilities. One perspective is embodied in the story of the meeting of Alexander the Great with the philosopher Diogenes; it has been told by many at different times, but one of the earliest versions is included in the *Lives of*

Eminent Philosophers of Diogenes Laertius (*c.* 180–*c.* 240). On visiting Diogenes, who was residing in a barrel in the marketplace in Corinth, Alexander identified himself and asked Diogenes if there was anything he wished from him. 'Yes,' replied Diogenes. 'You can get out of my light.'[2] The fable crystallizes the belief that the 'philosopher', here taken as the fantasy-epitome of the one-supposed-to-know, should keep power at a distance, preferring the luminous truth of Diogenes' light to Alexander's looming shadow. This is a direct rebuff to the Philosopher-Kings of Plato's *Republic* and to the Platonic principle, still being maintained by Christian Wolff in 1730, that 'a state can be happy when either philosophers rule or those who rule are philosophers'.[3] Peter Sloterdijk writes that the story of Diogenes

> demonstrates in one stroke what antiquity understands by philosophical wisdom – not so much a theoretical knowledge but rather an unerring sovereign spirit. The wise man of long ago knew best of all the dangers of knowledge that lie in the addictive character of theory. All too easily they draw intellectuals into the ambitious stream where they succumb to intellectual reflexes instead of exercising autonomy. The fascination of this anecdote lies in the fact that it shows the emancipation of the philosopher from the politician. Here, the wise man is not, like the modern intellectual, an accomplice of the powerful, but turns his back on the subjective principle of power, ambition, and the urge to be recognized. He is the first one who is uninhibited enough to say truth to the prince.[4]

And yet knowledge – perhaps especially for most academics and intellectuals – has become ever more dependent upon earthly powers, and those powers upon it. One might say that the most obvious contemporary form taken by philosophical sovereignty is pensionable, legally guaranteed academic tenure, which allegedly secures the freedom of an academic to pursue whatever researches they see fit, unobstructed by political fear or favour and, most importantly, without let or hindrance to their salaries. Sovereignty, the idea of absolute and autonomous dominion, is always paradoxical since it can never in fact be self-given nor ever really derive directly from unearthly powers, but academic tenure is a particularly strange mixture of absolute autonomy and abject dependence.

In his decretal *Cum inter nonnullos* of 12 November 1323, Pope John XXII began his attempt to dissolve the legal fiction established by Nicholas III in 1279 regarding the ownership of property by the Franciscan order, a principle which, by distinguishing between owner-ship and use, allowed Franciscans the use of property that was in fact held by the Church. John's argument was that the Franciscans not only did, in principle and in actual fact, own property – lots of it – they should, following the precedent of Christ and his apostles, be permitted to do so. This was another of the many episodes of hectic, heretical set-to between institutional religion and zeal. One of the things that annoyed Papal officials most about the Franciscans, apart from having to provide banking services for their growing wealth, was their exhibitionist insistence on wearing clothing of such nose-offending noxiousness that it actually threatened to bring religion into disrepute. The intervention of the philosopher William of Ockham, plying a politicized version of his famous nominalist razor, led him to conclude that John XXII was himself a stubborn and inveterate heretic.[5]

In academic life we participate in something like the genial imposture with which John XXII tried unsuccessfully to deal. In our meekly Franciscan self-understanding, we in the universities, and especially in the humanities, believe ourselves to be on the outside of power and privilege, and therefore the better able to deploy our knowledge on the side of the weak, the embattled and the displaced; to speak truth on their behalf to power. But this view depends on a weak, sentimental and increasingly superannuated understanding of the place and power of knowledge.

High-level knowledge workers are for the time becoming the ruling class, even if many of us also confusingly feel like members of an anonymously and humiliatingly grinding cognitariat. This contradiction is in fact a distinctive feature of an epistemocracy, and was percipiently pointed out by Peter Drucker, who wrote in 1969 that '[t]he knowledge worker is both the true "capitalist" in the knowledge society and dependent on his job.'[6] It is not an acci-dent that most university graduates, 25 per cent of whom in the UK now graduate with the kind of first-class degree that would a couple of decades ago have seen them shunted into a safely tenured academic occupation, struggle to understand why they are not rewarded with the positions of admired and index-linked intellec-tual autonomy which they have been induced to expect. A little more historical understanding might in fact instruct them that it is not at all uncommon for members of a ruling class to feel both privileged and precarious (otherwise what was the Tower of London for?).

What Drucker pointed to with brilliant prescience was the most powerful structural tension of an epistemocracy: the fact that it is necessary for maximum social and economic efficiency to educate future knowledge workers for rapid adaptability, which in fact means educating them far beyond the levels of specific technical knacks and know-how required for currently existing occupations. Knowledge workers must be trained as rapid-response units rather than infantry, able to adapt to volatile needs and conditions through retraining, like pluripotent stem cells capable of being reassigned to any required biological function. No society in the world today can hope to approach prosperity if it does not somehow find the resources for rapid and widespread education and training; but such social projects of education can only succeed politically if ways can be found to manage the crises of frustrated aspiration they tend to produce. If knowledge workers are special forces, we should remember how difficult it can be to integrate such persons into salaryman society. In order to perform the function of educating citizens for participation in a knowledge society, liberally conceived universities must work covertly or simply unknown to themselves to constrain their own declared aim of producing limitless numbers of maximally self-aware, questioning and intellectually autonomous citizens. In many rapidly developing economies, the tensions which can be produced by a rapid expansion of knowledge and intellectual adaptability are often contained by focusing investment (a word which, in an epistemocracy, will always have a hummingly affective as well as an economic signification) in narrowly technical areas like law, medicine, management and engineering, or at least in narrowly technical understandings of those subjects. In the declining economies of the North, more complex solutions to the problem of the mass production of unrealizable intellectual aspirations and self-understandings have had to be sought.

One of the ways of negotiating this transition has been found in the impressively sustained assault on the traditional liberal idea of the universal, unaligned, humanist intellectual. It is an assault mounted since the 1960s by both the Right and the Left, though it would surely have to be conceded that it has been much more energetically, ingeniously and effectively pursued by the Left. This allows for the annealing of the otherwise unpredictable energies of wastefully free-floating 'critical intelligence' into an evangelical zeal-machine of collective social reform, in which everyone is accorded the right and the duty of being on an imaginary clamatory outside demanding expurgation of a number of mutable yet at any given time universally acknowledged ills of social inequality or exclusion – like the issues of social injustice against which even the current Conservative govern-ment in the UK has committed itself, among them race, faith, gender, disability, sexual orientation, National Living Wage and workers' rights, regional disparities, intergenerational fairness, mental health, domestic violence and abuse, school and technical education reform and migration. The State thereby comes to consist of its own obedi-ently bureaucratized gadflies. It is not that one should object to such commitments; it is precisely the opposite, in that, like the extirpation of sin, they cannot be objected to.

To make knowledge over into an instrument of critique turns out to be an unexpectedly helpful first step in instrumentalizing critique itself in socially salvific projects. We are seeing that the result is a kind of authoritarian liberalism that can do the work done more crudely in theocratic, post-totalitarian or more frankly gangsterist societies by anti-liberal authoritarianism. One of the signal aims and advantages of this form of generalized, socially solidary auto-critique is the sys-tematic exclusion of self-exclusion, the outlawing of outlawry, or the decathecting of the decathexis which, as is hinted at by the history of hermits and holy fools encountered in Chapter Six, can otherwise be such a troublesome by-product both of religious instruction and higher education alike.

Campaigns against social sin are, however, like all such homeo-static arrangements, a temporary abatement of turbulence and very possibly short-lived. The maintenance of zeal, for example, requires belief that one is part of an embattled minority, whether within a society or within a world in which one is under siege from the out-side, and so tends to run out of jizz as it is generalized, and the booted-and-spurred sectarian settles down to become the cardiganed Anglican. On the other side, once it gets under way, zeal is notably zealous in forming new occasions and opportunities for itself. So it is very likely that we will see other structural tensions arising from the move to an economy that is increasingly organized around and replicated through knowledge.

The power identified with scientific knowledge was epitomized in the twentieth century in the development of atomic weapons, which became decisive in the outcome of the Second World War. The power of military knowledge has been extended and ramified over the second half of the twentieth century by the huge economic power embodied and invested in technical expertise of all kinds. Competitive advantage nowadays depends increasingly on more than the availability of resources and productive labour power. It has come to rely also on the capacity for technical innovation, for it is on this that we depend for our capacity to grow ourselves beyond the limits of our resources and to invent technological ways of continuing to balance the unbalanced energy books. It is certainly still possible to construct a life as a non-institutional 'intellectual', but the idea of an 'intellectual', especially in the form of what is called the 'public intellectual', is a category that belongs to what I propose in this final chapter to call an epistemocracy.

Like epistemopathy, the word 'epistemocracy' has been used by others before me, though at the time of writing it has not yet made its way into the *Oxford English Dictionary*. The word is most commonly used to refer to a government founded on or directed by the knowledge of the learned or expert. Among the earliest uses of the term in this sense was by Terence Ball in his 1988 book *Transforming Political Discourse*. 'Epistemocratic authority', Ball explains, 'refers to the claim of one class, group or person to rule another by virtue of the former's possessing specialized knowledge not available to the latter'; it is, as Ball neatly puts it, the assumption that one who is *an* authority should therefore be *in* authority.[7] A. James Gregor uses the word epistemocracy to refer to the system of rule 'by those who are informed and competent' which was called for by Italian Fascist theorists and ideologues, with the coinage 'epistemarchs' to refer to 'advocates of rule by the most gifted, most knowledgeable, and most committed'.[8] More recently the term has been whittled down to 'epistocracy' by David Estlund, probably because it usefully suggests a portmanteau contraction of 'expert aristocracy'. Estlund characterizes epistocracy simply as 'rule by the wise', specifying that an 'epistocrat' could be taken, depending on the context, to refer either to a wise ruler, or an advocate of epistocracy.[9] We might wonder whether there might not be a class of epistocrats who would correspond not to democrats, but to bureaucrats – that is, neither the leaders or advocates, but the functionaries of a knowledge system.

Most political philosophers who have considered the nature and desirability of epistemocracy have followed Estlund in assuming that it means government by a specific class of experts or the learned, and have therefore been concerned about its possible tensions with democracy. Jason Brennan goes further than most in arguing that the complexity of modern government combined with the dismaying levels of ignorance of most voters on most issues makes some form of expert-driven epistocracy preferable to democracy.[10] This view has been encouraged by recent political developments, which, as David Runciman has suggested, has produced among members of the intellectual elite (a group with which almost half of UK voters, those voting to remain in the EU, seem bizarrely to identify) the return of misgivings about the inherent weakness of democracy.[11] Runciman reports that, following the Brexit vote, the almost universal response in Cambridge (where both he and I teach, and where the vote to remain was stronger than anywhere else except Gibraltar and the postal district where I live in London) was vicious mockery of those who had voted in this unaccountable and self-harming fashion.[12] Vengeful thoughts and mutterings were abroad; Jeremy Paxman quoted with relish H. L. Mencken's sentiment that 'Democracy is the theory that the common people know what they want, and deserve to get it good and hard.'[13] I remember it very much as Runciman describes it and also remember moronically joining in the booby-baiting game. Writing in February 2017, John Naughton drew the lesson that '[i]t shows, in a picture, why a failure to invest in education and tackle educational underachievement eventually imposes massive social costs (possibly including the breakdown of democracy). It's not rocket science, either.'[14] So we apparently do not need knowledge to know that the answer is more knowledge. In fact, David Runciman's judgement is rather more nuanced: 'The educational divide that is opening up in our politics is not really between knowledge and ignorance. It is a clash between one worldview and another.'[15] In past eras, human beings struggled with the question of how to overcome their ignorance. In our era, the pressing question is what we are to do with our knowledge.

Most of the critical discussions of epistemocracy understandably centre on considerations of legitimacy and effectiveness, circling round the key question of whether it would be a good idea to hand over more decisions to experts. As Fabienne Peter frames the issue, 'Does political decision-making require experts or can a democracy be trusted to make correct decisions?'[16] The argument seems to come down to the choice between maximizing the chance of making correct (or at least good) decisions and maximizing people's sense of involvement in the decision-making process. Recognizing the pressure to refer more and more decisions about complex matters to experts, and the contribution that can be made by specialized knowledge in engineering, medicine and physics, Terence Ball resists the idea that politics itself can ever be regarded as merely technical procedure, since it is 'the art of collective deliberation, dialogue and judgement'.[17] Nadia Urbinati similarly argues that a focus on good decision-outcomes has risks for the maintaining of democratic procedures, which may be regarded as a good in themselves: 'Although for a noble cause and despite that [sic] it bestows wisdom to the crowd, the epistemic twist of the public sphere would deform democracy's distinctive cacophonic and imprecise character, which is essential to the enjoyment of political freedom'.[18] There are those who argue that it may be possible, despite David Estlund's misgivings, to institute limited forms of epistocracy that would avoid these distortions of the democratic process.[19]

These are complex and important issues, but they are not the only ones imaginable, and the question of how to make decisions is not the only one that may be asked about an epistemocracy. Perhaps one of the reasons that this kind of question has attracted so much attention in recent years is that it provides a set-up which allows for detailed theoretical modelling and testing of the process of decision-making, in the ways that characterize the work of Estlund and those who have responded to it. But however cognitively rewarding it may be, tightening the focus in this theoretical way reduces political life to formal systems of government, and reduces government to the asking and answering of questions. One might wonder whether in fact democracy remains strong, with elections, especially in the form of yes/no referendums, being the problem.

A more idealistic use of the term epistemocracy appeared in a chapter entitled 'Epistemocracy, A Dream', in Nassim Nicholas Taleb's *The Black Swan* (2007). Taleb uses the term 'epistemocrat' for somebody who exhibits 'epistemic humility' in that 'he holds his own knowledge to be suspect'.[20] This watchful, gently self-reproving creature is typified for Taleb by French Renaissance philosopher Michel de Montaigne, though one can imagine less attractive versions of epistemic humility – for example in the ceaseless self-doubt of the obsessive-compulsive, or the more bullying and corrosive forms that may be taken by universal scepticism – meaning that one's humility would ideally have to extend to one's own suspiciousness. Taleb then proposes the name 'epistemocracy' for 'the province where the laws are structured with this kind of human fallibility in mind'.[21] In fact, there are only a couple of paragraphs on this topic before Taleb gets drawn into more interesting, but largely unrelated, commentary on the difficulty of predicting the future, though he does fill things out somewhat in some remarks on the occasion of the second edition of *The Black Swan* in 2010: 'My dream is to have a true "epistemocracy"; that is, a society robust against expert errors, forecasting errors and hubris, one that can be resistant to the incompetence of politicians, regulators, economists, central bankers, bankers, policy wonks and epidemiologists.'[22] Taleb has been followed by Brent C. Pottenger, whose *Healthcare Epistemocrat* blog proclaims:

> Today, an epistemocrat is a person who, concerned with what he or she does not know, engages in life-long learning and erudition to hedge dynamically against and to embrace uncertainty.
>
> Essentially, an epistemocrat is a practitioner (a thinker and a doer; a Jesuit-spirited 'contemplative in action') who respects (via paradoxes) the humble limits of being human and searches (via thinkering) for practical, real-world solutions that help us live and grow together in our increasingly complex and recursive world: diversify.[23]

The epistemocracy whose stirrings and growth I think I can make out is a different kind of thing, in that it implies not just government by experts but the sedimentation and propagation of forms of expertise more generally, and implies the growing authority of the principle of knowledge rather than of a specific class of knowers. This is what might be called *distributive epistemocracy*, or knowledge-production if not exactly from below, then perhaps in more directions and dimensions than from the top down.

The questions enjoined by such a situation are: what would life be like in an epistemocratic condition? What is the tone and temper of a society that accords high and even ultimate authority to knowledge, whoever might possess it? Those who feel that settling the questions of efficiency and legitimacy are sufficiently to the purpose will be likely to say that if we are only able to do so – preferably, but not necessarily without damaging democratic functioning – life will simply be better, for we will be able to make better decisions, which will do us all good. The assumption here is that what makes people unhappy is poor decision-making and that good decision-making would make them happier. But government is much more than the making of decisions; it is also the process of deliberation, in the many different forms in which this occurs.

DELIBERATION

Decision-oriented deliberation assumes that we need to deliberate in order to decide the best ways of removing impediments to happiness. This has a lot going for it because we know of a lot of impediments to happiness: poverty, disease, oppression, ignorance among them. But it does not have everything going for it, for the unexpected reason that one of the impediments to happiness would be the removal of all impediments to happiness. It is assumed that human beings want to be happy, but it does not appear that they really do. What human beings seem most to want is to *want* to be happy, and so to be taken up in efforts to achieve it. We like to tackle problems; indeed, doing so makes us happier than almost anything else, not because we want to see the problems solved, but because we like there to be problems to tackle. We do not tackle problems in order to solve them; rather we project solutions to problems in order to make it worthwhile tackling them, and to make it possible for it to be necessary for us to engage in the problem-tackling activities that are so important to us. What we really seem to want is not to be happy but to *matter*, and knowledge is increasingly the means to this mattering.

Knowledge is useful and indeed often essential – if rarely fully sufficient – for overcoming difficulties. This is one of the strongest reasons for an epistocracy, or aristocracy of concentrated knowledge. But knowledge, as long as it is sufficiently distributed, is also an excellent way of creating and prolonging difficulties; indeed, one of the most important purposes of knowledge is to keep the difficulties coming. We do not deliberate in order to gain knowledge: we have knowledge in order to have something to deliberate over and with.

We have reason in order to maximize the opportunities for reasoning. This is in fact one of the strongest reasons for an epistemocracy, or government by distributed knowledge.

Knowledge is an important part of the process of deliberation, but it is not the only important thing about it. This is not only useful to know not knowing it can amount to a kind of madness. This is the reason that the performance or playing out of knowledge, in all the ways discussed in this book, matters so much to us. For the performance of knowledge is our way not just of finding solutions – for solution is dissolution – but of keeping things in play.

Knowledge is inseparable from playing at knowledge. The more intelligent an animal, it is often observed, the stronger its motivation to play. This is not the only reason for there to be reason, but it seems to be what reason is more and more drawn to as other reasons for its existence diminish through the successful overcoming of impediments to survival. We play at knowledge because the aim of knowledge is first of all to remove all impediments in play, and then to remove all impediments *to* play.

Knowledge comes about in order to enhance the survival chances of those who develop it (or those who have survived happen to have developed knowledge). But survival is itself only a means to ensure the possibility of play, for which knowledge is also a fundamental necessity. The notion of knowledge-play allows us to reconcile the distinction between instrumental and non-instrumental knowledge. Instrumental knowledge may be regarded as concerned with the existential problems of survival which threaten to make it impossible for knowledge games to occur. The point of surviving is in order to be able to continue to play; the pay-off is the play-off. We may surmise that instrumental problems also incidentally provide the possibility for knowledge-play in advance of the situation in which all existential threats will have been overcome. Under these circumstances, instrumental knowledge may be regarded as providing the seriousness necessary for there to be, as we say, something to play for. This knowledge of its playful purpose is something that instrumental knowledge must hide from itself. Indeed, perhaps instrumentality is the way in which knowledge conceals from itself the knowledge of its orientation towards play, thereby allowing a nesting of play within seriousness and seriousness within play that is itself a kind of play.

KNOWLEDGE COLONIES

Pessimism or wariness about epistemocracy emphasizes the role of the knower, or epistemocrat, in the process. Taleb's fragile optimism focuses rather on the wary rule of knowledge itself. I would like to propose a diagnosis that bisects the line separating the philosopher-king from the cautious agnostic. The epistemocracy about which I speculate here is a social condition in which the idea of knowledge dominates over every other social value. Its focus is not the utility but the idea of knowledge, an idea that I suspect we are unlikely to be able to separate from fantasy any time soon. It may perhaps be regarded not so much as a particular sociopolitical arrangement as a particular disposition – a kind of collective epistemophilia.

Important background is supplied by the growth of the theory of social rationalization, from the work of Max Weber onwards. Weber suggests that modern societies move away from traditional forms of authority and government – which depend on charismatic leaders and inherited modes of belief – towards forms of rational calculation, the two principal drivers of this being the growth of bureaucratic administration and the effects of economic markets. The growth of the idea of rationalization produced as its counterpart the curious notion of the *Lebenswelt*, 'lifeworld', the central principle being perhaps that the lifeworld was rationalization's object, or what it went to work on. For Edmund Husserl and Alfred Schütz the lifeworld was both a background – the 'given' of already existing meanings, assumptions and prejudgements – and an after-effect, in that processes of rationalization tended to disclose that innocently given lifeworld for the first time as what it was, but perhaps could never be again.

The idea that life can be – or simply has been – divided between its spontaneously 'living' part and its programmatically 'rational' part can scarcely survive a minute's sensible reflection, but nevertheless underpins much of the philosophy and social theory of the twentieth century onwards, whether or not it is explicitly formulated in these terms. It has also driven and legitimized much of the artistic and cultural practice of the twentieth century, as well as many of the ways of thinking about the formal work of thought and research – not least because this research is undertaken in institutions divided into intellectual estates having responsibility for specific areas of what are thought of as 'lived experience' on the one hand and technical knowledge on the other. Just as the lifeworld is thought to be the remainder or surplus part of life, the 'residual essence' left over from or excreted by the production of technical life, so those in the humanities who are supposed to make the investigation, defence and enrichment of the lifeworld their business are accustomed to see theirs as a residual form of knowledge, albeit a vital and redemptive one. What Jürgen Habermas described as the progressive 'colonization of the lifeworld by autonomous systems' has become an idea of very general application, which is extraordinarily and rather ingloriously shared between rightward thinkers from Spengler to Scruton and leftward thinkers from Adorno onwards to almost everybody.[24] The idea of a conflict between experience and autonomous systems of knowledge is so general as to have become part of the fabric of thought and so to cease even to be an idea. It is, in fact, part of the system of rationalization of social knowledge.

The prospect of epistocracy has often been understood as a further extension of the power and authority of calculative rationality over the lifeworld, through its reduction of politics to matters of expert calculation. My proposition here is to use the term *epistemocracy* to signal not the colonization of the lifeworld by calculative rationality, but rather something that looks very much like the opposite, the colonization of knowledge by the lifeworld. Rather than life being subordinated by knowledge or its self-serving impersonators, knowledge is in the process of being 'culturized', or lived out as lifeworld, in the systematic fantasy of 'experience'.

In my usage, epistemocracy would refer to a culture of knowledge. It would point to the government not of abstract systems, but of feelings about those systems which, due to the effects of rapid circulation through communications media, are increasingly lifted to the condition of abstract systems themselves. A culture of knowledge would depend not just on the production and propagation of knowledge but on the promise, proclamation and performance of the idea of knowledge. Knowledge would not just be valued, it would furnish something like a coordinating grammar of values and an increasingly universal medium of exchange. A knowledge society is describable in terms of what it is; a knowledge culture is what a knowledge society seems to itself to be. This must be regarded as an abstract distinction, rather than one that allows for clear and abstract distinctions between usages of the terms, and they undoubtedly blend and overlap such that ideas about what a knowledge society is start to feed back into the conditions of that society.

First introduced in 1969 in Peter Drucker's *Age of Discontinuity* and then identified as a leading feature of 'post-industrial society' by Daniel Bell in 1973, the phrase 'knowledge society' began to be used regularly in the mid-1980s and has become increasingly embedded during the 2000s both in official policy statements and in ordinary usage.[25] The effect of this embedding is simultaneously to encourage reflections on what a knowledge society might need, consist in and be capable of, and to make reflections on why we should think in such terms at all seem unnecessary. The success of the phrase shifted the sociorhetorical weather. Nico Stehr made the most important principle of a knowledge society the 'penetration of all its spheres of life by scientific knowledge', but subsequent accounts have observed a multiplication of styles and forms of knowledge well beyond the scientific or technical in knowledge societies.[26] Indeed, perhaps the most important and enabling condition of a knowledge society has been the development of computational technologies which now determine the ways in which not just information but the forms of social experience are stored, processed and exchanged.

For the time being the idea of a knowledge society still seems suffused with optimism and good intent. The UNESCO report *Towards Knowledge Societies* sees the increase in access to knowledge as an unconditional good, decreeing that

> A knowledge society should be able to integrate all its members and to promote new forms of solidarity involving both present and future generations. Nobody should be excluded from knowledge societies, where knowledge is a public good, available to each and every individual.[27]

A knowledge society might well be one in which there is more knowledge, and in which that knowledge is more important to the stability and prospering of that society than in other kinds of arrangement. But it is surprisingly hard to be sure how one would in fact register or measure or consequently regulate any of this. In fact, whatever measurement there could be would be bound to be of the appearances of knowledge-proxies and enactments of knowledge-relations – the performances of knowledge that are the vehicles of epistemopathic endowment and that have been the subject of this book. The most prominent of these knowledge-proxies are perhaps levels of economic investment and social participation in education. It is routinely assumed that this must mean that more people know more things and know how to do more things, but there is also room for doubt on this score: there certainly seem to be many things that people with rather limited levels of education were able to do in the past that people find challenging nowadays (maths, grammar and so forth), not to mention rudimentary life skills that are beyond many citizens of advanced societies.

One might even be justified in thinking that a knowledge society could be one in which there is on the whole a lower concentration of intelligence, since it would be one in which the capacity to access and communicate specialist expertise is more important than the possession of it. A knowledge society is therefore perfectly compatible with a situation in which individual members of that society know less than ever before about many more kinds of thing. In fact, a knowledge society requires and enables an increase in the quantity and variety of mediations of knowledge, and these furnish the conditions for a knowledge culture, that is, a society which mediates to itself through these mediations the idea and ideal of knowledge as such.

On the one hand there is an undoubted diversification in the kinds of thing that can count and weigh as knowledge: as Daniel Innerarity has observed,

> knowledge society is one in which knowledge, rather than science, is afforded great significance. We cannot fully understand a knowledge society without considering the fact that, in its functioning and its conflicts, it encompasses many different types of knowledge, some of them contradictory.[28]

On the other hand, the growing epistemocracy seems to make whatever does count and weigh as knowledge more important than anything else. This may not necessarily be a fortunate condition.

EXOPISTEMOPATHY

Gernot Böhme observed in an essay of 1992 that a knowledge society is not just a society in which there is more knowledge, it is also a society organized in such a way as to be able to know itself:

In order for society to be controllable through knowledge, it must itself be organized in terms of knowledge: social processes must be differentiated according to function and arranged according to models, and social actors must be disciplined in a way which makes their behavior amenable to data collection or makes their social role and activities relevant only insofar as they produce data . . . [I]f one wants to characterize modern society from this perspective as a knowledge society it is necessary to stress that it is not a matter of knowledge about how society may be in itself, but of knowledge of a society which is already organized with respect to its knowability.[29]

Perhaps the greatest conundrum thrown up by the contemporary examples of the knowledge society has been the separation of knowledge from human knowing brought about by computational technology. Artificial intelligence has been with us for a long time, perhaps even, as people nowadays say when referring to periods of more than about a week, 'the longest time', because all intelligence is artificial, since all intelligence (in the sense of a capacity for judgement) requires to be externalized in the form of intelligence (as the giving of report). What is knowledge for? Knowledge is to be communicated. If there is a strong urge to keep certain kinds of knowledge hidden away, this may be because the urge or imperative to communicate knowledge is otherwise so intrinsic to it. The word 'intelligence' lets on about this sufficiently: to be intelligent is to have some intelligence to pass on. Something similar applies to the word 'information': information is not just a given, it is something that must *be* given. Indeed, if the principle holds that 'I do not know what I think until I see what I say', then I do not know that I know something until I can tell it to myself. I can only cognize something I can recognize. The drive to know, if there is such a thing, is a drive to be able to tell of what one knows, in order that one may be one-taken-to-know. It does not ever seem to be enough to know: one must impart the news of what one knows or, at the very least, secure it from theft or forgetfulness so that it may be recalled as needed. I am making a book from the things I think about our concern with knowing as part of my own fulfilment of this pattern: finding out what there may be to know about our care for knowing is not for me easy to distinguish from finding out what there may be to be told about it.

But something unexpected happens when one tells what one knows. For that very process, which brings knowing into focus and fulfilment, also begins to separate me from my knowledge. As a consequence, I am much more likely to forget something to which I have given written form. Understandably, and politely, people sometimes ask me to represent the views or arguments that are articulated in things I may have written. Having externalized what I know, or my processes of coming to know, in written form, I am then asked to personify that knowledge, to act as convincingly as I can as the *sujet-supposé-savoir* of the knowledge. But the mere fact of having articulated the knowledge in some way that makes it intelligible means that the knowledge is no longer quite mine, and must become less and less mine as time passes. This is why, when people pay me the compliment of asking me to explain what I may have meant by something I have written, I have to put myself in their position, by reading it, in just the way they could do for themselves.

So there is no knowing without telling, and especially the kind of repeatable telling that is writing; but this writing is the ablation of my knowledge, even, as Socrates feared, the very vehicle of my amnesia. As in the sentence from Joyce's *Finnegans Wake* quoted in Chapter Six, every telling has a taling, a reckoning up; but it also has a tailing off. I act and sometimes speak as though I thought that I were stockpiling what I know in what I write, laying up knowledge against the day when knowledge may have gone from me, or I from it. But the more knowledge I accumulate in this way, the less actual knowing there is in me, of me. The knowing will always have to be in what I have written, in the warrant it provides for the fantasy of the one supposed by the writing to know; the one, that is, that provides the imaginary support for the writing that might otherwise impossibly seem to come from nowhere and rest on nothing, but which actually is itself the support for this supposition. How telling it is that I must always have something to rest on when I write, some support or hypothesis – a desk, a table, a lap, my palm, even a friend's accommodating back. It is the necessary support for the writing that provides my support, my supposition.

The desire to automate thinking has been recurrent throughout the history of thought about thought. This is perhaps a logical extension of the feeling that reason is itself a kind of mechanical operation to which mind submits itself. Sometimes, as in Francis Bacon's remarkable proposal in his *New Organon*, this seems to promise a purging from knowledge of the more dubious operations of mind:

> There remains one hope of salvation, one way to good health: that the entire work of the mind be started over again; and from the very start the mind should not be left to itself, but be constantly controlled; and the business done (if I may put it this way) by machines.[30]

For others, the mechanization and therefore exteriorization of calculative mental operations held out the promise of freeing capacity for other kinds of cognitive activity. Mary Boole, the collaborator and wife of mathematician George Boole, whose work on algebraic logic provides the foundation for all Internet searching, wrote in 1883,

> if I were asked to point out the two greatest benefactors to humanity that this century has produced, I think I should be inclined to mention Mr. Babbage, who made a machine for working out series; and Mr. Jevons, who made a machine for stringing together syllogisms. Between them they have conclusively proved, by the unanswerable logic of facts, that calculation and reasoning, like weaving and ploughing, are work, not for human souls, but for clever combinations of iron and wood.[31]

Boole proposes that the delegation of such sorting operations to arrangements of iron and wood will bring an understanding of the kinds of intellectual growth that is possible when they are transcended:

> If you spend time in doing work that a machine could do faster than yourselves, it should only be for exercise, as you swing dumb-bells; or for amusement, as you dig in your garden; or to soothe your nerves by its mechanicalness, as you take up your knitting; not in any hope of so working your way to the truth. You can get anything you please by artificial arrangements, whether of matter or of ideas; any thing, that is, any inorganic transformation of already existing materials; any thing you please, except growth.[32]

But this confidence in the cognitive powers that are to be liber-ated by the automation of calculative reason must also cope with the possibility that external systems might also be able to accede to these higher or more essentially human kinds of intelligence. In September 2017, Google's Deep Mind group reported at a conference entitled 'Memory and Imagination in Humans and Machines' on work with neural networks that they hoped would begin to allow machines to develop some of the capacities that are referred to as 'imagination'. The discussions at the conference were characterized by a certain optimistic humility on the part of those describing computing devel-opments and peevishly defensive responses from those who regarded themselves as representing the humanities, for some of whom this seemed a presumptuous attempt to appropriate the territory they held to be their inheritance. Both sides seemed to display a naive positiv-ism about the nature of 'imagination', as though it were perfectly clear what this was, even as it proved necessary to maintain in its definition a certain degree of ineffability.

What we mean by imagination is not just what it denotes, but what we do with that word. What we do with that word, as opposed to what the word denotes, is to add fantasy to denotation. It is possible to agree with the opponents of computing that the idea of machine imagination is a fantasy, not because the way in which a machine may be said to imagine must always fall short of, or be qualitatively different from, human imagination, but because the idea of human imagination is itself made up in large part of fantasy. We depend on imagination to decide what 'imagination' means. What is more, it is an ongoing work of fantasy, one that is still in process – with the idea of machine imagination always being part of that process. The fan-tasy of mechanical imagination has from the beginning been a part of the process of imagining human imagination. This is prosopopoeia, glossed in 1561 as 'the fayning of a persone'.[33]

English has a rhetorical advantage over some other languages because it is a combination of Latinate and Germanic (to use their Latin name) ingredients, two lexical streams that, for historical and political reasons flowing from the conquest of Britain by a Latin-speaking people, the Normans (to use their German name), is equipped with a readymade machine-code for translating between the sensible and the intelligible, or (in German) the felt and the known (you can play this game all day). Since our language conjoins a feeling-lexicon and a knowing-lexicon, it can provide a sensitive register of the alternations between feeling and knowledge, along with their recursive nestings (what, for instance, we feel about what we think we know about feeling).

One might think in particular of the fortunes of words that begin as knowing-words and become suffused with certain kinds of feeling. One would be the term 'data'. A couple of decades ago, data tended to mean the results of experimental procedures usually having a numerical form. Data was therefore the product of certain kinds of systematic investigation aimed precisely at the formation of data. So data was not in any sense what the word suggests it might be, things simply given to us; data had to be formed and captured in specific and deliberate ways, and in determinate contexts. But over the last two decades or so, the spread of personal computing has meant the production of large amounts of pre-coded data which is immediately available for processing operations – which can, of course, include surveillance, marketing and identity theft, because, although data still needs to be produced, it is also spontaneously emitted by many of our personal actions and interactions insofar as they take place in self-archiving, digitally mediated ways. Many human societies in the past have been extremely nervous about the magical uses that can be made of hair, fingernails and other kinds of personal exuviae; our concern nowadays is with the products of our data excretion. Data is not so much given, as the word suggests, as incontinently given off. The enormous growth in the shredding industry testifies to this concern about the risk posed to us by our shreddings. The word 'data' is becoming much more likely to allude to this kind of concern with the person rather than with abstract or merely technological matters.

Another word that oscillates between cognitive and affective registers is 'algorithm'. An algorithm is a computational procedure: as a professor of computing in my university said to me, 'it's just a recipe'. As such, it is one of the most familiar operations in all human life. You operate an algorithm every time you measure a wall and decide how many rolls of wallpaper you are going to need and every time you fry the onions at the beginning of cooking spaghetti bolognese, rather than leaving it until the end. If I look up the word 'algorithm' in the *OED*, which I have just done, I operate an algorithm to do it. The usefulness of an algorithm is precisely that it is a mixture of the purposive and the automatic: I don't have to devise a procedure for performing these actions every time I do it.

Algorithm, often in the form *algorism, algorym* or *augrim*, was in use from at least the thirteenth century to signify the Arabic system of decimal numbering and calculation, as distinguished from *abacism*, or the use of the abacus. It owes its name to the fact that the first arithmetical treatise translated from Arabic into Latin to explain the use of Hindu numbers was a ninth-century work by the Persian mathematician Muhammed ibn Mūsā al-Khwārizmī, the Latin rendering of whose name, for example in the *Liber algorismi de numero Indorum*, became the name for the practice he explained. *The Crafte of Nombrynge* from the early fifteenth century begins with the words 'This boke is called þe boke of algorym, or Augrym after lewder vse. And þis boke tretys of þe Craft of Nombryng, þe quych crafte is called also Algorym'.[34] The word seems to have blended with the Greek ἀριθμός, *arithmos*, number, and perhaps also to have been influenced by the word *algebra*, on which al-Khwārizmī also wrote and which also derives from his name. There is no etymological connection with *augury*, which is from Latin *avis*, bird, and Indo-European *-gar*, to call or make known, though the existence of forms like Anglo-Norman *augorime* for *algorism* suggests the possibility that the words have influenced each other. No doubt Greek *arithmos* (number) and the rise in the sixteenth century of the word *rhythm*, from Greek ῥυθμός, *rithmos*, for measured time or recurring order, will have contributed something to the magical overtones of the word.

Some of these overtones seem to have been reawakened in contemporary uses of the word algorithm. For some time, automated cognitive procedures, some of them mechanical but mostly electronic, have been becoming faster, more complex and autonomous of human beings. The word algorithm had been a part of the technical vocabulary of programmers and computer scientists, but has moved into cultural and political life, with the growing awareness of a world of automatic calculations – making decisions in an unregulated manner, in areas as diverse as financial trading, medical diagnosis, battlefield biometrics and the ordering of taxis – along with the concern about the way in which search engines provide information to users selectively through the use of algorithmic filters, meaning that the transmission of human knowledge is itself being governed by non-human mechanisms. The essays gathered together in the collection

Algorithmic Life (2015) indicate the rapid naturalization of this term as a shorthand for the effect of impersonal and autonomous information systems.[35] Not only has the idea of the algorithm been the subject of increasingly frequent and intense cathexis, but calculative procedures are increasingly able to be brought to bear to form and transform human feelings and perceptions, making for a rapid and somewhat unpredictable interchange between what we know, what we feel about what we know, and what we know about what we feel about what we know. The term 'algocracy', bred from Estlund's 'epistocracy', has recently been proposed for this alarming situation.[36]

An algorithmic society depends on what has been called datafication, the rapid transformation of communicative behaviour and other human phenomena into information capable of being processed and exploited. The most important transformation is the fact that what, at the beginning of statistics – in the mortality bills of the plague years in London, and the collection of large amounts of social information by the revolutionary government in France – used to be a laborious and time-consuming process, can itself now happen spontaneously, in systems of self-encoding data production. Artificial intelligence therefore does not merely name the intelligent operations performed on the natural and human worlds, but the production of 'intelligence' by intelligent systems. There is more knowledge than ever before because our capacities for generating knowable objects are increasing so rapidly. Under these circumstances, we might do well to pay attention less, as Steve Fuller has put it, to the physics of knowledge and more to its chemistry, so we might 'not be interested in finding an underlying unity that that distinguishes knowledge from other things, but rather principles for converting anything into a piece of knowledge'.[37]

An important part of our understanding and inhabitation of this system is the overheated cathexis of the idea of abstract system itself and the law of magical exception that systematically operates through it – that is, the law ensuring that one can never be fully assimilated to a system that one is able fully to explicate. We perhaps have need of an idea we might call 'exopistemopathy' as the response to the prospect of exopistemology, the mechanical rage against the machine of artificial systems for their theft or usurpation of what we just know (instinctively, which is to say, automatically) are properly human powers of knowing, learning and understanding. There is an unstable

compound of fascination, delight and dread in the idea of a knowledge that operates without our knowing it, perhaps partly because
that is a feature of all our knowledge. Such systems constitute what
I have previously called a dream machine, a machinery for producing dreams of machines and what they are capable of doing to us.[38]
Many fantasies of artificial intelligence can be seen as alien abduction
fantasies (fantasies of abduction by aliens and fantasies that abduct
us as aliens might). Indeed such fantasies may themselves be a kind
of artificial intelligence.

It is natural to assume that because unequal access to knowledge
has in the past been a class differentiator, that the widening of access
to knowledge will in itself act as a solvent of disadvantage. But knowledge is not necessarily a neutral good, nor does it necessarily lead to
depolarization and the intelligent sharing of interests. Indeed, there
is no better example than the university of how powerful a differentiator knowledge, rather than the lack of knowledge, can be. With
the sedimentation of epistemocracies we are just as likely to see the
development of powerful epistemic blocs or knowledge classes which
will cut across and perhaps even entirely displace the traditional affiliations of 'class', 'race', religion, gender, age, region, occupation and
income, as we are to generate republics, syndicates, factions, even
armies of shared understanding. The assumption is that the substantial populations who voted for Trump and Brexit did so because they
were misled, misguided and misinformed. This assumption is itself
a manifestation of epistemocracy, the resentment by a particular
knowledge class at the infringement of its prerogatives. 'How could
we accept that future knowledge societies will operate like so many
exclusive clubs only for the happy few?' ask the authors of the UNESCO
report *Towards Knowledge Societies*.[39] We may come to wonder how
we could have imagined that the propagation of knowledge would
simply and necessarily lead to more social convergence and consensus.
We can expect that conflicts over knowledge will increasingly express
themselves as epistemocratic conflicts in and through knowledge.

The UNESCO report goes to considerable lengths to distinguish
knowledge – which is always presented as positive, nurturing, careful
and desirable – from information and data, which latter can easily
alienate and overwhelm or be commodified or instrumentalized in
ways that reduce human freedom or create conflict. Knowledge is
assumed to be identical with what is called critical reflection, and is

assumed to be the result of education. But it is not at all clear that the liberal ideal of critical reflection will be the way in which knowledge and education are understood everywhere. There are, for example, powerfully authoritarian traditions in education that it would be foolish to expect to wither away on their own. They are, of course, among the diverse knowledge traditions that the UNESCO report urges us to preserve against colonization by the knowledges of the North.

The eight years that passed between UNESCO's *Towards Knowledge Societies* and the follow-up report *Renewing the Knowledge Societies Vision* (2013) seem to have deepened the rift between information and knowledge. Yet this has happened without much to fill out convincingly the difference between them, beyond the assertion that information can bring about bad effects while knowledge is both empowering and peace-enhancing, this proposed largely on the grounds that 'knowledge implies meaning, appropriation and participation'.[40] This seems to mean that, where information is It, knowledge is Us – 'Information and knowledge are not the same because knowledge requires interpretation by human beings' – as though to restate the Freudian ambition: *wo Es war, soll Wir werden* (where there was It, will be We).[41]

But this account is less a definition of knowledge than a compliment paid to an ideal of thinking and feeling about the ways of possessing and exchanging information. It is hard to share the confidence of the UNESCO report that 'despite their sophistication, machines will never replace the human being when it comes to the reflection necessary to transform information into knowledge', not least because the report itself acknowledges within the space of a few sentences that '[h]enceforth, a cognitive act can no longer be thought of on the model of the classical theories of knowledge, which treat it as an individual psychological act.'[42]

Among the predictable outcomes of open, or as one might prefer to call it, wild, data are terrorism, proliferation of weapons, every kind of fraud, theft, piracy and exploitation, the growth of systems of private and public menace and harassment, and the debasement of news reporting into an even more feculent slurry of sadistic mockery, witch-burning and the moralized pursuit of revenge. It is not of the feeblest use to quarantine 'information', as the bad, mechanical, inhuman kind of knowledge, from good knowledge, understood as information made meaningful by human interpretation. One can be quite certain that there is no shortage of interpretation by human beings or human meaning-making among ISIL, which indeed, like any group of militant zealots, handsomely meets all the essential requirements for a knowledge society.

The most important thing to understand about the kind of knowledge characteristic of knowledge societies is that it is less and less embodied in knowers and exists ever more in the capacity for passage and exchange, the cycles of information propagation and decay. The epistemic has become epidemic in its structure, production and rhythm; this is because knowledge has become ever more mediated, even as it has also become more immediately available. Mediation removes responsibility, immediacy makes it very difficult to limit effects. The most important principle of knowledge, therefore, is that it has become mobile. As long as 'knowledge' is arbitrarily restricted to the sort of thing that we would wish not to see restricted for the benefit of one group and the disadvantage of another, this mobility will seem desirable. But if knowledge includes every kind of information, true or false, dangerous or safe, useful and useless, enriching and debasing, it is naive to see the uncontrollable acceleration of its dissemination as an absolute good. Knowledge in the UNESCO sense requires detachment and delay, while the very means of growing knowledge societies closes every possibility of delay, deferral or distance.

There are two opposite dangers that are conceivable in developed, distributed epistemocracy. The first is the deepening disadvantage of the ignorant, which will paradoxically become more cruel and injurious for those subjected to it the more that knowledge and education spread. It is much better to have a 20 per cent illiteracy rate than a 40 per cent illiteracy rate, but it is much worse to be part of a 20 per cent minority of the illiterate than a 40 per cent minority, and to be part of the 2 per cent almost removes one from anything that could be called human existence altogether. The growth of a knowledge society cannot help but deepen the disadvantage to those not in the know. Poverty can be relatively speedily remedied by money, and even violence is susceptible to certain kinds of social and legal mitigation. But ignorance and the increasingly catastrophic exclusion from human life it implies is much more expensive to remedy and beyond a certain point may be irremediable. To be accounted stupid is already in most societies the most vicious and pitiless exclusion from participation in social life that is imaginable. Knowledge society has a capacity to create non- or prehumans, and that is much more powerful than any other set of power relations.

We can expect power to continue to leak away from the rich, the male, the white and possibly even the beautiful (always the last unearned advantage to come under investigation) and to accrue steadily and in spades to the smart, or maybe the merely fly. The incurious kowtowing to know-how in an epistemocracy may make it harder than ever to appreciate how long the list is of things that are worse than ignorance (cowardice, malice, pride, selfishness, treachery, indolence, unkindness, rage, cruelty, addiction and so on) and how considerable and precious too the back-catalogue of human graces and virtues that need have no necessary relation to intelligence – though it would be intelligent of us to honour and foster them (endurance, courage, resilience, loyalty, fairness, adventure, cheerfulness, tenderness, friendliness, forgetfulness, devotion, generosity, vivacity, joy, love, sentimentality, hesitation, humour, mercy, care). It has been part of the purpose of this book to try to suggest how complicated, irrational, unlovely and even sometimes dangerous the human infatuation with its own actual and imagined powers of knowledge can be, and along the way to acknowledge the work of thinkers (my personal list includes Erasmus, Montaigne, Hume, James and Serres) who manage to be not only percipient but lovable and who, when it came down to it, would place the knowledge of love over the love of knowledge. We should not regard our relation to our knowledge as unimprovable, but it will be important for us to try to become more intelligent about unintelligence; not least because, if the power to shame is toxically potent, the condition of shame, though the most exquisitely painful form of vulnerability, may also harbour surprising and dangerous powers of insurgence.

For the other danger of epistemocracy is not so much intellectual deficit as defection – and the door it opens gapingly wide for intensified conflict as knowledge becomes not just a resource to be fought over but a vehicle to be fought through and with. The principle that knowledge is power has been taken to mean either that knowledge is a means for 'Power', meaning established or state powers of various kinds, to assert its dominion, or it is a means whereby such Powers can be heroically stood up to. But it is important to recognize that, with knowledge increasing on all sides, knowledge is power everywhere and for everybody who has it. The growing tensions and conflicts over intellectual property rights, for example, as they concern drug patents, software and the ownership of music and other cultural productions are already far too complex and involve too many competing interest groups to be reduced romantically to a struggle between corporations and the commons.[43] In the absence of a willingness sometimes to sacrifice truth for peace, it is hard to see what will intervene to prevent the escalation of the epistemic rivalry and spite that had already, even before the election of Trump and the British vote to leave the European Union, become a feature of recent election campaigns. The Enlightenment aim of replacing *doxa* with *logos* will have to be given up in the face of the multiplication of every conceivable kind of doctrinal adherence and doxological authority. The growth of knowledge is likely to take place not just through increasing what individuals know and know how to do. It will also increase the opportunities and desires for making known, in the sense both of disclosing and of producing. The chances of epistemocracy in Taleb's sense – of a prudently and pragmatically self-limiting mode of knowledge, a knowledge capable of inhibiting as well as inhabiting its own excited investments and exaggerations – seem currently limited.

PRODUCTION OF KNOWLEDGE

This is acknowledged in the phrase 'knowledge production', which has strangely ceased to sound strange over the course of my lifetime. Not all human eras and communities have believed in the infinite producibility of knowledge, which is precisely why most human groups have devoted so much attention to its reproduction. Indeed, it seems likely that most human groups that have had any abstract conception of the temporality of knowledge have tended to see it steadily occupying more and more of a finite space of the knowable, or adequating nature to the human, rather than expanding outwards into an infinite space that it itself forms as it goes, like a locomotive laying down its own track before it. It seems strange that such a conception should have come to seem natural in the very period in which we are having to make such painful adjustments to the idea of the finitude of every other earthly resource that we had previously assumed to be without limit. One must surely suspect some principle of epistemopathic compensation here, as though knowledge needed to conjure up a superpower-equipped fantasy-double of itself, to make up for what it has glumly been forced to come to know of finitude. The prospect of the infinite horizon for knowledge production is probably a proxy for the godlike fantasy of boundlessly giving rise to oneself, an intoxication that, intrinsic though it may seem, has not always turned out well.

At the same time, there is a very long history of the performing of knowledge and knowledge-relations, some of which have been explored in the chapters of this book. This may suggest that knowing is inseparable from some kind of theatrical production (I do not mean to say uniquely so). Knowledge is never quite here or there, at the point where it is supposed to be: libido must supply the place of that *ibid*. It requires staging, ceremonies, impersonations, transmissions, tableaux and libretti, pageants and puppet plays to stand in for its always maddeningly truant here and now. The desire to know which Aristotle assumed was primary is endlessly deflected into the desire to make knowing knowable. There must always be some form through which knowledge can be performed, some plotting, characterization and laying of the scene. Some of these scenographies have been explored in the preceding chapters: in the Faustian phantasmagoria of the chalked circle commanding the macrocosm; the soul-searching and psychic surgery in the private chambers of psychoanalysis; the mystery plays and smoky places of secrecy; the adversary courts and show trials in which knowledge is made to own up to itself; the wastes and wilds, the fogs and fens and cunning corridors of unknowing; the studies, schoolrooms, libraries, laboratories and lecture halls in which the show is stopped, or must go on; and all the many ways and means in which we may be said to 'invest' in knowledge – be it sartorial, psychological, military or economic. The *mise en scène* that is most conspicuous by its absence from this book is the one on which all its deliberations depend for their delivery: the phantasmagoric space-time of the book itself, our most familiar and established form of artificial intelligence, which parses knowing into its places, occasions and parts of speech, spinning out its suppositions, prepositions and postponements.

None of what has been written here implies that we should weaken the resolve to widen, diversify and make more precise our knowledge, nor to extend knowledge to many more of the human population through education. Indeed, I have tried to argue that our social dependence on knowledge makes ignorance more of a deprivation now than at any other time. But it ought to suggest that we might be more carefully curious than we are about the kinds of affective investment we have already made in the idea of knowledge. When the UNESCO report *Towards Knowledge Societies* evokes what it calls 'genuine knowledge', it articulates what can only be a vague hope that we know what this means and that we will recognize it when we see it, while indicating an uneasy half-awareness that knowledge can be and do many unpredictable and intractable things.[44] What Nico Stehr maintained more than two decades ago, early in the formation of the idea of knowledge societies, is true now more than ever:

> The most serious theoretical deficiency of existing theories of modern society which assign a central role to knowledge is ... their rather undifferentiated treatment of the key ingredient, namely knowledge itself ... [O]ur knowledge about know-ledge is, despite, and, for a time, because of the sociology of knowledge, not very sophisticated or comprehensive.[45]

We are confident of knowing something about unconscious knowledge, but have scarcely begun to grasp the unconscious of knowledge. The madness of knowledge takes many different forms, but perhaps they all fix around one form of insanity, in the literal sense of the word *sanus*: not being sound, whole, integrated or all of a piece. Perhaps it could be articulated in an adaptation of the open-ing words of Nietzsche's *On the Genealogy of Morality* cited as the epigraph to Chapter Three: the more knowledge we have, the less we knowers seem to know of it.[46] This may be the irremediable uninteg-rity of a knowledge that will always put us beside ourselves, since for it to have done with itself would be to have done with our selves.

It is likely that we many centuries ago reached the operative limit of what it was possible for an individual human being to know and know how to do, meaning that any increase in human knowledge must take place entirely in our stores of collective or communicable knowledge rather than in things that any one of us may be said any more to 'know' in the antique, possessive sense. We are at this point in history more dependent than ever before on being able to increase and intensify what and how we know – gambling more feverishly, more intoxicatedly than ever before, for example, on being able to continue coming up with technical means of outpacing the physical limits within which we have come to realize we exist on this planet. This dependence on knowledge seems, as usual, to make us at once more powerful and weaker. If our forms of social organization behaviour make us less able than ever before to depend upon patterns of immunity against disease, we will depend as never before on medical expertise and economic investment that may make it possible to keep our noses in front of pathogen resistance. The only protection against the risks that come from the ever greater entanglement with one another's lives – politically, militarily, medically, environmentally – seems to be ever greater and more knowledgeable entanglement. These are technical difficulties that we need to try to equip ourselves to solve.

I have attempted to maintain a strategic separation through this book between epistemological questions to do with what we can know and epistemopathic questions concerning the dreams, dreads and desires we entertain about knowledge – our inveterate idealization of and devotion to knowledge, desire for mystery, mastery and discovery, the difficulty we have in separating knowledge from rivalry and dispute, our strangely mingled longing and loathing for fancied states of ignorance, the care we take to embody our veneration for knowledge in the places and spaces we build and our relation to the object world. If I have maintained this separation between what we know and what we feel about our knowledge, it has been with a growing sense that we will need to get better at understanding and managing the history of our ambitions and investments, as though it were a part of the known and knowable world. Perhaps our survival and well-being are no more at stake in this than they have been before, but we should perhaps not take the risk of assuming that they are any less. Knowledge is often uplifting, absorbing, honest, healing, liberating, enlarging, useful, enabling, irenic, dignifying, continent and civilizing. It is also, at various times, greedy, arrogant, aggressive, aggrandizing, egotistical, obsessive, enslaving, belligerent, myopic, colonizing, paralysing, conservative, devious, cowardly, lazy and ungovernable.

I have assumed throughout this book that the human experience of knowledge is strongly marked by the essential difficulty of knowing one's knowledge – not just being sure of the extent of one's knowledge but also being able to sense what knowing anything is like. I can know, to a certain extent at least, that I know and how I know, but it seems I cannot know my knowing – the very oddity of the phrase is a testament to the fact. The difficulty of knowing one's knowledge is analogous to the difficulty of feeling one's sensations, as pointed out by David Hume. I can feel cold, itchy or sad, but I cannot feel my feeling of those things; similarly, I can know how to ride a bicycle, ask for an omelette in Paris and communicate the second law of thermodynamics, but knowing my knowing of these things (as opposed to my learning, remembering or communicating of them) is not something I can naturally or easily feel or do. Knowing what I know is at best an assumption about what, under given conditions, I might be able to do. It is hard to say what having an experience of any of those forms of knowing might amount to. This essential unknowability of knowledge means that human beings are forced to seek and sustain their relationship to their own knowledge through various kinds of symbols and surrogates. Just as there is a kind of 'referred sensation' that happens in the body as a sort of stand-in pain for an organ unprovided with nerves (the left arm during a heart attack, for example), so there may be referred knowledges of knowing. Much of this book has been concerned with these forms of displacement or shadow-theatre.

One of the areas of human performance in which the noetic functions of reflection, observation, discovery, learning and memory have probably been more developed, and certainly more important for the survival of the earliest human settlements than in any other, is in agriculture. Knowing how to grow things became the defining skill for the development of what we tellingly still call human culture: the growth of human knowledge was hugely accelerated by the knowledge of growth. The epistemic potency of agricultural skills is redoubled by the fact that such skills required and rewarded the development of writing. Cultivating the land in one place rather than moving from place to place in search of fresh resources required the intellectual mobility provided by accountancy and reckoning, which made necessary the kind of externalized symbolism (perhaps originally of quantities) that would develop into writing. Orality is nomadic: writing is a necessity for settled peoples, because they need to have and be able to retain, recall, transmit and even transform much more knowledge of their environments. If one's environment is to be made a productive one, the relationship to it must become calculative. Nomadic lives involve projections and reckoning, to be sure, but these are immanent to the living choices made by the group, which are likely to be habitual. Nomadic peoples themselves are the calculations through which they live in their environments, where settled peoples perform acts of calculation abstractly. You can move, or you can know: perhaps that is why we have what are called Chairs in universities, and why the All-knowing God is usually depicted seated rather than on the run.

Agriculture makes possible and necessary the kind of second nature we call culture. It is striking how much of the work of knowing, especially when it is involved with writing, is still suggested through dimly figured agricultural and horticultural allusions. A seminary was originally a piece of ground on which seeds were sown; nurseries, of plants and sucklings, derive from Latin *nutrio*, to nourish, as an *alumnus* and *alma mater* are from *alere*, to feed or sustain; riddles and reading recall the operations of the sieve; gardens are libraries and libraries and anthologies are gardens, pages are fields. Human culture seems to be becoming ever more extraterrestrial, even as this conceals from ourselves the fact that we are as dependent as we have ever been on the capacity of the earth to fix energy from the sun. It seems likely that biochemistry will need to supplement and perhaps even replace cultivation, the old division between the industrial and the agricultural losing its meaning. But, as engineering – the maintenance and modification of the conditions of existence, physical, biological, psychological and symbolic – becomes the universal human occupation, there will be more need than ever to supplement our knowledge of cultivation with the careful cultivation of our knowledges. For this, we may need to get to know more about what knowledge means to us, we would-be knowers.

REFERENCES

INTRODUCTION

1 Anon., 'Jean Paul', *English Review*, VII (1847), p. 296.
2 Ralph Cudworth, *A Treatise Concerning Eternal and Immutable Morality* (London, 1731), p. 272.
3 James IV of Scotland, *Daemonologie In Forme of a Dialogue* (Edinburgh, 1597); Thomas Heywood, *Troia Britanica; or, Great Britaines Troy* (London, 1609), p. 288; Guy Miège, *A Dictionary of Barbarous French; or, A Collection, by Way of Alphabet, of Obsolete, Provincial, Mis-spelt, and Made Words in French* (London, 1679), sig. M2v.
4 Aristotle, *Metaphysics, Books I–IX*, trans. Hugh Tredennick (Cambridge, MA, and London, 1933), p. 3.
5 Jacques Lacan, *The Seminar of Jacques Lacan*, Book XX: *Encore: On Feminine Sexuality, The Limits of Love and Knowledge, 1972–1973*, ed. Jacques-Alain Miller, trans. Bruce Fink (New York, 1998), p. 121.
6 Peter Sloterdijk, *You Must Change Your Life*, trans. Wieland Hoban (Cambridge, 2013), pp. 83–106.
7 'Occasional Notes', *Pall Mall Gazette*, XL/6197 (21 January 1885), p. 3.
8 'A Merry Medico', *Punch*, LXXXVIII (17 January 1885), p. 26.
9 Sigmund Koch, 'The Nature and Limits of Psychological Knowledge: Lessons of a Century Qua "Science"', *American Psychologist*, XXXVI (1981), p. 258.
10 Sigmund Koch, 'Psychology's Bridgman vs Bridgman's Bridgman: An Essay in Reconstruction', *Theory and Psychology*, II (1992), p. 262.
11 David Hume, *A Treatise of Human Nature*, ed. Ernest C. Mossner (London, 1985), p. 462.
12 William James, *The Meaning of Truth: A Sequel to 'Pragmatism'* (New York, 1909), p. 120.
13 Peter H. Spader, 'Phenomenology and the Claiming of Essential Knowledge', *Husserl Studies*, XI (1995), pp. 169–99.
14 Ernst Cassirer, *The Philosophy of Symbolic Forms*, vol. III: *The Phenomenology of Knowledge*, trans. Ralph Manheim (New Haven, CT, 1957), p. xiv.
15 Francis Bacon, *The New Organon*, ed. Lisa Jardine and Michael Silverthorne (Cambridge, 2000), p. 44.
16 Sigmund Freud, *The Standard Edition of the Complete Psychological Works*

of Sigmund Freud, 24 vols, ed. and trans. James Strachey et al. (London, 1953–74), vol. XIII, p. 84.

17 Francis Quarles, *Emblemes* (Cambridge, 1643), p. 19.

18 Jerome S. Bruner, Jacqueline J. Goodnow and George A. Austin, *A Study of Thinking* (New Brunswick, NJ, 1986), p. 12; Niklas Luhmann, *Introduction to Systems Theory*, ed. Dirk Baecker, trans. Peter Gilgen (Cambridge and Malden, MA, 2013), p. 121.

19 T. S. Eliot, 'Gerontion', *Complete Poems and Plays* (London, 1969), p. 38.

20 Michele G. Sforza, 'Epistemophily-Epistemopathy: Use of the Internet between Normality and Disease', in *Psychoanalysis, Identity and the Internet*, ed. Andrea Marzi (London, 2016), pp. 181–207.

21 Randall Styers, *Making Magic: Religion, Magic, and Science in the Modern World* (Oxford and New York, 2004), p. 16.

22 Samuel Beckett, *Company. Ill Seen Ill Said. Worstward Ho. Stirrings Still*, ed. Dirk van Hulle (London, 2009), p. 8.

23 Richard Rorty, *Contingency, Irony, and Solidarity* (Cambridge, 1989), p. 21.

24 Michel Foucault, 'The Order of Discourse', in *Untying the Text*, ed. Robert Young (Boston, London and Henley, 1981), p. 60.

25 Slavoj Žižek, *The Sublime Object of Ideology* (London, 1989), p. 21.

26 Michel Serres, *L'Incandescent* (Paris, 2003), p. 141 (my translation).

27 Jacques Lacan, *The Seminar of Jacques Lacan*, Book XI: *The Four Fundamental Concepts of Psychoanalysis*, ed. Jacques-Alain Miller, trans. Alan Sheridan (New York and London, 1998), p. 232.

28 Steven Connor, 'Collective Emotions: Reasons to Feel Doubtful' (2013), http://stevenconnor.com/collective.html.

29 Lawrence Friedman, 'Drives and Knowledge – A Speculation', *Journal of the American Psychoanalytic Association*, XVI (1968), p. 88.

30 Ibid., p. 82.

31 Ibid., p. 93.

32 Bruno van Swinderen, 'The Remote Roots of Consciousness in Fruit-fly Selective Attention?', *Bioessays*, XXVII (2005), pp. 321–30.

33 Jakob von Uexküll, *A Foray into the Worlds of Animals and Humans, with 'A Theory of Meaning'*, ed. Dorion Sagan, trans. Joseph D. O'Neil (Minneapolis, MN, and London, 2010).

34 *The Holy Bible . . . Made from the Latin Vulgate by John Wycliffe and his Followers*, ed. Josiah Forshall and Frederic Madden, 4 vols (Oxford, 1850), vol. I, p. 85.

35 Freud, *Standard Edition*, vol. XVIII, p. 38.

36 Philip Larkin, *Collected Poems*, ed. Anthony Thwaite (London, 1988), p. 208.

37 John Dryden, *The Works of John Dryden*, vol. XV: *Plays: Amboyna, The State of Innocence, Aureng-Zebe*, ed. Vinton A. Dearing (Berkeley, CA, and London, 1994), p. 209.

38 E. Nesbit, 'The Things That Matter', in *The Rainbow and the Rose* (London, New York and Bombay, 1905), p. 5.

39 W. R. Bion, 'A Theory of Thinking', in *Second Thoughts: Selected Papers on Pyscho-Analysis* (London, 1984), pp. 110–19.

40 Samuel Beckett, *Samuel Beckett's Mal Vu Mal Dit/Ill Seen Ill Said:*

A Bilingual, Evolutionary, and Synoptic Variorum Edition, ed. Charles Krance (New York and London, 1996), p. 33.

41 Ibid., p. 32.

42 Samuel Beckett, *Complete Dramatic Works* (London, 1986), p. 148.

43 I. A. Richards, *Science and Poetry* (London, 1926), p. 25. References, to *SP*, in the text hereafter.

1 WILL TO KNOWLEDGE

1 Michel Serres, *Statues: Le Second Livre de fondations* (Paris, 1987), p. 209 (my translation).

2 Michel Serres, *Statues: The Second Book of Foundations*, trans. Randolph Burks (London, 2015), p. 119.

3 John Milton, *Paradise Lost*, ed. Stephen Orgel and Jonathan Goldberg (Oxford, 2008), p. 224.

4 Francis Bacon, *The New Organon*, ed. Lisa Jardine and Michael Silverthorne (Cambridge, 2000), p. 24.

5 Samuel Beckett, *The Unnamable*, ed. Steven Connor (London, 2010), pp. 37–8.

6 Bacon, *New Organon*, p. 24.

7 Arthur Schopenhauer, *The World as Will and Representation*, 2 vols, trans. E.F.J. Payne (New York, 1969), vol. 1, p. 149. References, to *WWR*, in the text hereafter.

8 Friedrich Nietzsche, *The Will to Power: Selections from the Notebooks of the 1880s*, ed. R. Kevin Hill, trans. R. Kevin Hill and Michael A. Scarpitti (London, 2017), p. 286. References, to *WP*, in the text hereafter.

9 Samuel Beckett, *Disjecta: Miscellaneous Writings and a Dramatic Fragment*, ed. Ruby Cohn (London, 1983), p. 86.

10 Michel Serres, *Malfeasance: Appropriation through Pollution?*, trans. Anne-Marie Feenberg-Dibon (Stanford, CA, 2010).

11 Michel Foucault, *Power/Knowledge: Selected Interviews and Other Writings, 1972–1977*, ed. Colin Gordon, trans. Colin Gordon, Leo Marshall, John Mepham and Kate Soper (New York, 1980), p. 132.

12 Ibid., p. 133.

13 Ibid., pp. 53–4.

14 Rex Welshon, 'Saying Yes to Reality: Skepticism, Antirealism, and Perspectivism in Nietzsche's Epistemology', *Journal of Nietzsche Studies*, XXXVII (2009), p. 24.

15 Friedrich Nietzsche, *On the Genealogy of Morality*, ed. Keith Ansell-Pearson, trans. Carole Diethe (Cambridge, 2006), p. 4.

16 Peter Bornedal, *The Surface and the Abyss: Nietzsche as Philosopher of Mind and Knowledge* (Berlin and New York, 2010), p. 32.

17 Welshon, 'Saying Yes to Reality', p. 23.

18 Nietzsche, *Genealogy of Morality*, p. 87.

19 Ibid.

20 Peter Sloterdijk, *You Must Change Your Life*, trans. Wieland Hoban (Cambridge and Malden, MA, 2013), pp. 8–10.

21 Christopher Marlowe, *Doctor Faustus and Other Plays*, ed. David Bevington and Eric Rasmussen (Oxford, 2008), p. 140.

22 Ibid., p. 142.

23 Ibid., pp. 140–41.

24 Arthur Lindley, 'The Unbeing of the Overreacher: Proteanism and the Marlovian Hero', *Modern Language Review*, LXXXIV (1989), p. 1.

25 Karl P. Wentersdorf, 'Some Observations on the Historical Faust', *Folklore*, LXXXIX (1978), p. 210.

26 Ibid., p. 205.

27 François Ost and Laurent van Eynde, *Faust, ou les frontières du savoir* (Brussels, 2002), p. 8 (my translation).

28 Ibid.

29 Ibid.

30 Oswald Spengler, *The Decline of the West*, vol 1: *Form and Actuality*, trans. Charles Frances Atkinson (London, 1926), p. 75. References, to DW, in the text hereafter.

31 W. B. Yeats, 'An Irish Airman Foresees His Death', *The Poems*, ed. Richard J. Finneran (New York, 1997), p. 136.

32 Oswald Spengler, *Selected Essays*, trans. Donald O. White (Chicago, IL, 1967), p. 145. References, to SESS, in the text hereafter.

33 C. G. Jung, *Freud and Psychoanalysis: Collected Works*, trans. R.F.C. Hull (London, 1961), vol. IV, p. 247.

34 C. G. Jung, *The Psychogenesis of Mental Disease: Collected Works*, trans. R.F.C. Hull (London, 1960), vol. III, p. 190.

35 A. A. Roback, *History of American Psychology* (New York, 1952), p. 259.

36 William McDougall, *An Outline of Abnormal Psychology*, 6th edn (London, 1948), p. 232.

37 Sigmund Freud, *The Standard Edition of the Complete Psychological Works of Sigmund Freud*, ed. and trans. James Strachey et al., 24 vols (London, 1953–74), vol. IX, pp. 197–8. References, to SE, in the text hereafter. Sigmund Freud, *Gesammelte Werke*, ed. Anna Freud et al., 18 vols (London, 1991), vol. VIII, p. 162. References, to GW, in the text hereafter.

38 Hyginus (Gaius Julius Hyginus), *Fabulae*, ed. Maurice Schmidt (Jena, 1872), p. 130.

39 Seneca the Younger (Lucius Annaeus Seneca), *Epistles 93–124*, trans. Richard M. Gummere (Cambridge, MA, and London, 1925), pp. 444–5.

40 Martin Heidegger, *Being and Time*, trans. John Macquarrie and Edward Robinson (Oxford, 1962), p. 243.

41 Edmund Burke, *A Philosophical Enquiry into the Origin of Our Ideas of the Sublime and Beautiful*, ed. Adam Phillips (Oxford, 2008), p. 29.

42 Ibid.

43 Samuel Beckett, *Molloy*, ed. Shane Weller (London, 2009), p. 177.

44 Guy de Chauliac, *The Cyrurgie of Guy de Chauliac*, ed. M. S. Ogden (London, 1971), p. 117.

45 Philip Larkin, 'An Arundel Tomb', *Collected Poems*, ed. Anthony Thwaite (London, 1988), p. III.

2 KNOW THYSELF

1 Pausanias, *Description of Greece*, Book 8, trans. W.H.S. Jones (Cambridge, MA, and London, 1935), p. 507.

2 Plato, *Euthyphro. Apology. Crito. Phaedo. Phaedrus*, trans. Harold North
  Fowler (Cambridge, MA, and London, 2005), p. 421.
3 Ibid., pp. 421–3.
4 Sir John Davies, *Complete Poems*, ed. Alexander B. Grosart, 2 vols
  (London, 1876), vol. I, p. 43.
5 Ibid., vol. I, p. 120.
6 Ibid., vol. I, p. lxxvii.
7 T. S. Eliot, 'Sir John Davies', in *Elizabethan Poetry: Modern Essays
  in Criticism*, ed. Paul J. Alpers (New York, 1967), p. 325.
8 James L. Sanderson, *Sir John Davies* (Boston, MA, 1975), p. 127.
9 Davies, *Complete Poems*, vol. I, pp. 15–16.
10 Ibid., p. 16.
11 Louis I. Bredvold, 'The Sources Used by Davies in *Nosce Teipsum*', *PMLA*,
   XXXVIII (1923), pp. 745–69; George T. Buckley, 'The Indebtedness of *Nosce
   Teipsum* to Mornay's *Trunesse of the Christian Religion*', *Modern Philology*,
   XXV (1927), pp. 67–78.
12 Davies, *Complete Poems*, vol. I, p. 21.
13 Ibid.
14 Ibid.
15 Philip Skelton, *Complete Works*, ed. Robert Lynam, 6 vols (London, 1824),
   vol. VI, p. 201.
16 Fulke Greville, *The Complete Poems and Plays of Fulke Greville, Lord Brooke
   (1554–1628)*, 2 vols, ed. G. A. Wilkes (Lewiston, Queenston and Lampeter,
   2008), vol. II, p. 273.
17 Ibid.
18 Ibid., vol. II, p. 274.
19 Ibid., vol. II, p. 303.
20 Ibid.
21 Anne S. Chapple, 'Robert Burton's Geography of Melancholy', *Studies
   in English Literature, 1500–1900*, XXXIII (1993), 99–130.
22 Robert Burton, *The Anatomy of Melancholy*, ed. Thomas C. Faulkner,
   Nicolas K. Kiessling and Rhonda L. Blair, 6 vols (Oxford, 1989–2000),
   vol. I, p. 24.
23 Richard Hedgerson, 'Epilogue: The Folly of Maps and Modernity',
   in *Literature, Mapping and the Politics of Space in Early Modern Britain*,
   ed. Andrew Gordon and Bernhard Klein (Cambridge, 2001), p. 243.
24 Ayesha Ramachandran, *The Worldmakers: Global Imagining in Early
   Modern Europe* (Chicago, IL, 2015), p. 224.
25 Dioscorides Pedanius of Anazarbos, *De Materia Medica: Being an Herbal
   with Many Other Medicinal Materials*, trans. T. A. Osbaldeston and
   R.P.A. Wood (Johannesburg, 2000), p. 706.
26 Ibid., p. 707.
27 Burton, *Anatomy of Melancholy*, vol. I, p. lxii.
28 William Alley, *Ptochomuseion: The Poore Mans Librarie* (London, 1565),
   fol. 126v; A. M., *The Reformed Gentleman; or, The Old English Morals
   Rescued from the Immoralities of the Present Age . . .* (London, 1693), p. 4.
29 Timothy Bright, *A Treatise, wherein is Declared the Sufficiencie of English
   Medicines, for Cure of All Diseases, Cured with Medicines* (London, 1615),
   p. 17.

30 Thomas Pope Blount, *Essays on Several Subjects* (London, 1692), p. 162.
31 Lionardo Di Capua, *The Uncertainty of the Art of Physick together with an Account of the Innumerable Abuses Practised by the Professors of that Art*, trans. J. L. (London, 1684), p. 47.
32 Burton, *Anatomy of Melancholy*, vol. 1, pp. 100–101.
33 Ibid., vol. 1, p. 115.
34 Ibid., vol. 1, p. 58.
35 Stephen Frosh, *For and Against Psychoanalysis*, 2nd edn (London, 2006), pp. 29–81.
36 Quoted in Darius Gray Ornston, 'The Invention of "Cathexis"', *International Review of Psycho-Analysis*, XII (1985), pp. 391–8, p. 393.
37 Peter T. Hoffer, 'Reflections on Cathexis', *Psychoanalytic Quarterly*, LXXIV (2005), p. 1129.
38 Adam Phillips, 'Psychoanalysis and Education', *Psychoanalytic Review*, XCI (2004), p. 786.
39 Sigmund Freud, *The Standard Edition of the Complete Psychological Works of Sigmund Freud*, 24 vols, ed. and trans. James Strachey et al. (London, 1953–74), vol. XIX, p. 216. References, to *SE*, in the text hereafter.
40 Ernest Jones et al., 'Discussion: Lay Analysis', *International Journal of Psycho-Analysis*, VIII (1927), p. 265.
41 Sigmund Freud, *Gesammelte Werke*, ed. Anna Freud et al., 18 vols (London, 1991), vol. IX, p. 105. References, to *GW*, in the text hereafter.
42 Sigmund Freud, *The Correspondence of Sigmund Freud and Sándor Ferenczi*, vol. 1: *1908–1914*, ed. Eva Brabant, Ernst Falzeder and Patrizia Giampieri-Deutsch, trans. Peter T. Hoffer (Cambridge, MA, and London, 1993), p. 457.
43 Sigmund Freud and Sándor Ferenczi, *Briefwechsel*, Band 1.2: *1912–1914*, ed. Eva Brabant, Ernst Falzeder and Patrizia Giampieri-Deutsch (Vienna, Cologne and Weimar, 1993), p. 185.
44 Ibid.
45 Johann Wolfgang Goethe, *Faust: Der Tragödie Erster Teil* (Stuttgart, 1956), p. 9 (my translation).
46 C. G. Jung, *Memories, Dreams, Reflections*, ed. Aniela Jaffé, trans Richard and Clara Winston (London, 1963), pp. 147–8.
47 Ibid., p. 148.
48 Ibid., pp. 147–8.
49 Sándor Ferenczi, *First Contributions to Psycho-Analysis*, trans. Ernest Jones (London, 1952), p. 241. References, to *FC*, in the text hereafter.
50 Bertram D. Lewin, 'Education or the Quest for Omniscience', *Journal of the American Psychoanalytic Association*, VI (1958), p. 395.
51 Bertram D. Lewin, 'Some Observations on Knowledge, Belief and the Impulse to Know', *International Journal of Psycho-Analysis*, XX (1939), p. 429.
52 Ibid., pp. 429–30.
53 Lewin, 'Education or the Quest for Omniscience', p. 395.
54 Ibid., p. 410.
55 Melanie Klein, *Love, Guilt and Reparation, and Other Works, 1921–1945* (London, 1998), p. 70. References, to *LGR*, in the text hereafter.

56 Ernest Gellner, *The Psychoanalytic Movement: The Cunning of Unreason*, 2nd edn (London, 1993), p. 124.

57 Ibid.

58 Rachel Bowlby, *Freudian Mythologies: Greek Tragedy and Modern Identities* (Oxford, 2009), p. 124.

59 Julia Kristeva, 'The Need to Believe and the Desire to Know, Today', in *Psychoanalysis, Monotheism and Morality: Symposia of the Sigmund Freud Museum 2009–11*, ed. Wolfgang Müller-Funk, Ingrid Scholz-Strasser and Herman Westerink (Leuven, 2013), p. 79.

60 Sophia de Mijolla-Mellor, *Le Besoin de savoir: Théories et mythes magico-sexuels dans l'enfance* (Paris, 2002), p. 4 (my translation).

61 Liran Razinsky, *Freud, Psychoanalysis and Death* (Cambridge, 2013), p. 39.

62 Mary Chadwick, 'Notes upon the Acquisition of Knowledge', *Psychoanalytic Review*, XIII (1926), pp. 257–80, pp. 267–9.

63 Ibid., p. 279.

64 Mary Chadwick, *Difficulties in Child Development* (London, 1928), pp. 371–2.

65 Marie-Hélène Huet, *Monstrous Imagination* (Cambridge, MA, 1993), p. 5.

66 Chadwick, 'Notes upon the Acquisition of Knowledge', p. 269.

67 M. B. Bill, 'Delusions of Doubt', *Popular Science Monthly*, XXI (1882), p. 788.

68 Mary Chadwick, *Adolescent Girlhood* (London, 1932), p. 233.

69 Mary Chadwick, 'A Case of Kleptomania in a Girl of Ten Years', *International Journal of Psycho-Analysis*, VI (1925), p. 311.

70 Ibid., p. 312.

71 Mary Chadwick, 'Im Zoologischen Garten', *Zeitschrift für psychoanalytische Pädagogik*, III (1929), pp. 235–6, p. 235 (my translation). References, to 'IZG', in the text hereafter.

72 Mary Chadwick, *Difficulties in Child Development* (London, 1928), p. 364.

73 Susan Stanford Friedman, *Analyzing Freud: Letters of H.D., Bryher, and their Circle* (New York, 2002), p. 100.

74 Ibid., pp. 188, 142.

75 Rachel B. Blass, 'Psychoanalytic Understanding of the Desire for Knowledge as Reflected in Freud's *Leonardo da Vinci and a Memory of his Childhood*', *International Journal of Psycho-Analysis*, LXXXVII (2006), p. 1269. References, to 'DK', in the text hereafter.

76 Ludwig Wittgenstein, *Philosophical Occasions, 1912–1951*, ed. James C. Klagge and Alfred Nordmann, trans. various (Indianapolis, IN, and Cambridge, MA, 1993), p. 125.

77 John Farrell, *Freud's Paranoid Quest: Psychoanalysis and Modern Suspicion* (New York and London, 1996), p. 46.

78 Steven Connor, *Dream Machines* (London, 2017), pp. 61–3.

79 W. R. Bion, *Attention and Interpretation: A Scientific Approach to Insight in Psycho-Analysis and Groups*, in *The Complete Works of W. R. Bion*, ed. Chris Mawson (London, 2014), vol. VI, pp. 242–3.

80 W. R. Bion, *Second Thoughts: Selected Papers on Psycho-Analysis* (London, 1967), pp. 93–109.

81 Ibid., p. 165.

82 W. R. Bion, *Learning from Experience* (London, 1962), p. 36.

83 W. R. Bion, *A Memoir of the Future*, Book One: *A Dream*, in *The Complete Works of W. R. Bion*, ed. Chris Mawson (London, 2014), vol. XII, p. 45.

84 Gellner, *The Psychoanalytic Movement*, p. 3.

3 SECRECY

1 Richard Dawkins, 'Theology Has No Place in a University', Letters to the Editor, *The Independent*, 6539 (1 October 2007), p. 30.

2 Peter Sloterdijk, *You Must Change Your Life*, trans. Wieland Hoban (Cambridge and Malden, MA, 2013), pp. 83–107.

3 Ibid., p. 34.

4 Wilhelm Reich, *The Mass Psychology of Fascism*, trans. Vincent R. Carfagno, ed. Mary Higgins and Chester M. Raphael (New York, 1970), pp. 115–42.

5 Sigmund Freud, *The Standard Edition of the Complete Psychological Works of Sigmund Freud*, 24 vols, ed. and trans. James Strachey et al. (London, 1953–74), vol. XIV, p. 76.

6 E. M. Cioran, *Drawn and Quartered*, trans. Richard Howard (New York, 1983), p. 82.

7 *The Owl and the Nightingale: Text and Translation*, ed. Neil Cartlidge (Exeter, 2008), p. 34.

8 Anon., *The Kalender of Shepherdes: the edition of Paris 1503 in photographic facsimile: a faithful reprint of R. Pynson's edition of London 1506*, 3 vols, ed. H. Oskar Sommer (London, 1872), vol. III, p. 180.

9 Samuel Taylor Coleridge, 'Frost at Midnight', in *The Major Works*, ed. H. J. Jackson (Oxford, 2008), p. 87.

10 James Joyce, *A Portrait of the Artist as a Young Man*, ed. Seamus Deane (London, 1992), p. 43.

11 James Joyce, *Ulysses: The 1922 Text*, ed. Jeri Johnson (Oxford, 2008), p. 274.

12 Freud, *Standard Edition*, vol. XVII, pp. 224–5.

13 Ibid., p. 225.

14 John Palsgrave, *Lesclarcissement de la Langue Francoyse* (London, 1530), fol. cclxxiii(v).

15 Thomas More, *The Debellacyon of Salem and Bizance* (London, 1533), sig. O3r.

16 Francis Bacon, *The Essays*, ed. John Pitcher (London, 1985), p. 126.

17 Steven Connor, 'Channels' (2013), www.stevenconnor.com/channels.html.

18 Emily Dickinson, *Complete Poems*, ed. Thomas H. Johnson (London, 1975), p. 620.

19 Edward W. Legg and Nicola S. Clayton, 'Eurasian Jays (*Garrulus glandarius*) Conceal Caches from Onlookers', *Animal Cognition*, XVII (2014), pp. 1223–6.

20 Alex Posecznik, 'On Anthropological Secrets', www.anthronow.com, 1 October 2009.

21 'Secret Intelligence Service' (n.d.), www.sis.gov.uk, accessed 23 September 2018.

22 Georg Simmel, 'The Sociology of Secrecy and of Secret Societies', *American Journal of Sociology*, XI (1906), p. 452. References, to 'ss', in the text hereafter.

23 Evelyn Lord, *The Hell-fire Clubs: Sex, Satanism and Secret Societies* (New Haven, CT, and London, 2009).

24 John Robison, *Proofs of a Conspiracy against All the Religions and Governments of Europe, Carried on in the Secret Meetings of Free Masons, Illuminati, and Reading Societies* (London and Edinburgh, 1797), pp. 11–12.

25 Ibid., pp. 25–6.

26 Neal Wilgus, *The Illuminoids: Secret Societies and Political Paranoia* (London, 1980).

27 Michel Foucault, *The History of Sexuality*, vol. 1: *An Introduction*, trans. Robert Hurley (New York, 1980), p. 35.

28 Michael Taussig, *Defacement: Public Secrecy and the Labor of the Negative* (Stanford, CA, 1999), p. 51.

29 Samuel Beckett, *Murphy*, ed. J.C.C. Mays (London, 2009), p. 38.

30 Georg Simmel, *The View of Life: Four Metaphysical Essays with Journal Aphorisms*, trans. and ed. John A. Y. Andrews and Donald N. Levine (Chicago, IL, and London, 2015), p. 5.

31 Procopius of Caesarea, *The Anecdota, or Secret History*, trans. H. B. Dewing (Cambridge, MA, and London, 1935), p. 5.

32 Procopius of Caesarea, *The Secret History of the Court of the Emperor Justinian* (London, 1674), p. 48.

33 Rebecca Bullard, *The Politics of Disclosure, 1674–1725: Secret History Narratives* (London, 2009), p. 37.

34 Melinda Alliker Rabb, *Satire and Secrecy in English Literature from 1650 to 1750* (Basingstoke, 2007), pp. 73–4.

35 Bullard, *Politics of Disclosure*, p. 11.

36 John Pudney, *The Smallest Room* (London, 1954), p. 33.

37 Ibid.

38 Samuel D. Warren and Louis D. Brandeis, 'The Right to Privacy (The Implicit Made Explicit)', in *Philosophical Dimensions of Privacy: An Anthology*, ed. Ferdinand David Schoeman (Cambridge, 1984), p. 76.

39 Ibid.

40 Ibid., p. 77.

41 Kocku von Stuckrad, *Western Esotericism: A Brief History of Secret Knowledge*, trans. Nicholas Goodrick-Clarke (London and Oakville, CT, 2005), p. 11.

42 Jan Assmann, *Religio Duplex: How the Enlightenment Reinvented Egyptian Religion*, trans. Robert Savage (Cambridge and Malden, MA, 2014), pp. 3–4.

43 Irenaeus, *The Writings of Irenaeus*, trans. Alexander Roberts and W. H. Rambaut, in *Ante-Nicene Christian Library: Translations of the Writings of the Fathers Down to AD 325*, ed. Alexander Roberts and James Donaldson, vol. v, pt 1 (Edinburgh, 1868), p. 22.

44 Stuckrad, *Western Esotericism*, p. 26.

45 Katherine Raine, 'Thomas Taylor, Plato, and the English Romantic Movement', *Sewanee Review*, LXXVI (1968), p. 231.

46 Thomas Taylor, *A Dissertation on the Eleusinian and Bacchic Mysteries* (Amsterdam, 1790), p. iii.

47 Ibid., pp. 52–3.
48 Ibid., p. 127.
49 Ibid., pp. iii–iv.
50 Margot K. Louis, 'Gods and Mysteries: The Revival of Paganism and the Remaking of Mythography through the Nineteenth Century', *Victorian Studies*, XLVII (2005), pp. 329–61.
51 Helena Petrovna Blavatsky, *The Secret Doctrine: The Synthesis of Science, Religion, and Philosophy*, 2 vols (London, 1888), vol. I, p. xxiii. References, to *SD*, in the text hereafter.
52 W. B. Yeats, 'The Statues', *Collected Poems* (London, 1951), p. 323.
53 Peter Sloterdijk, *God's Zeal: The Battle of the Three Monotheisms*, trans. Wieland Hoban (Cambridge and Malden, MA, 2009), p. 130.
54 Ambrose Bierce, *The Devil's Dictionary* (London, 2008), p. 42.
55 Jonathan Black, *The Secret History of the World* (London, 2007), p. 20.
56 Ibid., p. 33.
57 Ibid., p. 34.

4 QUISITION

1 Walter J. Ong, *Fighting for Life: Contest, Sexuality, and Consciousness* (Amherst, MA, 1989), pp. 27–8.
2 Ibid., p. 35.
3 Shlomith Cohen, 'Connecting Through Riddles, or The Riddle of Connecting', in *Untying the Knot: On Riddles and Other Enigmatic Modes*, ed. Galit Hasan-Rokem and David Shulman (New York and Oxford, 1996), p. 298.
4 Annikki Kaivola-Bregenhøj, *Riddles: Perspectives on the Use, Function and Change in a Folklore Genre* (Helsinki, 2016), p. 57.
5 Cora Diamond and Roger White, 'Riddles and Anselm's Riddle', *Proceedings of the Aristotelian Society*, LI (1977), p. 145.
6 Emily Dickinson, 'The Riddle we can guess', *The Complete Poems*, ed. Thomas H. Johnson (London, 1975), p. 538.
7 Galileo Galilei, *Opere*, ed. Antonio Favoro, 20 vols (Florence, 1890–1909), vol. IX, p. 227 (my translation).
8 Diamond and White, 'Riddles and Anselm's Riddle', p. 156.
9 Sophocles, *Ajax. Electra. Oedipus Tyrannus*, trans. Hugh Lloyd-Jones (Cambridge, MA, and London, 1997), pp. 363–5.
10 Ludwig Wittgenstein, *Tractatus Logico-Philosophicus*, trans. C. K. Ogden (London, 1960), p. 187.
11 Lee Haring, 'On Knowing the Answer', *Journal of American Folklore*, LXXXVII (1974), p. 197.
12 Ibid., pp. 200–202.
13 Ibid., p. 207.
14 John Blacking, 'The Social Value of Venda Riddles', *African Studies*, XX (1961), p. 3.
15 Ibid., p. 5.
16 Ibid.
17 Roger D. Abrahams, 'Introductory Remarks to a Rhetorical Theory of Folklore', *Journal of American Folklore*, LXXXI (1968), p. 150.

18 Ibid.
19 Rafat Borystawski, *The Old English Riddles and the Riddlic Elements of Old English Poetry* (Frankfurt am Main, 2004), p. 47.
20 Ibid., p. 8.
21 Ibid., p. 19.
22 Lewis Carroll, *Alice's Adventures in Wonderland and Through the Looking-Glass and What Alice Found There*, ed. Roger Lancelyn Green (Oxford, 1998), p. 63.
23 Johan Huizinga, *Homo Ludens: A Study of the Play Element in Culture*, trans. R.F.C. Hull (London, Boston and Henley, 1980), p. 108.
24 Abrahams, 'Introductory Remarks to a Rhetorical Theory of Folklore', p. 156.
25 Rudolph Schevill, 'Some Forms of the Riddle Question and the Exercise of the Wits in Popular Fiction and Formal Literature', *University of California Publications in Modern Philology*, II (1911), pp. 204–5.
26 Plutarch, *Moralia*, trans. Frank Cole Babbitt (Cambridge, MA, and London, 1928), vol. II, p. 375.
27 Ibid., p. 377.
28 Eleanor Cook, *Enigmas and Riddles in Literature* (Cambridge, 2006), pp. 7–26.
29 Galileo, *Opere*, vol. IX, p. 227 (my translation).
30 Ella Köngäs Maranda, 'The Logic of Riddles', in *Structural Analysis of Oral Tradition*, ed. Pierre Maranda and Ella Köngäs Maranda (Philadelphia, PA, 1971), p. 214.
31 Ibid., pp. 192–3.
32 Ian Hamnet, 'Ambiguity, Classification and Change: The Function of Riddles', *Man*, new ser., II/3 (1967), p. 379.
33 Matthew Marino, 'The Literariness of the *Exeter Book* Riddles', *Neuphilologische Mitteilungen*, LXXIX (1978), p. 265.
34 Ilan Amit, 'Squaring the Circle', in *Untying the Knot: On Riddles and Other Enigmatic Modes*, ed. Galit Hasan-Rokem and David Shulman (New York and Oxford, 1996), p. 284.
35 Huizinga, *Homo Ludens*, p. 112.
36 Daniel 2.5, *The Holy Bible . . . Made from the Latin Vulgate by John Wycliffe and his Followers*, ed. Josiah Forshall and Frederic Madden, 4 vols (Oxford, 1850), vol. III, p. 623; Claudius Hollyband, *The Treasurie of the French Tong* (London, 1580), sig. oir.
37 Huizinga, *Homo Ludens*, p. 108.
38 Sarah Iles Johnston, *Ancient Greek Divination* (Chichester, 2008), p. 56.
39 Huizinga, *Homo Ludens*, pp. 105–18.
40 Ibid.
41 Ibid., p. 110.
42 Ong, *Fighting for Life*, pp. 130–33.
43 Ibid., pp. 122, 123.
44 Brian Tucker, *Reading Riddles: Rhetorics of Obscurity from Romanticism to Freud* (Lewisburg, NY, 2011); Daniel Tiffany, *Infidel Poetics: Riddles, Nightlife, Substance* (Chicago, IL, and London, 2009).
45 Tucker, *Reading Riddles*, p. 168.

46 Donald Felipe, 'Post-Medieval Ars Disputandi', PhD dissertation, University of Texas (1991), p. 4, http://disputatioproject.files.wordpress. com.

47 Marcus Terentius Varro, *On the Latin Language*, trans. Roland G. Kent, 2 vols (Cambridge, MA, and London, 1938), vol. I, p. 231.

48 Ibid.

49 Ku-ming Chang, 'From Oral Disputation to Written Text: The Transformation of the Dissertation in Early Modern Europe', *History of Universities*, XIX/2 (2004), p. 132.

50 Ibid., p. 140.

51 Ibid., pp. 133–4.

52 Robin Whelan, 'Surrogate Fathers: Imaginary Dialogue and Patristic Culture in Late Antiquity', *Early Modern Europe*, XXV (2017), p. 19.

53 Janneke Raaijmakers, 'I, Claudius: Self-styling in Early Medieval Debate', *Early Modern Europe*, XXV (2017), p. 84.

54 Graham Chapman, *The Complete Monty Python's Flying Circus: All the Words*, vol. II (London, 1989), p. 88.

55 Jakob W. Feuerlein, *Regulae praecipuae bonae disputationis academicae* (Göttingen, 1747), p. 5 (my translation).

56 William Clark, *Academic Charisma and the Origins of the Research University* (Chicago, IL, 2006), p. 79.

57 Ong, *Fighting for Life*, p. 127.

58 John Rodda, *Public Religious Disputation in England, 1558–1626* (Farnham and Burlington, VT, 2014), pp. 74–8.

59 Ibid., p. 203.

60 Theophilus Higgons, *The First Motive of T. H. Maister of Arts, and Lately Minister, to Suspect the Integrity of his Religion which was Detection of Falsehood in D. Humfrey, D. Field, & other Learned Protestants . . .* (Douai, 1609), p. 52.

61 Chang, 'From Oral Disputation to Written Text', p. 159.

62 Clark, *Academic Charisma*, p. 139.

63 John Milton, *Complete Poems and Major Prose*, ed. Merritt Y. Hughes (New York, 1957), p. 632.

64 Lorraine Daston, 'Baconian Facts, Academic Civility, and the Prehistory of Objectivity', *Annals of Scholarship*, VIII (1991), p. 345.

65 Mary Poovey, *A History of the Modern Fact: Problems of Knowledge in the Sciences of Wealth and Society* (Chicago, IL, and London, 1998).

66 Oswald Dykes, *Moral Reflexions Upon Select British Proverbs: Familiarly Accommodated to the Humour and Manners of the Present Age* (London, 1708), sig. A3v.

67 *The Fanatick Feast: A Pleasant Comedy* (London, 1710), p. 6.

68 Maria Edgeworth, *Patronage*, 4 vols (London, 1814), vol. I, pp. 82–3.

69 'Epilogue to the New Comedy of Speculation', *Britannic Magazine*, III (1795), p. 410.

70 C. H. Wilson, ed., *The Myrtle and Vine; or, Complete Vocal Library*, 4 vols (London, 1800), vol. III, p. 82.

71 George Gordon, Lord Byron, *Byron's Don Juan: A Variorum Edition*, 4 vols, ed. Truman Guy Steffan and Willis W. Pratt (Austin, TX, and Edinburgh, 1957), vol. III, p. 203.

72 Ibid., vol. III, p. 512.

73 Thomas Moore, *Life of Lord Byron: With his Letters and Journals*, 6 vols (London, 1854), vol. III, p. 201.

74 John Collins, *Scripscrapologia; or, Collins's Doggerel Dish Of All Sorts* (Birmingham, 1804), p. 163.

75 'Philip Harmless', 'To the Quiz Club', *The Quiz*, I (1797), pp. 81–2.

76 Charles Dibdin, *The Etymology of Quiz, Written and Composed by Mr Dibdin, for his Entertainment called The Quizes, or A Trip to Elysium* (London, 1793), p. 3.

77 'Wanted', *The Spirit of the Public Journals for 1809*, XIII (1809), pp. 168–9.

78 Anthony Pasquin (John Williams), *The Hamiltoniad; or, An Extinguisher for the Royal Faction of New-England* (Boston, MA, 1804), p. 45.

79 Richard Polwhele, *The Follies of Oxford; or, Cursory Sketches on a University Education, from an Under Graduate to his Friend in the Country* (London, 1785), p. 12; *Advice to the Universities of Oxford and Cambridge, and to the Clergy of Every Denomination* (London, 1783), pp. 37–8.

80 *Advice to the Universities*, p. 38.

81 Ibid., pp. 39–44.

82 Ibid., p. 44.

83 'Quizicus', 'Address to the Freshmen of the University of Cambridge', *Sporting Magazine*, V (1794), p. 157.

84 Ibid.

85 Ibid.

86 Steven Connor, *Beyond Words: Sobs, Hums, Stutters and other Vocalizations* (London, 2014), pp. 172–3.

87 Samuel Pratt, *Harvest-Home: Consisting of Supplementary Gleanings, Original Dramas and Poems* (London, 1805), p. 143.

88 Alexander Rodger, *Stray Leaves from the Portfolios of Alisander the Seer, Andrew Whaup, and Humphrey Henkeckle* (Glasgow, 1842), p. 127.

89 'Central Criminal Court, Sept. 20', *The Times* (22 September 1879), p. 12.

90 Alex Boese, 'The Origin of the Word Quiz', www.hoaxes.org, 10 July 2012.

91 'Origin of the Word Quiz', *London and Paris Observer*, DIX (15 February 1835), p. 112.

92 Ibid.

93 Ibid.

94 Ben Zimmer, 'Here's a Pop Quiz: Where the Hell Did "Quiz" Come From?', www.vocabulary.com, 9 February 2015.

95 'Quoz', *The World*, 816 (15 August 1789), n.p.

96 Ibid.

97 Ibid.

98 *The World*, 821 (22 August 1789), n.p.

99 *The Diary; or, Woodfall's Register*, 138 (5 September 1789), n.p.

100 Thomas Paine, *Rights of Man, Common Sense and Other Political Writings*, ed. Mark Philp (Oxford, 2008), p. 247.

101 James Joyce, *Ulysses: The 1922 Text*, ed. Jeri Johnson (Oxford, 2008), p. 286.

102 'Domestic Intelligence', *European Magazine and London Review*, XLI (1802), p. 500.

7 Robert Lowth, *Lectures on the Sacred Poetry of the Hebrews*, 2 vols, trans. G. Gregory (London, 1787), vol. II, p. 127.

8 Charles Dickens, *Hard Times*, ed. Kate Flint (London, 2003), p. 193.

9 Antoine Arnauld, *The Coppie of the Anti-Spaniard Made at Paris by a French Man, a Catholique*, trans. Anthony Munday (London, 1590), p. 29.

10 Randle Cotgrave, *A Dictionarie of the French and English Tongues* (London, 1611), sig. Q2r.

11 Ben Jonson, *The Alchemist and Other Plays*, ed. Gordon Campbell (Oxford, 2008), pp. 237–8.

12 Ibid., p. 236.

13 George Ripley, *The Compound of Alchymy; or, The Ancient Hidden Art of Archemie [sic], Conteining the Right & Perfectest Meanes to Make the Philosophers Stone, Aurum Potabile, with Other Excellent Experiments* (London, 1591), sig. K2v.

14 Jonson, *Alchemist*, p. 238.

15 Ibid., p. 219.

16 Ibid., p. 297.

17 Piero Gambaccini, *Mountebanks and Medicasters: A History of Italian Charlatans from the Middle Ages to the Present*, trans. Bettie Gage Lippitt (Jefferson, NC, and London, 2004), p. 5.

18 Nicholas Jewson, 'The Disappearance of the Sick Man from Medical Cosmology, 1770–1870', *Sociology*, X (1976), pp. 232–3.

19 Roy Porter, *Quacks: Fakers and Charlatans in English Medicine* (Stroud, 2000), p. 43.

20 James Adair, *Medical Cautions, for the Consideration of Invalids* (Bath, 1786), p. 13.

21 Henry John Rose and Thomas Wright, *A New General Biographical Dictionary*, 12 vols (London, 1848), vol. I, p. 84.

22 Porter, *Quacks*, p. 100.

23 Alexander Pope, *The Major Works*, ed. Pat Rogers (Oxford, 2006), p. 24.

24 Porter, *Quacks*, p. 93.

25 John Corry, *The Detector of Quackery; or, Analyser of Medical, Philosophical, Political, Dramatic, and Literary Imposture* (London, 1802), pp. 64–5.

26 Tom Gunning, 'The Cinema of Attraction: Early Film, its Spectator and the Avant-garde', *Wide Angle*, VIII (1986), p. 66.

27 Porter, *Quacks*, p. 157.

28 Steven Connor, *Dream Machines* (London, 2017), pp. 103–17.

29 Johann Burkhard Mencken, *The Charlatanry of the Learned*, trans. Francis E. Litz, ed. H. L. Mencken (London, 1937), pp. 59–60.

30 Plato, *Euthyphyro. Apology. Crito. Phaedo. Phaedrus*, trans. Harold N. Fowler (Cambridge, MA, and London, 2005), pp. 565–7.

31 Abraham Andersen, *The Treatise of the Three Impostors and the Problem of the Enlightenment: A New Translation of the 'Traité des Trois Imposteurs' (1777 Edition)* (Lanham, MD, 1997); Georges Minois, *The Atheist's Bible: The Most Dangerous Book that Never Existed* (Chicago, IL, and London, 2012).

32 K. R. St Onge, *The Melancholy Anatomy of Plagiarism* (Lanham, New York and London, 1988), p. vii.

33 Stanley Cavell, *Must We Mean What We Say? A Book of Essays*, 2nd edn (Cambridge, 2002), p. 264.

34 Ibid., p. 266.

35 Pauline Rose Clance and Suzanne Imes, 'The Imposter [*sic*] Phenomenon in High Achieving Women: Dynamics and Therapeutic Intervention', *Psychotherapy Theory, Research and Practice*, XV (1978), pp. 241–7.

36 Joe Langford and Pauline Rose Clance, 'The Impostor Phenomenon: Recent Research Findings Regarding Dynamics, Personality and Family Patterns and their Implications for Treatment', *Psychotherapy*, XXX (1993), p. 496; Rebecca L. Badawy, Brooke A. Gazdag, Jeffrey R. Bentley and Robyn L. Brouer, 'Are All Impostors Created Equal? Exploring Gender Differences in the Impostor Phenomenon–Performance Link', *Personality and Individual Differences*, CXXXI (2018), pp. 156–63.

37 Dana Simmons, 'Impostor Syndrome, a Reparative History', *Engaging Science, Technology, and Society*, II (2016), pp. 119–20.

38 Ibid., p. 123.

6 UNKNOWING

1 Thomas A. Fudge, *The Trial of Jan Hus: Medieval Heresy and Criminal Procedure* (Oxford, 2013), pp. 64–70.

2 Sharon Henderson Taylor, 'Terms for Low Intelligence', *American Speech*, XLIX (1974), p. 202.

3 John Donne, 'The True Character of a Dunce', *Paradoxes, Problemes, Essayes, Characters . . .* (London, 1652), p. 67.

4 Henry Cary, *The Slang of Venery and its Analogues* (Chicago, IL, 1916), p. 51.

5 Nicholas Breton, *Crossing of Proverbs, Crosse-answeres and Crosse-humours* (London, 1616), sig. A8r.

6 John S. Farmer and W. E. Henley, *Slang and its Analogues Past and Present: A Dictionary, Historical and Comparative, of the Heterodox Speech of All Classes of Society for More than Three Hundred Years*, 7 vols (London, 1890–1904), vol. II, p. 280.

7 Ibid., vol. II, p. 281.

8 Jeannie B. Thomas, 'Dumb Blondes, Dan Quayle, and Hillary Clinton: Gender, Sexuality, and Stupidity in Jokes', *Journal of American Folklore*, CX (1997), p. 282.

9 Geoffrey Chaucer, *The Riverside Chaucer*, 3rd edn, ed. Larry D. Benson (Oxford, 2008), p. 69.

10 Walter Scott, 'Marmion: A Tale of Flodden Field', *Poetical Works*, ed. J. G. Lockhart (Edinburgh, 1841), p. 103.

11 Sigmund Freud, *The Standard Edition of the Complete Psychological Works of Sigmund Freud*, 24 vols, ed. and trans. James Strachey et al. (London, 1953–74), vol. XVII, pp. 223–4. References, to *SE*, in the text hereafter.

12 Christopher Marlowe, *Dr Faustus and Other Plays*, ed. David Bevington and Eric Rasmussen (Oxford, 2008), p. 308.

13 Hermann Varnhagen, 'Zu den sprichwörtern Hendings', *Anglia: Zeitschrift für englische Philologie*, IV (1881), p. 190.

14 'Cuthbert Cunny-Catcher', *The Defence of Conny-catching; or, A Confutation of those Two Iniurious Pamphlets Published by R. G. against*

the Practitioners of Many Nimble-witted and Mysticall Sciences (London, 1592), sig. A3r.

15 Robert Greene, *A Notable Discouery of Coosenage Now Daily Practised by Sundry Lewd Persons, Called Connie-catchers, and Crosse-byters* (London, 1591); *The Second Part of Conny-catching Contayning the Discouery of Certaine Wondrous Coosenages, Either Superficiallie Past Ouer, or Vtterlie Vntoucht in the First* (London, 1591).

16 Thomas Dekker and Thomas Middleton, *The Honest Whore, with The Humours of the Patient Man, and the Longing Wife* (London, 1604), sig. F3r.

17 Anon., *The Cony-catching Bride who After She Was Privately Married in a Conventicle or Chamber, According to the New Fashion of Marriage, She Sav'd her Selfe Very Handsomely from Being Coney-caught* (London, 1643).

18 Francis Beaumont and John Fletcher, *Cupids [sic] Revenge* (London, 1615), sig. H3r.

19 B. E., *A New Dictionary of the Canting Crew in its Several Tribes of Gypsies, Beggers, Thieves, Cheats &c.* (London, 1699), sig. C3v.

20 Ibid., sig. D1v; sig. C8v.

21 Daniel Heller-Roazen, *Dark Tongues: The Art of Rogues and Riddlers* (Cambridge, MA, 2013).

22 Keith Briggs, 'OE and ME *cunte* in Place-names', *Journal of the English Place-name Society*, XLI (2009), p. 29.

23 Kit Toda, 'Eliot's Cunning Passages: A Note', *Essays in Criticism*, LXIV (2014), pp. 90–97.

24 T. S. Eliot, 'Gerontion', *Complete Poems and Plays* (London, 1969), p. 38.

25 Richard Holt and Nigel Baker, 'Towards a Geography of Sexual Encounter: Prostitution in Medieval English Towns', in *Indecent Exposure: Sexuality, Society and the Archaeological Record*, ed. Lynne Bevan (Glasgow, 2001), p. 210.

26 Ibid., p. 202.

27 Briggs, 'OE and ME *cunte*', p. 29.

28 B. E. *New Dictionary*, sig. D1v; John Cleland, *Memoirs of a Woman of Pleasure*, 2 vols (London, 1749), vol. I, p. 196.

29 James Joyce, *Ulysses: The 1922 Text*, ed. Jeri Johnson (Oxford, 2008), p. 548.

30 Lisa Williams, 'On Not Using the Word "Cunt" in a Poem', *Virginia Quarterly Review*, LXXXII (2006), p. 151.

31 Sigmund Freud, *Gesammelte Werke*, 18 vols (London, 1991), vol. XII, p. 247.

32 Ibid., vol. XVII, p. 47.

33 Briggs, 'OE and ME *cunte*', pp. 36, 28, 31.

34 James Joyce, *Finnegans Wake* (London, 1975), p. 213.

35 Ibid., p. 203.

36 Ibid., p. 310.

37 John Stephens, *Essayes and Characters, Ironicall, and Instructiue* (London, 1615), p. 33; George Ruggle, *Ignoramus: A Comedy as it was Several Times Acted with Extraordinary Applause before the Majesty of King James*, trans. Robert Codrington (London, 1662).

38 Richard Chenevix Trench, *On the Study of Words: Five Lectures Addressed to the Pupils at the Diocesan Training School, Winchester* (London, 1851), p. 74.

39 William Tyndale, *An Answer to Sir Thomas More's Dialogue, The Supper of the Lord after the True Meaning of John VI and I Cor. XI*, ed. Henry Walter (Cambridge, 1850), pp. 48–9.

40 Thomas Blount, *Glossographia, or, A Dictionary Interpreting All Such Hard Words of Whatsoever Language Now Used in Our Refined English Tongue . . .* (London, 1661), sig. KK4v.

41 John Donne, 'The True Character of a Dunce', in *Paradoxes, Problemes, Essayes, Characters* (London, 1652), pp. 68–9.

42 Christopher Marlowe, *Dr Faustus and Other Plays*, ed. David Bevington and Eric Rasmussen (Oxford, 2008), p. 145.

43 Mikaela von Kursell, 'Faustus as Dunce: The Degeneration of Man and Word', *The Explicator*, LXXI (2013), p. 304.

44 Cecil Adams [pseud.], 'What's the Origin of the Dunce Cap?', *The Straight Dope*, 21 June 2000, www.straightdope.com.

45 Charles Dickens, *The Old Curiosity Shop: A Tale*, ed. Norman Page (London, 2000), p. 190.

46 Yadin Dudai et al., '*Dunce*, a Mutant of *Drosophila* Deficient in Learning', *Proceedings of the National Academy of Sciences of the United States of America*, LXXIII (1976), pp. 1684–8.

47 J. S. Duerr and W. G. Quinn, 'Three Drosophila Mutations that Block Associative Learning Also Affect Habituation and Sensitization', *Proceedings of the National Academy of Sciences of the United States of America*, LXXIX (1982), pp. 3646–50.

48 T. W. Adorno, *Minima Moralia: Reflections from Damaged Life*, trans. E.F.N. Jephcott (London and New York, 2005), p. 197.

49 B. E., *A New Dictionary*, n.p.

50 James Frederick Ferrier, *Institutes of Metaphysic: The Theory of Knowing and Being* (Edinburgh and London, 1854), p. 400.

51 Ibid., pp. 414–15.

52 John Skelton, *Poetical Works*, ed. Alexander Dyce, 3 vols (Boston, MA, and Cincinnati, OH, 1856), vol. II, p. 126.

53 William Hazlitt, 'On Prejudice', in *The Collected Works of William Hazlitt*, vol. XII: *Fugitive Writings*, ed. A. R. Waller and Arnold Glover (London and New York, 1904), p. 391.

54 Michael Deacon, 'Even Stupid People Have Feelings – Let's End This Bigotry', www.telegraph.co.uk, 2 August 2010.

55 John Saward, *Perfect Fools: Folly for Christ's Sake in Catholic and Orthodox Spirituality* (Oxford, 1980), pp. 16–17. References, to *PF*, in the text hereafter.

56 Peter Sloterdijk, *God's Zeal: The Battle of the Three Monotheisms*, trans. Wieland Hoban (Cambridge and Malden, MA, 2009), pp. 23–4.

57 William Wordsworth, *The Major Works*, ed. Stephen Gill (Oxford, 2000), p. 70.

58 Ibid., p. 79.

59 Ibid., p. 80.

60 John Lyly, *Mother Bombie* (London, 1594), sig. E5r.

61 Patrick McDonagh, *Idiocy: A Cultural History* (Cambridge, 2011).

62 Martin Halliwell, *Images of Idiocy: The Idiot Figure in Modern Fiction and Film* (Abingdon and New York, 2016), p. 233.

63 Genese Grill, 'Musil's "On Stupidity": The Artistic and Ethical Uses of the Feminine Discursive', *Studia Austriaca*, XXI (2013), p. 94.

64 Richard Vaughan, *Matthew Paris* (Cambridge, 1958), p. 60.

65 F.E.J. Valpy, *An Etymological Dictionary of the Latin Language* (London, 1828), p. 544.

66 Alfred Ernout and Alfred Meillet, *Dictionnaire étymologique de la langue latine: Histoire des mots*, 4th edn (Paris, 2001), p. 659.

67 Flannery O'Connor, *Mystery and Manners*, ed. Sally Fitzgerald and Robert Fitzgerald (New York, 1969), p. 77.

68 Robert Kugelmann, 'Imagination and Stupidity', *Soundings: An Interdisciplinary Journal*, LXX (1987), p. 87.

69 Ibid., p. 89.

70 Ibid., p. 90.

71 Tony Jasnowski, 'The Writer as Holy Fool: A Virtue of Stupidity', *Writing on the Edge*, IV (1993), p. 26.

72 Ibid., p. 30.

73 Ibid., p. 31.

74 Natalie Pollard, 'The Fate of Stupidity', *Essays in Criticism*, LXII (2012), p. 136.

75 Avital Ronell, *Stupidity* (Urbana, IL, 2002), pp. 6–9. References, to SY, in the text hereafter.

76 Sianne Ngai, *Ugly Feelings* (Cambridge, MA, 2005), pp. 271, 280.

77 Ibid., p. 278.

78 Ibid., p. 284.

79 Ibid., p. 297.

80 Ibid., p. 261.

81 Dale C. Spencer and Amy Fitzgerald, 'Criminology and Animality: Stupidity and the Anthropological Machine', *Contemporary Justice Review*, XVIII (2015), pp. 414, 417–18.

82 Christopher Prendergast, 'Flaubert: Quotation, Stupidity and the Cretan Liar Paradox', *French Studies*, XXXV (1981), p. 266.

83 Robert Musil, 'On Stupidity', in *Precision and Soul: Essays and Addresses*, ed. and trans Burton Pike and David S. Luft (Chicago, IL, and London, 1990), p. 270.

84 Ibid., pp. 283–4.

7 EPISTEMOTOPIA

1 Melanie Klein, *Love, Guilt and Reparation, and Other Works, 1921–1946* (New York, 1975), p. 59.

2 Sigmund Freud, *The Standard Edition of the Complete Psychological Works of Sigmund Freud*, 24 vols, ed. and trans. James Strachey et al. (London, 1953–74), vol. IV, p. 273.

3 Ibid., vol. IV, p. 274.

4 Klein, *Love, Guilt and Reparation*, p. 59.

5 Ibid., p. 60.

6 Ibid.

7 Ibid., p. 66.

8 Deborah P. Britzman, *After-Education: Anna Freud, Melanie Klein, and Psychoanalytic Histories of Learning* (Albany, NY, 2003), p. 3.

9 Ibid., p. 7.

10 Scott Olsen, *Golden Section: Nature's Greatest Secret* (New York, 2006), p. 8.

11 Anon., *Ad C. Herennium de Ratione Dicendi (Rhetorica ad Herennium)*, trans. Harry Caplan (London and Cambridge, MA, 1954), p. 209. References, to *RH*, in the text hereafter.

12 Mary Carruthers, *The Craft of Thought: Meditation, Rhetoric, and the Making of Images, 400-1200* (Cambridge, 1998), p. 12.

13 Joannes Tzetzes, βιβλιον ιστορικησ τησ δια στιχων πολιτκων/*Historiarum variarum chiliades*, ed. Theophilus Kiesslingius (Leipzig, 1826), p. 322.

14 Martin Heidegger, *Introduction to Metaphysics*, 2nd edn, trans. Gregory Fried and Richard Polt (New Haven, CT, and London, 2014), p. 141.

15 Jorge Luis Borges, 'The Library of Babel', in *Collected Fictions*, trans. Andrew Hurley (New York, 1998), pp. 113–14.

16 Ibid., p. 115.

17 Ibid.

18 Ibid., p. 118.

19 Justus Lipsius, *A Brief Outline of the History of Libraries*, trans. John Cotton Dana (Chicago, IL, 1907), pp. 36–7, 52–4.

20 Lina Bolzoni, *The Gallery of Memory: Literary and Iconographic Models in the Age of the Printing Press*, trans. Jeremy Parzen (Toronto, Buffalo and London, 2001), pp. 65–82.

21 Carruthers, *Craft of Thought*, pp. 22–3.

22 Steven Connor, *Dream Machines* (London, 2017), pp. 153–4.

23 Giulio Camillo, *L'idea del theatro* (Florence, 1550); Francis A. Yates, *The Art of Memory* (London, 1966), pp. 129–59.

24 Quoted Yates, *Art of Memory*, pp. 130–31.

25 Quoted ibid., p. 132.

26 Ibid., p. 144.

27 Robert of Brunne, *Robert of Brunne's 'Handlyng Synne' AD 1303*: Part I, ed. Frederick J. Furnivall (London, 1901), p. 158.

28 Dora Thornton, *The Scholar in his Study: Ownership and Experience in Renaissance Italy* (New Haven, CT, and London, 1997), p. 137.

29 Ibid., p. 77.

30 Jacobus de Voragine, *The Golden Legend; or, Lives of the Saints, as Englished by William Caxton*, 6 vols (London, 1900), vol. V, pp. 202, 207.

31 David Hume, *A Treatise of Human Nature*, ed. Ernest C. Mossner (London, 1985), p. 301.

32 Donald Beecher, 'Mind, Theaters, and the Anatomy of Consciousness', *Philosophy and Literature*, XXX (2006), p. 3.

33 Ibid., p. 14.

34 Steven Connor, 'Thinking Things', *Textual Practice*, XXIV (2010), pp. 1–20.

35 Seamus Heaney, 'Villanelle for an Anniversary', *Opened Ground: Poems, 1966–1996* (London, 1998), p. 289.

36 John Milton, *Paradise Lost and Paradise Regained*, ed. Gordon Campbell (London, 2008), p. 351.

37 Henry Peacham, *Minerva Britanna; or, A Garden of Heroical Devises* (London, 1612), p. 185.

38 Charles Augustin Sainte-Beuve, 'Pensées d'août', in *Poésies* (Paris, 1837), p. 152.

39 Gaston Bachelard, *The Poetics of Space*, trans. Marie Jolas (Boston, MA, 1994), p. 22.

40 John Henry Newman, *The Idea of a University*, ed. Frank M. Turner (New Haven, CT, 1996), pp. 16–17.

41 Robert Burton, *The Anatomy of Melancholy*, ed. Thomas C. Faulkner, Nicolas K. Kiessling and Rhonda L. Blair, 6 vols (Oxford, 1989–2000), vol. I, p. 236.

42 William Camden, *Britain; or, A Chorographicall Description of the Most Flourishing Kingdomes, England, Scotland, and Ireland*, trans. Philémon Holland (London, 1610), p. 486.

43 Philip Larkin, 'Whitsun Weddings', in *Collected Poems*, ed. Anthony Thwaite (London, 1990), p. 116.

44 Jet Propulsion Laboratory, 'NASA Spacecraft Embarks on Historic Journey into Interstellar Space', www.jpl.nasa.gov, 12 September 2013.

45 Lewis Carroll, *Alice's Adventures in Wonderland and Through the Looking-Glass and What Alice Found There*, ed. Roger Lancelyn Green (Oxford, 1998), p. 105.

46 Wilhelm Worringer, *Abstraction and Empathy: A Contribution to the Psychology of Style*, trans. Michael Bullock (Chicago, IL, 1997), p. 15.

47 Bachelard, *The Poetics of Space*, p. 91.

48 Émile Durkheim, *The Elementary Forms of Religious Life*, trans. Karen E. Fields (New York, 1995), p. 217.

49 Christopher Marlowe, *Dr Faustus and Other Plays*, ed. David Bevington and Eric Rasmussen (Oxford, 2008), p. 254.

8 EPISTEMOCRACY

1 Steve Fuller, 'Knowledge as Product and Property', in *The Culture and Power of Knowledge: Inquiries into Contemporary Societies*, ed. Nico Stehr and Richard V. Ericson (Berlin and New York, 1992), p. 174.

2 Diogenes Laertius, *Lives of Eminent Philosophers*, trans. R. D. Hicks, 2 vols (London and New York, 1925), vol. II, p. 41.

3 Christian Wolff, 'On the Philosopher King and the Ruling Philosopher', in *Moral Enlightenment: Leibniz and Wolff on China*, trans. and ed. Julia Ching and Willard G. Oxtoby (Nettetal, 1992), p. 187.

4 Peter Sloterdijk, *Critique of Cynical Reason*, trans. Michael Eldred (London and New York, 1988), pp. 160–61.

5 Patrick Nold, *Pope John XXII and his Franciscan Cardinal: Bertrand de la Tour and the Apostolic Poverty Controversy* (Oxford, 2003), pp. 140–77; Melanie Brunner, 'Pope John XXII and the Michaelists: The Scriptural Title of Evangelical Poverty in *Quia vir reprobus*', *Church History and Religious Culture*, XCIV (2014), pp. 197–226.

6 Peter F. Drucker, *The Age of Discontinuity: Guidelines to our Changing Society* (London, 1969), p. 259.

7 Terence Ball, *Transforming Political Authority: Political Theory and Critical Conceptual History* (Oxford, 1988), p. 115.

8 A. James Gregor, *Mussolini's Intellectuals: Fascist Social and Political Thought* (Princeton, NJ, and Oxford, 2005), pp. 27, 142.

9 David M. Estlund, *Democratic Authority: A Philosophical Framework* (Princeton, NJ, and Oxford, 2008), pp. 29, 278 n. 16.

10 Jason Brennan, *Against Democracy* (Princeton, NJ, 2016).

11 David Runciman, 'How the Education Gap is Tearing Politics Apart', www.theguardian.com, 5 October 2016.

12 Ibid.

13 H. L. Mencken, *A Little Book in C Major* (New York, 1916), p. 19.

14 John Naughton, 'The Education Gap and its Implications', *Memex 1.1: John Naughton's Online Diary*, http://memex.naughtons.org, 6 February 2017.

15 Runciman, 'Education Gap'.

16 Fabienne Peter, 'The Epistemic Circumstances of Democracy', in *The Epistemic Life of Groups: Essays in the Epistemology of Collectives*, ed. Michael S. Brady and Miranda Fricker (Oxford, 2016), p. 133.

17 Ball, *Transforming Political Authority*, p. 119.

18 Nadia Urbinati, *Democracy Disfigured: Opinion, Truth, and the People* (Cambridge, MA, and London, 2014), pp. 5–6.

19 Anne Jeffrey, 'Limited Epistocracy and Political Inclusion', *Episteme* (2017), pp. 1–21.

20 Nicholas Nassim Taleb, *The Black Swan: The Impact of the Highly Improbable* (London, 2007), p. 190.

21 Ibid.

22 Nicholas Nassim Taleb, 'Black Swan-Blind', *New Statesman* (5 July 2010), CXXXIX/5008, p. 30.

23 Brent C. Pottenger, 'What is an Epistemocrat?', *Healthcare Epistemocrat*, 2007, http://epistemocrat.blogspot.co.uk.

24 Jürgen Habermas, *The Theory of Communicative Action*, 2 vols, trans. Thomas McCarthy (Boston, MA, 1987), vol. II, p. 333.

25 Drucker, *Age of Discontinuity*, pp. 247–355; Daniel Bell, *The Coming of Post-industrial Society: A Venture in Social Forecasting* (New York, 1973), p. 212.

26 Nico Stehr, *Knowledge Societies* (London, Thousand Oaks and New Delhi, 1994), p. 9.

27 UNESCO, *Towards Knowledge Societies* (Paris, 2005), p. 18.

28 Daniel Innerarity, 'Power and Knowledge: The Politics of the Knowledge Society', *European Journal of Social Theory*, XVI (2012), p. 4.

29 Gernot Böhme, 'The Techno-structures of Society', in *The Culture and Power of Knowledge: Inquiries into Contemporary Societies*, ed. Nico Stehr and Richard V. Ericson (Berlin and New York, 1992), p. 42.

30 Francis Bacon, *The New Organon*, ed. Lisa Jardine and Michael Silverthorne (Cambridge, 2000), p. 28.

31 Mary Everest Boole, *The Message of Psychic Science to Nurses and Mothers* (London, 1883), pp. 246–7.

32 Ibid., p. 247.

33 Heinrich Bullinger, *A Hundred Sermons vpon the Apocalips of Iesu Christe* (London, 1561), p. 199.

34 Robert Steele, ed., *The Earliest Arithmetics in English* (London and Oxford, 1922), p. 3.

35 Louise Amoore and Volha Piotukh, *Algorithmic Life: Calculative Devices in the Age of Big Data* (London, 2015).

36 John Danaher, 'The Threat of Algocracy: Reality, Resistance and Accommodation', *Philosophy and Technology*, XXIX (2016), pp. 245–68.

37 Fuller, 'Knowledge as Product and Property', p. 158.

38 Steven Connor, *Dream Machines* (London, 2017).

39 UNESCO, *Towards Knowledge Societies*, p. 22.

40 Robin Mansell and Gaëtan Tremblay, *Renewing the Knowledge Societies Vision: Towards Knowledge Societies for Peace and Sustainable Development* (Paris, 2013), p. 1.

41 Ibid., p. 13.

42 UNESCO, *Towards Knowledge Societies*, p. 50.

43 Sebastian Haunss, *Conflicts in the Knowledge Society: The Contentious Politics of Intellectual Property* (Cambridge, 2013).

44 UNESCO, *Towards Knowledge Societies*, p. 96.

45 Stehr, *Knowledge Societies*, p. 91.

46 Friedrich Nietzsche, *On the Genealogy of Morality*, ed. Keith Ansell-Pearson, trans. Carole Diethe (Cambridge, 2006), p. 3.

FURTHER READING

Adams, Cecil [pseud.], 'What's the Origin of the Dunce Cap?',
  www.straightdope.com, 21 June 2000
Amoore, Louise, and Volha Piotukh, *Algorithmic Life: Calculative Devices
  in the Age of Big Data* (London, 2006)
Andersen, Abraham, *The Treatise of the Three Impostors and the Problem of
  the Enlightenment. A New Translation of the Traité des Trois Imposteurs
  (1777 Edition)* (Lanham, MD, 1997)
Batsaki, Yota, Subha Mukherji, and Jan-Melissa Schramm, eds, *Fictions
  of Knowledge: Fact, Evidence, Doubt* (London and New York,
  2012)
Beecher, Donald, 'Mind, Theaters, and the Anatomy of Consciousness',
  Philosophy and Literature, XXX (2006), pp. 1–16
Berkman, Marcus, *Brain Men: The Passion to Compete* (London, 1999)
Bill, M. B., 'Delusions of Doubt', *Popular Science Monthly*, XXI (1882),
  pp. 788–95
Bion, W. R., *Learning from Experience* (London, 1962)
Birdsall, Carolyn, Maria Boletsi, Itay Sapir and Pieter Verstraete, eds,
  Inside Knowledge: (Un)doing Ways of Knowing in the Humanities
  (Newcastle upon Tyne, 2009)
Boese, Alex, 'The Origin of the Word Quiz', www.hoaxes.org, 10 July 2012
Brady, Michael S., and Miranda Fricker, eds, *The Epistemic Life of Groups:
  Essays in the Epistemology of Collectives* (Oxford, 2016)
Bullard, Rebecca, *The Politics of Disclosure, 1674–1725: Secret History Narratives*
  (London, 2009)
Camillo, Giulio, *L'idea del theatro* (Florence, 1550)
Carruthers, Mary, *The Craft of Thought: Meditation, Rhetoric, and the Making
  of Images, 400–1200* (Cambridge, 1998)
Cassirer, Ernst, *The Philosophy of Symbolic Forms*, vol. III: *The Phenomenology
  of Knowledge*, trans. Ralph Manheim (New Haven, CT, 1957)
Chadwick, Mary, 'Notes upon the Acquisition of Knowledge', *Psychoanalytic
  Review*, XIII (1926), pp. 257–80
Clark, William, *Academic Charisma and the Origins of the Research University*
  (Chicago, IL, 2006)

Connor, Steven, 'Modern Epistemopathies' (2017), www.stevenconnor.com/
modern-epistemopathies.html

——, 'Thinking Things', *Textual Practice*, XXIV (2010), pp. 1–20

Cook, Eleanor, *Enigmas and Riddles in Literature* (Cambridge, 2006)

DeLong, Thomas A., *Quiz Craze: America's Infatuation with Game Shows*
(New York, Westport and London, 1991)

Donne, John, 'The True Character of a Dunce', in *Paradoxes, Problemes,
Essayes, Characters* (London, 1652), pp. 67–71

Drucker, Peter F., *The Age of Discontinuity: Guidelines to our Changing Society*
(London, 1969)

Felipe, Donald, 'Post-Medieval Ars Disputandi', PhD dissertation, University
of Texas, 1991, https://disputatioproject.files.wordpress.com

Ferrier, James Frederick, *Institutes of Metaphysic: The Theory of Knowing and
Being* (Edinburgh and London, 1854)

Gambaccini, Piero, *Mountebanks and Medicasters: A History of Italian
Charlatans from the Middle Ages to the Present*, trans. Bettie Gage Lippitt
(Jefferson, NC, and London, 2004)

Halliwell, Martin, *Images of Idiocy: The Idiot Figure in Modern Fiction and Film*
(Abingdon and New York, 2016)

Haring, Lee, 'On Knowing the Answer', *Journal of American Folklore*, LXXXVII
(1974), pp. 197–207

Harms, Arnold C., *The Spiral of Inquiry: A Study in the Phenomenology of
Inquiry* (Lanham, MD, 1999)

Hasan-Rokem, Galit, and David Shulman, eds, *Untying the Knot: On Riddles
and Other Enigmatic Modes* (New York and Oxford, 1996)

Haunss, Sebastian, *Conflicts in the Knowledge Society: The Contentious Politics
of Intellectual Property* (Cambridge, 2013)

Heller-Roazen, Daniel, *Dark Tongues: The Art of Rogues and Riddlers*
(Cambridge, MA, 2013)

Hoerschelmann, Olaf, *Rules of the Game: Quiz Shows and American Culture*
(Albany, NY, 2006)

Innerarity, Daniel, 'Power and Knowledge: The Politics of the Knowledge
Society', *European Journal of Social Theory*, XVI (2012), pp. 3–16

Kaivola-Bregenhøj, Annikki, *Riddles: Perspectives on the Use, Function
and Change in a Folklore Genre* (Helsinki, 2016)

Kugelmann, Robert, 'Imagination and Stupidity', *Soundings:
An Interdisciplinary Journal*, LXX (1987), pp. 81–93

Lewin, Bertram D., 'Education or the Quest for Omniscience',
Journal of the American Psychoanalytic Association, VI (1958),
pp. 389–412

——, 'Some Observations on Knowledge, Belief and the Impulse to Know',
International Journal of Psycho-Analysis, XX (1939), pp. 426–31

Lipsius, Justus, *A Brief Outline of the History of Librairies*, trans. John Cotton
Dana (Chicago, IL, 1907)

Lord, Evelyn, *The Hell-fire Clubs: Sex, Satanism and Secret Societies*
(New Haven, CT, and London, 2009)

McDonagh, Patrick, *Idiocy: A Cultural History* (Cambridge, 2011)

McGann, Jerome J., *Towards a Literature of Knowledge*
(Oxford, 1999)

Mansell, Robin, and Gaëtan Tremblay, *Renewing the Knowledge Societies Vision: Towards Knowledge Societies for Peace and Sustainable Development* (Paris, 2013)

Maranda, Ella Köngäs, 'The Logic of Riddles', in *Structural Analysis of Oral Tradition*, ed. Pierre Maranda and Ella Köngäs Maranda (Philadelphia, PA, 1971), pp. 189–232

Mencken, Johann Burkhard, *The Charlatanry of the Learned*, trans. Francis E. Litz, ed. H. L. Mencken (London, 1937)

Mijolla-Mellor, Sophia de, *Le Besoin de savoir: Théories et mythes magico-sexuels dans l'enfance* (Paris, 2002)

Musil, Robert, 'On Stupidity', in *Precision and Soul: Essays and Addresses*, ed. and trans. Burton Pike and David S. Luft (Chicago, IL, and London, 1990), pp. 268–86

Nagel, Jennifer, *Knowledge: A Very Short Introduction* (Oxford, 2014)

Nesbit, E., 'The Things That Matter', in *The Rainbow and the Rose* (London, New York and Bombay, 1905), pp. 3–5

Nietzsche, Friedrich, *The Will to Power: Selections from the Notebooks of the 1880s*, ed. R. Kevin Hill, trans. R. Kevin Hill and Michael A. Scarpitti (London, 2017)

Ost, François, and Laurent van Eynde, *Faust, ou les frontières du savoir* (Brussels, 2002)

Pollard, Natalie, 'The Fate of Stupidity', *Essays in Criticism*, LXII (2012), pp. 25–38

Porter, Roy, *Quacks: Fakers and Charlatans in English Medicine* (Stroud, 2000)

Poovey, Mary, *A History of the Modern Fact: Problems of Knowledge in the Sciences of Wealth and Society* (Chicago, IL, and London, 1998)

Posecznik, Alex, 'On Anthropological Secrets', www.anthronow.com, 1 October 2009

Procopius of Caesarea, *The Anecdota, or Secret History*, trans. H. B. Dewing (Cambridge, MA, and London, 1935)

Rabb, Melinda Alliker, *Satire and Secrecy in English Literature from 1650 to 1750* (Basingstoke, 2007)

Richards, I. A., *Science and Poetry* (London, 1926)

Ronell, Avital, *Stupidity* (Urbana, IL, 2002)

Rudnytsky, Peter L., and Ellen Handler Spitz, eds, *Freud and Forbidden Knowledge* (New York, 1994)

Runciman, David, 'How the Education Gap is Tearing Politics Apart', www.theguardian.com, 5 October 2016

St Onge, K. R., *The Melancholy Anatomy of Plagiarism* (Lanham, New York and London, 1988)

Saward, John, *Perfect Fools: Folly for Christ's Sake in Catholic and Orthodox Spirituality* (Oxford, 1980)

Sforza, Michele G., 'Epistemophily-Epistemopathy: Use of the Internet between Normality and Disease', in *Psychoanalysis, Identity and the Internet*, ed. Andrea Marzi (London, 2016), pp. 181–207

Simmel, Georg, 'The Sociology of Secrecy and of Secret Societies', *American Journal of Sociology*, XI (1906), pp. 441–98

Simmons, Dana, 'Impostor Syndrome, a Reparative History', *Engaging Science, Technology, and Society*, II (2016), pp. 106–27

Spengler, Oswald, *The Decline of the West*, vol 1: *Form and Actuality*, trans. Charles Frances Atkinson (London, 1926)

Stehr, Nico, *Knowledge Societies* (London, Thousand Oaks and New Delhi, 1994)

——, and Richard V. Ericson, eds, *The Culture and Power of Knowledge: Inquiries into Contemporary Societies* (Berlin and New York, 1992)

Stuckrad, Kocku von, *Western Esotericism: A Brief History of Secret Knowledge*, trans. Nicholas Goodrick-Clarke (London and Oakville, CT, 2005)

Taussig, Michael, *Defacement: Public Secrecy and the Labor of the Negative* (Stanford, CA, 1999)

Thomas, Jeannie B., 'Dumb Blondes, Dan Quayle, and Hillary Clinton: Gender, Sexuality, and Stupidity in Jokes', *Journal of American Folklore*, CX (1997), pp. 277–313

Thornton, Dora, *The Scholar in his Study: Ownership and Experience in Renaissance Italy* (New Haven, CT, and London, 1997)

Tucker, Brian, *Reading Riddles: Rhetorics of Obscurity from Romanticism to Freud* (Lewisburg, PA, 2011)

UNESCO, *Towards Knowledge Societies* (Paris, 2005)

Walsh, Dorothy, *Literature and Knowledge* (Middletown, CT, 1969)

Wilgus, Neal, *The Illuminoids: Secret Societies and Political Paranoia* (London, 1980)

Winter, Sarah, *Freud and the Institution of Psychoanalytic Knowledge* (Stanford, CA, 1999)

Wood, Michael, *Literature and the Taste of Knowledge* (Cambridge, 2009)

Yates, Francis A., *The Art of Memory* (London, 1966)

INDEX